*f*P

ALSO BY OWEN WEST

Sharkman Six
Four Days to Veracruz

THE SNAKE EATERS

★ ★ ★

AN UNLIKELY BAND OF BROTHERS
AND THE BATTLE
FOR THE SOUL OF IRAQ

OWEN WEST

WITHDRAWN

FREE PRESS

New York London Toronto Sydney New Delhi

Free Press
A Division of Simon & Schuster, Inc.
1230 Avenue of the Americas
New York, NY 10020

First Free Press hardcover edition May 2012

FREE PRESS and colophon are trademarks of Simon & Schuster, Inc.

For information about special discounts for bulk purchases,
please contact Simon & Schuster Special Sales at
1-866-506-1949 or business@simonandschuster.com.

The Simon & Schuster Speakers Bureau can bring authors to
your live event. For more information or to book an event contact the
Simon & Schuster Speakers Bureau at 1-866-248-3049 or
visit our website at www.simonspeakers.com.

Credits for insert photography: All photos on page 1; the SBVIED and
Humvee photos on page 2; the group photo of July 2006 on page 3; and the
mine digger on page 4 are courtesy of Mike Troster. Photo of Khalidiya street
on page 4 and photo of enemy KIA on page 8 are courtesy of Alex Connor.
All other photos are courtesy of the author.

Manufactured in the United States of America

1 3 5 7 9 10 8 6 4 2

Library of Congress Cataloging-in-Publication Data

West, Owen.
The Snake Eaters : An unlikely band of brothers and the battle for the soul of Iraq /
Owen West.—First Free Press hardcover edition.
p. cm.
1. West, Owen 2. Iraq War, 2003—Campaigns—Iraq—Anbar (Province)
3. Iraq War, 2003—Personal narratives, American. 4. Counterinsurgency—Iraq—
Anbar (Province) 5. United States. Marine Corps—History—Iraq War, 2003–
6. Military assistance, American—Iraq. 7. Iraq—Armed Forces—Training of.
I. Title.
DS79.764.A63W47 2012
956.7044'342—dc23
2011051715

ISBN 978-1-4516-5593-3
ISBN 978-1-4516-5597-1 (ebook)

To combat advisors around the world
fighting their own small wars

CONTENTS

★　★　★

INTRODUCTION

From 2005 through 2007, the battle for the grubby city of Khalidiya became so intensely personal that an Iraqi battalion, its American military advisors, and the insurgents they hunted knew each other by name. Victors of conventional battles secure terrain and move forward. The anonymous villagers are part of the landscape, like trees. In Khalidiya, however, the central task was rooting guerrillas out of the local human terrain, stripping them of their anonymity.

U.S. forces are not built for this form of warfare, called counterinsurgency. Our enemies in both Iraq and Afghanistan posed as civilians, and our firepower-based Army struggled to cleave them from complicit local populations. The lesson from both wars was clear: America must train indigenous security forces to fight their own insurrections. Local forces, who speak the language and share the culture, can, with the right tactics and support, convince skeptical inhabitants to turn against the insurgents in their midst. The combat advisors who mentor these forces thus become paramount.

Advisors are not new battlefield entrants. For a century, the United States has deployed small teams of American soldiers alongside foreign armies to show them how to defeat insurgencies and take control of their own countries. In military jargon, advisors are "combat multipliers"—a good twenty-man team can leverage the services of a thousand foreign troops at a sliver of the cost of deploying a similarly sized U.S. unit.

The problem is, the role of the military advisor remains a mystery to the public and misunderstood by politicians. Reflecting a common misperception, President Obama has several times declared that advising is not a "combat mission."[1] But the exact opposite is true. Only an advisor's aggressive willingness to share risk—his performance under fire—with local troops gives him credibility with and influence over them.

This gap in understanding is not limited to civilians. Our generals are uncomfortable prescribing advisors as a solution to these twenty-first-century wars. Advising a foreign military requires nontraditional training that takes years; soldiers need a wonk's cultural awareness, the rudimentary language capability of a border cop, a survivalist's skills, and the interpersonal savvy of a politician. Military hierarchy is built on control, so it feels unnatural for the leadership to dispatch these small bands of advisors, who on paper cannot give orders, to live among foreign, sometimes hostile soldiers in an effort to stabilize their countries. As a result, our instinctive way of responding to the recent insurgencies in Iraq and Afghanistan has been to send hundreds of thousands of troops at a cost of billions a year rather than rely on advisors.

In the spring of 2004, the Iraq insurgency flared and the U.S. military found itself with no local uniformed partners. America had dismantled Iraq's army a year earlier. More than a thousand advisors were suddenly needed to rebuild and train the New Iraqi Army. It was the largest advising requirement since Vietnam, and the mission was treated like a live grenade. The U.S. Army Special Forces teams, the only units trained for the task, were in short supply, splitting their focus between hunting most-wanted terrorists and advising a few Iraqi Special Forces units.

The next logical source for advisors was one of the active-duty American divisions scheduled to deploy to Iraq. But their leaders had no appetite for advising—they considered it an inferior mission and, besides, the U.S. military promotion structure rewarded the commanders leading the big conventional units, not advisors.

So the advising mission in Iraq fell to reservists. It was a controversial assignment; the mission to raise a competent military force was extremely tough and the reservists were considered inferior soldiers. Many senior generals predicted they would fail. That was a reasonable assumption. They were part-time soldiers whose real expertise was in civilian trades like plumbing and firefighting. Worse, their minimal predeployment training was misdirected—for a few weeks before shipping out, the reservists were prepared to teach Iraqi recruits on secure bases.

In 2005, a tiny minority of advisor teams was assigned to Anbar Province. It was a dreaded duty station—40 percent of all U.S. fatalities occurred in Anbar. By comparison, Baghdad, with a population six times bigger than Anbar's, was the site of 30 percent of U.S. deaths.

This is the story of one of those teams—ordinary soldiers used in an extraordinary way. Thrust onto a lethal battlefield with little infantry experience and no preparation to fall back on, this isolated team showed that no matter how we enter these murky twenty-first-century wars, all roads out lead through the combat advisor.

★

That Khalidiya had any path to stability was doubtful when in the fall of 2005 the first New Iraqi Army Nissan truck puttered into the city. For two years, bigger U.S. battalions had failed to bring the city to heel. Now the task had been handed to Iraqi Battalion 3/3–1, the "Snake Eaters" (the nickname referred to their shoulder patch that depicted a hawk clutching a fanged snake), one of the first battalions borne of the New Iraqi Army. The 3/3–1 officers, a mix of Shiites and Sunnis, were secular career soldiers but knew better than to predict rationality when dealing with tribal Sunni Anbaris, whom they considered *majnoon*—crazy. Serving under the experienced Iraqi officers were about five hundred soldiers, or *jundis,* who were predominantly Shiite and had joined for the paycheck.

Like their advisors, the 3/3–1 jundis were despondent over their assignment to Anbar Province. Upon learning of the posting, many had deserted. Anbar was home to the Sunni terror group al Qaeda in Iraq (AQI). The archterrorist Abu Musab al-Zarqawi had seized control of the Khalidiya area in 2004 by hiding his agents among local workers. Zarqawi had released a letter warning: "Shiism is the looming danger and the true challenge. They are the enemy. Beware of them. Fight them."[2] In Anbar Province, Shiite jundis were as much a target as the Americans.

Anbar's deadliest stretch was a road that connected the heart of the Sunni rebellion against American-imposed Shiite control, the capital city of Ramadi, with its soul, Fallujah, where a year earlier Zarqawi had made a fateful stand against the invaders before slipping away as it was destroyed. Between them lay the no-stoplight city of Khalidiya. Home to twenty-five thousand, it brimmed with tough loiterers willing to kill for $100, local tribesmen—including hundreds of Saddam Hussein's Mukhabarat secret police retirees—clawing for power, and transient assassins from al Qaeda in Iraq who moved between Ramadi and Fallujah and were known as "commuters from hell."

Khalidiya's southern border is Lake Habbaniyah, formerly a stopover for flying boats carrying wealthy Brits to India in the 1930s. The Khalidiya tribesmen would sell cheap trinkets to the tourists and the RAF pilots stationed at the lush air base across the street. In 1958, business dried up when the pro-British monarch, King Faisal II, and his family were machine-gunned by Iraqi troops. The British occupation disintegrated and the air base was abandoned.

I arrived in Iraq in October 2006 as a casualty replacement. I was an infantry officer turned Wall Street trader, but grunts are replaceable parts. I was routed to the overgrown Camp Habbaniyah air base, headquarters of the "new" 1st Iraqi Division, which in Khalidiya was considered a hostile occupying force, same as the British. I was assigned to the twelve-man Army advisor team embedded in the Iraqi Battalion 3/3–1. When I arrived, the Snake Eaters and their advisors lived on a barren hilltop outpost overlooking Khalidiya. The American combat casualties had been replaced with Marines like me. I was the third fill-in. As our Humvee approached the outpost that first night, a nervous jundi with an AK-47 inspected us with a penlight. Here in the flesh was the best hope for an American withdrawal from Iraq.

Three and a half years into the war, it was unclear whether the advisor model was working. Senior Marine intelligence officers had concluded that al Qaeda in Iraq controlled the citizens of Anbar Province. Enemy attacks in Khalidiya had never been higher. Headlines echoed the obvious—the war was over and we had lost.

Our advisor team's call sign was "Outcast." It seemed a well-earned nickname. Ours was the fourth team to mentor the Snake Eaters in its thirty-three-month existence, a multiyear effort by reservists, National Guardsmen, soldiers, Marines, and interpreters who built the unit from scratch and passed it along in various forms like jockeys switching atop a thoroughbred during a race. My role was small. After fighting from within an Iraqi battalion, I became convinced that our own country could accomplish more with fewer forces and less money if we changed the way we fought and, yes, ran higher risks due to the exposed position of advisor teams.

No team ran higher risks than the group of Army reservists that served from September 2005 to July 2006, preceding my mixed team. They are the focus of this book. Led by Lieutenant Colonel Mike Troster, a DEA agent, the team had adopted an aggressive approach to advising that clashed with schoolhouse instruction. Reading Troster's after-action reports in the fall of 2006, I was initially surprised by his emphasis on hunting the enemy. The Pentagon was circulating a new counterinsurgency field manual that was eagerly co-opted by the press for its highbrow, "graduate-level" philosophy that emphasized winning over the people by raising the local standard of living. But it is 20-year-olds who apply the theory on the streets. Our team adopted Troster's clear ethos over the complicated official manual.

The battle for Khalidiya required different tactics. Rooting out guerrillas is morally bruising warfare. Insurgents don't wear uniforms and they don't fight in the open. Instead they plant bombs in front of shops, snipe from houses where children are sleeping, and occasionally blow themselves up in markets if soldiers get too close. It is an effective resistance as long as the people don't betray them. At the height of the Anbar insurgency, few locals ever told the truth and nothing happened without a fight.

The culture of a war is revealed not in formalized theoretical works but in small, daily acts of kindness and cruelty, of duty and shirking. On the hilltop outpost, jundis and their advisors worked to overcome their cultural differences because they knew that on patrol in Khalidiya, they fought and died for people who would despise them until the battle was won.

★

The need to tell the story of the American advisors in Iraq was driven home to me in no uncertain terms by the nightly outbursts of "Alex," the primary interpreter for my team. Because Alex was an Outcast for twenty-four months, his brother was tortured to death in Baghdad. The murderers drove the family from their home, then harassed them by phone for several months, promising to return the boy's body parts for money.

I sponsored Alex for a special immigrant visa. He lived with my family in New York City and then Connecticut while he tried to pass the entry test for the Marine Corps. He later volunteered to return to Iraq with another advisor team.

Like any Iraqi man, Alex was obsessed with politics. He was riveted by the 2008 American presidential campaign. He memorized what American generals, politicians, and commentators said about Iraq and Afghanistan on the cable news networks. When I came home at night, he'd unload.

"How can they understand so little?" he'd ask. "Tell the story of the Snake Eaters. Then they'll know what it's really like."

CHARACTERS

September 2005 to July 2006

BATTALION 3/3–1 SNAKE EATERS

Colonel Falah (battalion commander)
Lieutenant Commander Fareed
 (executive officer)
Major Aamr (operations officer)
Major Mohammed (company commander)
Captain Dhafer (company commander)
Captain Walid (company commander)
Captain Haadi (company commander)
Captain Hamid (company commander)
Lieutenant "GQ" Ali (platoon commander)
Lieutenant Khalid (platoon commander)
Lieutenant Abbas (platoon commander)
Lieutenant "Bez Boz" (platoon commander)

ADVISORS

Lieutenant Colonel Michael Troster
Major Walter Roberson
First Lieutenant John Bennett
Sergeant First Class Eliezer Rivera
Sergeant First Class Mark Huss
Sergeant First Class Mark Gentile
Staff Sergeant Christopher Watson
Staff Sergeant Richard Blakley
Staff Sergeant Shawn Boiko
Sergeant Greg Bozovich
Sergeant Joseph Neary

Interpreters

GW
Joe
Reyes
Alex

Combat Replacements

First Lieutenant Bill Rusher
Sergeant First Class Stephen Alban
Staff Sergeant Saul Cardenas
Staff Sergeant Larry Dehart

July 2006 to February 2007

BATTALION 3/3–1 SNAKE EATERS

Lieutenant Colonel Fareed
   (battalion commander)
Lieutenant Colonel Sammi
   (executive officer)
Lieutenant Colonel Aamr
   (operations officer)
Major Mohammed (operations chief)
Captain Dhafer (company commander)
Captain Haadi (company commander)
Captain Ma'ath (company commander)
Lieutenant Khalid (company commander)
Lieutenant "GQ" Ali (platoon commander)
Lieutenant Abbas (platoon commander)
Lieutenant Faisal (scout commander)
Lieutenant "Fredo" Mohammed (scout)

ADVISORS

Major Mac
Major Steven Sylvester
Major Pierre Dupuy
Captain David Coyle
Captain Milton Perez
Sergeant First Class Tod Caldwell
Sergeant First Class Robert Akin
Sergeant First Class Andrew Himes
Staff Sergeant Matthew Mattern
Staff Sergeant Dave Cox
Staff Sergeant Gordon Solomon
Sergeant Brian Schwarzman
Lance Corporal Timothy Smith
Lance Corporal Shaun Lester

Interpreters

Alex
Reyes

Combat Replacements

Major Owen West
Captain William Stoesser
Captain Jeffrey Foisy
Gunnery Sergeant James Newton
Staff Sergeant Wayne O'Donnell
Staff Sergeant Anthony Povarelli

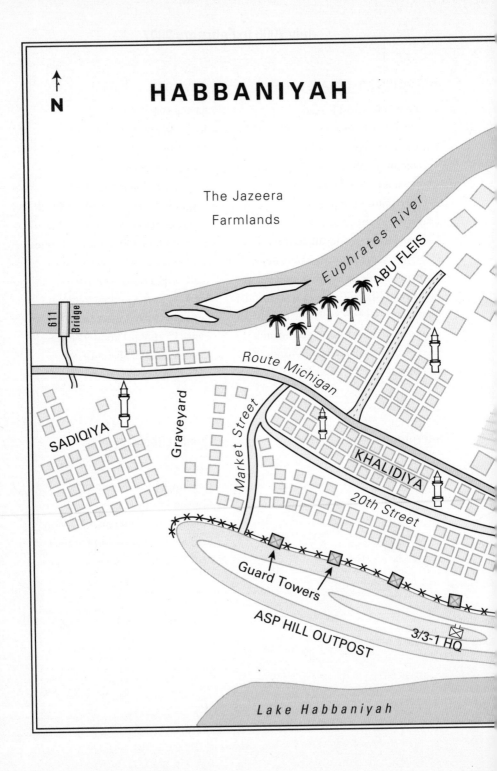

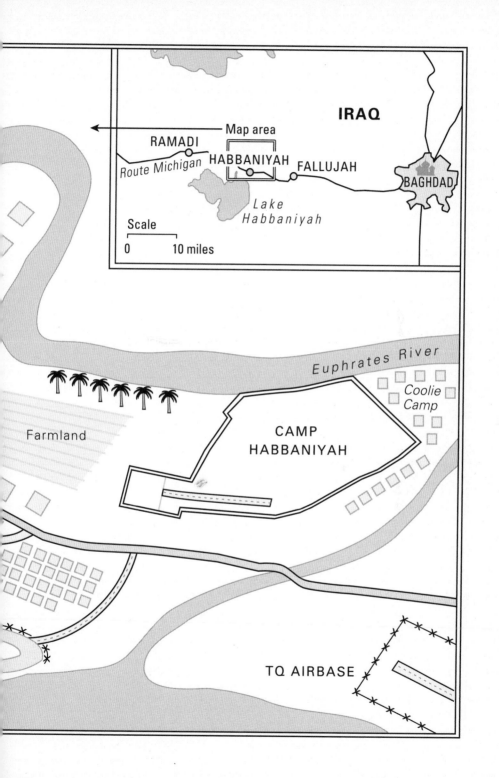

IRAQ

RAMADI

Map area

HABBANIYAH

FALLUJAH

Route Michigan

BAGHDAD

Lake Habbaniyah

Scale

0   10 miles

Euphrates River

Coolie Camp

Farmland

CAMP HABBANIYAH

TQ AIRBASE

PART ONE

INTO THE HAZE

★ ★ ★

1

Into the Haze

★   ★   ★

September 2005

Hunched over the steering wheel of his Humvee, U.S. Army Staff Sergeant Chris Watson, 26, cursed. His was the last of four vehicles in a tiny convoy headed into Khalidiya. Watson turned on the wipers to brush away the dust stirred by the heaving troop carrier barely visible ten meters ahead.

Through the scratched Plexiglass of his bulletproof windshield, Watson could see a dozen Iraqi enlisted soldiers, called jundis, packed tightly against the troop carrier's sandbagged walls, their AK-47s swaying like cattails as the big vehicle heaved. Two jundis were perched dangerously on the tailgate. The Iraqi privates were either too junior to claim shelter against the leaking sandbags or too fatalistic to care if they lived, *Insha'Allah,* to fight again tomorrow.

It was September 16, 2005. Watson was part of a ten-man advisor team of Army reservists that had deployed to Iraq expecting to teach jundis basic training on a secure, sprawling base with a Burger King, a Green Bean coffee shop, and a fitness center. Their combat tour, they thought, would consist of posting cell phone videos of AK-47 shoots and barracks antics on YouTube. Instead, they were embedded in 3/3–1—the 3rd Battalion of the 3rd Brigade of the 1st Iraqi Army Division—and ordered to remake themselves as infantry combat advisors in Khalidiya, living and fighting as Iraqi soldiers.

The lead vehicle was a sputtering white Nissan truck carrying the Iraqi patrol commander and his bodyguards. Behind it were two armored troop carriers filled with jundis and driven by U.S. National Guardsmen stationed on Camp Habbaniyah. Last came Watson's Humvee, which was occupied by two fellow combat advisors. The convoy roared out of the barbed-wire gates of Camp Habbaniyah into "Indian country," soldierspeak for enemy territory since the Dakota Wars of the 1860s when U.S. cavalrymen from isolated forts pursued indigenous tribes. Watson knew from the single predeployment class he'd had on Iraqi religion that there were Sunni tribes in his area and that they hated the Shiites, but that was about it. He was more concerned with the awful road conditions. Death came three ways in Iraq: sniper shots, roadside bombs, and suicide car bombs, which were the most catastrophic.

An Iraqi car swerved to the side of the road as the convoy bore down the highway. Watson could barely see it through the cloud of dust. For a moment he thought the shifting image was a car bomb, but then the troop truck full of jundis barreled right past the idling car and Watson followed tight in its contrail, squinting at the expressionless civilian driver while his own heart hammered.

Joseph Conrad's *Heart of Darkness,* a cult favorite of Special Forces advisors, describes British gunboats, a century before, bombarding a dark green African jungle—a metaphor for the gulf between two civilizations. In Iraq, the Humvee had replaced the gunboat. In the hot, dusty haze, Watson could barely see through the four inches of armored Plexiglas.

In the Humvee, Sergeant Shawn Boiko, 24, could see better. Standing on the gunner's platform above Watson, his torso poked through the hole in the roof where the turret was mounted. A wet cotton T-shirt wrapped over his mouth, Boiko surveyed the bouncing pile of jundis over his 7.62mm machine gun. They were younger and skinnier than he expected, and it scared him. Everything about the mission did.

On paper, Boiko was expected to "advise" the jundis on how to fight like U.S. soldiers. Like the rest of his teammates, he was only a part-time soldier—a flooring manager from California. He figured that before he passed whatever soldiering skills he had on to the jundis, the first order of business was keeping his teammates alive.

This was only his second trip into Khalidiya. On Boiko's previous journey, a handover ride with the outgoing advisors to give the newcomers an overview of their area of responsibility, they had heard the dull crump of a distant explosion, followed by high-pitched shouts over the radio. Advisors patrolling with a different Iraqi battalion two kilometers away yelled of casualties as they traded rounds with insurgents.

One of the experienced advisors conducting the turnover had said, "Khalidiya. Biggest city in the area. It's a very bad area. People hate our guts. Couple days and it's all yours. Can't say I'll miss it."

This time, Boiko was no longer a spectator. He grasped the hand wheel that swiveled the heavy machine gun, cranking like a yachtsman turning the winch on his sail. The wheel's teeth bit into the turret base ring, shifting the half-ton steel doughnut fluidly to let Boiko's barrel sweep over one car after the other as Iraqi drivers peeled off the road to let the three trucks of jundis and the Humvee pass.

As the up-gunner, the Humvee's only defense, Boiko figured he had about two seconds to decide to open fire if one of the hundreds of erratic Iraqi motorists suddenly sped directly at the Humvee. He pointed the jiggling front sight post of his gun at one car, then another, and slightly depressed an imaginary trigger finger for the fifth—or was it the fiftieth?—time.

The convoy was on Route Michigan, the most heavily mined road in Iraq, averaging a dozen firefights and twenty roadside bombs every day between Ramadi, the capital of Anbar Province, and Fallujah. On the route-planning maps it was labeled "black," or closed to logistics convoys, but not to combat patrols like Boiko's. Anbar itself, which is larger than North Carolina, was held by just twenty-two thousand U.S. soldiers and Marines dispersed over twenty thousand square kilometers. That was just 20 percent of the total U.S. force in Iraq, yet Anbar was responsible for almost half the American deaths in the entire country.

Boiko didn't know the statistics. He just sensed that Khalidiya, which was halfway between Ramadi and Fallujah, was bad news because of the local vibe. Vehicle patrols were Iraq's version of safari. Boiko and his fellow advisors had been told to memorize the web of roadways into Khalidiya, but it was hard to keep his eyes off the people loitering along Route Michigan, the mustached men in dirty knockoff designer sweat suits and the women hidden inside abayas who scurried nervously into doorways as the convoy passed. There was an air of impending doom.

"Don't let some jackass crash into us," Chris Watson shouted.

"I'd say 'watch for IEDs,' but I doubt it'd do any good," Sergeant First Class Mark Huss, 36, yelled up to Boiko over the engine roar.

As the senior advisor on the patrol, Huss sat in the right-hand seat next to Watson. Looking out the blast window, he was horrified by the mounds of trash that hemmed them in on both sides. They had been told by a stateside trainer to look for anything out of the ordinary, but there was enough garbage littering the macadam to conceal a hundred bombs. Besides, everything here was "out of the ordinary."

"If they want to hit us," said Huss, "there's not much we can do about it."

Except react. But the three rookie advisors did not know how they would react under fire. They hadn't experienced combat, and they were not infantrymen, or even regular soldiers. Watson was a cop from Virginia. Huss ran a plumbing company in Iowa. Since being activated, Watson and Boiko were his new direct reports. With the team's other seven teammates back in Camp Habbaniyah—including his team leader, Lieutenant Colonel Mike Troster, a DEA agent—Huss felt a crushing weight of responsibility. He vowed never again to be stressed by a call about a burst pipe.

★

By the fall of 2005, reservists like Mark Huss had become, haphazardly, the main effort in America's exit from Iraq. President George W. Bush had explained the strategy earlier that year in an address to the nation, saying, "As the Iraqis stand up, we will stand down."[1] The New Iraqi Army was being built from scratch, so that they could take over control of the country, but the "new" jundis were mostly poor volunteer recruits with little military experience, and the officers—many of whom had served in the "old" Iraqi army under Saddam—had neither the experience to lead troops in the absence of ruthless conscription nor a plan to break the insurgency in their own country.

Hundreds of Iraqi units in various stages of development needed to be mentored by U.S. advisor teams. Many Iraqi units were still in training and required basic classes that mimicked American boot camp. A few, like 3/3-1—one of the first New Iraqi Army battalions—were in the fight and needed experienced combat advisors to show them how to defeat insurgents firsthand and link them to U.S. medical and fire support.

The U.S. military had few trained advisors. Although the Army's traditional counterinsurgency instructors, the Special Forces, took great pains to select and train advisors in three-year training blocks, many of their teams had been assigned to raiding units designed to kill or capture high-level insurgents. Even if they were reassigned, the Special Forces had enough teams to fill only 10 percent of the billets. Conventional active-duty infantry commanders, in turn, desperately avoided the mad scramble to embed small groups of Americans in fledgling Iraqi units. They didn't want to break their units into autonomous parts, effectively ceding control of their men to Iraqi colonels. So the advisor mission fell to reservists.

Confusion over the mission pervaded the highest ranks of the U.S. military. Advising was considered basic training in garrison instead of building counterinsurgency skills in combat. The Army handed the advisor assignment to its two reserve institutional training divisions, the 98th and the 80th, which specialized in classroom education and static training. Neither unit had deployed since World War II, and even then the 98th saw no combat. Selection for advisor duty was not rigorous. Soldiers could not be overtly prejudiced, handicapped, or too fat to deploy. Infantry training was not required, and combat experience was scant among the seven hundred reservists in each division. The soldiers in the 98th were given forty-two days of stateside "advisor training," where they drilled for a tour training jundis on a giant forward operating base (FOB), a theme that reflected the confusion at the top.

The 98th was the first division to ship out, in the fall of 2004. The advisors posted to Iraqi Battalion 3/3–1 included a lumberjack, a T-shirt salesman, and a trombone player in the U.S. Army band. They soon found themselves in combat. After graduating from training in December 2004, Iraqi Battalion 3/3–1 was ordered into Mosul, north of Baghdad, to fight alongside an American motorized infantry battalion. The advisors went wherever their host unit went. They were classroom instructors no more. The ten-man team was expected not only to teach the fledgling Iraqi battalion how to defeat insurgents, from the jundis all the way up to the commanding officer, but also to manage the relationships their protégés formed with nearby U.S. units and even local sheikhs. It was widely considered the trickiest job in Iraq.

Because of the flawed selection process and the brief, misguided training program, performance of the advisors was uneven. Many teams failed to adequately progress their Iraqi units. Complaints about the underprepared reservists stretched from the battlefield to the high command in Baghdad, where one colonel threatened to write a book titled *Blame It on the 98th*.[2] The general in charge of the military advisors, a former Special Forces commander, doubted the reservists had the requisite skills for advising.[3] Even the senior U.S. commander in the Middle East, General John Abizaid, criticized the decision to assign the advising mission to reservists. "We didn't give you the best and the brightest," he told Lieutenant General David Petraeus, who in the summer of 2004 had been brought in to run the entire Iraqi security rebuild. "We put the third team on the field."[4]

Huss's 80th Institutional Training Division replaced the 98th in September 2005. Recipients of the same misguided training that had plagued the 98th a year earlier, Huss's ten-man team had two additional obstacles to overcome upon being assigned to Iraqi Battalion 3/3–1: The Iraqi unit had six months of combat experience and required tactical advice that was a step above other Iraqi units emerging from training, and they were stationed in Anbar Province, which meant tough combat and interservice friction. Anbar was sometimes called "Marineland" because it was run by Marines. There were only two other Army advisor teams in the entire province, the vast majority being Marine teams. Several members of the original advisor team from the 98th assigned to 3/3–1 in 2004 had been forcibly replaced, including the team leader, an Army major, who had been replaced by a Marine captain.

When Huss's team reported to Camp Habbaniyah in September 2005, their Marine bosses tried to comfort them by saying they didn't need to reinvent the wheel. They just had to "keep up the mentorship," a senior advisor told them, and "unfuck the Iraqis." What that meant exactly, the rookie advisors did not know. They were average Americans handed an extraordinary mission. Somehow they had to build confidence and competence in the Iraqis to take the lead in the war, and ultimately defeat the insurgency, so the Americans could leave. With little understanding of the situation, no doctrine or training on advising to lean on, and zero combat experience to provide rules for staying alive, the rookie advisor team had been shoved into the dragon's mouth.

Lieutenant Colonel Troster, the advisor team leader, hoped to lean on the nearby U.S. "partner unit." The plan to have the Iraqi security forces take over the war was not limited to advisors. Each Iraqi battalion was partnered with a conventional American battalion for logistics and medevac support, and to operate alongside in combat until they were ready for independence. This way the jundis could mimic regular U.S. infantrymen on patrol as well as their few advisors, and the advisors could supervise the relationship between the units and reinforce the salient day-to-day lessons.

In Habbaniyah, 3/3–1's partner unit was an ad hoc U.S. National Guard task force called Task Force Panther, built around the 1–110th National Guard infantry battalion from Pennsylvania. TF Panther had arrived in Iraq two months earlier, in July 2005, as a mishmash of National Guard units that included tanks from Vermont, artillery from Utah, infantry from Michigan and Pennsylvania, and dozens of individual augmentees from across the United States. Panther deployed with only three undersize infantry companies in part because many of the guardsmen balked at the original activation order. Only a handful of guardsmen had been activated during a decade of war in Vietnam. Few expected to be called to fight in Iraq after just two years of war.

Troster, Huss, and the rest of the 3/3–1 advisors were, in turn, surprised that their Iraqi battalion was partnered with a Guard unit. Why in the world, they wondered, was a skeleton National Guard battalion that should have been sandbagging a river in Allegheny County assigned to one of the toughest combat zones in the country?

The Marine command in Fallujah regarded the situation in Camp Habbaniyah with deep skepticism. The Pentagon had placed National Guardsmen from Pennsylvania—who had no training in counterrevolutionary warfare—into the heart of the Sunni insurgency in July. Following them in late August were Iraqi soldiers who had no armored vehicles, no tactical sense, no discipline, and could not even shoot straight, yet had been labeled the critical factor for stability. And who had arrived in September to train the most important troops in Iraq? Army reservists like Mark Huss who, one weekend a month—and two weeks in the summer—satisfied his reserve duties by teaching soldiers how to maintain laundry facilities.

As far as most Marines were concerned, the totem pole was clear enough. At the top were Special Forces teams, then the Army Rangers, Marine infantry, and the famous Army units like the 101st Airborne. In the middle somewhere were Marine reservists and the Army units they'd never heard of. At the bottom were Army reservists and National Guardsmen.

Expectations were not high for an Iraqi battalion partnered with a National Guard battalion and advised by Army reservists.

★

As they motored down Route Michigan, the wind whipped hot across Boiko's sweating face, goggled like the Plexiglass on his Humvee. Every gust swirled up to his turret the stink of piss, feces, garbage, and the wet rotting fur of dog carcasses—the fate of unlucky strays nosing in the sewage and trash for dinner, hit by Iraqi motorists, or blasted by bombs. They, too, didn't know where the explosives had been buried overnight.

The city of Khalidiya, home to twenty-five thousand Sunnis and a couple hundred besieged Christians and Kurds, seemed to swallow the patrol. A dozen minarets marked the mosques that divided Khalidiya's endless cluster of two-story concrete houses into neighborhoods. Many of the imams at these mosques were Takfiri—a Sunni Muslim sect that claimed the right to punish *kuffars,* or nonbelievers, as well as Iraqi soldiers who had committed apostasy by serving the Americans. The elder imams called for "resistance" against the *Amerikee* occupiers and their puppets. The popular up-and-coming preachers called for bombings and beheadings.

In their training, the advisors had been sternly lectured to avoid the topic of religion. It was considered too highly charged for the U.S. soldiers to broach with their protégés; in the Iraqi ranks, the jundis were poor Shia, and the officers were a mix of well-connected Shia and career-military Sunnis. Some of the men in the advisor team did not know one sect from another.

It hadn't rained for months, but soon the tires were dripping wet from the exposed sewers. Boiko swiveled his machine gun at the shadows cast before every house, every pedestrian, every alley; Watson, at the wheel, tried to avoid hitting the throngs of shoppers in the narrow streets; Huss stared at the map on his lap, their way into town highlighted in yellow marker.

Huss puzzled over the map. Either he couldn't figure out where he was or the convoy had taken a wrong turn. Should he ask the Iraqi lieutenant in the Nissan or the National Guardsmen driving the two transports?

They were lost.

Boiko cranked his machine gun turret to the rear, toward a street that the shoppers had suddenly vacated. The Humvee slowly followed the trucks into a dark alley. Webs of dangling power lines, like thick ropes of cypress trees, drooped onto the jundis from above.

The soldiers used their rifles to hold up the live wires to form an arch so the convoy could crawl under without snagging too many lines. A handful of boys darted across the street in front of Boiko's gunsight, bounding over the trash heaps, brown shimmers in the heat mirage.

"This sucks," he shouted down into the Humvee. "I think we're gonna get hit."

The two U.S. troop trucks lurched to a stop in front of an empty schoolyard. The only sound Boiko could hear was the light splatter from dripping water tanks atop the roofs. Then the Iraqi lieutenant gave a sharp order, and jundis slowly got down from the trucks, like senior citizens stepping off a tour bus.

The National Guardsmen driving the heavily armored troop trucks felt a different sense of urgency. As soon as the jundis were down, they roared out of Khalidiya, leaving the Iraqi Nissan pickup, the advisor Humvee, and three squads of jundis alone on foot in a town that wanted them dead.

Where the hell are they going? Huss wondered.

Throughout Iraq, standing rules required American vehicle convoys to have a minimum number of vehicles—usually four—in case of the total destruction of one by a mine followed by a small-arms ambush on the others. Huss figured because his team was embedded with Iraqis, these rules might not apply—the entire 3/3–1 battalion had only three armored troop trucks, which broke down constantly, and a handful of Nissans that labored under the thinnest sheets of welded steel. With two vehicles, he felt marooned in a foreign city. He could try to raise the National Guard transports on the radio and call them back. One duty of the advisors was to act as liaison between Iraqi battalions and nearby U.S. conventional units like the guardsmen, who were also stationed on Camp Habbaniyah and were supposedly the 3/3–1 "partners." But in training, the instructors had emphasized that the Iraqis were in charge. If the patrol order called for the U.S. trucks to drop off the jundis and bolt, it wasn't something Huss was going to override in the field.

"Let me guess," said Watson. "The Guard left us and this ain't the drop-off spot."

"Correct," Huss replied as he unsealed the battle-locked five-hundred-pound armor door of the Humvee and headed toward the Iraqi lieutenant.

It was the first rule they would break. The outgoing advisors had told them the armor would keep them alive and to avoid getting out of a Humvee in hostile territory.

Huss approached Lieutenant Qatan, the 22-year-old Iraqi platoon leader in 3rd Company (Iraqi soldiers used just one name for fear of being outed as American puppets and assassinated). Qatan spoke a little English. Huss had received three nights of Arabic classes in the States. The advisors had no interpreter.

"Hey! This the right place or the wrong place? Good or bad?" asked Huss.

"Bad," said Qatan. "One kilometer."

Huss looked down the vacant street, increasingly annoyed that Qatan had let the National Guard trucks leave.

"One klick. Not too far. Okay, let's walk down Route Michigan," said Huss.

Qatan looked stunned. To the American, a grid coordinate on a map was of the most vital importance. To the Iraqi, the map spot was just another unexpected change to accept, like the weather. They were where they were. That was enough.

"No," Qatan said. "Michigan too dangerous. Patrol from here."

Huss didn't like it. He didn't know where they were going, so he couldn't accurately alert the advisor radio net back at Camp Habbaniyah. Idling on Khalidiya's deserted streets felt as reckless as walking along mined Route Michigan, but it was his first day and he didn't want to get off to a bad start with Qatan.

Qatan shouted and his men began clomping up stairs to get to the rooftops, where they could watch over the town. The residents said nothing. Huss figured the last thing the patrol needed was an American inspecting bedrooms while mothers muttered and children shadowed him, so he turned back to the truck.

Boiko stood up in his turret, motioning for Huss to avoid the gutter, convinced it was about to detonate. He remembered the chubby instructor during training who made it sound so easy—all you had to do to spot the mines was *look for the suspicious wires, the teddy bear, the fluorescent flags*. Right. All Boiko could see were blocks and blocks of chipped-up pavement, sewage-filled potholes reflecting the sun, and heaps of trash.

"Get back here, Huss!" Boiko yelled. "They're lighting fires on the roofs."

Coils of kerosene smoke spiraled up from the rooftops. Morning meals? Signal fires? Boiko couldn't decide. Movies remind Vietnam vets of the war they fought decades ago. For Americans new to combat in Khalidiya, war reminded them of their DVD collections. Was this like the beginning of *Black Hawk Down*?

Watching the jundis, Boiko was surprised there was no solidarity between them and the Khalidiya residents, who brushed off all requests for information. Wasn't the whole point of putting the Iraqis, rather than the Americans, in the lead based on the fact that shared language and country would lead to better cooperation from the civilians?

Huss retreated to the Humvee and again sat in the right-hand seat, sealing himself inside several thousand pounds of armor. Some jundis, frustrated by their inability to connect with the local Sunnis, wandered back to their flimsy Nissan with the thin steel slats welded on the sides. Others stood in the deserted alleyways, smoking nervously and watching the Humvee, wondering what the hell the Americans had gotten them into this time. That it had been the National Guardsmen, not the advisors, who had taken the wrong turn didn't really matter. After all, the advisors were supposed to coordinate with fellow Amerikees.

Inside the Humvee, Huss pondered the opposite. *Why is this on me?* In training, the advisor team had been told, "If the Iraqis see your CamelBak, you're wrong!" Meaning: Never get out in front. The U.S military strategy in Iraq had been made crystal clear to them—transition the war to the Iraqis. They were to lead. Advisors were to, well, advise somehow.

Stay in the Humvee, Huss thought. *It's their war.*

He watched a tired jundi amble over to the Nissan where he used the bumper as a boot rest. Huss and his teammates had not been selected for their skills, trained to a standard, or given a defined role. It was up to them to decide how to fit in. The former lecturer on laundry facilities knew little about urban infantry tactics and, despite a crash course, even less about advising. But he'd worn the U.S. uniform for thirteen years and he now understood what he had to do. The advice about staying inside the Humvee's armor was just plain wrong.

Huss popped open the heavy Humvee latch.

"Where are you going?" yelled Boiko.

"Where do you think I'm going?" answered Huss as he stomped back toward Lieutenant Qatan.

Huss was acting on a hunch, but it was a smart one. Special Forces have long followed the dictum "Lead from the rear of the front." Huss wasn't SF, but he knew he had to share the dangers with his foreign protégés and give his best impression of a seasoned urban infantryman. He adjusted his body armor and ammo and trotted toward the jundis at a quick, alert glide, like a ballroom dancer. Keeping his rifle tight in his shoulder, he splashed through sewer water, darting among the parked cars and staying as low as possible without blowing out his back, occasionally taking a knee and springing back up. Wherever his eyes went, his rifle barrel followed. When he reached the jundis, his trousers were mucked up to the knees.

The jundis didn't seem impressed. He didn't realize that they culturally deferred to pomp, not grunt work, whether that was a highfalutin sheikh, a well-fed colonel, or an American advisor out on his first real mission.

"You men find some cover," Huss said to the jundis surrounding the Nissan. "And get your weapons outboard."

The soldiers smiled and nodded politely. They didn't understand a word. Lieutenant Qatan walked up.

"Let's get outta here, Lieutenant," said Huss. "We're in the wrong area."

"No trucks," said Qatan.

"Well, let's get out on Michigan and speed-march."

"Michigan too dangerous," the lieutenant repeated.

"This is dangerous," said Huss. He didn't want to insult Qatan by being overly demonstrative, so he checked his motions and voice, like a batter mumbling under his helmet to an umpire.

Huss turned around, convinced he had won the argument. Qatan might have imagined the same thing. Huss trotted back to the Nissan, tapped on the window, and gestured for the Iraqi driver to maneuver the truck so that his rear machine gunner could cover the street. The Nissan crept back fifty meters in the direction of Route Michigan but stopped short of geometric efficacy, where it could cover the rear avenue of approach with bullets. Huss waved his arms like a traffic cop. The driver smiled, shook his head, and refused to move.

In the meantime, after a desultory search of the nearby homes, the jundis had abandoned any pretence of military discipline. They chatted idly to pass the time like vacationers stuck on an obligatory condo tour, oblivious of the dangers lurking in the street. Lieutenant Qatan had entered a house, but Huss had no idea what he was doing in there.

If they understand that this is a bad place, why don't they leave?

Ten minutes later, Qatan walked back out to the alleyway. Relieved, Huss went to meet him halfway. Just as he began to speak, a hunk of shrapnel whizzed like a buzz saw between him and Qatan, smashing apart the wall behind them.

His ears throbbing as if they'd been hammered, Huss was knocked flat by the explosion. The mine had gone off next to the Nissan, right where he had just stood, and the alley was whirling in smoke. Jundis howled like wounded animals, but in the haze he couldn't tell who was hurt. When his ears cleared, Huss heard cries of "Wounded!" and "Dead! Dead!"

Jundis were screaming at Huss in English. In their six months in Mosul they'd taken some casualties. Third Company had come out of it with the nickname "Unlucky Company." They didn't speak English, but they knew how to call for American medevac.

Huss sprinted back to the Nissan. Three jundis inside the blood-splattered cab moved. The soldier behind the machine gun had a deep gash across his chest, just above the body armor plate. He was dead. Another jundi slumped against the curb, moaning and holding his blood-soaked arm.

Bullets snapped the air. With his blown eardrums, Huss could hear only faint cracks. His pulsating skull was fuzzing his vision. But he could see a nearby jundi shouldering his AK-47 and firing blindly into town.

"Spread out and take cover!" Huss screamed. "Hold fire until you have a target!"

The jundis watched Huss, who at six feet and in full battle gear waddled like a football center. Deciding the American's size afforded them the best protection, a few soldiers huddled behind him and peeked out. Others decided to capitalize on the idea as well and began running toward him, only to be turned away when his hand began swiping at the sky.

"Spread out!"

Perched in the Humvee turret, Sergeant Boiko, the flooring manager, couldn't believe how calm Huss was. Bullets continued to chip at the neighboring houses while jundis trailed behind Huss, darting like a school of fish, mimicking his every move.

Boiko had heard of the Iraqi "death blossom," but here it was playing out. Jundis fired at everything, the way a porcupine sheds quills. Some revolved in a full circle, shooting at everything and nothing.

Boiko ducked into the Humvee below his waist.

"I can't see what they're firing at!" he shouted to Watson, the cop, who urged him to stay down as he eased the Humvee forward.

Watson parked next to Huss, who was helping a wounded jundi out of the Nissan.

"Dude, they're trying to kill us!" shouted Boiko. "You okay?"

"Setting up a casualty collection point here," Huss said.

Fisting a radio mike, he called for tank support from TF Panther. A tinny voice replied that the tanks were busy watching a suspicious Iraqi man walk down Route Michigan.

Huss would have to rely on the Iraqi quick reaction force (QRF) coming from their base about three kilometers away on the edge of the town dump. The QRF was the battalion's 911 force, an on-call group of jundis who would blast out as reinforcements in whatever vehicles they could cobble together.

"The dude in the back of the truck did a somersault when he got hit," said Watson.

"Want me to help him?" asked Boiko. He was the closest thing to a doctor on the team. He had served as a paramedic before landing the flooring gig.

"That jundi is dead," said Huss, grabbing several smoke grenades. "Get to Michigan, set up a blocking position, and guide in the QRF. I'll stay here."

Watson and Boiko drove away. The Humvee began to take fire, but Boiko couldn't see the shooter. He might have been up high in the minaret a block away. The sergeant couldn't unleash his belt of rounds without positively identifying the sniper in the mosque. There were dozens of rules of engagement for U.S. troops in Iraq, including advisors, but none as strict as those dealing with mosques. Knowing this, guerrillas often used mosques as weapons caches and shooting hides.

Tearing onto Michigan, their Humvee stood at the entrance to the village across the street, Abu Fleis, a sprawl of large ornate homes and farms that was favored by wealthy Baathist retirees of Saddam Hussein's Mukhabarat secret police force.

A crowd of men in sweat suits, dark trousers, and cheap Western-style dress shirts began to form, a silent jumble of crossed arms and brazen stares. An Iraqi sedan careened out of the alley behind the crowd and sped onto Michigan, pounding along the median and scattering the wild dogs before slowing toward the Humvee.

With a whole fifteen minutes of experience in the turret to draw upon, Boiko picked up his M-4 rifle and fired into the oncoming car. The driver swerved wildly, then slowed and clawed west, toward Ramadi and a group of Army vehicles rushing toward them, coming to a halt.

"I think you got him," said Watson in his Richmond cop's drawl.

"Hell yes I did."

Boiko looked over his gunsight at the mob. They watched him back, then watched the immobile car.

Why had the driver suddenly come closer to a firefight? What was he thinking? Was he thinking at all? Boiko asked himself.

The crowd did not reveal an opinion. They didn't shout. They didn't spit or throw rocks. They just stared.

The loudspeakers attached to the walls of one of the town's five minarets sprang to life, the imam's sharp words echoing through the rank urban canyons.

It's going to be a long tour, thought Boiko.

★

Like most firefights in Iraq, this one ended in less than two minutes. The Iraqi QRF scooted away the five wounded jundis. Qatan kept the dead man with them, wrapped in sheets taken from a nearby house. He gathered the remnants of his patrol, shushing the occasional outburst of tears. All stole glances at their new American chaperones.

Huss didn't know Arabic, but he understood that Qatan was blaming the outsider, the new advisor who didn't know how to do his job. It confused him. He didn't think he'd screwed up. By the time the troop trucks arrived to take the jundis back to base, Huss was feeling guilty. Perhaps if he had stayed out of sight in the Humvee the whole time, the jundis would have walked around for a while and left town without incident.

When a big Marine wrecker arrived to take the smoking Nissan to the car graveyard, Qatan reacted with stiff pride. "We will take the Nissan back the Iraqi way," he said. "We don't need them." He backhanded the air with his hand.

"Well, who the hell called for a wrecker, then?" asked an annoyed Marine corporal. The Marine tow crew was stationed in the nearby American air base TQ, where false alarms along deadly Route Michigan were not easily forgotten.

Huss knew Qatan was just reclaiming the leadership that had slipped in the moments after the bomb went off, when the jundis had huddled behind Huss. He pulled the Marine aside. "I called for the tow. We lost a man today. Now it looks like the Iraqis want to clean up the mess. I'd appreciate it if you didn't make a big deal of it."

The Marines in the wrecker took in the whole sorry scene and shrugged.

"You one of their advisors?"

"Yeah, I am."

"Good luck, man. I mean it."

The jundis ran large tow straps from the back of a truck to the broken axle of the crumbled Nissan. Qatan shouted confidently to move out. The three advisors watched from their Humvee. In one of their classes they had been taught the T. E. Lawrence gospel: "Better the Arabs do it tolerably than that you do it perfectly. It is their war, and you are to help them, not to win it for them."[5]

Iraqi trucks dragged the broken Nissan along Michigan like a fallen rider towed by a horse. The U.S. Humvee trailed, each of the advisors wondering if they should put a halt to what they called a goat rodeo. Small sparks emerged from the heated axles of the Nissan, then ribbons of aluminum peeled away. Less than a kilometer from Camp Habbaniyah, the spark shower was so hot that even the hungriest strays gave up the chase. The air reeked of scorched rubber and the madness of it all.

Boiko ducked his head inside the Humvee. "Jesus, it's gonna catch fire!"

Flames curled up toward the Nissan's fuel tank. The jundis jumped from their truck, sawed through the tow straps, and fled in all directions. Fire reached the fuel and flared. Watson threw the Humvee in reverse.

"Man, they are all kinds of stupid," said Watson. "Look at 'em run. Bet they got ammo in there!" He wondered how he could look out for men who could not look out for themselves.

The ammo inside the Nissan cooked off like popcorn. It started with a single pop, reached a crackle, and rose to a crescendo, with bullets zinging in every direction while the jundis tried to press themselves into the ground.

It took an hour for the fire to burn out. After five hours and one death in 100° heat, the exhausted patrol limped back to Camp Habbaniyah. The advisors faced a twelve-month tour. To a man, they wondered why they had volunteered for such lonely, frustrating duty and whether they would hold up. They were all close to tears but not one cried.

As was common in battle, their future civilian lives suddenly burst with potential. They wouldn't sweat the paycheck. They would be better fathers. If they could just survive three hundred more patrols in Khalidiya.

Three hundred.

Their first simple patrol had been FUBAR—fucked up beyond all recognition. Was it going to be like this every day?

★

As the Humvee rolled into Camp Habbaniyah, the rest of the team came out to greet the advisors returning from patrol. Lieutenant Colonel Mike Troster, who was in charge of the advisor team, gave the downcast Huss a half hug. For the 44-year-old reserve infantry officer, this was an enormous gesture. He wasn't a coddler, but he knew the toll exacted by helplessness in a climate of relentless violence.

Troster had joined the Drug Enforcement Administration in 1988, after a stint as a cop in Richmond, Virginia, during the nationwide crack cocaine epidemic. He had raided the stinking dens and seen the strung-out bodies, baked minds, and ruined lives. Troster's civilian job had prepared him to face an urban insurgency far better than any military course. He joked that twenty years of lies had robbed him of his head of hair, which he now kept shaved.

He patted Boiko on the back of the neck. It was dusted with dry sweat.

"It's serious out there, Troster," Boiko said.

"I know it is."

Troster was no martinet. He allowed his subordinates to call him "sir," "Colonel," or even "Troster" so long as they avoided his first name. Looking over his exhausted men, he was sick with guilt that as the team leader he'd missed the patrol.

But Troster couldn't go on every mission. He needed three men to accompany the Iraqis, plus another three to stand by as a QRF. That left only four men to train four seventy-five-man Iraqi infantry companies; track the patrols outside the wire; inspect the supply, logistics, and hospital sections; attend endless meetings with the Iraqi brigade staff; recover from the last patrol and plan the next one.

With only ten men, something had to give. So Troster constantly tried to flatten the rank hierarchy like Special Forces commandos do. Everyone on the team did every chore, period.

Military manuals preached the virtue of decentralized decision making, but the wartime reality was that most superiors overcontrolled their subordinate units, minimizing both casualties and junior initiative. Twenty-first-century radios and tracking devices made it even easier to micromanage.

Troster knew that reservists were more relaxed than full-time soldiers by nature. They spent most of their professional lives interacting with civilians. Even when they donned their weekend uniforms, rules were different from those guiding the active-duty force. There was no contractual bond with a specific unit. If reservists decide you're an overbearing jerk, they often vote with their feet, joining another unit.

Once activated, however, the men under his command could not flee Habbaniyah. But Troster knew their pride and grit could abandon them. And if that happened, they were in for a year-long sufferfest.

"We lost a jundi today," said a dejected Huss.

"You can't control random death," said Troster.

"I'm not sure what we did wrong," said Huss.

"You did good," Troster said. "Go get out of your battle rattle. We'll clean up."

The rest of the advisor team relieved the three men back from patrol. Like a pit crew, they stripped and oiled the machine gun, tossed the spent water bottles, washed the windshield, and scrubbed blood out of the seats, leaving the cushions to bake dry in the sun. Boiko and Watson paced alongside their seven teammates, telling them the story, and everyone listened.

Troster encouraged this locker room–style banter. The team greeted every returning patrol to learn the small details of the day's contact, helping the soldiers overcome feelings of isolation and giving them a nod of accomplishment that comes from peer recognition.

War tends to make men sentimental. Troster refused to let soldiers returning from outside the wire to be met with silence that turned bravado into self-pity. If that happened, Khalidiya would sense it. And when the people sensed it, the enemy sensed it, too.

★

Inside his concrete barracks room on Camp Habbaniyah after the patrol, Mark Huss took a long pull of cool water and stripped the sweaty armor from his body. He hung it on pegs where it dripped into pools. The rooms hadn't been upgraded in fifty years. More salt wouldn't matter.

Five hours ago, Huss had fancied himself a teacher watching his new pupils during recess from the schoolhouse. What a joke. Now he understood that to be an advisor, he had to set the example in combat, showing the jundis leadership without showing up the Iraqi officers.

The 3/3–1 officer cadre was a mix of Sunni and Shia career soldiers, with several veterans of Saddam Hussein's elite special units among them. They treated the jundis—the junior enlisted men—like mules. It had little to do with religion. The old Iraqi Army was built around patrimony. The closer you were to Saddam's circle, the better the pay. Influential Shia had always been a part of Saddam's officer corps. The Shia conscripts, however, had been born into Iraq's underclass and had no bloodline connection to the elite. The caste system was stark. Officers sometimes used pistol bullets as corrective action.

Huss was a senior enlisted man, a noncommissioned officer (NCO) with decision-making power, the backbone of the U.S. Army. He showed deference to officers, of course, but he expected respect. In the New Iraqi Army, as in Saddam's Army, the officers made all the decisions for the jundis. He knew that no advisor could ever change that, and he suspected that the Iraqis resented taking advice from enlisted men, American NCO or not.

Huss was determined to be an older brother to the jundis. Although the Iraqis had been in combat for months, while the Americans had just arrived, they needed serious help. They lazily walked the battlefield, clustered up as a defensive instinct, and fired blindly. That included Qatan, but Huss had to protect the lieutenant's reputation if he was going to break through to the other officers. Officers tend to be professionally defensive, no matter their nationality.

Huss was too tired to eat so he slept hungry. After sunset, he fought the grogginess and a sharp headache, pulled on his muddy boots, put a loaded 9mm pistol in his pocket, slung his M-4 across his chest, and trudged across the camp to the memorial ceremony for 3rd Company's fallen man.

Unlucky Company, *his* company.

A few candles flickered near a photograph of the fallen jundi. It was quiet except for a few jundis sniffling in their bunks and some grainy Arab music spun from a cassette player. It smelled of strong tobacco. The Iraqis watched him, wet eyes reflecting the light. Huss had the feeling he should say something, but of course he didn't speak Arabic, so he stood there with his hand over his heart. On the laminated Iraq country card the Army had issued him, a cultural sheet of dos and don'ts that included a few Arabic pronunciations like "Good Morning," and "Stop! Hands up," the hand-over-heart gesture meant either a promise or sincerity, Huss couldn't remember which.

An angry Lieutenant Qatan approached.

"The jundi Hussein was a very good soldier. The men are very sad."

Meaning Hussein would be alive if I hadn't insisted on moving the Nissan, Huss thought. "I'm here to honor Hussein," he said.

Qatan softened and translated for Unlucky Company's commander, Captain Walid. He was a thin, bald Iraqi who wore the same thick mustache as every other officer. Huss had been warned that Walid was lazy and rarely left the guarded wire walls of Camp Habbaniyah. But now he was every inch the indignant warrior, glaring up at the massive Huss while barking at him in Arabic so all could hear.

"Captain Walid is angry because the trucks left us at the wrong place," said Qatan. "And because you wanted us to walk on Michigan."

All on me, Huss thought.

"That's war," Huss said. "You go where you're supposed to go and do what you're supposed to do."

Qatan translated. Walid said nothing, but the jundis seemed to accept this. They had been fighting for eight months and Huss had been fighting for about eight hours, but the American projected authority.

Huss stood there for a few awkward minutes listening to the sad music, nodded politely, then walked back to his room where he tried to flush the day's memories so he could sleep, a pistol on his nightstand. Huss wasn't worried about the loyalty of the jundis; he feared their ability to secure the area. Insurgents mortared Camp Habbaniyah several times a week. The team lived with the 3rd Iraqi Battalion right next to the perimeter concertina wire. The week before, several insurgents had sidled to the guard post and shot a jundi to death. When an advisor to the 2nd Iraqi Battalion, Marine Sergeant Brian Dunlap, had rushed forward to fight, the attackers ran away.

That night, AlertNet, a humanitarian news service run by the Thomson Reuters Foundation, posted the blurb: "Four Iraqi soldiers were killed and five were wounded when a roadside bomb struck their vehicle in Khalidiya, 85km west of Baghdad, policeman Mohammed Abbass said."[6]

There were no police in Khalidiya, but that did not stop the concocted story from being repeated on leftist American websites like Common GroundCommonSense.org and DemocraticUnderground.com, and eventually reprinted on icasualties.org, a well-respected site used by U.S. reporters and soldiers to track battlefield trends.[7]

In the space of a few hours, the killing of jundi Hussein and three ghosts from the 3rd Company, 3rd Battalion, 3rd Brigade, 1st Iraqi Division was read around the world.

★

When Huss left the Unlucky Company barracks, Captain Walid and Lieutenant Qatan walked over to the officers' mess, where Qatan told the story of the failed patrol.

"Sergeant Huss was like a hyena," concluded Qatan. "He was strong in the battle but clumsy with his mind."

"We will find out what he does in America," Walid offered.

The other Iraqi officers, who sat riveted throughout the story, turned to hear the appraisal of their battalion commander, Lieutenant Colonel Falah, a smart, trim officer in his early forties whose youthful looks masked a cruel streak. "It is important to learn the information of their real jobs," Falah said. "I am surprised the Americans again sent us reserves. We are Special Forces and our advisors should be Special Forces, especially here in Anbar."

The others nodded in agreement. Several of the officers had served in Saddam Hussein's elite infantry units, but even they were still digesting their deployment to Habbaniyah, where they were fighting for their lives.

If the advisors entered Habbaniyah as underdogs, so did Battalion 3/3–1. They had arrived at the camp only a month earlier as one of three elite battalions in the Iraqi 3rd Brigade. For a week they gingerly probed the Euphrates-fed farm hamlets surrounding the base with a few two-hour patrols, and then the entire 3rd Battalion had gone on an eleven-day leave. They returned to orders from their Iraqi brigade headquarters—which was advised by a team of Marines—handing them sole responsibility for Khalidiya, the poisonous capital of the Habbaniyah area and its only real city, two kilometers west of Camp Habbaniyah. It was devastating news. The 3/3–1 officers had assumed that Khalidiya, whose urban box land was ideal landscape for snipers and bombers, would be patrolled by all three battalions in the 3rd Brigade. Worse, the previous advisor team had given way to yet another group of rookies, for the third time in twenty months.

Iraqi Battalion 3/3–1 had rolled off the assembly line in the fall of 2004 and fought acceptably well during its initial six-month tour in Mosul. Their reward for this trial run was a transfer to Habbaniyah. When they heard they were going to Anbar Province, dozens of jundis deserted rather than face what they saw as a death sentence. Many had hoped to redeploy to Baghdad, where they could defend their own neighborhoods. Instead, they had been ordered to help the Americans bring the Habbaniyah region to heel. The local Sunnis—especially the hard-bitten, uneducated ones in the wasteland towns surrounding the moldering British air base—were seen by the Shia soldiers as a lost tribe, ungrateful for help, unwilling to abandon murderous traditions, and unworthy of salvation. Even the Sunni officers were fearful of the "crazy hicks," as they called the Anbar tribesmen.

No man personified the local fanaticism more than arch-terrorist Abu Musab al-Zarqawi, who declared war on the Shia a week after the 3/3–1 arrived in Camp Habbaniyah.[8] Two kilometers west on Route Michigan in Khalidiya, Zarqawi stationed about a dozen AQI lieutenants. They were aided by a half dozen radical imams who arranged housing for foreign Arab fighters—Sunni jihadists from other countries who had come to kill Americans or Shia—using Route Michigan as their main thoroughfare between Ramadi and Fallujah. Three hundred U.S. soldiers and Marines had died in the corridor.

AQI also relied on several hundred cooperative Sunni tribesmen as part of the "honorable resistance"—men who earned money by fighting and were morally reinforced by their sheikhs and imams, no matter the collateral damage involved in attacks. None of these warriors wore a uniform. Most lived at home, from where they were summoned to snipe at American soldiers, plant roadside bombs once or twice a month, and otherwise act like a street gang.

It wasn't uncommon for AQI and their confederates to build a bomb, pay a local digger to plant it along the highway, recruit a different lookout to detonate it by remote control, and then drive home for dinner at a farmhouse ten kilometers away, where they could watch it all play out on a DVD delivered by a hired cameraman.

AQI controlled the everyday lives of the Habbaniyah tribes. It sold the fuel and taxed the trucks that used it to move along the highway, charged protection fees to the rare business that wasn't shuttered, and coerced imams to skim for the mujahideen, or freedom fighters, contributions made in the mosques. AQI operatives married tribal women to insert themselves into the traditional hierarchy and murdered any sheikh who objected to the practice.

Americans occasionally strung barbed wire across the highway so they could check the faces of travelers against grainy, grimy Xeroxed photographs of suspected terrorists. In early 2005, a small caravan carrying Zarqawi encountered an American checkpoint near Khalidiya. According to the Americans, the wily Zarqawi jumped from his truck, leaving his laptop in haste.

Local Khalidiyans remembered it differently. Zarqawi calmly got out of the backseat of the car while the Americans sorted through the queue. He stopped to piss by the side of the road and then slipped down a back alley. The villagers hid him while Americans searched between houses.

To protect a fellow Sunni was the duty of every Khalidiyan. Even if they didn't love AQI, they were socially connected to, and literally enriched by, the local insurgency. In the same way small Texas towns follow their football teams, everybody in Khalidiya knew an active resistance fighter and kept score. The Americans promised security but had brought a hurricane of damage. They passed through Khalidiya in their armored trucks like tourists on glass-bottomed boats admiring exotic fish.

The Khalidiya sheikhs, a title loosely used in Anbar for any man with influence, implored the AQI fighters to remain cautious. If they paraded in their black balaclavas too prominently in town, mugging for pictures on al Jazeera, they would draw the attention of Marine headquarters in nearby Fallujah. It was best to inflict some casualties on each American unit that rotated through the area—enough to keep the Americans on the defensive but not so many that the Marines would mass their forces to crush the city, as they had done in Fallujah in 2004.

Khalidiya had perfected this war of the flea: A sniper shot on Monday, a roadside bomb on Tuesday, a street protest of the disproportionate American response on Wednesday, soliciting medical supplies from the Americans on Thursday, an attack in Ramadi early enough on Friday to return for noon prayer, a mortar attack on Camp Habbaniyah on Saturday, and planning to rout incoming transients on Sunday.

Since September 2003, when the first U.S. battalion took residence in Camp Habbaniyah, Khalidiya insurgents who pretended to be civilians had steadily taken American lives while bolstering their own influence. Now it was September 2005, and a battalion from the New Iraqi Army had arrived. AQI and its local social network of bombers and shooters planned to give the Shia soldiers and their Sunni puppet officers the same bright welcome they'd given the maladroit American units that had shuffled in and out for the previous two years.

2

You Do Not Give Me Orders

★   ★   ★

September 2005

Huss slept for fifteen hours the day after the bomb blast, but couldn't shake the fatigue. He opened his door and squinted. The sun was high. Huss did his best to steel himself for a patrol that was scheduled to leave Camp Habbaniyah in an hour, give or take. The battalion sent out one or two patrols daily and punctuality wasn't expected.

Huss had learned that lesson a week earlier. An advisor he was replacing, the Army musician, told him an Iraqi formation was scheduled for 0700. Huss waited in the empty Camp Habbaniyah courtyard for twenty minutes before checking on the American advisors. They were asleep. Eventually the jundis rolled out for physical training, organized by a sharp Iraqi lieutenant named Khalid who wanted to impress the new advisors on deck. The exercises were so ridiculous that Huss, a former wrestler, excused himself to chuckle privately.

Huss wasn't laughing now. Punch-drunk, he was so tired he could barely lace his boots. His head hurt.

Sergeant First Class Eliezer Rivera, 40, a post office supervisor from Virginia, stopped him. "I'm taking your place this afternoon," said Rivera.

"It's my patrol."

"You got to go out yesterday. I want to see the sights," said Rivera, who was the same rank as Huss but had been promoted earlier and thus was the team's senior NCO.

Rivera was no expert on combat fatigue. He had no instruction on the subject. Nor had he heard of traumatic brain injury (TBI) caused by explosions. A year later, Pentagon health experts would label such battlefield concussions the "signature injury" of the war and institutionalize screening procedures, but Rivera didn't have the benefit of future science. He just knew that Huss was hurting.

All the advisors were. They now understood that their daily task would be to lead Iraqi soldiers into a deadly city that had struck down a man on their first patrol. The Army had established a training program to show new advisors what they were supposed to do in a pinch—shoot from a moving vehicle, throw a grenade, say "excuse me" in Arabic—but the initiative never specified what the teams were supposed to accomplish on the murky counterinsurgency battlefield.

That was up to junior soldiers like Boiko. Because the team had no medic, his civilian paramedic experience attracted jundis at all hours, and he'd been with them only a week. His ambulance runs were years gone, but when he told one inquisitive English-speaking jundi about his past, the rumors of a surgeon in their midst spread like bomb fragments.

Today was Boiko's turn to be vehicle commander of the three-man advisor Humvee, accompanying three trucks the Iraqis had scrounged up. They didn't want to ride with the National Guardsmen of TF Panther today. The patrol roster was twenty jundis, one Iraqi officer, and three American enlisted men. Boiko checked his personal radio and walked over to where the jundis were gathered listening to an Iraqi lieutenant delivering the patrol brief in the shade of one of the hundred eucalyptus trees planted by British soldiers seventy years earlier.

Camp Habbaniyah was built in 1935 on the west bank of the Euphrates to boost air support during the forty-year British occupation of Iraq. It was lavishly designed, a precursor to the monstrous consumer FOBs built by the Americans for their own foray. There were so many trees on the two-kilometer-wide camp that shade was always a few steps away, and in the summer the Brits could plunge into the Olympic-size swimming pool near the Rest Center, or visit the sailing club that adorned the shore of Lake Habbaniyah, a few kilometers south of the base, where King Faisal sometimes water-skied with the RAF pilots. The Brits abandoned the air base in 1959, after Iraqi soldiers murdered Faisal.

Boiko was surprised that the Iraqi patrol leader, Lieutenant Khalid, was a platoon commander. It was the second time in as many days that an Iraqi company commander—first Captain Walid and now an Iraqi captain known as "Big Mustache"—sent a subordinate in his place. But Khalid was impressive. He briefed his troops on time. He arranged to bring an Iraqi medic along, which took pressure off Boiko. Khalid wore American kit he had paid for himself, including a first aid pouch and a fighting knife. Most Iraqis went into combat with a magazine in their weapon and a miniature Koran in their pocket.

"All set?" Boiko asked Khalid.

Khalid smirked. He spoke some English, but in Iraq, the language was Arabic. If American enlisted men were going to lord it over him, they should a least be able to communicate.

Salam Aleykum *to you too, brother,* thought Boiko. He walked back to his idling Humvee, which was parked under a giant camouflage net, a leftover from Iraq's feeble defense against U.S. airstrikes on Habbaniyah at the outset of the war. A short Iraqi wearing a faded American camouflage uniform and a green Kevlar helmet approached the American Humvee. "Boiko! Boiko! I am GW, the terp."

The interpreters, mostly middle-class Shia from Baghdad, used nick-names to shield their identities from both the locals and the jundis, who once back home on leave might blab to the wrong militiaman. Boiko grinned broadly at the terp, another huge relief.

"I'm Shawn Boiko. You can call me Boiko."

"I already call you Boiko."

Boiko took an instant liking to GW. "Hot today."

"Hot for Wahabi, too," said GW.

The jundis sometimes called the insurgents Wahabi, Takfiri, or irhabi, referring to a politicized Sunni theology that in Iraq's chaos had come to stand for insane murderers.

Boiko and GW hopped into the Humvee. Above them in the turret, Rivera jerked back the charging handle of the machine gun, opened the feed tray cover, and inspected, then reinspected, the empty chamber. Watson, the driver, tossed water bottles into the backseat.

"You ready for this?" asked Rivera.

"The Army says so," said Boiko.

The patrol left the wire in the early afternoon. The temperature rose well over 100°, driving Khalidiya residents indoors. Lieutenant Khalid wanted to sneak into town instead of parading up Route Michigan, where insurgent lookouts were posted every few hundred meters. So he used a little-known camp gate to the north. The convoy resembled a circus caravan. A Nissan pickup, a boxy Iraqi ambulance, an ancient British turned Iraqi Army trans-port, and Boiko's Humvee turned down a Khalidiya side street onto Market Street. If you wanted to earn your combat infantryman's badge, which dis-tinguished soldiers who'd experienced enemy contact, the corner of Market and 20th streets, Khalidiya's main intersection just north of the police station that had been blown up by insurgents in 2003 and the hospital that had been abandoned by doctors and nurses in 2004, was your best chance.

Loiterers crushed their cigarettes and disappeared into a labyrinth of alleys and walled houses. No one knew why it was called Market Street.

There were no open shops. The only imports were the myriad bombs that made Market one of the most heavily mined thoroughfares in Iraq. The going rate was $70 to plant a mine, double that if the bomb killed a jundi or an American.

The Iraqi ambulance smacked an irrigation rut and skidded in the mud. The driver hit the gas, sinking the wheels in deeper. The axle bent. The Iraqi medic got out. He shook his head and lit a cigarette. Today, his war was over.

Khalid scowled. They were at "Crows' Feet," the point where the streets began to cobweb at the edge of town. Khalid ordered the jundis to dismount. Khalidiya's reputation for snipers pushed Rivera low behind the gun. Insurgents shot exposed turret gunners every week, their final seconds replayed on the Syrian Al Zwar satellite television channel, a loop of snuff videos the jundis sometimes watched for macabre scares. The enemy posted the same clips on YouTube for the U.S. soldiers. The doomed Americans always looked lazy in their final moments. After five minutes of slouching in the turret under the weight of his armor, Rivera understood why. His back was inflamed. He inched back up, bobbed his head to frustrate anyone glassing him with a scope, and gave up after ten minutes. It was just too damned hot to dodge bullets.

Crouching in the cool shadows of the wheel wells, five jundis stayed back to guard the vehicles. The rest trailed Khalid on foot like baby ducks. Boiko slowly worked his way up the long column of jundis with GW at his side, leaving Rivera and Watson in the Humvee. As they moved deeper into the city, his thermometer read 107°. Sweat spilled down his body, pooling in his trouser cuffs before welling in the bottom of his boots.

Boiko wore a four-and-a-half-pound helmet, a fifteen-pound day pack, a water bladder, a first aid kit, a long-sleeve camouflage uniform thick enough for winter, fireproof gloves, knee pads, a sixteen-pound armor-plated vest hung with another seven pounds of bullet magazines, grenades, flares, and a radio. A Kevlar crotch flap dangled between his legs. A heavy throat protector turtlenecked his vest. His "desert boots" were thick enough to ford snowdrifts. All together his kit weighed more than fifty pounds and added fifteen degrees.

Boiko looked like a mountaineer. He felt like he was scaling a peak built out of running hair dryers. His thighs were burning under the strain and the sun. The jundis, who wore lightweight helmets and a single armor chest plate—instead of the six pieces of armor—seemed to be keeping up just fine. *Whatever they can do, I can do better,* thought Boiko.

Khalid dashed from one shaded pathway to another to avoid snipers. Potholes from explosives scarred the road, one deep enough to swallow a small car. Rows of squat houses with high concrete walls had been stacked next to thousands of multistory cinder-block buildings, one roof just a meter away from the next. Each house had barred windows and a tiny courtyard ringed by stout walls, the equivalent of an urban fortress.

Boiko noticed that the people of Khalidiya again refused to engage with the jundis on patrol. Most did the soft scatter. They eased off the street and silently let the strange army pass. Doors closed on children inside, their lingering eyes causing sharp warnings from mothers to look away.

The heat turned the jundis' sprints into shuffles. They knelt at the end of every block, scanning the rooftops while they sucked water from their canteens. Gunfire cracked somewhere, but Boiko didn't stop. He was too tired. It had to be aimed somewhere else. GW grabbed him and pulled him down.

"What the hell?" Boiko exclaimed.

"We're taking fire," said GW.

"Us?"

"Yes, us!"

The shots continued. Boiko was too hot to tell whether the fire was coming from close or far away. Flipping the channels on his high-tech encrypted American radio, Boiko heard nothing. Using a cheap Iraqi walkie-talkie, GW heard everything.

"A jundi has been shot," GW reported. "Back at the vehicles."

"Find Khalid and tell him we gotta get back there."

Khalid was already running back. The sound of gunfire increased as they approached Crows' Feet. Boiko keyed the radio as he ran: *Dagger Whiskey, this is Dagger Bravo. Someone shot?*

No clue, Watson replied on the Humvee radio. *We're taking fire, though.*

"The jundi is okay," GW interrupted. "Hit him in the plate!"

"Yeah!" Boiko shouted joyfully. The thought of losing someone on the first patrol he led terrified him. He slapped GW on the shoulder as they ran.

The patrol's vehicles were circled like covered wagons. Watson put his Humvee closest to the gunfire to shield the thin-skinned Iraqi trucks. In the turret, Rivera scanned the area, looking for muzzle flashes. Not a single puff of dust. Where was the firing coming from?

"We good to get outta here, GW?" asked Boiko.

"I'm sorry to tell you, but a jundi has been shot in the chest. Very hurt."

"You said it hit his plate," snapped Boiko.

"I was wrong."

The gawking crowd of jundis parted for the former paramedic. Shedding his fireproof gloves, Boiko knelt by the wounded Iraqi and found a pulse. It was fading as fast as his color.

"Throw him in the Humvee," said Boiko. "We need to get him to TQ."

A medical shock trauma unit stood ready to treat urgent casualties at the air base, just seven kilometers east on Route Michigan. They might just make it.

"No. We're putting him in our truck. Not yours," Khalid said as his jundis placed the stretcher in the Iraqi ambulance. Boiko had no time to point out that the ambulance was stuck in the mud. He removed a battle dressing from his first aid kit, stuffed an expanding fabric ball into the wound, and grabbed the nearest jundi.

"Hold it tight, man."

Khalid rigged a single tow cable from the troop truck to the moored ambulance. The line quivered under the strain and then yanked the ambulance free. Speeding toward TQ, the advisors followed in the Humvee, watching the Iraqi medic work on the wounded jundi, the ambulance doors flapping open and shut with every bump.

Enemy bullets plinked off the armor. Boiko and Watson pleaded with Rivera to move down the turret, but the senior NCO just slid down a bit, hands still on the machine gun.

"Still got no targets," Rivera said.

"Well, somebody sure has you."

The tow cable popped. The frayed steel line snapped like a whip into the back of the British troop truck, severing a steel stanchion and nearly decapitating a jundi. The ambulance stopped and the Humvee skidded abreast. The Iraqi medic looked at Boiko and shook his head.

Boiko had seen enough final pronouncements as an EMT to know what it meant, but he'd also seen the dying claw their way back to life. Watson and Boiko sprinted to an ambulance awash in blood. A hole in the jundi's chest drained red in lazy spurts, like a sump pump.

"We need to get this soldier to TQ now, Khalid!"

"We'll put him in the big truck," Khalid replied through GW.

"No you won't," Watson calmly countered. "The Marines at TQ will light you up, you roll up in that thing. You're putting him in the Humvee. We'll take him to TQ."

Khalid was furious. Who was Watson? A driver! The jundis responded to power, *wasta,* and here were two sergeants undercutting an Iraqi officer.

"You don't give me orders."

The jundi was bleeding out. This was no time for pulled punches. Boiko turned to GW. "You tell Khalid that the only way his soldier will live is if we get him to TQ. Otherwise, when he dies, it's on him."

Hearing the translation, Khalid lunged forward and shoved Boiko. Boiko shoved back and the two locked like crabs, handfuls of harnesses, helmet to helmet.

"You tell him his soldier is dying!" said Boiko. "He's killing him by wasting time!"

They were separated, and Khalid and his men tried to slide the stretcher into the U.S. Humvee, but they couldn't get it into a groove. Eventually they jammed it, sending grenades and flares clattering into the foot wells. To make room, Rivera inched his feet forward in the turret while GW and the Iraqi medic squeezed in.

Rushing toward TQ, the bleeding jundi pitched and rolled. The men held him like parents cradling a new baby, terrified to hold too tightly, terrified to let go. The Iraqi medic stroked the jundi's hair, mumbling in Arabic.

"You don't know what the hell you're doing, do you?" said Boiko. He clambered onto the center ridge with his head tucked behind Rivera's knees. He shoved a pressure bandage into the pool of blood welling in the sunken chest of the skinny jundi and watched for air filling what was left of his lungs.

"Come on, dude."

The jundi opened his eyes and fixated on Boiko as if to say, "Bring me back, bring me back." Then his eyebrows shot up in terror. He reached out, hugged Boiko fiercely, and gurgled.

"Stop the vehicle," said Boiko. "He's dead."

Boiko and Watson exited to get some fresh air, but the heat quickly sapped any relief the desert air gave their nostrils. The Iraqi Nissan, packed with crazed jundis, driver leaning on the horn, skidded toward them. Khalid gestured the Americans to get back into the Humvee and drive.

"They've lost their freaking minds," said Watson.

Boiko felt like he'd been poisoned. He wanted to tell Khalid about the death himself, a healing moment for them both. Look him right in the eye like a soldier. Maybe even hug it out. Iraqis liked that, right?

Too late. GW slashed his hand vigorously across his throat. Boiko started to tell him to pick a friendlier hand signal but the Iraqis erupted in a screaming rage. Americans tended to brood after a fellow soldier's death, plotting revenge and then quietly seeking solace with one another. The Iraqis just unbridled their emotions and rode them until spent.

The jundi gunner standing behind the Nissan's cab screamed and pulled the trigger back on his PKC machine gun, rounds arcing into the sky. The news of the death rippled through the crowded flatbed truck. Other jundis fired. All the gunfire caused the Americans to wince. Then the crazed machine gunner leveled his barrel at the Americans.

Only six meters away, Rivera pivoted his machine gun and put the sights on the Iraqi gunner. The Iraqi gunner pointed at Boiko and screeched, while GW hastily translated.

"Drive him to your hospital or I will kill you!"

"He's dead," said Boiko.

"He is not dead. Take him or you will be dead."

"Watch your mouth, asshole," Boiko said. "It could get you killed out here."

"I will kill you!"

Boiko glared, turned his back, and walked to the Humvee

"GW, tell Khalid to get over here and see for himself," Boiko yelled. "I'm sick of these goddamned Iraqis! Tell 'em they best stay the hell away from me. Forever!"

Khalid and his men tugged the stretcher out of the Humvee and stood around the dead soldier, the way boys stare at a dead bird. A jundi poked the corpse with his boot, while another checked for a pulse. A third took off his helmet and held his face in his hands, wailing. Another lay facedown, pounding his fists into the dirt.

Then the corpse twitched. The jundis jumped back, shouting and pointing. Some clapped and smiled. Others waved at their medic to help the dead man. After a few frantic minutes, the jundi was once again pronounced dead. The Americans and GW climbed back in the Humvee as Khalid and his jundis resumed their screaming.

"What're they saying?" Boiko asked.

"It's not important," GW said. "We should leave right now, okay?"

Like a good terp, he knew better than to translate everything.

★

An hour later in Camp Habbaniyah, the advisors watched the jundis say good-bye to their dead friend. The corpse was cleaned, wrapped in a white sheet, and carefully lifted into a truck for transportation to the morgue at TQ. From there it would be flown to Baghdad and sent to an Iraqi hospital for collection by the family. The death notification system was simple: A sobbing jundi called the family or some relative nearby. Some bodies were lost for weeks, so tangled was the tracking system.

"They hate us," Boiko told his teammates.

"They don't," Troster said firmly. "They're just in mourning."

"Boiko. Watson. We should pay our respects," said Rivera.

Boiko, Rivera, and Watson walked over to the dormitory where the Iraqi officers were quartered. Boiko had filled his helmet with cold soft drinks and offered them around to his Iraqi charges. The perspiring cans felt cool in his hand, but the Iraqis refused them. Khalid wouldn't even greet him.

The advisors trudged over to the quarters of the Iraqi enlisted men, a concrete hut where two dozen jundis sat cross-legged in a circle around a pot of rice. They smiled when they saw the sodas and invited the advisors to sit with them. Their own officers rarely visited, and they never brought sodas. The jundis chugged the sodas and the Americans pawed at the rice bowl, sharing their meal.

One jundi popped three cheap cigarettes into his mouth, sucked them alight, and offered them up. The Americans politely declined and returned to their hooch, stripping off lukewarm armor and rancid cotton T-shirts. You couldn't wear more comfortable synthetics because in a fire the fibers melted into your skin. In their boxers, the advisors huddled around portable air conditioners, guzzling Cokes and eating Pop-Tarts, while they read letters from home for the twentieth time. The night was hot, and the sweaty gear made the compound smell like a locker room. One advisor excused himself to take a piss, burst into tears behind the barracks, and vowed never to read letters from his kids in company.

GW poked his head into the room. The Iraqi Army had no death benefits so he was collecting money to send to the family of the dead jundi. Boiko, Watson, and Rivera pitched in $200.

"There's a sniper out there who knows his business," Watson commented.

"Those Khalidiya people hate their own countrymen," said Huss, who had volunteered to go on the next patrol despite the fact that he still had a headache. "I think even the jundis are surprised."

"If it's like this every day, we'll lose the whole battalion in six months," Watson rejoindered. "This makes policing look like crossing-guard duty."

"The way the officers are acting, it looks like we've already lost them," Boiko added. "This mission . . ."

The men needed to vent, and as team leader, Troster couldn't be party to it. Not when they were so wrung out. The common Army phrase, *If the troops ain't bitching they ain't happy,* was true insomuch as shared misery bonded men, but Troster's presence, even if silent, would be interpreted as complicity. To prevent a loss of esprit de corps, he'd have to step in to douse the inflamed language with conviction. There'd be words, maybe words that would linger. It was hot enough already. Besides, his men's instincts were correct. The insurgents were buried in the city of Khalidiya like ticks, the jundis were as alien outside the wire as his advisors and had no meaningful contact with the locals, and the Iraqi officers were undercutting his team.

In his running shorts and combat boots, an M-4 carbine slung under his right arm, Troster left the room and walked toward the Euphrates, which was sliding lazily by just a hundred meters away. He stopped to watch two jundis inspecting rooftop damage from a recent mortar strike. Just across the river was Jazeera, farmland the Americans rarely patrolled and that as a result was dominated by insurgents.

Mortars fell on the camp nearly every day. They hit with flat, crunching claps, like library books dropped on linoleum. TF Panther had tucked the Iraqis in a far corner of camp, close to the Jazeera mortarmen and away from their HQ. Many Panther guardsmen believed the jundis were calling for the mortars and adjusting the strikes by cell phone. This was not isolated paranoia. U.S. headquarters in Baghdad issued an intelligence report claiming the Iraqi units assigned to Anbar had been infiltrated by insurgents, and that Iraqi officers in Habbaniyah had indeed guided mortars onto American troops.

To Troster, who was watching the jundis pour a bucket of tar into the shrapnel divots on the roof, the report was an absurd accusation. The 3rd Iraqi Brigade had lost several vehicles so far, and a few jundis had been grievously wounded. Any traitor would have been smoked out.

GW tentatively approached Troster, his head bowed. He was wrung out, caught between the advisors who paid him and the countrymen who wanted new, more experienced advisors.

"What are you hearing, GW?" Troster asked.

"It's bad, sir. The officers are complaining about you advisors."

In the American military, officers know that they must firmly quash rumors. Humor is tolerated, but no disciplined unit allows malevolent gossip and backbiting to fester in the ranks. Society under the dictatorship of Saddam Hussein had dined on gossip. Each family would talk only to those they thought they could trust, but deceit was common. In Khalidiya, few Sunnis ventured far from home. If strangers appeared on the street, the residents alerted their neighbors. Accurate information was scarce, so what was heard on the street was exchanged like currency, even after rumors spread beyond facts.

Iraqi military units weren't immune. The rumors racing through camp insisted that the new Americans didn't care about Iraqis. Huss had exposed the patrol to the attack on Michigan. Boiko and Watson had dumped a jundi out of their Humvee before he died. Rivera had wanted to kill Lieutenant Khalid.

"GW, please tell Colonel Falah that I wish to meet with him," Troster said.

"Tomorrow?"

"Tonight. I'm conducting an investigation into the jundi's death now."

There was nothing to investigate. Troster was sure his men had acted properly. But he had to restore his team's image, and to do it he needed to meet the Iraqi officers halfway and play the blame game deftly or they'd reject him outright. His goal was to buy a few weeks for his advisors to demonstrate their mettle. They had no good training to lean on and would have to learn how to survive in combat on the job even while "teaching" the more experienced jundis.

★

Troster's team had graduated from advisor training only a month earlier, a ninety-day period of instruction at Indiana's Camp Atterbury. Because of all the wasted time, the advisors described the infuriating training as forty-five days of ill-conceived classes crammed into ninety. Most of their teachers had never been to Iraq; none had advised foreign militaries. Instructors taught soldiers to stick their rifles out of Humvee windows as they rolled through dangerous areas. In Anbar, however, roadside bombs were so prevalent that stupidly compromising an armor seal was punishable by court-martial. Only two men per team received heavy-machine-gun training. But advisors in Iraq rotated the job daily. Radio training was limited by specialty, yet every advisor in Iraq had to know how to use the radio. Instructors crammed language and cultural classes into a single week, the briefs given by soldiers who had never been to Iraq, much less survived combat there. The courses at Camp Atterbury packed eight hours of Arabic-language immersion into two nights, right after critical but exhausting combat lifesaving classes. Future advisors were taught to toss grenades by throwing baseballs over a parked minivan. The Army failed to supply common training aids like butcher paper or Magic Markers, so Troster's men bought their own at Wal-Mart.

Troster expected to receive counterinsurgency, or COIN, training at Atterbury. He assumed the Iraq War would be won on the streets, face-to-face with a city forced to choose between the coalition and the insurgency. But Atterbury didn't do COIN.

He sent emails to friends already in Iraq asking for the latest COIN best practices. While waiting to hear back, he decided to teach his advisors what he already knew. One example was "combatives training," or hand-to-hand combat. Soldiers were trained to deliver killing blows, but Troster doubted Iraq's insurgents would come close enough to kill them with bare hands. Much of the time, he suspected, advisors would be grappling like cops with suspects, so he taught his men choke holds and arm bars used by law enforcement.

The command sergeant major of Troster's 80th Division spotted the group practicing the moves. The 80th had guidelines on close combat training and a set physical fitness schedule. "Who authorized this training?" the top enlisted man asked.

"I did," said Troster.

"Well, you're wrong. This is not a combatives day and those aren't even proper combatives. Follow the training schedule."

Troster stood his ground. "No, Sergeant Major."

Atterbury loved fake mortar drills, and camp rules mandated that soldiers sprint away from imaginary shells into imaginary bunkers. Once a trainer caught Troster's team in their hooch playing cards during a drill. "You're all dead!" she screamed.

"We died weeks ago," Boiko replied.

The largest emphasis during training was placed on protecting big bases from attack. The advisors spent hours guarding fake ammo. They were placed without night-vision goggles into towers, staring at the taillights leaving base, and then ordered to shoot the hell out of the Hoosier countryside during inevitable attacks by hundreds of invisible Iraqi insurgents. It was as if Atterbury was preparing the advisors to defend a log fort against a Sioux attack in 1863.

The implication of this training was clear: Combat was what advisors did only a fraction of the time, with a fraction of the force. The instructors claimed that even in the rare case of being assigned to an Iraqi unit that was in the fight, like 3/3–1, the jundis knew how to act outside the wire. According to the instructors, advisors needed to focus on best practices inside the wire, like hired consultants. They weren't supposed to run the corporation.

FOBing—drawing combat pay stationed on a giant forward operating base— might have been the lifestyle for Troster's team had one of his fellow colonels not fallen ill in Kuwait. Troster was tapped to take the man's place. Now he had several problems. Disillusion pervaded both his men and the Iraqi soldiers they were supposed to advise, the jundis were not as well trained as advertised, and the advisors' credentials to give advice were in question. Overarching this internal fracture was the fact that neither side had a strategy for gaining control of Khalidiya. Troster needed to unify the effort so his advisors could eventually influence operations. Shared risk taking in combat was sure to create the bond, and steely professionalism under fire was sure to create influence. To demonstrate that, Troster had to convince his counterpart, the Iraqi battalion commander, Lieutenant Colonel Falah, to give them a chance.

★

Later that night, Chai Boy shot up from his wooden camp stool when Troster walked into the small waiting room outside the office of the Iraqi battalion commander.

"*Masah il khair,*" Troster said, an evening greeting. "Please find Colonel Falah."

Chai Boy was a young jundi who served tea, lit cigarettes, ran petty errands, and never left the wire. As he scurried off, one of Lieutenant Colonel Falah's bodyguards opened the door. Falah's security contingent included a brother and several cousins. All held military rank, drew military pay, and had only one mission—to prevent Falah's assassination.

The aristocratic colonel rose from behind a desk that was decorated with trinkets from his military service under Saddam Hussein, including an Iraqi unit trophy from fighting the Americans in the 1991 Gulf War and a plaque given to him by the American unit he worked with in Mosul in the winter and spring of 2005. That signaled power. He was chatting with another veteran of Saddam's army, his operations officer, Major Aamr.

Aamr was peering at a photo map of Khalidiya poked with red pins indicating recent attacks. Burly and with a thick handlebar mustache, Aamr was talkative, self-deprecating, and muscular. But Aamr wasn't a bully. And his droll wit reminded advisors of Peter Sellers playing Inspector Clouseau. He looked at Troster and smiled.

In 2003, Aamr had commanded a company in Saddam's Special Forces and was ordered to hold a small bridge spanning the Diyala Canal in south Baghdad against attacking U.S. Marines. His men dug trenches and chopped down palm trees to build bunkers. When he saw Marine vehicles across the river, his men opened up. The Americans responded by shooting everything—buildings, the bridge, abandoned cars, trench lines, trees, dogs, even the river, which they bombed and strafed.

Aamr was a good leader and his men held fast, but they had no air cover, no artillery cover, and no contact with their higher command. Those other units had already fled the battlefield. Aamr finally gestured for his men to run up the trenches and ordered them to take off their uniforms and boots, don the civilian clothes in their packs, and go home. He warned them to cheer wildly whenever they saw American tanks. He also told them to stay in touch with each other and to give their unit number when the victorious Americans would, he believed, order Saddam's army to reassemble. He would return to take command of the Special Forces company.

But America's top civilian official in occupied Iraq, Paul Bremer, officially disbanded the Iraqi Army in June 2003 and thus unwittingly replaced Saddam as the man most hated by Iraq's professional military caste. All the leaflets had pledged that an honorable surrender would lead to continued service. Now that the army was disbanded, what was Aamr supposed to do for a living? Become a professional looter like the Iraqis who paraded past his house in Baghdad each day under the weight of stolen goods, like ants carrying bread crumbs? He drove a bus for the rest of year, waiting for the Americans to come to their senses.

In early 2004, word spread through the underground community of former Iraqi Army officers, who had been secretly meeting in small groups over tea and tobacco in Baghdad hookah bars, that the Americans wanted them back. Aamr was part of a group of hard-core officers, mostly Special Forces with good reputations, Sunni and Shia both, that immediately joined the effort to rescue what they considered a foundering American project in Iraq.

"*Masah il khair,*" Troster said respectfully.

The Iraqi officers clucked approvingly.

"*Masah il noor,*" the Iraqis said in concert, returning the greeting.

"You like chai?" asked Falah.

Without waiting for Troster's answer, Falah barked loudly at the door. "Chai! Chai!"

Troster winced.

There was a scramble outside, and one of Falah's bodyguards chased Chai Boy for effect.

"*Nam, shukran,* Colonel," said Troster. Yes, thanks.

Troster waited while the Iraqis lit cigarettes and poured themselves sugary tea. A television flickered Arab and American soap operas, which were officer favorites (the jundis preferred Shiite mullahs thundering sermons for hours).

"It was very hot day," said Falah. "It will be better weather soon."

In Iraq, just like the rest of the world, small talk helps all parties in a negotiation establish a cordial, neutral atmosphere. Troster knew he couldn't start with his immediate concern, but he also wanted to reassert his power, or Falah would treat him as a supplicant. Some advisors addressed Iraqis of equal or higher rank as *saydi,* or sir. Troster never did. Senior Iraqi officers sensed and exploited any gap in perceived power, a habit they learned as they approached general, a promotion determined by cronyism, political maneuvering, and bribery.

"I'm from Virginia, Colonel, a very hot state in the summertime," said Troster as the chitchat petered out. "I was very sorry to learn about the death of the jundi today. How can we help his family?"

After decades of Saddam's wars and police state brutality, Iraqi officers rarely dwelled on the loss of one more soldier. The mourning was done by jundis. Falah seemed puzzled by the offer.

"The Iraqi Army does nothing for him," said Falah. "We are trying ourselves."

Troster knew GW hadn't told the Iraqi officers about the money they'd collected.

"My soldiers gave two hundred dollars for his family," Troster said. "Please let me know if you want us to do more."

The Iraqis exchanged quick bursts of Arabic. The officers earned $600 a month and the jundis about half that. Troster's team had relieved them of a heavy financial burden. And set a difficult precedent.

"You have done much," Falal said. "Thank you."

They sipped tea. The fan sounded louder.

"Have you been told why the jundi died? Medevac took too long," said Falah.

"Colonel, I wasn't there and you weren't there," said Troster. "Sometimes our men tell us one side, but as officers we must choose the truth. I can tell you with all my heart that my men did everything they could."

"Lieutenant Khalid says the Humvee stopped on the road," said Falah.

"The Humvee stopped because the jundi was dead. Then your jundis pointed their AKs and a PKC at my advisors. Very dangerous."

Troster kept sipping his tea as he let the statement sink in. As a civilian, he had worked undercover, recruiting snitches. He had spent countless hours in intellectual combat with dangerous men inside DEA interrogation rooms, tapping for the right psychological buttons to elicit a confession or crack a case. Falah wasn't his enemy, but Troster believed that every conversation moved a relationship forward or backward.

"But the jundi wasn't dead," Falah pressed. "He moved on the ground. Many jundis saw it."

"Ever slaughter a sheep, Colonel?"

"Of course."

"Ever see the animal move after you killed it?"

"Many times."

"That was God's will with the jundi. My soldiers did the right thing. Your soldiers did the wrong thing," said Troster.

Falah traded a look with Aamr.

"Colonel, I know they are just frustrated," Troster continued. "You told me that in Mosul, the Americans worked with you more closely than Task Force Panther. Now here you are in Khalidiya on your own, and you have new advisors on top of it. I'm here tonight to tell you my soldiers are honored to be part of such an elite battalion, the only Iraqi unit in the country to have its own battle space. We are soldiers, not civilians, and we have come here to help you kill Takfiris and take Khalidiya back from the insurgents. But if my men don't have your support, tell me now. Maybe brigade can make different arrangements."

It was Falah's turn to sip tea. Was he being called out by a rogue advisor on the hot seat? Or did Troster have the support of the Marine advisors to his own HQ, the 3rd Iraqi Brigade—and the ability to get him fired?

★

In the summer of 2004, Falah, Aamr, and their comrades from two other battalions formed the 3rd Brigade of the fledgling 1st Iraqi Division at Taji, an American-run training center north of Baghdad. The 3rd Brigade was an elite force designed to hunt insurgents, and they were told they would receive special training after boot camp.

They were born fighting. On their first day at camp, they scrapped with an Iraqi National Guard (ING) unit going through basic training. The ING was considered by the career officers of 3rd Brigade to be an amateur operation filled with civilians who had tricked the foolhardy Americans into high ranks and had never heard a shot fired outside a wedding celebration.

The goal of boot camp is to break men down, stripping them of their individuality so they can be rebuilt as a team. The first group of advisors allowed the 3rd Iraqi Brigade to brag about receiving special urban warfare training. The Americans didn't see roof hopping and room clearing as anything special, but the Iraqis didn't have to know that.

In fall 2004, the brigade received an order to rush 150 kilometers north to Mosul, Iraq's second-largest city, to prepare for the upcoming national election. They ended up patrolling alongside U.S. units for six months.

From Mosul, 3/3–1 went to Camp Habbaniyah, where Troster joined them with a new advisor team, their third. For more than a year, Iraqi officers had watched American soldiers fill their canteens with chai and chug it like Gatorade, plaster their rooms with pictures of half-naked women, strip to their shorts to lift weights, always swearing mercilessly and teasing the unwitting jundis. They cleaned their weapons with toothbrushes, stayed up all night writing operations orders, slept for a few hours with their boots on, lined up at the gate ten minutes before the scheduled patrols, and rushed toward the sound of gunfire.

"The jundi was probably dead, *saydi*," said Aamr.

"Yes, the jundi was dead," Falah concurred. "I will tell the officers. More chai?"

"*Shukran*," Troster thanked him.

Chai was Iraq's social lubricant. The gravity of a tribal dispute could be measured in sips. A truly aggrieved party refused to drink until an acceptable settlement, weakening the host's position by invoking a centuries-old silent protest. Troster took a spoonful from the sugar tin and stirred, sipped, and smiled. So did the Iraqis.

"Tomorrow we go back to Khalidiya," Falah said. "We will search many houses. Can you get trucks?"

Troster was surprised. He didn't see how Falah's schedule of two short patrols per day for a five-hundred-man battalion could ever secure Khalidiya. But now Falah was proposing a battalion-size operation. Both the Iraqis and the advisors were trying to impress each other.

"I'll get the trucks. Have you picked out which houses to hit?" Troster asked.

"It makes no difference. We talk to the people and they will tell us where the terrorists live. It is the Iraqi way."

3

The Usual Suspects

★ ★ ★

Lieutenant Colonel Falah tasked Major Mohammed, the tough 4th Company commander, with leading the mission the following night, September 18. The plan was for three companies of jundis to leave the Camp Habbaniyah wire when IED triggermen were asleep, cordon a few city blocks, and interview residents.

Mohammed smoked a cigarette while the advisors herded excited jundis onboard two massive U.S. Army trucks called six-bys on loan from TF Panther. A few of the advisors inspected the jundis' canteens. If the Americans wanted to do menial work, that was fine with Mohammed, as long as they didn't bother him.

A platoon commander who fought in the Iran-Iraq War, Mohammed rose to the rank of major. He quit Saddam's army in 1998 in disgust over the sycophancy necessary to advance. For five years, he built houses. Then he rejoined the New Iraqi Army in 2004.

Peers who had stayed in Saddam's army were brought back as colonels by the Americans, but Mohammed liked being a major. That meant he could lead his beloved company. Tall for an Iraqi, thin except for a slight potbelly, Mohammed never wore body armor or helmet.

"I can't chase terrorist dogs with all that armor on," he explained.

The jundis thought he was crazy. Americans called him "ballsy." Mohammed didn't care one way or the other.

Jundis crowded around an advisor who had run out of signal flares. They flocked to handouts of any sort—batteries, muscle magazines, fighting equipment, DVDs, Cokes, candy. Mohammed was disgusted by the groveling, and he blamed his own Shia-dominated government for not outfitting

41

its own soldiers. Mohammed was a secular Sunni and his hatred for politicians was universally applied. The least the Shia could do now that they were in charge was look after their own.

Most of his men admired the combat aggressiveness of American soldiers. Mohammed considered them mercenaries on temporary loan from a fickle nation. Of the Iraqi officers, Mohammed gave the advisors the least respect. So the advisors liked him the most. No ass kissing, no lies, no body armor, no spray and pray—holding back the trigger with your eyes closed—in a firefight. Just business.

In the trucks a jundi whistled. Lieutenant Colonel Falah walked from his office trailed by staff officers in shiny new gear, much of it provided by Americans. Many jundis wore rags and dented armor. The Americans tried to make up the difference, but half the donated gear ended up in Baghdad markets on the next liberty.

Falah extended his arms so that his bodyguards could slip on his armor. The last thing that went into his pocket was a signal flare, regally presented for his inspection.

Mohammed felt the familiar anger with Falah rising until he caught sight of Troster, the new advisor team leader, who looked as disgusted as he felt. Mohammed chuckled.

Mohammed and his 4th Company had lived outside the wire in Mosul for six months, during which period Falah visited them only five times. When Mohammed's company raided an insurgent safe house and detained two guerrillas, Falah took credit. But Mohammed hadn't sulked. In the Iraqi Army, combat success was measured by the speed with which credit was stolen from you.

The convoy snaked down Route Michigan and stopped along the northern edge of Khalidiya. All was still except for the clacking of portable generators. Then a tailgate slammed down and dozens of jundis spilled into the street, rushing to the nearest houses.

Mohammed thought the operation was just a show for the Americans. Most men in town who weren't in the fight were unemployed. They loitered and smoked and gossiped. Women raised their children. And gossiped. All of them shielded the insurgent network, refusing even to speak of its existence to Iraqi soldiers. There was no chance a massive house-to-house sweep would result in useful information. Intelligence would come one hard source at a time. Some sources would be volunteers whose allegiance switched from shielding insurgents to helping the New Iraqi Army, the kind of informants American advisors preferred, because there was no arm twisting involved, but the best ones, thought Mohammed, would be suspects who were hunted relentlessly, interrogated, and convinced to betray their comrades.

Mohammed watched the jundis from the other two companies pound on doors with the well-worn stocks of their AK-47s. Lights flickered on in the chosen houses, but the rest of the street remained dark. Khalidiya was used to nightly mayhem—whether insurgents forcing a family to dig in a mine or American SEALs kidnapping a suspect. The other families kept their windows shuttered to the passing plagues.

Mohammed's 4th Company was in charge of securing the operation perimeter. He was setting up his jundis when Falah and his entourage approached. Mohammed counted eleven bodyguards.

"I thought I'd observe 4th Company tonight," Falah told Mohammed.

"It would be our honor, saydi. I'm putting a blocking position near Michigan to seal it off. Sergeant Mustafah will lead. You can go with him."

Having diverted Falah, Mohammed continued with a single reliable jundi to a house that had aroused his suspicions on a previous patrol. An hour later he returned with two prisoners. Dozens of blindfolded suspects sat on the curb next to American trucks already brimming with captives. Jundis ran from house to house, yanking out more.

Flashlight beams, shouting jundis, sullen detainees, quiet families. Watching the operation, Mohammed knew that most of the prisoners were innocent—no one protested an arrest more vociferously than the mother of a guilty boy.

Mohammed manhandled his two prisoners into line with the others. The detainees babbled to one another. Mohammed kicked a loudmouth in the thigh, warning that the next open mouth would find a bullet. To show weakness now would double the calamity.

Mohammed summoned the nearest guard. "Who are these men?" he asked.

"I don't know, saydi," the jundi said.

"Why have we arrested them?"

"I don't know, saydi."

Mohammed searched out Falah, who was talking through the interpreter GW to a bemused Troster at an abandoned storefront. Like Mohammed, Troster couldn't imagine that the dragnet was doing any good. In fact, he was pretty sure goodwill was draining.

"The trucks are full," Troster said. "We can't process all these prisoners tonight."

"Yes, the operation is now finished," Falah concluded.

"You know, Colonel, we may have created more enemies tonight," said Troster.

"Most of them help the terrorists already. But now they know I know. The important thing is to not apologize for the operation and show weakness," Mohammed told the skeptical Troster. "If you don't have water, then you must piss on a tree to bear fruit."

To Mohammed, having advisors was like an arranged marriage—he had to live with it. New advisors were especially irritating. These plumbers, mechanics, and teachers—who were they to judge the decisions of Iraqi officers until they understood the culture?

A group of old men tried to push their way past the jundis on the perimeter but were rebuffed with short jabs of rifle barrels. Mohammed walked over to where they stood in protest, some of them hissing. In the dark, he eavesdropped on their conversation for a few minutes, then approached the ringleaders whose aftershave could be smelled even though they were smoking. Al Qaeda occasionally beat smokers senseless on the street, citing the Koran, but the rule was enforced only on people who didn't have connections.

Mohammed told the local men that he was a Sunni, like them, and his battalion would fight for a united Iraq. But if their sons chose al Qaeda, then he would throw them in Abu Ghraib, where a crazy American woman would ride their naked bodies like a child on a goat. The old men chuckled, clucking their tongues at the major's dark humor.

"If another of my soldiers is killed," Mohammed said in a low voice, "I will hunt down the killers and drag their bodies on this street."

The old men complained about the 2nd Iraqi Battalion that had arrived the previous week, when 3rd Battalion was on leave. One claimed the jundis dragged his son down an alley and shot him in the head to avenge a bombing. A young boy told Mohammed that his mother had been killed when the jundis shot blindly at the houses, and that he would someday exact revenge. Houses had been ransacked, gold and jewelry stolen. Jundis took several men to an abandoned base hangar, beat them, and threw them onto Route Michigan. And the American advisors had been present for the kidnapping!

"That wasn't 3rd Battalion," Mohammed told the crowd. "They will not come back. This is our town now."

Mohammed was livid. Temporary units were bad policy when fighting an insurgency. They had no long-term ownership of the complex battlefield and little investment in the consequences of their actions. Americans were typically the worst offenders, with their paid-by-the hour contractors and their trigger-happy convoys, but now the 3rd Iraqi Brigade HQ had allowed 2nd Battalion to smash up Khalidiya and then handed the city over to 3rd Battalion with no warning.

Mohammed wasn't sure which accusations were true or false, but they seemed plausible. He didn't think highly of the other two battalions in the brigade. Jealousy and backbiting among Iraqi units bordered on fratricide.

Bribes affected which unit went to a given sector. Religious devotion, Sunni or Shiite, provoked gossip about disloyalty. Mohammed didn't doubt that some Shiite jundis, if discipline grew lax, would steal from, beat, and murder Sunnis in Khalidiya.

Whether crazed jundis, insurgents, or car accidents were the actual culprits didn't matter, Mohammed thought. The rumors had already spread. Khalidiya now believed the story of rampaging jundis, which made it effectively true even if stitched out of lies.

Jundis began boarding trucks, but they were overcrowded with detainees. To make room, they randomly released prisoners. Mohammed asked the old men to point out relatives and he ordered them freed, too. It was a gesture of good faith. And power.

Before dawn, the convoy rumbled to the Camp Habbaniyah Detention Facility, which was run by TF Panther. The brig looked like an enormous chicken coop surrounded by five-meter-high concrete barriers. Blindfolded prisoners were roughly passed down a long line of jundis that resembled an old-fashioned fire bucket line into the prison's narrow entrance, where American guards from TF Panther took custody of them. In all, thirty-six detainees were placed into concrete cells awaiting legal review, a joint ruling by a lawyer from TF Panther and its commander. There were two options: free the prisoners or forward them up the chain of command with evidence packages solid enough to withstand another set of lawyers.

Sunrise came. In the daylight, Troster felt bad for some of the younger prisoners, teenagers who were quaking in their pajamas. Falah drove off to enjoy breakfast as the advisors and jundis set to work on writing down whatever flimsy evidence the jundis had gleaned from the household interviews. Processing each prisoner required twenty minutes of paperwork, one set in English and another in Arabic. Some jundis could barely write. Others attempted Roman letters and produced mere scrawls. Charge sheets were torn up and rewritten. Jundis munched on Doritos and smeared the papers with orange dust. After three hours, Troster handed a mound of papers to a frowning guardsman who knew that whatever charges the strange Iraqi soldiers had come up with would not hold up against U.S. evidentiary standards.

The lieutenant in charge of the jail could not be found and the guards didn't seem to care where he was. The prisoners would be released by afternoon, they told Troster. As Troster left the lockup, Mohammed cynically commented that at least there could be no accusations his jundis had mistreated civilians.

"Khalidiya believes the 2nd Battalion looted the city," said Mohammed. "There are claims of murder. Probably lies."

"I can't speak to the murder, but it's not all lies," Troster said.

Troster surprised Mohammed by telling him that a week earlier he had been quietly ordered to run an investigation on the 2nd Iraqi Battalion and its advisors by his boss, Marine Colonel Daniel Newell, the senior advisor to the 3rd Iraqi Brigade (the headquarters of the 1st, 2nd, and 3rd Iraqi battalions). Local Khalidiyans had alleged retaliatory abuse by 2nd Battalion jundis stemming from a bomb blast in Khalidiya and complicity on the part of their advisors.

After the Abu Ghraib scandal broke in 2004, American commanders began probing thousands of accusations that ranged from traditional war crimes to the petty loss of a helmet. One probe actually looked into an incident in which a U.S. soldier ate two lunches instead of the one he was entitled to. At any given time, an American battalion had up to a dozen ongoing probes. Advisors were required to investigate their own teams and the Iraqis they were advising.

Troster wasn't happy conducting a probe into another advisor team, especially considering he had just arrived in Camp Habbaniyah. He had interviewed the Marine advisors and written up his investigation findings, short and to the point:

During the first week of September 2005, when 3rd Battalion was on leave, 2nd Battalion was sent into Khalidiya in their place. Three jundis were killed in a blast on Market Street. In a simmering rage, 2nd Battalion jundis struck citizens with their rifle stocks, smashed up cars, and tore into nearby houses. Eventually the heat wore them down and the battalion returned to base with five prisoners. Instead of depositing the prisoners at the American jail, as per the TF Panther requirement, the jundis—in the company of a U.S. Marine advisor—stashed the detainees overnight in an abandoned hangar for interrogation and released them the following morning. The identity of the bomber was never found.

In the report's conclusion, Troster wrote that the Marine advisors to 2nd Battalion should not be held criminally responsible for the rampage. After all, U.S. training made it clear that advisors could only advise, "not give orders."

Troster felt proud of his report. It seemed like a wise observation to send to lawyers at Marine headquarters who couldn't fathom life on the streets. Walking out of the jail a week later, however, he was not so sure. The overnight dragnet had shaken his understanding of the advisor mission.

After two patrols, his men had correctly concluded that their key task was mentoring jundis and junior Iraqi officers in combat. Troster had to do the same on patrol, but he also had to break through with Falah and influence his tactical decision making. The operation had clarified that. On paper, U.S. advisors acted as a link to the world's most powerful military and managed the relationship with the American partner unit—TF Panther in Troster's case. The idea was to provide Iraqi Battalion 3/3–1 with sufficient operational support so the Iraqi soldiers could focus on stripping the insurgents of their anonymity, as they knew the enemy best.

That was nonsense. Troster considered what he did know: TF Panther seemed to have little interest in joining 3/3–1 in Khalidiya, and the jundis, who were perceived as invaders, did not know the enemy at all. AQI sought to erect a thirteenth-century caliphate, enforced by execution. The Sunni tribes weren't interested in building a caliphate. But they forged alliances with hard-liners and foreign fighters to keep their power base and revenue streams. Almost all Sunnis in Anbar applauded attacks on Americans and jundis.

Falah's operational tempo and tactics were deeply flawed. By patrolling just once or twice a day, and spending most of its time behind the walls of Camp Habbaniyah, 3/3–1 was repeating the same old mistakes of past American units instead of demonstrating commitment to the city of Khalidiya. The people would not come forward with information if they failed to receive fair and consistent treatment in return.

Certainly not after last night.

4

Ambush

★　★　★

September 2005

For two days after the roundup, Khalidiya was quiet. The daily 3/3–1 patrols walked through town unmolested. Troster was eager to take advantage of the respite by flooding the city with jundis at all hours.

Over a breakfast of hot samoon bread and jam on September 21, Troster pressed Falah. "With our current patrol schedule, the insurgents can dig in bombs or terrorize the people without any fear of being caught," he said. "Driving into Khalidiya once or twice a day just makes us easy targets. If we patrol more, we will hurt less."

"It is impossible. In Mosul, the Americans patrolled with us and treated us as partners and friends. It's not like that now. Panther does not like us. We are doing what we can."

That afternoon, 3/3–1 received a memo from the U.S. Army National Guard Brigade HQ, nine kilometers away in Ramadi, requiring Iraqi units to patrol in armored vehicles. That order reflected the gulf between American headquarters and the reality of Iraqi outfits. The Iraqi battalions had no armored Humvees. Their pickup trucks looked like eighth-grade metal shop projects.

Troster was frustrated. Abandoning the battlefield for six hours was an invitation for even the most paranoid bombers to start replanting bombs. Twenty-four hours was an eternity. He hopped into a Humvee and drove toward the "American side" of Camp Habbaniyah where TF Panther was headquartered, desperate to find an available armored transport to take the jundis into Khalidiya. Camp Habbaniyah was a divided base. The Panther guardsmen felt threatened by their Iraqi partners and were erecting a giant sand-and-concrete wall the Iraqi soldiers called the Great Wall of Habbaniyah, which would soon cleave the base in half. Iraqi soldiers weren't allowed to depart Camp Habbaniyah even from their own "side" without an American escort. The sign inside the west gate read: STOP HERE! MILITARY CHECKPOINT! DO NOT MOVE FORWARD FROM THIS POINT OR DEADLY FORCE WILL BE USED AGAINST YOU. The sign was printed in English with fading Arabic below in smaller font. Troster thought the policy was bad enough for Iraqi Army vehicles entering the "Iraqi side" of camp, but he couldn't understand why TF Panther would block the exits.

Troster flashed his ID for two sets of roadside guards and wheeled the Humvee up to the TF Panther HQ, which was about the size of a small elementary school and located adjacent to the long runway that paralleled Route Michigan. He found the operations officer, or OpsO, in a room with a giant map board that depicted the huge area of responsibility TF Panther had been assigned by its parent National Guard brigade in Ramadi.

"I need two trucks to take the jundis into town each day until your brigade headquarters rescinds this no armor, no Iraqi patrol order," Troster told the Panther OpsO, a major.

"Sir, we build the transport assignments each week at the operations planning meeting," said the major. "I'd like to help you, but we can't swing it."

"You drove the other night, when we made all those arrests."

"Sir, that was a one-time thing. We had only a day to plan the mission and had to jump through our ass."

"Are you saying you need a week to plan operations?" Toster asked, incredulous.

"I'm saying we're short-handed as well, sir. That's why we hold the meeting."

"Let me try this again," said Troster. "Forget about driving. I know it's a pain to drive the jundis around like bus drivers. How about we act like real partners? We'll embed a hundred jundis into each of your companies, and you send them into Khalidiya together. The jundis get training, and Khalidiya gets security troops."

It took the OpsO a few seconds to realize Troster was serious. "That's not the plan right now, sir."

"What is the partnership plan?" Troster asked.

"You'll have to take that up with the CO, sir."

Troster could not find Panther's commanding officer. He left the Panther HQ in a funk. He knew the guardsmen were chronically undermanned for their battle space, which included a four-kilometer, heavily mined stretch of Route Michigan, the Abu Fleis peninsula town of three thousand due north of Khalidiya on the other side of Route Michigan, Civil/Coolie Camp, a converted shantytown of five thousand abutting Camp Habbaniyah that had originally been built by the British in the 1930s to house workers on the airfield, and thirty thousand additional inhabitants in the hundreds of farm hamlets spread over twenty-five square kilometers.

But Falah was right about the so-called partnership with Panther. There wasn't one that Troster could see. U.S. partner battalions were supposed to help the advisors train Iraqi units for independence, but the partnership varied enormously from unit to unit. In the same way a fresh troop depended on the attitude and expertise of the old hand who'd been there, done that, so too did the new Iraqi battalions respond to the cues of their American counterparts.

During its six-month deployment to Mosul, from January to July 2005, mixed patrolling was exactly what 3/3–1 experienced. Platoons of jundis were regularly folded into the ranks of U.S. infantry companies. That's what they expected out of Panther when they arrived in Habbaniyah in August 2005.

Panther had a different plan for the incoming 3rd Iraqi Brigade: plugging gaps in its battle space, starting with Khalidiya. Following the lead of previous U.S. units stationed in Habbaniyah, TF Panther employed a forward operating base campaign, meaning that the majority of its personnel spent the majority of their time on the base. Securing Camp Habbaniyah alone required a hundred men. Two motorized QRFs stood by in case of emergencies—medevacs, firefights, and vehicles damaged by explosions—which arose often. One infantry company manned a sandbagged redoubt plopped atop the 611 Bridge separating Khalidiya from the Jazeera farmlands. The TF Panther tank unit constantly patrolled Route Michigan. That left a single infantry company to patrol with Humvees kilometer after kilometer of cities, river roads, and farms. They returned to Camp Habbaniyah to sleep, while the company of tanks and armored gun trucks held the highway at night.

There was no official Iraqi mentoring program in Anbar. The Marine provincial command headquartered in Fallujah was busy with its own campaign. Starting in the summer of 2005 and intensifying that fall, Marines had focused on large-scale search-and-destroy missions in a dozen cities west of Ramadi. The idea was to drive insurgents out of the towns so Iraqi soldiers following in trace could more easily secure them, but results were mixed. Pacification depended not only on the unpredictable availability and capability of Iraqi battalions but also on American partnership plans. Some U.S. battalions integrated at the squad level. Others, like TF Panther, did not integrate period.

★

Another day came and went without patrols in Khalidiya. Troster imagined that the credibility of his Iraqis had plummeted in the city. On the night of September 22, he tried a different plan to get the marooned 3/3–1 into town. Across Route Michigan from Camp Habbaniyah, overlooking Khalidiya and the rest of the green Euphrates valley, an abandoned ammunition supply point (ASP) sat atop the small ridge that formed the northern edge of Lake Habbaniyah. Troster wanted 3/3–1 to leave the walled confines of Camp Habbaniyah and instead operate from ASP Hill, right in Khalidiya's back-yard. From the bombed-out bunker complex, a U.S. target in the opening days of the war, 3/3–1 could walk right into the city, just four hundred meters downhill.

The benefits were physical proximity to Khalidiya and an isolated exis-tence—only two kilometers from Camp Habbaniyah, ASP Hill would still be within range of logistics support, but the rustic living conditions would bond his advisors and 3/3–1, and focus the mission. The obvious drawback was lack of security and comfort. ASP Hill was vulnerable to attack, and it lacked the creature comforts of Camp Habbaniyah, including a mess hall, reliable electric power, and trees. Food and water would have to be trucked up the hill.

"This will not work," said Falah when Troster broached the subject after dinner. "The whole brigade is here." The 1st, 2nd, and 3rd Iraqi battalions lived in relative comfort together on Camp Habbaniyah.

"You want to win in Khalidiya? You have to live where you fight," said Troster.

"Khalidiya is close to Camp Habbaniyah! There is no need live on the ASP."

Risk aversion wasn't limited to Iraqi commanders. Most American units were encouraged to be extra careful. They lived on large bases and were ordered to travel outside the wire only in large armored vehicle convoys. But "commuting to the fight," as this tactic became known, unwittingly turned mines into the most lethal threat in Iraq.[1] As soon as the soldiers returned to their heavily guarded bases, the insurgents would begin to lay new bombs for their next excursion out.

"Please think about it, Colonel," said Troster.

"Colonel Troster, there is really nothing more to think about," Falah replied.

Troster and his advisors lacked the battlefield credibility needed to influence operations. Examining his own position, he knew words would not sway Lieutenant Colonel Falah, no matter how militarily sensible. He needed to bolster his arguments with performance.

Troster got his chance on September 24. The rule requiring Iraqi units to patrol in armored vehicles was finally rescinded after a lobbying effort by Colonel Newell, Troster's boss, advising the 3rd Iraqi Brigade, 3/3–1's parent unit. Troster invited Newell along on the next 3rd Battalion patrol; he wanted to show the Marine what his Army reservists could do, and he hoped Newell would apply some top-down pressure on Falah to relocate to ASP Hill by putting a bug in the ear of Falah's boss, the 3rd Iraqi Brigade commander.

Newell agreed, and Troster circled back to Falah, who was in his hut studying the day's patrol plan. "The brigade advisor, Colonel Newell, would like to accompany a patrol into Khalidiya. He is eager to see how 3rd Battalion operates," Troster told Falah.

"This is very good," Falah said carefully. "Is the brigade commander coming with his advisor?" Meaning, was Falah's boss, the Iraqi brigade commander, accompanying Troster's boss?

"No. Newell wants to keep a small impact."

Falah was relieved. By impressing Newell with a single patrol, he would have a friend in higher headquarters, and since the Iraqi commander wasn't going along, he didn't have to go along either. The advisors could go have their fun.

The next morning, September 24, jundis assembled the patrol in the Camp Habbaniyah courtyard, the drivers testing the engines of a hillbilly Nissan and a derelict Iraqi transport called a Leyland that looked like a white school bus without a roof. Four mortar rounds and six rockets roared into camp, exploding like thunderclaps. Shrapnel chipped the building walls and left scars like chicken pox. No one was hurt, but it was the fourth attack in six days.

Deep inside Camp Habbaniyah, the TF Panther counterbattery radars locked on the arcs of the enemy rounds and fed the angles into a computer. In under a minute, howitzers fired a salvo back into Jazeera. It was an everyday greeting between combatants, though the Iraqis felt—wrongly—that the guardsmen fired more response rounds when the enemy struck closer to their side of the base.

Two patrols left the gate. The 2nd Battalion headed to Abu Fleis. An American Humvee packed with five advisors followed the two Iraqi trucks from 3rd Battalion and headed toward Khalidiya. Troster sat in the right command seat. Sergeant First Class Rivera drove. Newell and his weapons expert, Chief Warrant Officer "Gunner" Dave Kenison, an experienced member of the Marine team who Troster suspected was along to evaluate, took the rear seats of the truck. Army Reserve Staff Sergeant Greg Bozovich, 22, one of Troster's men, was perched in the turret.

Bozovich, or "Boz" as he was known, was working at a Loew's department store when he was activated. He was a hard case who scorned those reservists who came all the way to Iraq only to end up on desk duty. A finance specialist in the reserves, he had been originally slotted in a cushy billet in Baghdad filing paperwork. He begged his commander to let him join an advisory team and was denied repeatedly. But when Troster fired one of the men during training, Bosovich had become available—his commander had come to see him as a troublemaker.

"Rivera, swing into the lead," Troster said.

"Copy."

Troster fired up the Warlock jamming system to block selected radio frequencies as Rivera passed the other vehicles in the convoy. Warlock is software that is supposed to blaze an electronic path through minefields detonated by cell phones and other gadgets that electronically sparked the detonations. By positioning themselves at the head of the convoy, the advisors could protect the Iraqi vehicles that followed from roadside bombs.

Leading also demonstrated to the Marines that the reservists were steely.

The Humvee bounced along a hard-packed dirt road behind Khalidiya. Here the insurgents would dig holes, bury the explosives, and repack the soil. So everything looked like a bomb hole. Behind the wheel, Rivera knew the bomb threat was just something he and his advisor teammates had to accept. The fact that they were always bracing for an explosion in a world in which anything can blow up caused constant combat stress, which Rivera also added to the list of things to accept, right next to jundis who pointed machine guns at him.

As they approached the first asphalt road marking the city limits, they drove past mounds of bottles, cans, petrol containers, plastic wrap, broken crates, and animal carcasses. Two young boys squealed, *"Jibli* ("Give me") candy! Jibli soccer ball!"—a sign that U.S. units had been in town for some time. Kids unfamiliar with Americans asked for footballs.

"Welcome to Khalidiya," said Troster.

"Lovely," said Newell.

With no warning, a bomb detonated behind the rear Iraqi Nissan, fifty meters behind the Humvee, showering everyone with mud pellets. Bozovich ducked into the Humvee, his heart pounding.

"Relax, killer," joked Kenison. "That one wasn't even close."

Some mines were detonated by driving over manual triggers, and others were initiated via radio signals that penetrated Warlock or were far enough away from the jammer not to be blocked. The advisors in the Humvee suspected the latter.

Boz smiled. He pulled himself back up to the machine gun when a second blast lifted the six-ton Humvee up with a plume of dust, then slammed it down.

"Boz, you okay?" yelled Troster.

"I'm good."

"Tires blown?" Troster asked Rivera.

"Don't think so."

They sat quietly for a moment. A near miss. An insurgent in Khalidiya was cursing because he pressed a cell phone digit a second too late after the Humvee drove past a mark on the road.

"I can see this is going to be fun," Newell said.

Troster popped his door and ran out to check on the Iraqis. They sat immobile. The driver, visible now that the haze cleared, was waving either hello or get away.

"Y'alla! Y'alla!" Troster shouted. Let's go! Let's go!

He wanted the trucks to get away from the road's flotsam of garbage in case there were more secondary mines—bombs that were exploded minutes after an initial blast, when troops were milling about their damaged vehicles. The Iraqi trucks slowly followed the Humvee over a dirt rise and onto a field only partially covered with debris. Rifle fire rang out. Troster figured it came from an insurgent cell moving from house to house along 20th Street, the main street in Khalidiya. Bozovich pointed his machine gun along the rooftops but saw no muzzle flashes. Jundis hopped off the Leyland and spread out. A few began blasting away at echoes of enemy gunfire skittering through the alleys.

An Iraqi lieutenant Troster did not recognize darted over.

"What were you waiting for?" Troster asked.

"We thought you were dead," said the lieutenant. "Boom. Whole Humvee gone."

"Let's see if we can grab a flank." Troster wanted to encircle the band of insurgents and then fire at them instead of running straight at them.

The Iraqi winced. He glanced at the maneuvering advisors seeking covered firing positions and then back at Troster. "Keep going on the patrol?"

"Of course we keep going. We just got here."

Troster pressed ahead on foot. The mounted machine guns atop the vehicles had a decent elevated position and followed them into town, providing sporadic bursts of cover fire. The Iraqi lieutenant lingered behind his jundis, ducking every time a few rounds snapped nearby.

"Hey! Spread your people out!" Troster shouted.

The officer looked at Troster, shrugged, and then scoured the ground as if he'd lost his watch. Troster's eyes fixed on Lieutenant Khalid. He knew Khalid and Boiko had gotten into a fight. He figured the kid had guts.

Troster turned back to the scared officer. "You're fired! Khalid, you're in charge of this mission now. Let's get them."

Khalid brightened, glad that the American colonel recognized what his NCOs couldn't. That advisors had no authority to fire Iraqis was a complaint for another day. Khalid began a house sweep, indicating that the Americans should fall in behind.

There was a distant pop to the north, across Route Michigan, followed by a rumble so loud it scattered Khalidiya's yapping dogs. Both sides stopped firing. A mushroom cloud of dust rose about ten football fields away, expanding like a slow-bursting firework.

Troster rolled to the brigade frequency and waited for a transmission from 2nd Battalion patrolling in Abu Fleis. High-pitched, barely intelligible screams interrupted the static. The Marine advisors in Abu Fleis were communicating with brigade headquarters on Camp Habbaniyah. *Roadside bomb! Getting the hell out of there! All we have is his body armor!*

Say again about the body armor and slow down. Over.

Roger. One MiTT and one terp were foot mobile when the IED went off. The terp is WIA. The MiTT [member of the military transition team] *is missing. We found his body armor.*

Is that because it got blown off him or because he was captured? Over.

We don't know. Over.

Who is it?

Sergeant Dunlap.

The sergeant had ridden the lead Humvee into Abu Fleis. When a small mine detonated in front of his truck, he hopped out with his interpreter to inspect the damage. It was a trap. A secondary bomb planted nearby spun the terp over the hood and into the irrigation channel. Dunlap evaporated.

The TF Panther QRF was already rolling toward the blast. They stopped at the rear gate and demanded details before leaving the wire. The tower guards were clueless. SEALs in two Humvees plowed past the TF Panther guardsmen. News of a missing American was all they needed to dive in.

The SEALs were the grand old men of Habbaniyah. They had operated from the camp since 2004 and knew more about the area than anyone else. Leaving the wire on the hunt was an everyday thing. With them was Command Sergeant Major Jeff Mellinger, the senior enlisted man in Iraq, who happened to be visiting the SEALs. Mellinger, who at 51 was the last Vietnam-era draftee in the Army, patrolled relentlessly. By the time his continuous thirty-three combat months—three back-to-back tours—ended, he had survived twenty-seven mine blasts.

The SEALs began the manhunt by tracking footprints and collapsed stalks of river growth, signs Dunlap might have been dragged off by insurgents. Mellinger's eyes were drawn elsewhere. A downtrodden Marine advisor to the 2nd Battalion was trudging down the middle of the road carrying his rifle by its optic. The Panther soldiers, having finally appeared on scene, had placed some questionable suspects on their faces. Mellinger saw one of the soldiers kick a detainee. The entire scene reeked of cruel incompetence.

"What do you think you're doing!" screamed Mellinger, taking control.

Mellinger reported the incidents of indiscipline, but months later, on another trip to Camp Habbaniyah, he saw the very same Panther soldier in a mess hall, and the man had the gall to say, "Well, good morning to you, Command Sergeant Major!" without a care in the world.

A SEAL found Dunlap's remains. He hadn't been kidnapped. He'd absorbed the full blast of the bomb and been shredded.

★

Back in Khalidiya, Khalid's patrol searched a dozen houses, asking the inhabitants questions. No one had seen or heard digging on the road. There were no irhabi—terrorists—in Khalidiya, they said. Abu Fleis, across the street, sure, plenty of Republican Guard generals there. Have you seen the size of their houses! Didn't you just hear those explosions? But not in Khalidiya. *La. La. La.* No. No. No.

Khalid knew they were lying. He shrugged them off.

Troster was impressed with the young lieutenant. Five nights earlier, the Iraqi had seen his own battalion commander arrest dozens of citizens for no reason, fueling more hatred. Now that he was put in charge, Khalid behaved differently. Troster sensed that the lieutenant's instincts paralleled his own experiences cultivating a DEA informant network. Interviewing residents in a firefight's aftermath, when the insurgents were still mingling on the streets or hiding in nearby houses, was about as effective as walking up to local gawkers at a murder scene and loudly asking for the names of the assailants.

A string of artillery rounds from Camp Habbaniyah streaked through the sky, trailing the sound of ripping newspapers. They thudded on a deserted island on the Euphrates that was used as a dock for fishing boats from Abu Fleis.

"What the hell is going on?" Bozovich yelled from the turret.

First we stop patrolling and give the enemy time to plant simultaneous ambushes in Khalidiya and Abu Fleis, thought a befuddled Troster. *Now TF Panther has decided to pitch in with artillery bombardment?*

He keyed the radio and asked brigade HQ what the guardsmen were shooting at.

Could be suspected POO sites. Over.

POO—points of origin—referred to ground used by the enemy for mortar and rocket attacks. That didn't make any sense to Troster.

I'm seeing the impacts and they're shelling the island west of Abu Fleis. No mortar team would shoot from an island. Over, radioed Troster.

Roger. It's a terrain denial mission. Over.

"Terrain denial" meant picking a grid coordinate on the map and repeatedly blowing it up to prevent insurgents from using it as a POO in the future. The advisors and the jundis watched as shrapnel shredded the trees, the shock waves blowing the swamp grass flat. Civilians appeared on balconies to watch the pointless fireworks.

In the 1920s, British occupation troops had bombed Iraqi villages to quell tribal uprisings. Inflicting pain on a rebellious population was an accepted counterinsurgency tactic. British Major General C. E. Callwell, author of the era's most influential book on guerrilla warfare, *Small Wars: Their Principles and Practice,* argued that locals who refuse friendship should be brought to reason "by the rifle and sword, for they understand this mode of warfare and respect it. Sometimes, however, the circumstances do not admit of it, and then their villages must be demolished and granaries destroyed."[2]

Callwell's point wasn't as bellicose as it sounded. To deprive an agrarian people in rebellion of the means of sustaining a revolt was a brutally efficient method of starving guerrillas. But Callwell never would have understood lobbing artillery shells at meaningless undergrowth.

The advisors couldn't figure it out, either.

5

Survivor on Steroids

★ ★ ★

September 2005

In Iraq, every unit had a home base and the fallen were ceremonially mourned. The army advisors did not know Sergeant Dunlap well, but the service so upset Boiko that he refused to attend another. By the time they called Dunlap's name for the third time during the ceremonial roll call, Boiko wanted to scream, "He's gone, man!"

He wondered who would be next. Insurgents made that decision two days later. A mortar round landed in Camp Habbaniyah between two 3rd Battalion cooks scrubbing pots, killing them both. Soon the courtyard filled with screaming jundis.

This time the frenetic expressions of feeling didn't abate, as they usually did after a while. Trucks revved. Orders in Arabic echoed in the square. Jundis ran pell-mell. They thrust iron bunk beds into flatbed Leyland trucks and piled mattresses into the Nissans.

Troster found Falah in an agitated state. "What's happening?"

"We are leaving for ASP Hill."

"Now?"

"Yes. The brigade commander has just given the order. Second Company will do reconnaissance. The rest of the battalion will follow in a day."

Troster wasn't happy that the constant stream of indirect fire was the spark for this decision, but he thought it was a huge step for the battalion to leave Habbaniyah and go live on a hilltop outpost right in sullen Khalidiya's backyard.

Here come the pain, al Qaeda, Troster thought.

Boiko and Watson drove up ASP hill with 2nd Company. At the top of the ridge was a two-kilometer-long plateau that stretched down to shimmering Lake Habbaniyah in the south and ran parallel to Khalidiya from east to west. The hill itself was a windswept moonscape largely devoid of trees and ground scrub. Four concrete buildings marked the main entrance. Beyond the buildings, dozens of abandoned ammunition bunkers—hulking mounds of cement ten meters high and thirty meters long—dotted the grounds like giant tents on an abandoned circus ground. Evidence of countless American missile attacks abounded, from half-buried tail fins jutting ominously out of the sand to gaping holes in the roofs of some bunkers. The jundis thought they looked like fallen elephants.

A year earlier, insurgents had overrun a local Iraqi ING unit trying to hold ASP Hill. The guerrillas stole hundreds of AK-47s and heavy machine guns. Now a small contingent of TF Panther guardsmen ran a radio relay station there, retransmitting electronic messages from Camp Habbaniyah to units on patrol.

An excited guardsman rushed up to Boiko, Watson, and the Iraqi soldiers who were replacing his unit on the hill. He explained the defensive plan they had worked out in case insurgents from Khalidiya attacked and showed them the living quarters, a cement structure called the Horseshoe because of its shape. It had just nine small rooms, a pipe for a shower, a hole in the ground for a toilet, and two air conditioners.

"Where are the Iraqis going to sleep?" the guardsman asked.

"The jundis are checking out the bunkers."

"I wouldn't recommend that. Hot as hell in there, and they're full of bats."

"Yeah, well, you wouldn't recommend a lot of what the Iraqis do," said Watson. "The officers are sleeping right here with us. A few jundis are going to be posted as lookouts on the roof."

It took a few moments before the guardsman realized the advisor was serious.

"What's your internal security plan?" asked the guardsman.

"If you mean defending ourselves from our own Iraqis, there is none."

Advisor teams are vulnerable to attack by any one of the thousands of jundis they train. In 2004, jundi recruits murdered two advisors. Protection plans in this regard varied. Most advisor teams lived in separate quarters from their trainees. Others slept in the same building but in segregated areas that were guarded by a single advisor, called a "firewatch."

Advisor team 3/3–1 was in a very tiny minority. On ASP Hill, they would bunk alongside Iraqi officers like in a dormitory, with no firewatch.

Boiko and Watson made a quick tour. From the perimeter of the hilltop, marked by a few broken strands of barbed wire, Khalidiya was just a few hundred meters downslope. The city looked so close that Boiko thought he could reach it with a Frisbee and a breeze blowing off the lake. Today wind was blowing the stink uphill from Khalidiya.

When they returned to the Horseshoe, the guardsmen were already packed up and sitting in an idling truck.

"That was quick," Watson said to their guide.

"I'll be blunt. It sucks up here," said the guardsman. "We'll leave the Porta-John, the two AC units, and the generator. It's barely enough juice for a company, let alone a battalion."

"Who empties the Porta-John?"

The guardsman shrugged. "Good luck."

That night, Boiko and Watson grabbed a few jundis to patrol the wire, probing the ASP from an insurgent's point of view. They exited friendly lines through a hole in a dilapidated fence and looked back at the outpost. A cluster of lights marked 2nd Company as they worked into the night, shoveling ammonia-laced bat guano from their new home in an ammo bunker.

ASP Hill was far larger than they'd expected. The perimeter was three kilometers long and two kilometers deep. Four guard towers marked the northern wire, closest to Khalidiya, but the strands disappeared underground in places, buried by long ago sandstorms.

"It'd take the entire battalion just to watch the wire," said Boiko.

"And any jundis in those towers are just RPG bait," Watson agreed.

The small patrol crept toward Khalidiya. Staying on the high ground, they followed a ridge to a graveyard a hundred meters from the town's center. Generators hummed along the deserted streets. They stared into the urban emptiness for hours and saw only one man loitering under a streetlight.

They took a different route home. A pack of wild dogs, barking and howling, intercepted them as they neared camp. They cut back toward Khalidiya and tried a different approach. Again they were attacked by strays.

"I think we just found our security unit," Boiko said.

★

The next morning, Troster scrounged up transport trucks and the rest of the battalion headed like refugees up to the hill. Jundis had stripped their Camp Habbaniyah barracks of anything useful. They stuffed trucks with wall lockers, aluminum desks, wooden chairs, electrical wire, curtains, lamps, and even doorknobs. Motoring up the rising ASP Road, they were met by a bored jundi who lifted the gate with a rope.

"This is what they call security?" Troster's XO, the second in command of the team, commented. Since their arrival in Camp Habbaniyah, the XO had grumbled aloud about the lack of comforts that were available on larger FOBs, like personal Internet. ASP Hill made Camp Habbaniyah look like the Ritz. Troster might have tolerated the complaints had the man been stalwart on patrols. But so far his deputy had avoided them. One of the benefits of Marineland, thought Troster, was supposed to be their quick dismissal of officers who did not cut it. He had the feeling he'd soon be testing that theory.

The advisors looked back at Camp Habbaniyah, plainly visible from their new perch. Gone were Bangladeshi sanitization crews, menthol piss pucks, sloshing buckets of Pine-Sol, and endless alcohol hand squirt stations. Gone were the billowing air-conditioning units, computers littered with racy Yahoo Messenger chats, and mountainous piles of Pop-Tarts.

Boiko and Watson had staked out a room with one of the two air conditioners the guardsmen had left behind. Troster and Rivera lived with the radios so they could monitor the team. The radios needed air-conditioning, so Troster and Rivera crammed into the four-meter by four-meter room with Boiko and Watson.

Boiko was irritated by their intrusion, and sleep deprived from a night spent nervously walking the defensive lines. "We've been working our asses off up here," he told Troster. "Find someone else to play rank games with."

Senior advisors like Troster faced two team-building challenges. They had to ensure that the Americans were bridging the Iraqi cultural gap while keeping their own teams cohesive. Internal friction set a bad example for the Iraqis and acted like a cancer that could ruin their shared mission.

Troster knew that Boiko—ten years his junior and prone to voicing his opinions—was just dealing with a crisis of expectations. The austerity of ASP Hill magnified personality quirks. But Troster couldn't allow the chain of command to be compromised.

He didn't like to pull rank. In his view, leadership built cohesion, while invoking legal authority could fracture it. Still, the chain of command was the bedrock of managing combat. "Move your stuff over now, Boiko."

"No, thank you, Colonel."

In a typical military unit, the XO would have played bad cop, allowing the commander to make unpopular decisions while avoiding the appearance of doing so. But Troster's XO was looking for a satellite provider and power for the NFL Sunday Ticket.

Watson stepped between Troster and Boiko.

"You're fine in here, sir. Boiko's brain has been contaminated by the constant smell of garbage. All he can think about is sleeping under the AC and making it home to see his daughter."

The team broke up in laughter. Troster and Rivera packed in with Watson and Boiko, and the rest of the men separated into two other rooming groups, leaving the majority of the rooms for the Iraqi officers. The advisors filled their rooms with dirty packs and sleeping bags and ammunition, hammering nails into the cement to hang their rifles and armor next to their children's artwork. Most of the pictures depicted Americans helping smiling Iraqi children, a fairy tale image the soldiers in turn imported to Anbar.

Until the mines started blowing them up.

Move-in smacked of the first day of camp. The Iraqi officers' rooms looked tidier, but they had less gear, which gave them more space to hang things like religious banners on the wall. The mixed unit inspected each other's rooms, lingering over cultural anomalies like Maxim posters ("This girl lives next door to you *and* you?") and prayer beads ("I didn't know Muslims used Rosaries!").

Major Mohammed stood watching the socializing from the small sand courtyard in the middle of the Horseshoe. He had dark circles under his eyes that his jundis joked were reservoirs of rage. After a few minutes, he shouldered his pack and marched to live with his 4th Company troops in their bunker.

Specialist Joseph Neary, 22, was the youngest man on the advisor team. In civilian life, he was a heating technician by day and a rock-and-roll guitarist by night. Neary had joked his way through training, often showing up late for class. What Neary really liked was Iraqi culture. He spent as much time as he could with the Iraqis, quickly picked up Arabic, and was soon known as "Yusef the Amerikee," the boy soldier who gave the children candy.

He asked Troster if he could live with the terps, who were bunking in a single room at the top of the Horseshoe.

"Don't worry, Neary. Rivera will find you a home."

"Sir, it's not like that. I really want to live with them."

Troster approved the move, and Neary bounded down the hall for total immersion. The lieutenant colonel knew from Neary's lackluster performance at Atterbury that his youngest soldier wasn't cut out for straight infantry duty, which required discipline and bravado, but many superb infantrymen lacked the creative flexibility to make it as advisors. Two types of behaviors soldiers exhibited most typically disrupted advisor teams: feeling frustrated by the Iraqis and becoming a rejectionist, or using the Iraqis as a means of rebelling against U.S. military norms and "going native."[1]

Neary was susceptible to the latter behavior. The colonel discussed it with senior enlisted men Rivera and Huss. Neary could benefit from the challenge of learning a different culture, but he also needed extra attention to ensure he didn't drift apart from his American teammates.

The rest of the advisors took stock of the outpost. From the hill, Lake Habbaniyah shimmered cool and inviting. They were tempted to swim, except someone mentioned the human waste sluicing from the sewers. And the occasional floater.

Sergeant First Class Huss accompanied Captain Dhafer, a 29-year-old Shiite platoon commander who was a favorite to patrol with because he spoke good English, on a walking tour of the jundi sleeping quarters. Dhafer pointed at one of the many explosive scars that etched the big bunkers, which looked to Huss like concrete aircraft hangar bays.

"This is how I was introduced to America," Dhafer said, whose first exposure to Americans occurred during President Bill Clinton's punitive bombings for Saddam's failure to cooperate with UN weapons inspectors in 1998. Dhafer, then a second lieutenant, was driving to an aircraft maintenance depot when a Tomahawk hit a hangar bay. His ears popped. He never forgot the power of it. Five years later, in 2003, Dhafer had hoped the Americans would invade, cut the rot out of the Iraqi Army, and raise his salary, but Bush took so long to fix the army that his hopes faded. Maybe all armies were corrupt. The move to the ASP with his new advisors had boosted Dhafer's spirits. He hoped to do his job in isolation from Baghdad military politics and be rewarded.

"Any chance the insurgents attack us up here?" Huss asked.

"That would be too easy," said Dhafer, tilting his head toward Khalidiya. "We could kill them in an hour. No, they will make us go into the city and dig them out."

Staff Sergeant Mark Gentile, 50, went to inspect the motor pool. Gentile, a mechanic, had been volunteered for an advisor team by his unit in Pennsylvania and was told he'd be instructing jundis on vehicular maintenance. He was still trying to adjust to infantry combat and now had to learn how to live like a survivalist on ASP Hill. He walked past 4th Company's bunker. The jundis were using two full pallets of water—hundreds of bottles of purified water—to scrub bat shit from their new digs. He was going to say something about it, but Major Mohammed was glaring at him in the sun so he continued his walking tour.

He found two jundis at the motor pool trying to jump-start a Nissan. The old cables were colorless. He was about to stop them when one tripped the ignition. There was a flame and a sharp pop. A spark shower doused them. They had reversed polarity, frying the electrical systems. They showed him the cables and shrugged.

"Next time, come find me," Gentile told them.

Across from the motor pool, a platoon of jundis was unloading a Nissan truck piled high with the supplies smuggled out of Camp Habbaniyah. Its shock absorbers were compressed under the weight. Supervising the off-load was First Lieutenant John Bennett, 28, a former enlisted military policeman who had gone to college on an ROTC scholarship and emerged as a reserve officer, only to be funneled into Troster's advisor team as a logistics expert, though he had no experience. Not that military supply schooling would have helped on ASP Hill. Bennett had expected to receive an Iraqi convoy of life-sustainment goods like freeze-dried meals, crates of water bottles, ammunition, and batteries befitting outpost living. Instead, the items, which ranged from a giant box of tea leaves to a rusted bicycle, reminded him of a garage sale.

"Where's the rest of the supplies?" Bennett asked the 3/3–1 supply officer, a weak-willed young Iraqi captain who had been assigned the billet because there was so little to do. "Blankets. Shovels. Sandbags. Generators?"

The Iraqi captain shrugged. "The Amerikees give us these things."

"Not up here, they don't," said Bennett. "You need to let your brigade know you can't survive up here without a ton of supplies."

The captain shrugged again. Frustrated, Bennett walked over to the Horseshoe to check on the Iraqi electrician who was trying to run power lines to the generator. He found the electrician holding his hand in pain because he had tied a birds' nest of low-voltage wires to the generator and had been shocked unconscious.

"You okay?" Bennett asked, after finding GW to translate.

"I did it," said the electrician, smiling. "The companies have power."

Several other advisors gathered to check on the electrician's health, and they noticed a facial tic when he retold the story for the crowd. The advisors nicknamed him "Twitch."

Before sunset, the Iraqis raised their flag at the small headquarters building. The 3/3–1 unit symbol was a falcon under a parachute. The advisors thought the bird resembled Woodstock from the comic strip *Peanuts*. The flag hung limply atop the pole, which was hot to the touch after absorbing sunlight all day. The Americans and Iraqis cracked open warm sodas and toasted their new surroundings. To mark the moment, a Khalidiya insurgent fired his rocket at them. It whooshed over the ASP and exploded near a lake back channel.

"Independence day," said Troster.

Later that first night, Bosovich found GW and convinced him to translate during a visit with Major Mohammed.

"If you don't make it back in an hour, we'll come with backup," Huss joked.

On Boiko's advice, Boz and GW filled their hands with rocks and jogged from the Horseshoe to the 4th Company bunker, taking turns throwing stones at the ravenous strays that took halfhearted runs at them.

Major Mohammed started a small fire in a cement pit. They sat in the dark while Mohammed prepared the chai, which he made himself, waiting for the jundis to connect a thin strand of slash wire to the overloaded generator at the Horseshoe.

GW said something in Arabic to Mohammed, and Boz detected annoyance. Mohammed was lukewarm to terps. Their loyalty was to the Americans, whose relentless culture eventually morphed them into lost souls who ate beef jerky, salivated over pornographic videos, and wore iPods everywhere.

"I'm here to learn," Boz said. GW quickly translated.

"There is much to learn," said Mohammed. "What did you do before?"

"I worked in a department store. But I volunteered to be an advisor."

"Why?"

"Because I wanted to help the jundis," Boz said, adding, "Okay, and mostly I wanted to fight."

Mohammed chuckled. "If what you say is true, then you have come to the right city. And you have come to the right company."

★

Personal relationships were the foundation of advising. The rookie advisors knew this from their very first welcome-aboard speech at the Phoenix Academy, but in practice it was vacuous guidance. It was like shoving a transfer student into a football locker room before a bowl game, announcing him as the player-coach, and telling him to "relate."

Advisors who had been to college compared those first few days on the ASP to a freshman dormitory. Others thought the TV show *Survivor* was a better analogy, a notion that gained currency as they watched the Iraqi characters around them.

The cast included Lieutenant Ali, whom the advisors nicknamed "GQ" because he spent hours, it seemed, grooming himself for patrol in front of the warped mirror in the bunker. Advisors jockeyed to walk behind him in Khalidiya because the powerful smell of his aftershave dampened the rot of the streets.

Then there was "Bez Boz," or Baby Falcon, a tiny, incompetent lieutenant who owed his rank to his father, a general. Iraqi companies chose birds of prey for their call signs. Bez Boz exuded neither majesty nor power. A notorious sycophant, Bez Boz so relentlessly flattered the advisors that they used him as a sounding board for their worst ideas, including a raid in canoes, which he promised to take straight to Lieutenant Colonel Falah.

The junior advisors had arrived in Iraq with only the most cursory knowledge of its many cultures. They weren't allowed to attend several Atterbury classes for lack of space. Troster, Rivera, and Huss were senior enough to attend the culture classes, but even those courses emphasized what *not* to do around the Iraqis, delivering a lesson in tact that Troster now believed to be unfounded paranoia. Most cultural friction was smoothed over by the Iraqis themselves on a case-by-case basis.

Once, for example, when Falah had returned from leave, Troster asked how his wife was doing. Falah smiled and pulled him aside politely.

"Colonel Troster, we do not ask this question. We say, 'How is your family?'"

"Yes, of course. I apologize, Colonel Falah."

"No, there is no apology in a situation like this. Just an understanding that we are different. But together in the war against irhabi terrorists."

The advisor training had incorrectly focused on avoidance. Certainly there were sensitive topics to be avoided, but they were minor given the enormous importance of proactive collaboration and camaraderie.

The Iraqis wanted to talk about religion, the military retirement system, George Bush, the awful state of American soccer, even welfare. The younger advisors like Boiko and Boz were able to broach touchier subjects because they were clearly curious, instead of purposely seeking pressure points.

Each night on ASP Hill, dinner for the officers was prepared by a pair of 50-year-old jundi cooks who kept a gas-fired stove at the small staff quarters where Falah, Fareed (the 3rd Battalion XO), Aamr (OpsO), and the rest of the senior battalion headquarters officers lived. The American enlisted advisors were always welcome in the officers' mess, partly because the conversational choices of the younger Americans provided a regular distraction.

"Do any of you guys have two wives?" asked Boz one evening.

The officers burst out laughing.

"No, it is too difficult," said Aamr. "A colonel we know has two wives, and it is tougher than war. In Islam, you must follow *al Adallah,* justice, and treat the ladies exactly the same."

"Exactly?" asked Boz.

"Exactly the same."

"That *is* tough," said Boz, stopping there. The one subject the team did not discuss was sex.

The rustic isolation of ASP Hill encouraged bonding. Troster couldn't change the fact that his men were inexperienced reservists, but he knew that they had an advantage over most active-duty soldiers when it came to being advisors. As reservists, they had already crossed cultures as citizen-soldiers and were comfortable making interpersonal connections in both worlds. That applied to foreign military units like 3/3–1.

Now the advisors had to prove themselves in combat.

6

Mass Casualty

★   ★   ★

October 2005

The advisor team shared a single mirror with the Iraqi officers—a dirty distorted slab in the communal latrine. The stench from the nearby dung hole made showers quick for the Americans, but a few Iraqis used the latrine as a personal spa. The day before leave, they shaved their torsos before going home. The floor resembled a dead dog's hide. Thicker flip-flops were on order.

When they did study themselves in the mirror, the advisors saw that their heavy body armor built muscles and melted away fat. After ten days of patrolling from ASP Hill, where snack food was scarce, the soldiers looked wiry and strong, like wrestlers awaiting weigh-in. Care packages started arriving from home to augment their diet, but their metabolisms seemed impervious to the junk diet of Twizzlers, ramen noodles, Khalidiya mystery meat, and the addictive samoon bread the jundi cooks baked at all hours in an oven the Americans bought with special funds allocated for "must-have" military items.

The jundis soon realized that the advisor team's mail, which was driven up from Camp Habbaniyah every few days, meant sugary treats and pictures of muscled American male athletes and barely dressed women. U.S. Humvees rolled up to the dented aluminum gate at ASP Hill's entrance and often the jundi guard would say, "Mail call?" Many jundis, like the children in Khalidiya, constantly asked for material goods. It was the one cultural tic that vexed the advisors. On the streets, children screamed, "Mister! Jibli soccer ball, jibli dollars! You Amerikee, jibli jibli!" On ASP Hill, the jundis said, "Jibli cookie! Jibli magazine!" while the poorest Iraqi soldiers demanded big-ticket items, like fighting knives and Ironman watches, for which they offered little thanks.

Each advisor had his own approach to the constant requests and culti-vated his own following. Huss gave his food to jundis who were vigilant on patrol, like Jundi Hussein, a young kid who was always smiling and never accidentally swept the muzzle of his AK-47 across Huss's body as other jun-dis were prone to do on patrol when they turned to tell you something.

The advisors had completed eighteen patrols with 3/3–1 in ten days without complaints from the Iraqi officers. There were no kudos, either. The reservists were still figuring out their role on a confusing battlefield. To Troster it was nothing to celebrate—they still lacked the performance under fire that would enable operational influence—but it did indicate that their protégés had at least accepted them.

On October 8, Troster looked in the Horseshoe mirror and saw a mar-ble-size lump in his chest. He was sent to Baghdad for a biopsy. Before he left, he asked his boss, Colonel Newell, to send his deputy, Major Sean Mey-ers, and Gunner Kenison up to ASP Hill to augment the team.

"I'll be back in two days," said Troster, "but I don't want to leave my XO in charge even for an hour."

"He's that bad?" asked Newell.

"He's that bad."

"Would he get someone killed out there?"

"He doesn't go outside the wire, so I don't rightly know."

"Let's go over our options for replacing him when you return," said Newell.

Bearing a log of Copenhagen chewing tobacco as a gift, Kenison and Meyers drove up ASP Hill. Troster hopped a C-130 to an American hospital in Baghdad on October 9, and the following day, he learned his MRI was negative. He was sitting in the clinic's receiving area when a group of ban-daged jundis limped past. They shuffled toward the examination tables with their arms held away from their sides, as if they had terrible sunburns. Blast victims. One of the jundis walked over.

"Troster?"

Then it hit him: These men were from his battalion. Something terrible must have happened while he was in the hospital.

"*Salam Aleykum,*" Troster said. Peace be upon you. "What happened?"

The Iraqi moved his hand like a car, then opened his fingers.

"Car bomb? Suicide car bomb?"

"Yes. Big boom. Many dead."

★

Every day at least at least one patrol went down Khalidiya's 20th Street, which was heavily mined, but it was the city's spine. To avoid it meant conceding the town to the insurgency.

On October 10, Huss accompanied Unlucky 3rd Company. He drove the Humvee. Neary, the youngest advisor, took the turret. Lieutenant Qatan sat in the right-front command seat and was acting as Huss's interpreter. Troster's unit lacked the manpower to meet minimum U.S. vehicle requirements and they didn't have enough interpreters to cover every patrol. As the other advisors saw it, the XO was not adventurous and did not like to patrol, and the team had just lost Gentile, the mechanic. Newell's brigade team back at Camp Habbaniyah was also shorthanded and Gentile was reassigned to help them. Advisor team 3/3–1 was down to eight men.

Two lightly armored Iraqi deuce and a halfs—two-and-a-half-ton open-backed trucks—from hard-luck 3rd Company followed the Humvee. Each carried two jundis in the cab, six in the cargo hold, and one standing behind the roof, holding on to a vibrating PKC Soviet-style belt-fed machine gun like a fire hose.

This is Dagger 3 exiting friendly lines with two Americans, twenty IA [Iraqi Army], *and no terps,* radioed Huss.

Two kilometers on, the convoy thumped over the median and approached an alley near Khalidiya's tiny Christian neighborhood. Qatan was trying to find an approach into town that the insurgents had ignored. Huss slowed near a turnoff.

"Here?"

Qatan shook his head and waved Huss forward.

Huss idled near another alley.

"This one?"

"No. Maybe next road," said Qatan.

To Huss it was like flipping a coin. Either the route was mined or it wasn't. But the odds of being attacked sure as hell went up when you dragged ass near the city, looking for a way in. The shops on the edge of Route Michigan were crowded, however, a good sign on a sunny morning.

The Humvee began to turn. A white minivan lunged out of an alley toward the Iraqi truck. There was no time for Neary to rotate his gun.

"Oh, no."

The minivan exploded. The blast pitched Neary forward. Flames swept over the Humvee in a flash, combing his hair back. Shock waves threw Huss into the steering wheel. Fire swirled across the windshield. This was a much bigger detonation than three weeks earlier. Qatan and Neary's screams could be heard when the explosion's roar faded.

"You hit?" asked Huss. "Neary, are you hit?"

"I'm hit! I'm hit!"

Neary's neck ached and his hair smelled like sulfur. He swiped his brow, looked at his bloody gloves, and then showed them to Huss.

Huss pressed the pedal to the floor. Piles of brown soot spilled off the hood in swirls. Buildings reappeared through the dust on both sides. He flipped off the Warlock jammer and grabbed the handset.

Dagger, this is Dagger Three. That was us.

The Humvee bounced back onto Michigan. Nothing in thirty-eight years had prepared Huss for what he saw. No disaster movie, no CNN report on a school massacre. Nothing.

Flames engulfed the two deuce and a halfs, cooking his jundis alive. All that remained of the minivan was a smudge. Wounded jundis and civilians crawled on the streets, dragging trails of blood. Others drowned in puddles of offal, crumpled and charred.

"Jesus Christ."

Enemy automatic weapons fire stitched the hood. Some bullets dove into the engine block, others were deflected and sped screaming toward other resting places. Huss skidded to a halt behind one of the burning trucks, hugging it for cover. He checked Neary's neck wound—"It's just slashed-up skin, Neary, you're okay"—then grabbed his carbine.

"Let's go," Huss told Qatan, who was unhurt.

"What do I do?" Neary coughed, the stench of melting rubber and burning diesel choking him.

"Get up in that turret and fight."

Huss opened the door and was gone. Neary stood up in the turret and sprayed bursts to suppress the enemy shooters. *The only way to live is to fight,* he thought.

In the meantime, Huss ran to a burning truck and looked in the cab. The jundi in the passenger seat had a massive head wound. *One killed in action* he counted in his head.

The driver, charcoal. *Two KIA.*

Huss rushed past the flames roaring over the truck. Three jundis flopped down on the road behind the tailgate, shooting at an apartment building. Enemy bullets snapped back. Huss emptied a magazine into a corner apartment. Then he looked inside the rear of the truck.

Four jundis lathered with blood were still breathing, but barely. Fragments of the suicide vehicle had splashed the truck like a bucket of hot coals, the shrapnel coming in low and fast under the armor plating. Huss recognized one of his favorite jundis, Hussein. Red strips from his lower back dangled past his T-shirt. Hussein held out his bloody hands.

"*Lalla? Lalla?* We are good guys." He was asking *why.*

"You're gonna live, Hussein," Huss reassured him.

The metal of the hold scalded any skin that touched it. Huss handed Hussein a first aid pouch. Rounds pinged against the truck. Wounded jundis could choose either to cook inside the kettle or get shot in the street, but Huss thought they stood a better chance inside.

"Stay here until I say so!" yelled Huss.

"Very bad!" Hussein replied, fanning his own tear-streaked face.

"I said stay here!"

Huss jammed in a fresh magazine just as a jundi with a PKC finished reloading. They both cut loose and the enemy's shots trickled off.

Huss sprinted to the second vehicle.

Dead driver. Three KIA. The passenger was missing. Huss shouted encouragement at the wounded jundi machine gunner who continued to shoot into the apartments, then raced back to his Humvee.

"We got three KIA and fifteen WIA, not including you," said Huss.

"The whole company," said Neary.

"All but Qatan and one jundi. The WIA are badly burned."

Huss grabbed the spare medical kit and a bandoleer of ammo, then sprinted back to the truck, firing at enemy muzzle flashes as he ran. He thought there was a fair chance they'd be overrun and he'd end up on CNN wearing an orange jumpsuit for his beheading. It felt like forever, but it had been only a few minutes since the attack.

Neary got on the radio. *Dagger 3 been hit by a SVBIED on Michigan. Three IA KIA. One-five IA WIA. One MiTT WIA.*

Three jundis were dead, fifteen jundis were wounded, and one advisor was wounded. It wasn't an unusual tally for a SVBIED, a suicide-vehicle-borne improvised explosive device, which caused the most casualties of any single explosive in Iraq.

Give me a situation report, Dagger 3.

The sitrep is a mass casualty. I say again, MASS CASUALTY!

Neary clipped the handset to his ammo vest, rotated his gun, and searched the balconies for targets. His heart was thundering—was it pumping blood out his neck? He fired another volley of suppressive rounds and touched his seared head and neck. Not too bad.

"Keep firing!" he shouted at some jundis nearby.

Neary realized they couldn't hear him. But he wanted them to see he was still fighting and that he'd never abandon them. He thought it important that the townspeople, who marveled at his Arabic, see another side of him, too. From his position he could see an Iraqi man sprawled in the street, his *dishdasha* riding up his charred torso, half pink, half black. He was howling. And dying. An eight-year-old boy had propped himself up with one arm. Neary could see right through him. He was missing half his rib cage. His lung or some other organ inflated and deflated like a balloon. He looked more like a burst watermelon than a human being.

Huss dumped bandages for the wounded men where they had sprawled in a pile behind a concrete median wall. He tried to rally the jundis, but most were too scalded to shoulder a weapon. Huss tried to find an enemy fighter he could plug in retribution.

The soldiers and Khalidiya's citizens screamed as one. And they would keep screaming. Huss listened, feeling desperately alone in all the noise. He could not shake the sinking feeling that he had failed 3rd Company. He was responsible for Unlucky Company no matter what anyone said.

On ASP Hill, Bozovich had been trying to sleep, lathered in his own sweat. The SVBIED blast shook him awake. He bolted on his armor and ran to the trucks.

"Don't leave without me!" he shouted, racing toward a rolling Humvee.

Boiko hopped out of the driver's seat and waved him in. Kenison took shotgun. George, a portly terp addicted to American junk food, jumped in back alongside Watson.

"Let's go, let's go! You drive," said Boiko.

Boz raced down the highway. George told him to cut left at the soccer field to make a less obvious approach.

"They're right on Michigan. Look at the smoke!" Boiko countered.

George tapped his Motorola. High-pitched Arabic. He could hear gunfire on both the radio and outside rising to one long roar.

"Better this way," said George. "It is the sneaky way. They are fighting."

"Then let's roll right up on them!" said Boiko.

Boz swerved left and weaved his way through eastern Khalidiya, just as George suggested. Boiko was hurt that his teammate had trusted an interpreter's judgment over his. George wouldn't stop talking. He was trying to translate the radio static.

After a few meandering turns, Boz realized Boiko was right and that he shouldn't have listened to George. He rammed the Humvee toward the smoke, pedal jammed into the foot well.

"No, no, no. We must go the back way!" shouted George.

"You can shut up now," said Kenison.

Bradley Fighting Vehicles and Humvee gun trucks from the TF Panther QRF beat them to the carnage. Boiko took it in: scattered fire, potshots from stubborn insurgents that were answered by long strings of automatic weapons fire blasts from the Americans. And screaming. Always screaming.

Kenison hopped out of the Humvee. Boz grabbed his rifle and followed.

"Hey, man, where you going?" Boiko asked. "You're the driver."

"You drive. I'm in the fight!"

They came upon Huss tending the wounded, begging the TF Panther guardsmen for extra bandages.

"This your casualty collection point?" asked Kenison. "I got it now."

Boiko exited the vehicle and took his bearings. It looked like a tornado had ripped through a county fair. Dozens of civilians writhed on the pavement, caked in blood, motor oil, and dirt. Others staggered around, shouting at the sky.

He trotted over to Huss. "You okay?"

"I'm fine. Neary got hit. Savages."

Boiko saw the TF Panther medevac crew with Neary. Boiko darted toward his friend. Right then a Bradley's 20mm cannon erupted, hosing the apartment building with bullets. Terrified, Boiko ducked behind a Humvee.

Huss had never heard a chain gun up close. Slugs banged into the apartments. Sections of mortar peeled off. They cheered. They couldn't help it. Kill them all. Then the cannon stopped.

Khalidiya was so quiet that even the wounded took a few moments to savor the calm.

Then an enemy sniper put a round into the thick of vehicles but hit no one. Five minutes later, another shot was fired from a different location.

Kenison helped a wounded boy lying on his back with a broken leg twisted up next to his ear, a pressure bandage covering his disgorged guts. Huss didn't think the kid stood a chance.

An older boy tugged at Kenison's armor.

"He asks us to please fix his brother," George translated. "His father will beat him if he doesn't come home with the little one soon."

"You tell him to tell his brother . . ." Huss started before trailing off. He felt a tingling come up out of his stomach and across his face like a wave. Was he going to cry right here on the street? No. Not until someone paid. "We need to clear these apartment buildings. I'm taking 3rd into this one."

He gathered the startled reinforcements from 3rd Company who were arriving with the rest of the ASP's reaction force. Then they stormed the structure.

It was abandoned. They found a dozen forged Iraqi police ID cards and two fighting positions carved into the floor. Then they bounded to the roof. A blob of the suicide driver's charred guts slumped there, blown skyward by the blast. There was no other explanation for the intestinal mess.

An enraged Huss stared down at the smoldering trucks and turned toward the jundis. "Let's find some others," he said.

On the street, Boz joined GW, the terp. They rushed to the burning trucks. An insurgent started shooting at them from across Route Michigan, in Abu Fleis. Boz grabbed his jundis and ran into the gunfire. "Do it again!" screamed Boz in English. That scared off the gunner and they returned to the mayhem of Khalidiya.

GW prodded a severed leg with his boot, cursing the irhabi. Then he found the driver's head that went with it.

"Forever like this," he mumbled. Whether he was talking about the terrorists or the war, Boz didn't know.

Residents emerged with pitchers of water, splashing the heads of the wounded and dribbling droplets from their fingers onto parched lips.

What the hell are they waiting for? Boiko wondered of the civilians. "Get your people to the hospital!"

Then Boiko realized the locals were waiting for him.

"Start loading civilians in my Humvee," Boiko said to George. "We're takin' 'em to the TF Panther aid station."

In the driver's seat, Watson had already radioed the TF Panther command post on Camp Habbaniyah. But the guardsmen told him that bringing so many Iraqi civilians inside the secure compound violated regulations and too many casualties would overwhelm the hospital.

Blood-soaked Iraqi civilians pressed to get into the Humvee, screeching in Arabic. Boiko closed the door behind them, hopped into the command seat next to Watson, and picked up the radio handset.

We're coming in with three civilian pax. All are urgents.

Negative. I say again, you cannot bring civilians to the BAS. How copy? Over.

Boiko twisted the radio off. "Guess I copy nothing at all."

Watson sped past the gate guard on Camp Habbaniyah. One yelling match with the guardsmen later and they were inside the hospital compound, which was located near the airstrip. Boiko opened the rear door and a bloody Iraqi unfolded like a jack-in-the-box. A bulky medic from the TF Panther stood there with stretcher teams. His battalion surgeon, a doctor who held the rank of captain, also stood by, looking like he wanted to kill Boiko.

"You disobeyed a direct order, Sergeant!" said the captain. "Who the hell do you think you are?"

"Sir, they're bleeding out. Without us they'll die. There's a mass casualty out there, in case you haven't heard."

"You watch your mouth. I'm not going to explain my order to you. Just follow it."

"I'm a former paramedic. Now that they're inside, you'll treat them, Doctor."

The guardsman medic lifted the last groggy Iraqi out of the Humvee and set him gently on a stretcher as his trauma team rushed the victims inside the aid station. The captain glared at Boiko. Then he turned away to treat them.

"Bring any more in here and I'll bring you up on charges," he said over his shoulder. "We don't have the supplies to handle all these people, and if an American unit gets hit, we'll be empty. How's that going to feel?"

Boiko swore at the captain. The weight-lifting medic, an enlisted man like Boiko, spun Boiko and pulled him around the vehicle.

"You need to leave."

The medic seemed friendly and was also too huge to argue with.

"I need to find out about my buddy. He's here somewhere," said Boiko.

"What's his name?"

"Neary."

"I'll find out. Now go before someone comes out here and arrests you."

Then he insistently tucked Boiko back into the blood-soaked Humvee.

"You know I'm coming back with more, right?"

"You get them here, we'll treat them," said the medic with a wink.

Watson and Boiko made two more runs, ensuring a dozen locals got emergency treatment. No Iraqi thanked them on the street. They simply expected medical treatment from the Americans. Well, the kids never thanked them for soccer balls or candy. Why would parents be any different?

The jundis were driven to TQ air base and evacuated to Baghdad. After Watson and Boiko saw them off, they drove back to Camp Habbaniyah where Boiko searched the hospital for Neary. A lieutenant intercepted him at the entrance.

"You're not welcome here, Sergeant."

"Get out of my way or I'll beat the hell out of you."

"You just got yourself court-martialed."

Colonel Newell was visiting the wounded. He approached the tangled pair.

"This is one of my best soldiers, Lieutenant. What's the issue?"

Both men paused to consider the senior officer's intentions. The giant medic who had earlier helped Boiko grabbed him by the elbow and ushered him out of the hospital.

"Neary got a scratch on the neck. We sent him to TQ and he'll be back in a couple days. Now get the hell out of here and don't come back. Ever."

★

Back at the explosion site, Huss was sitting in front of a shuttered grocery shop trying to catch his breath. It was late afternoon, six hours after the blast. He, Falah, and Aamr had been chasing the sniper around Khalidiya for four hours, since the Iraqi officers arrived on scene. Huss hadn't eaten anything and he had been sweating so much his boots sloshed. He had plodded up dozens of staircases, kicked open dozens of doors, all the while carrying sixty pounds of armor and ammo. As the senior advisor on scene, he wasn't going to take himself out of the fight. His XO had not come down from ASP Hill to relieve him as did Falah and Aamr for their junior officers. He doubted he could make any more climbs.

Falah reached into the abandoned shop and plucked a cucumber from a rack. He handed it to the American.

"Eat this, Sergeant Huss. Take a break. Then we'll go up the next stairs."

Huss devoured it and thought perhaps he could make one more ascent after all. They climbed and climbed. Evidence of the enemy's stakeout was everywhere. From behind a locked door came hushed whispers. Aamr took lead position, and when the others hesitated, Huss took the second position in the stack, his forehead resting on Aamr's back.

In they went. Aamr thumped into a screaming old lady and Huss wheeled toward the right corner with his weapon shouldered, powered only by adrenaline. His sights centered on a screaming 12-year-old-girl. He tried to move past her to finish clearing his sector, just like he was trained to do, but she backed up with him, bawling.

Huss had a daughter her age. He lowered his rifle, scanned the room, and when one of the jundis called the apartment "clear," he sat next to the crying girl, removed his helmet, and wiped his face with his hand. Overheated, he cracked open his flak vest. He thought he might die in an Iraqi apartment.

The old lady was no longer angry. She took pity on the worn-out soldiers and filled a bowl with cool water. She handed it to Huss.

He stared at the black flecks spinning on the surface. He'd been warned in a dozen classes that unfiltered Iraqi water could put a man down for months. He put the bowl to his lips, coated his mustache, then gulped and gulped. He handed the bowl to Falah, who drank next and passed it on.

It was standard operating procedure to destroy any building the insurgents prepared for an ambush site, or they would use it again. It also sent a blunt message. They informed the old lady.

"She will not leave," said Falah. "She says her husband is dead and her sons are in jail. No one to protect her and her daughters."

"Tell her she has thirty minutes to get out before the bomb comes," said Huss.

The search party proceeded to escort families from the building, rounding them up as they worked their way downstairs. On the street, Falah told Huss that the old woman refused to move.

"We can go get her," said Falah, "but there will be a fight."

"You're kidding, right? We have aircraft inbound," said Huss.

"I am most certainly not kidding."

Huss was exhausted. He searched his confused instincts and then switched to the book. SOPs were written for moments like these, to help soldiers make decisions in extremis.

"They used that place to kill our guys today. It could happen again. I say we go ahead and drop."

Falah didn't have a problem with it. The jundis cheered.

But Kenison was controlling the aircraft from the ground. While it was true that the population of Khalidiya seemed to respond to the stick and not the carrot, he wasn't going to bring down a redwood on these people and drop a thousand pounds of explosives into their apartment.

"I'm aborting the mission. We can't drop with those pricks in there. Okay, Huss?"

"That's fine with me," said Huss, who was too tired to think.

★

The Iraqi mortuary officers needed someone to identify the jundis in the TQ morgue. Falah and Aamr volunteered, but they needed an American escort to enter the base. So Huss accompanied them, along with Colonel Newell. For Huss it was as if the day would never end.

The morgue AC was cranked high and it chilled their sweat. A Marine unzipped a body bag. Huss had been on his feet for eight hours at this point and was terribly dehydrated. He hoped he wouldn't puke. His head clanged. The Marine removed a mass of bandages from the inside of the cadaver's skull.

"So that's where all the damn bandages went," Huss said. "We can't have the jundis wasting meds on dead bodies when we're under fire, Colonel. This jundi was dead from the moment I saw him!"

"No, we cannot," said an incredulous Falah.

"Pass it along, please, Colonel."

Falah nodded. A Marine sergeant major looked Huss over outside the morgue. Huss was rocking back and forth on his feet.

"Better get your head checked out," the Marine said.

The morgue was connected to the shock trauma facility. Huss took a seat in the waiting area and fought the urge to vomit. Thirty minutes later the sergeant major walked back up to Huss, who was staring blankly at the wall. "Ready to go, Huss?"

"I haven't even seen anyone yet."

"Do they know you're here?" asked the sergeant major.

"They've been peeking at me."

The sergeant major was furious. He yanked open the door and growled at an attending physician. The doctor glanced at Huss and said he would get someone.

"No, sir, you won't get anyone else," said the senior enlisted man. "This man was blown up a few weeks back and he was blown up today while you and I were eating breakfast. He's been fighting for eight hours. His head is killing him. You treat him, sir. Right now."

The doctor examined Huss. He had a concussion, which explained the nausea. He prescribed ten days of rest.

Ten days, thought Huss. *Right.*

The massive chow halls at TQ were air-conditioned, with polished chrome and tile. With a fried-food lane, a pasta bar, and an ice cream sundae station, it was a huge improvement over MREs.

Approaching the facility, they smelled the fried food and they smiled. Newell vouched for Falah and Aamr, leading Huss and the Iraqis inside. At Taji, where 3/3–1 had trained, the base commander had barred Iraqis from eating in the mess hall for fear of infiltration. The Marines on TQ allowed it, but only if the Iraqis were escorted by a colonel.

The dining room grew quiet as Huss played tour guide. Dozens of "Fobbits," the soldiers and contractors who inhabited the lavish forward operating bases, studied the unusual group. Huss knew it was unfair to hate the support soldiers. But their quiet seemed to mean that they hated Iraqis, and they had no right to do that.

If anyone should hate the Iraqis, it was Huss, and he didn't. Not all of them, anyway.

★

It was a tough night for the team. Troster was still in Baghdad. Neary was wounded. Three jundis were dead, many more wounded. Was this the future? To be whittled down, one man at a time, by suicidal murderers willing to kill children?

The suicide car bomb had rattled the men. Iraqi Battalion 3/3–1 never found out who the bomber was. The blackened husk of the minivan sat on the shoulder of Michigan for months. Their job seemed tougher now. Every swerving jackass driver in Khalidiya already unnerved them, but now the images from the car bomb would send their hearts racing. Back home, young men were unselfish if they passed a basketball. In the murderous wake of the car bomb, turret gunners in Khalidiya—with fractions of a second to decide if an Iraqi driver was sinister or just stupid—chose civilian lives over their own several times each day.

When the sun finally closed out the horrible day, Boiko sat on the berm outside the advisor bunker smoking a cigarette but inhaling only the quiet. Evenings were relaxing in Khalidiya. Whether that was because the American and Iraqi soldiers rarely patrolled at night or because the insurgents worked union hours had yet to be determined. Colonel Newell rolled onto the ASP to check on the team. Boiko was too tired to stand up.

"You here for my court-martial, sir?" Boiko asked.

"Who said anything about a court-martial?"

"I pissed some people off today."

"I hear you piss people off every day," joked Newell. "I'd serve with you anytime, Boiko."

The colonel sought out the other 3/3–1 advisors. Boiko took a long pull on his cigarette to cover the growing stink of the Iraqi latrine across the road. He whistled the smoke across his nostrils as an air freshener. Then Boiko went to find Rivera so he could lobby to take the next patrol.

When Huss reached the ASP that night, he was running on fumes. He had a splitting headache. "Blown up" was a physical state he now accepted, like dehydration. Before he hit the rack he felt it was his duty to visit the 3rd Company bunker. He was shocked to find just twelve jundis. When he'd taken over as their advisor, he had had close to eighty men.

The company had lost four dead and five times as many wounded in only three weeks. A dozen men deserted after the first IED. The rest went on leave. When those jundis heard about the car bomb, chances were that they would stay home, too. The whole damn unit would disappear.

"Lalla?" a jundi asked. It was the same question Hussein had asked from the back of the burning truck.

"I don't know why."

"But we're good guys," said another jundi in English.

"Not to the insurgents, you're not," said Huss.

Huss trudged back to the advisor hooch. The Americans were outside listening to Gunner Kenison give a pep talk. Overhead, big Air Force jets started their evening runs from TQ to Kuwait, and then on to the United States, their homeward route cruelly right over ASP.

Huss wasn't in the mood for speeches, but something Kenison said held him upright for just a few more seconds.

"I came up here to see if you could fight," Kenison told the team. "To be honest with you, we weren't sure when you all showed up. After today, there's no doubt. You all did everything right out there. Especially you, Huss."

Huss sure as hell didn't feel that way. He had lost the entire patrol. He had come to Iraq to advise the Iraqis, and there was no one left for him to advise. He had failed. The Marines could sugarcoat it all they wanted, but Khalidiya was beating them.

★

The night after the car bomb, First Lieutenant Bennett stared into the fire pit. It was mid-October, and in the late evening it was almost cool enough at

70° for a fire. The Iraqis thought the Americans were pyromaniacs. They saw little sense in prolonging the day's heat over a fire. But for the advisors it was a chance to bond, one of the few benefits of the ASP, like cleaning a weapon without a shirt, Vietnam style, or letting a five o'clock shadow grow until Troster or Rivera barked for them to shave.

Bennett had just received a Dear John letter. He had been married for six years to a woman he had dated since he was a teen. Absence may help civilian hearts grow fonder, but military deployments often have the opposite effect on young couples.

In Iraq, Bennett read the Bible twice a day. His first month had been uneventful, partly because he was serving as the team logistics guru inside the wire some days. But Bennett also believed his regular prayers gave him a little more wiggle room than the average soldier.

"It's funny," Bennett said to Huss and Bozovich sitting around the fire. "You men have had a few close calls. I haven't seen squat. I thank God I haven't."

"That's a good thing, Lieutenant," said Huss.

"I don't dispute it."

Huss stared at Bennett. Satisfied that the young officer was serious, he turned his attention back to the flames.

"Now you probably gone and jinxed yourself, sir," said Boz. "You going out tomorrow?"

"Bright and early. But there are no jinxes," said Bennett.

The next morning, Bennett steered the Humvee down ASP Hill toward 20th and Market. Rivera manned the turret. An Iraqi Nissan trailed them. The pickup halted at the outskirts of town. A group, mostly children, approached the jundis and soon George the terp's radio cackled.

"These kids know where there is an IED!" he shouted

"Where?" Bennett asked.

"Farther up there."

Bennett and George trotted up to GQ, the Iraqi platoon commander, who pointed down Market Street and waited for Bennett's reaction. To Bennett, it felt like the scene from *Raiders of the Lost Ark* when the native guides led Indy to the entrance of the cave, then refused to continue.

Bennett narrowed the bomb's location to five possible places: three piles of trash, a broken patch of concrete, and a hump of dirt. But the sharp launch of a rocket-propelled grenade broke his concentration.

RPGs didn't whoosh like the bottle rockets Bennett recalled from movies, trailing soft plumes of exhaust. They boomed. The warhead ripped overhead and exploded somewhere behind him. Bullets cracked but Bennett saw no muzzle flashes. Another RPG tore into ASP Hill closer to him.

"You see 'em?" he asked George.

The portly terp lost his nerve and raced to the Humvee, faster than Bennett ever could have imagined him moving. The jundi PKC gunner atop the Nissan cut loose, firing in a great semicircle—a half ration of "death blossom."

"See anything?" Bennett yelled up at Rivera in the turret.

"If I did, I'd be firing, sir."

Spurred by Bennett, GQ rallied a group of jundis and off they went into town.

In the meantime, a Humvee filled with advisors bounced down the rutted hill from the ASP, Bozovich behind the gun. Enemy bullets bracketed the vehicle, bursts sailing high above the ASP guard towers and then low, kicking up dirt clouds just meters in front of Bennett. The vehicle swerving into a firing position, Bozovich shouldered the 240 and aimed at a low wall three hundred meters away, where muzzle flashes could be seen.

Red tracers ripped past Bennett. The enemy's were green.

"Cease fire!" Bennett screamed at Boz. "Cease fire! Cease fire!"

Boz didn't hear him, but he was firing at a group of terrified jundis GQ had tucked behind a wall. Bozovich sent another burst into the wall.

George came staggering up the hill, gasping and crying. Boiko, the driver, pulled him into the cracked door of the Humvee.

"What's up, George?"

"No! No! Jundis there!"

"Jesus Christ."

Boiko grabbed Bozovich's calf and squeezed as hard as he could.

"Cease fire, Boz! Cease fire!"

Boz's ears were ringing. He thought he heard Boiko urge him to keep firing, keep firing. Clear as day. *My rounds must be doing something good,* thought Bozovich. *Here comes the pain!* He put the sight post on the distant wall, held the trigger back, and walked the rounds across the cinder blocks, chewing through the cement. He emptied the ammunition can.

Below him, in the Humvee, Boiko was pounding on his calf.

"Cease fire, I said!"

Bozovich saw Boiko's lips this time. Saw George crying like a child. The red light on the terp's Motorola radio was steady with transmission. *Oh no,* thought Boz. His eyes moved reluctantly back to the wall while his trembling fingers attached a new can to the gun and slapped the feed tray cover home.

"My bad," said Boz.

It turned out there was no bomb. The kids had set them up. More important to Boz, there were no injuries. Just a squad of badly shaken jundis who demanded to know why Boz had shot at them.

★

That night, Troster returned from Baghdad. He went over the incident in detail with a deflated Boz; this one would be tougher to rebut than previous arguments. Friendly fire ruined battlefield reputations, and Troster doubted the Iraqi officers would deflect blame.

"It is different than you think," said GW, reporting from the officers' mess.

"Let me guess," said Boz. "Since we're on an Iraqi outpost, living under Iraqi rules, they're going to hang me right now."

GW laughed. "It is the opposite! 4th Company told 3rd Company you fired warning shots to correct their poor tactics. At dinner, Major Moham-med insisted that you signaled them to get low and stay down. Now the jundis call you Angry Sergeant. Angry *Areef.*"

"So there's no problem?" asked a stunned Troster.

"The only problem is that the jundis want to patrol with Huss or Boz all the time. The officers said Huss was the bravest man in Khalidiya yesterday, after the bomb."

Troster was buoyed. He shook Boz's hand and excused himself to find Huss. A month earlier, when relations with the jundis were fractured, Boz would have been cast as the idiot villain, as Huss had been on his first patrol. But Boz emerged from the bad shoot with his reputation bolstered. The 22-year-old finance specialist, who preferred to accompany Major Moham-med's 4th Company, had formed a bond with the no-bullshit Iraqi company commander who intimidated the other advisors.

Before he went to sleep, Boz walked down to the 4th Company bunker to check on the jundis and visit Mohammed, as had become his habit.

"I want to thank you," Boz told Mohammed over tea.

"This thing does not need thanks," said Mohammed. "I want our jundis to stay low, too. Words don't work. An angry areef might!"

7

Ranger Danger

★   ★   ★

October 2005

On the evening of the 15th, Troster stood in the back of the small Iraqi ops center on ASP Hill watching Lieutenant Khalid brief his patrol plan. Watson and Boiko, who were scheduled to escort him, leaned over the giant satellite photo that had been taped to the sandy map board and studied the proposed route into the center of Khalidiya. Bright red and yellow pushpins were scattered throughout town, indicating sites of past explosions and small-arms fire.

"I like the plan, Khalid," said Boiko, "but you need to spread out the dismount points so we're not clustered in a goat rodeo if the muj bomb us."

Troster studied Khalid's reaction. The proud Iraqi lieutenant still hadn't forgiven Boiko for embarrassing him over the evacuation of the dying jundi. His face tightened for a moment before he relented and said, "Yes. That is the proper tactic."

Satisfied with Khalid's plan and Boiko's input, Troster excused himself and walked a hundred meters to the barbed wire delineating the edge of the ASP Hill. Downslope, Khalidiya was close enough to see shadows pass through the spills of light from wealthier homes that had generators—and solid ties to the insurgency.

After a month on the job, Troster's men had gained enough credibility with the 3/3–1 officers and jundis to influence the conduct of individual patrols without jeopardizing camaraderie. But Troster remained unable to convince Falah to send patrols into Khalidiya more than twice a day without more American support.

Troster wanted to replicate the model the 3rd Armored Cavalry Regiment had used in early September to drive insurgents out of Tal Afar, a city of 175,000 up near the Syrian border. Troster had followed the operation via *Stars and Stripes* newspaper reports and email with friends. The 3rd ACR sent thirty-five hundred Americans and five thousand Iraqis into Tal Afar where they patrolled the streets together, a ratio of twenty citizens per soldier. Khalidiya had a population of twenty-five thousand. If TF Panther dedicated two motorized companies to a joint operation with 3/3–1, together they could occupy Khalidiya with nine hundred soldiers, about four hundred from Panther and five hundred from 3/3–1, a ratio of twenty-five citizens per soldier.

This technique for controlling infested cities was called the "oil spot" in military schools.[1] The idea was to flood a key city like Khalidiya with a mix of U.S. and local troops, controlling the movements of guerrillas. The Americans provided the logistics, armor, and firepower—and set the soldiering example on an individual level—while the indigenous soldiers under this umbrella of support engaged the local population. Civilian leaders were cultivated and encouraged to come forward. Some money for civic improvements was given out, controlled by these leaders. As the population turned against the insurgents, hometown police were recruited to keep insurgents out, and these changes reverberated in nearby communities. Most of the soldiers then moved on, like an oil spot spreading outward.

Troster thought a sudden, sustained burst of joint security in Khalidiya could crack the insurgency's foundation, while giving Falah and his men the reassurance and example they sought in operating alongside their U.S. partner unit. After a month, the TF Panther troops could return to Camp Habbaniyah and run just a few joint patrols a week, leaving the bulk of the work to 3/3–1.

But Troster had no control over TF Panther, and the Army had illuminated no official path to success in defeating urban insurgencies, nor issued any guidance on training Iraqi soldiers. Panther's main mission was securing Route Michigan. It had been assigned the security of a hundred square kilometers, not one city. As for mentoring Iraqi units, senior generals were prescribing a relationship with Iraqi forces that was in direct contrast with Troster's vision and Falah's expectations.

Two weeks earlier, on October 1, General George Casey, who was in charge of the Iraq War, and General John Abizaid, in charge of all U.S. troops in the Middle East, had told Congress that U.S. troops in Iraq created a dangerous dependency for Iraqi forces. Their plan called for quickly turning the war over to the Iraqis, while U.S. forces, which were described as stoking the insurgents, consolidated on bases. Reducing U.S. presence on the streets was essential to prodding Iraqi forces onto the front lines.[2]

By emphasizing transition instead of combined team operations, headquarters had sent a muddled message to units like TF Panther, which told the Iraqis to pacify Khalidiya on their own, even if three separate American units three times as large had not done so in two years.

Joint patrols were rare. Since moving to ASP Hill over two weeks earlier, the jundis had patrolled just a single time with one of the Panther companies, and even that had not gone well. A Panther captain had spat a never-ending stream of tobacco while briefing the jundis. Accidentally breaking Iraqi cultural taboos—like spitting while talking—was understandable.

"Sir, if you please," GW interrupted. "The jundis don't like very much when you spit. It is like giving them the bird."

"I can't stop," said the captain.

"It would be very good thing if you did, sir."

"You tell 'em not to spaz out, okay? Just keep it in their pants."

"Sir . . ."

"Tell 'em!"

If Troster wanted more presence in Khalidiya, he knew his plan could not count on the other Americans.

Watson approached Troster in the dark. "Sir, I gotta talk to you. A few of us overheard the XO telling his wife he wasn't gonna leave the wire if he could help it. I called him out and told him I'd be talking to you."

"A lot of us say things like that so we don't scare the home front, Watson. Hell, some wives have no idea what conditions we're living in."

"It wasn't a line, Colonel."

Troster believed that was true. In a small team on a small hill, the others knew, too, and that was a huge morale liability. Troster called Colonel Newell at Camp Habbaniyah and told him he wanted to fire his XO, even though it would leave 3/3–1 with only eight advisors. He would summarize the case over the next few days and submit it to his 80th Division headquarters for consideration.

"You're one of us now," said Newell. "No need to tangle yourself in red tape. Request approved. Send him down in the morning to join my team. I'll see what I can do about a replacement."

★

Fifty kilometers away in Baghdad, Army Major Walter Roberson was trying to get to a unit in contact with the enemy. Roberson, 36, was an active-duty Ranger-qualified officer who had left his Ranger training unit to get into the fight. He wangled his way to Iraq as an aide to a Special Forces general. Once there, another aggressive officer stole his slot.

"You don't want to be tagging around with me anyway, Walt," said the general. "Want to join a MiTT? I have a hot fill."

"What's a MiTT?'" asked Roberson.

"A military transition team. Advisors. There's an opening on a team in Anbar Province. They're eight reservists living on an outpost with an Iraqi battalion in a hot zone."

"Reservists? From where?"

"I don't know."

"I'll do it," said Roberson.

"I thought so."

★

On October 16, Troster drove down to Camp Habbaniyah. Roberson was standing stoically in front of the Iraqi brigade headquarters. The Ranger, who had heavy-barreled his way onto the first available helicopter leaving Baghdad for Anbar, wore old school desert camouflage instead of the Army's new digital outfit—the army combat uniform, or ACU. He looked like a giant jundi.

"You must be my new XO," said Troster. Replacements didn't come quickly. There was probably something wrong with the new guy who had the grim mug.

"I want to let you know straight off, sir. I'm an asshole," said Roberson.

"Good," said Troster. "I can use one of those."

"I mean it, sir." Roberson shouldered his bulky pack, grabbed his duffel bag, and jerked his thumb at the soldier climbing out of the turret. "Who's that?"

"That's the guy you're replacing."

★

That night the team packed into Troster's room beneath the air conditioner to feed on hot chow Troster and Roberson had brought back from the TF Panther mess hall in Habbaniyah. Between the radio static and the wheezing AC unit, the soldiers had to speak up a bit, and it was grating on Roberson's nerves. He didn't realize that several of the men, especially Huss and Boiko, had suffered hearing loss from explosions.

While Troster was ferrying Roberson, the other advisors had spent their day chasing a rumor that Zarqawi was hidden in a Khalidiya mosque. To enter a mosque, U.S. soldiers required permission from a general officer. While the advisors dithered outside, Major Mohammed, a Sunni, had set down his rifle and walked right inside over protests from his Shia jundis, who screamed warnings of Takfiri kidnapping. An hour later, Mohammed strolled out with nothing more than a request from the imam for a generator.

"Next time there's a bad guy in the mosque, I'm not asking permission, I'm going in!" said Boiko.

"Zarqawi was never even in K-Town today!" Huss retorted.

"There's a reason we have rules about mosques, bigger than any one man or any one team," Troster rejoindered.

"Well, screw that!" Boiko shouted. "I'm going in hard!"

Roberson's first impression of the ASP was awful, although an infantry career that started at West Point had presented him with plenty of hovels around the world. He would get used to the heat and smells. It was the team dynamic that really worried him. Some of the men had little regard for rank, and Troster, a lieutenant colonel, let them get away with it.

The living situation had to change, too. Roberson didn't want Boiko and Watson, relatively junior enlisted men, living with Troster, filling his free time with their chatter. A good XO kept good order and discipline so his boss could focus on tactics.

"Do you all know you're shouting?" Roberson asked sharply.

The advisors had rigged a bungee cord to the aluminum door to trap the precious cool air. There was a loud tin slam as the new XO exited.

Troster visited Roberson that night. In the stifling heat of Roberson's room, which was not air-conditioned, they sat side by side on a metal bunk bed poached from the TQ scrap yard, occasionally firing a battery at one of the hundreds of rats that also called the concrete kiln home.

"I'd like to make some changes, sir," said Roberson.

"Fine. Just understand the method behind the madness. They've had a lot of adjusting and a long tour in front of them. They're doing well with the Iraqis. We've built up some solid relationships."

"I'm not a people person," Roberson said quickly. "I'd like to leave the Iraqis to you and focus on operations and the field, if that works."

"Walt, the best thing you can do is help me design a plan to get the Iraqis patrolling in K-Town around the clock. Right now we send in a couple of patrols a day. Falah doesn't seem to understand that we're getting hit so often because we haven't committed to the fight yet," said Troster. "The key to security is presence. The people won't help us until they see commitment. Can you help?"

"I'll look at the patrol schedule and draw up a proposal."

They were interrupted by a scream. GQ, naked, ran out of the shower hutch, cursing in English. Many Iraqis picked up swearing as a second language from the U.S. soldiers. GQ shook the water from his hand, bellowed in Arabic, and returned to the shower. The water storage unit was on the roof. Twitch, the Iraqi electrician, rushed up a ladder and yanked a live wire free. He had been heating the water with a three-thousand-watt element, waiting for the splatter of steam from a rolling boil, or a circuit breaker to trip, before opening the shower, but he'd fallen asleep. GQ was lucky to have escaped with only a few scalded fingers.

"It's different up here, Walt," said Troster.

★

The reservists may not have been hard-core infantry, but Roberson quickly concluded that they were brave. The new XO was drafting the new ops plan the following night when 4th Company pulled up to the gate for a patrol. Bozovich hopped in a Humvee and wheeled it around the Horseshoe, taking lead position. When the dust cleared, Roberson walked out to see them off. Boz was the only American in the vehicle. Major Mohammed sat in the command seat. GW was in back. A jundi stood in the turret, holding a battered PKC with one hand while sipping on a Gatorade bottle with the other.

"Um, isn't patrolling alone illegal?" Roberson asked.

"I'm not alone, sir."

"You're the only American."

"Oh, that. Sure as hell should be," said Boz, grinning maniacally.

That Bosovich thought highly enough of the jundis to patrol without any other Americans stunned Roberson. He was pretty sure it violated a number of regulations. It certainly violated his own survival instincts.

"Got room for me?" Roberson asked.

"Sure, hop in, sir."

Night patrols were generally uneventful. The insurgents chose when to strike and the local fighters retired at sunset to eat and pray. Major Mohammed wanted to visit a pair of sick children he had heard about from their uncle while conducting a house search. He fought the insurgents on their terms, like a mafia don who was just as kind to women and children as he was cruel to his rivals. When he heard that the Marine motto in Iraq was "No better friend, no worse enemy," even the dark circles under his eyes brightened a bit. Mohammed embodied the phrase.

That evening in Khalidiya, Mohammed left Boz and Roberson in the idling Humvee to take a brief look at the children inside the house. Roberson watched a group of jundis sift through a trashy drainage ditch, looking for bombs, while a separate pair seemed to be practicing dance moves.

"What the hell are those two doing?" Roberson asked.

"They're scaring the dogs," said Boz.

Glowing green in Roberson's night scope, the jundis looked as alien as the tactics.

Mohammed returned and slammed the hatch hard. "Tell Colonel Troster that we must get a doctor to see these children. One of them is a girl. We need a lady doctor."

"That could be a tough one, Major," said Boz.

"But advisors can do anything!" Mohammed chuckled.

★

In the morning, Troster drove up to the shock trauma unit at TQ and recruited a female navy corpsman to treat the sick girl and perform check-ups on the mother and her sisters. The navy doctor in charge worried about his medic, but Troster told him they weren't out to take any stupid chances.

The next day, advisors led a small patrol to the boy's house to treat his polio and a rash he'd contracted playing in the garbage. The female corpsman couldn't do much to help him, but her presence cheered the family and their neighbors, who hadn't seen a doctor in years.

They reached the sick girl's house an hour later, and soon a small crowd of infirm locals gathered. Gossip traveled faster than most Iraqi cars. Most women hadn't had a gynecological checkup in years. The strongest men pushed their way to the front of the line. Bez Boz, the Baby Falcon, was nervous. Armed with a squeaky voice, the ninety-five-pound Iraqi lieutenant had neither the personality nor the physical presence for crowd control. GW rushed to the steps. "Please, we are here today to treat a little girl, and maybe some ladies."

The crowd hissed. Disgusted that women were receiving medical treatment before them, several men began to openly threaten an attack.

"We have to leave soon," GW told Troster, back inside.

"Roger that. Tell the people that we want to do this more often, and even reopen the hospital, but we need their support."

"They will not give it today. We must go."

The family thanked the doctor profusely, the girls lingering for long hugs. Troster hustled the medic to the door with a group of jundis acting like Secret Service guards.

"We need to do this again, Colonel," the corpsman said.

"It's not over yet," said Troster.

They were hit by small-arms fire before they reached Route Michigan. Long strings of AK-47 bullets fanned the alleys, most soaring high. It degenerated into a running gunfight. The U.S. Humvee took the lead, swerving to a halt at each intersection so the Iraqi Nissans could dart across, then repeating the leapfrog drill, guns blazing.

When Troster arrived at the ASP after the patrol, he was infuriated that a simple medical engagement had so quickly been dissolved by some hostile men and a few guerrillas. He jogged up to the Iraqi HQ building, sweating so much that he drenched Chai Boy's towel before entering the office.

"We can't keep going like this, Colonel. The reason that town is out of control is because the insurgents dominate when we aren't there, which is 90 percent of the time. We need more patrols," said Troster.

"It is a difficult situation. The Panthers . . ." stammered Falah.

"Enough about Panther. We can triple patrols ourselves."

"Ministry of Defense does not give me enough jundis to do that."

"We have enough jundis. On paper, at least. What's our current strength?"

"I will have to check with my staff," Falah said carefully.

Head count was a touchy subject with the Iraqis. Everything from food rations to fair pay depended on inflated numbers. Any Iraqi unit reporting honest figures would go hungry.

"Anyway, we do not have the radios to call for medevac," said Falah. "Chai?"

Troster knew from Falah's face that he'd come on too strong. Anyway, he'd tried the same push before, with zero success. It was time to give something in return.

"Chai, um, I am . . . *nam, shukran.*" Yes, thanks.

Falah pointed out a seat. Troster removed his body armor and flopped it onto the chair like a booster so he didn't soak it with sweat. He sat down.

"Colonel Falah, if you increase the patrols, you'll have medevac and fire support. We advisors will accompany every one."

"Every patrol?" asked a surprised Falah. "Your nine men will go on four patrols every day?"

"We can do it if I send just two advisors at a time," said Troster, knowing the dangerous position he was putting his men in. If a mine blew up their Humvee, the Iraqis would have to medevac them. "If that's what it's going to take."

Falah said nothing. What was there to say in the face of such gumption?

"Besides, higher headquarters sent a message by assigning Major Roberson as my new deputy," Troster continued, lowering his voice. "He is a West Point graduate. Some Special Forces general sent him here. Maybe to report back on tactics."

Chai Boy arrived with his tea set.

Falah's thoughts were elsewhere. He had seen advisors reach into the Iraqi chain of command before—Falah was named commander of 3/3–1 in Mosul when U.S. advisors engineered the firing of his predecessor. Troster figured Falah was trying to discern his advisor's intentions. Was Troster a rogue, or did he, or his new deputy, Roberson, have the connections to get him replaced, as he had done his own advisor team's XO?

Troster watched the sugar crystals disappear in the swirling brew, and still Falah said nothing. It was time for him to light the way.

"Colonel Falah, may I suggest something? Tomorrow I will meet with your personnel officer. I will take his numbers to Roberson. Perhaps he and Major Aamr can find a way to increase patrols with the current number of jundis. If so, we will present the plan to you tomorrow night for your consideration. *Coolish zien?*" Very good?

Falah smiled. "*Insha'Allah,* Colonel Troster. *Insha'Allah.*" God willing.

★

Troster met the 3/3–1 personnel officer, a Kurdish captain, the next morning. The officer had battled to win acceptance from the Baghdad soldiers his whole military career. He wasn't going to sell out to Troster. He handed Troster a ream of loose-leaf rosters written by hand in Arabic, then a steaming-hot chai. The battalion numbers didn't match Troster's, so they tried the company-level reports, each with about one hundred men. Still, no matches.

Jundis weren't under contract and could disappear for weeks without being reported AWOL. Others had been shifted to compensate for the 3rd Company casualties. Many shared the same name. After two hours and two pots of tea, it was clear that the personnel officer would bluff into the night and that Troster was perspicacious enough to keep up with each parry.

"Shukran, Captain," said Troster, ending the stalemate. "You have a difficult job. My job is patrolling. If we can find enough jundis to do it more often, I don't care what roster they come from. And I'll never ask about the numbers again."

The Iraqi went to brief Falah, and Troster checked on Roberson and Aamr. They were huddled over a flip chart.

"How's it looking?" Troster asked.

"Good, sir," said Roberson. "Major Aamr here has designed a way to get twenty-four-hour coverage in Khalidiya."

"Wow. That's better than I expected. You want to brief Falah ahead of time, or should we go in together?" Troster asked Aamr.

"Is better if we go all at once. Like General Powell says, 'Use many men and make it end very fast.' Yes?"

Troster agreed with Aamr. One-on-one, Falah tended to get stubborn, but when he was uncertain about controlling leaks, or outnumbered, he generally yielded. The trio worked for another few hours and then practically burst in on Lieutenant Colonel Falah.

Aamr delivered the brief in Arabic while the advisors stood firm, waiting, studying the plaque from Mosul for the hundredth time. Finally Falah said in English, "It is done. I have ordered Major Aamr to try this schedule, with eighteen hours of patrols every day."

"We will rotate the schedule so the insurgents will not know what eighteen hours, so it will be like twenty-four hours," Aamr said quickly. The advisors knew there would be some compromise and this one was small, deftly negotiated by Aamr while they stood hanging on the two words of Arabic they recognized.

"I will let the company commanders know my decision this evening," said Falah. "We shall start tomorrow. I will inform the brigade commander, and you will tell the brigade advisor about this achievement?"

"Of course, Colonel. Third Battalion leads the way again. In the Army, we call this 'initiative,' and we have it," said Troster. "Major Roberson and I have just one thing to add: This is going to get a lot worse before it gets better. Once we increase the pressure, the insurgents will respond. We need to prepare the jundis for a very hard month."

"The 3rd Battalion will be ready. The people will see who is the real Iraqi: the terrorist or the jundi."

8

Bombs Away

★   ★   ★

October 2005–January 2006

As ops officer, Major Aamr designed the continuous patrol rotation by increasing each company's weekly mission total from seven to eighteen patrols. Each patrol ran two to three hours, about the amount of time you could walk under the hot sun while remaining vigilant. The typical jundi now left the wire once every day. With only nine men, the advisor team had to adjust to a patrol tempo experienced by only the most heavily engaged regular units, and rarely sustained over longer periods of time. Working in pairs in a single U.S. Humvee, some men went out four times a day. Before their mission was over, soldiers like Rivera, Huss, and Bozovich would each log more than 450 patrols, an astonishing number considering how many enemy attacks in their zone awaited them.

The Iraqis didn't have enough vehicles to keep up such a high tempo, so Troster requested sustained transportation support from TF Panther. Four times a week, a platoon from Panther's headquarters company, call sign Pyro, would ferry jundis from ASP Hill to their patrol location and back in hulking armored transport trucks. Led by Second Lieutenant Ed Fonseca, 24, Pyro was an ad hoc motorized unit that now had three missions: transporting prisoners to the U.S. brigade jail in Ramadi, shepherding jundis in their armored vehicles, and at dawn and dusk driving Filipino mechanics who worked at the Camp Habbaniyah scrap yard back and forth to their quarters on the mammoth Marine air base, TQ.

The private contractor who ran the scrap yard was supposed to drive his workers himself. To woo TF Panther, the contractor loaded Pyro down with ice cream from giant freezers on TQ each evening, which was to be delivered to the Panther officers and NCOs at headquarters.

On the hottest days, the Pyro drivers had to push the pace to avoid exchanging a barrel of slop for an ass chewing from a salivating senior NCO. Fonseca himself had once returned from TQ without ice cream. The senior staff officers screamed at him, and from then on the soldiers joked that there was no debating Pyro's mission priority at headquarters: ice cream.

"There's no ice cream on ASP Hill," Troster had joked with young Lieutenant Fonseca.

"We're a mutt unit, sir," said Fonseca. "I've got a lot of people assigned to me that other officers did not want. Doesn't bother me. My only requirement is bravery."

"You're going to do just fine, Fonseca," said Troster.

On October 21, Boiko and Bozovich buddied up for the morning patrol on the new schedule, into Khalidiya alongside the Iraqi QRF to probe reports of a mine. For three hours they glassed the baked dirt with their binoculars. The mine was nowhere to be found. They tried to buy some samoon or falafels, but no shop was open. When they returned to ASP Hill, they had ninety minutes before their next patrol, so they nudged some advisors who were filling out paperwork out from under the AC and wolfed Pringles and knockoff Cokes. Boiko debriefed Troster while radios hissed and hummed.

"Good luck," said Troster.

"Oh, yeah, there's a lotta that around here," said Boiko on his way out.

Boz and Boiko then patrolled with 2nd Company. A jundi nicknamed "Private Crazy" was in their turret. Crazy cursed in English and loved to fight. Boiko tapped Crazy's leg to get his attention and felt a steady tremor. To comfort him, Boiko yelled, "Good to go?"

Private Crazy leaned down into the Humvee. "Good. Very good."

"Bet you like this armor, don't you?"

GW translated and Crazy smiled broadly and gave a thumbs-up. The best thing about riding with the advisors, next to the good food and free equipment they handed out, was the massive armor.

"You gonna kill an irhabi today?"

"Very many irhabi!"

"Well, we have to see one first," said Boz.

The enemy initiated the fighting in Khalidiya. The attacks were hit-and-run. In their first five weeks in Khalidiya, the advisors had been shot at or bombed more than twenty times, but had yet to sight an enemy fighter in action.

Despite Private Crazy's boast, the patrol proved uneventful, another long slog down 20th Street swiveling their heads toward every piece of trash and, out of respect, away from the very few women—mostly dressed in black abayas and niqab face veils—allowed outside by their patriarchs, usually to run errands.

Boiko and Boz escorted 2nd Company safely back to the ASP and picked up 4th Company. No break, their third patrol before noon. They were too tired to joke with the new jundi in the turret. They raced into the Horseshoe and emerged with packets of beef jerky and coffee, which they sometimes dipped like tobacco because the caffeine and the sting from the grounds across their gums kept them awake.

Back in the city, Boiko fiddled with the air-conditioning slots, but nothing came out. The AC had been on maximum cool since the first patrol that morning and seemed spent. The sun was high and cast the dusty city in sparkling glare. The residents of Khalidiya watched the strange Americans from whatever shade they could find, mostly beneath concrete awnings. They held their hands over their eyes to shield them from the sun.

Near the intersection of 20th and Market, a man darted up a narrow alley. With the instincts of a hunter, Major Mohammed was out and running before his vehicle had even stopped, followed quickly by Boz and a group of confused jundis who ran as a pack.

Boiko wheeled the Humvee and accelerated down the alley in support. Seeing him, the soldiers fell back behind the armored car. A mine detonated beneath the vehicle's rear bumper, pitching it onto Route Michigan. Soldiers never wore seat belts in Humvees. Boiko hit the roof and then the driver's side door. When he regained consciousness, Boz was standing there in the broiling dust shaking him awake.

"Boiko! Boiko!"

"Why are you yelling, man?"

"Christ, I thought you were dead."

"What's happening?"

"IED and now a small-arms ambush," Boz said, tugging at Boiko's bloody sleeve to get his attention. "You got a cut on your arm but no holes. I checked."

"Go fight, man. I'm good."

Boz didn't need further prodding. He shouldered his rifle, raised the sights to eye level, and sprinted around the open door of the Humvee toward a group of jundis who were watering the pavement with spent brass casings.

The bloody jundi in the turret slid down the side of the cab and stumbled toward his platoon. Pebbles from the mine blast had peppered his face, but he could see because his advisors had lent him a pair of ballistic goggles.

Boiko pitched his tingling feet outside the Humvee and let them dangle. He saw what appeared to be men with AK-47s approaching from the flank.

He sighted in and fired a magazine down the road. The apparition disappeared. A Bradley Fighting Vehicle rolled up and a guardsman yelled, "Dude, you know you're bleeding?"

"I know it."

The Bradley's gun banged and all other firing stopped. Heavy weapons had that effect on insurgents, who fought with a magazine in the AK-47 and two more in the pockets of their tracksuits. They weren't looking to attract bullets the size of cigars steered by magnifying glasses that could read a car license plate at four hundred meters. Guardsmen from the Bradley bandaged the cut on Boiko's arm and gave him cold water. Boiko drove the fractured Humvee back to the ASP where the pit crew awaited.

"You okay?" asked Troster.

"Another day at the office," Boiko replied. His back throbbed but he didn't say anything about it. Troster and Roberson took his place on the evening patrol with Boz. Boiko lay in his cot drinking nonalcoholic Beck's beer, listening to Boz on the radio. He went to sleep feeling guilty.

Inside the Humvee on patrol that night, Troster smacked Roberson, who was gunning in the turret, on the calf hard enough to attract his attention. "We knew the insurgents would respond to increased patrols, but on day one?" shouted Troster.

"Their operations cycle is faster than ours," said Roberson.

"It sure as hell is faster than Panther's," said Troster, who had given up on joint patrols. Instead, he had settled for transportation support. Of the five or six patrols that would now depart ASP Hill each day, TF Panther would drive the jundis on one or two, as long as they were scheduled in advance.

Troster knew that the insurgents still had plenty of time gaps to plant bombs like the one that had wounded Boiko. But shrapnel didn't discriminate. During advisor training, instructors claimed that if the insurgents accidentally killed civilians, the locals would eventually switch sides or at least expose the bombers to the jundis before they killed more innocents.

Troster saw two obvious problems with the theory. The rational people in the city had long ago decided that terror was more persuasive than government services. Most guerrillas were local boys, but even the hard-core AQI soldiers slept in the city when they operated in Khalidiya, and roamed freely enough to terrorize any local who aroused suspicions. The American units that had been there two years before the arrival of 3/3–1, on the other hand, had promised a better life for Khalidiya and then gone home to sleep in Camp Habbaniyah at night, leaving the flock to the wolves.

The other problem was that in some Khalidiya tribes the irrational outnumbered the rational. Their deep hatred of Americans and Shiites was stoked by radical imams and sheikhs. They blamed civilian casualties on the

American invaders and their traitorous "Persian puppets" fighting for Iran. And many people believed it.

If they were going to beat the insurgents, 3/3–1 had to show unwavering commitment to Khalidiya.

★

When Boiko awoke on October 22, he saw he had been removed from 4th Company's morning patrol, giving him an extra three hours' rest. Rivera made the switch and was paired with him on the next patrol.

Only twenty-two hours after being wounded by the bomb strike, Boiko was back in the rotation, following the example set by Huss. They crept through the eastern sector of Khalidiya on foot, winding through tight alleyways until they emerged at the city's soccer field. Every street seemed awash in litter, but the soccer pitch was relatively clean, though it had no grass either. Shared responsibility was an alien concept among most of the locals, but respect for soccer was universal.

Noon passed and the field stood empty, heat cracks widening in the shadowless town center. The troops retreated to the shade of their vehicles. Snipers could hit the field from one of a hundred apartments. Motorolas crackled in Arabic.

"What's the deal?" Boiko asked GW.

"The terrorists do not bomb the field. But there is no one playing so Lieutenant Khalid is careful," said GW. "He wants to cross very fast, in vehicles, and he wants us to lead. We have the Warlock."

"I can't decide if Khalid is smart or just paranoid," said Boiko. "I thought you said they never bomb the field."

"It would be very unlucky."

"Hold on," said Rivera, stomping on the gas. The Humvee ripped onto the field. Massive contrails of dust bloomed, slowly expanding in the dead air. Khalid had borrowed some Iraqi Panhards for his troops, armored vehicles that resembled turtles, and they spread out behind the U.S. vehicle.

Rivera braked on the north side of the field, near Michigan. Boiko stepped out and the dust caught up to him, washing like a wave across the scarf that acted as a filter. Khalid was out of the Panhard and moving fast toward Boiko.

A bomb exploded close by. Khalid tumbled and was almost halved by automatic weapons fire coming across the highway from Abu Fleis. Boiko regained his bearings, saw enemy muzzle flashes, and shot back.

At three hundred meters, it was impossible to differentiate between a good shot and effective suppression, but the firefight ended with the jundis staging along Michigan, relentlessly pouring bullets into Abu Fleis like volunteer firemen using up their allotment of water on an annual exercise.

Troster and Roberson raced downhill as part of the QRF and tried to pinpoint the enemy firing point in Abu Fleis, but children had already picked the area clean of fallen brass. "Two fights in two days. We're in for a long one if it's like this every day," said Troster.

"This is what I signed up for," said Roberson without irony.

"I know you did, Walt. But remember that some of the guys didn't. They're doing a hell of a job, but we have to watch for signs of burnout."

Roberson didn't respond. He'd judge their performance himself. But Troster was right about their endurance. For a bunch of carpenters and cops, they were a pretty determined bunch.

★

A routine developed on ASP Hill. Day after day the advisors critiqued the Iraqi mission briefs, inspected gear, checked radios, and ate cereal floating in Mountain Dew on the hoods of their Humvees while they prodded the Iraqi officers to depart on schedule. Loaded and locked, they rolled out the gate, drove slowly down a dozen streets swiveling their heads and sucking in their breath at each unexpected bump or clunk, dismounted for the long slog through neighborhoods where the residents never knew anything, the kids begged relentlessly, and the jundis looked bored. They sprinted for cover when the sniper shot or explosion came, yelled at the jundis when they returned a fusillade on a crowded street, called in mines, returned to base, debriefed the jundis, cleaned weapons, devoured junk food, asked about mail, mercilessly harassed each other like brothers, and fell into the rack.

In late October the weather broke, but the men felt cooler only after the sun had set. Major Mohammed led a night patrol through the wealthy section of Khalidiya on October 25. He spotted two men relaxing against a stone wall. There was a sunset curfew, but the jundis didn't want to rob the locals of their first cool evenings.

At first the men ignored the Iraqi major, continuing their conversation as he stood over them. Boz backed off to watch. Some Iraqi officers liked the Americans close and fed off their power. Major Mohammed wanted advisors to stay in the shadows.

"Peace be upon you," Mohammed said after a few minutes.

"And upon you, peace," the men answered.

"God the most merciful desires peace. Tonight you're going to give God what he wants. Show me where a bomb is buried."

"W'allah ma'aruf," said one. I swear to God I don't know.

Mohammed wasn't a yeller, but he was confrontational by nature, even with friends. He put his head between the two locals. Boz heard harsh whispers. Then the men crushed their cigarettes and led the patrol down an alley toward Route Michigan.

"What do we got, GW?" asked Boz.

"IED," said GW.

The locals pointed at a rice bag half buried in a gutter and tried to back up. Major Mohammed grabbed one of the men by the forearm, shaking his head. If it was a trap, they were all going up in flames. Together the trio squatted next to the bag. Mohammed slit the bag open with his knife and peered inside with a penlight. Then he lit three cigarettes and handed two over.

"Together we did God's will tonight," Mohammed told them. "You can go now."

"You will not say we helped you. It would be very bad," one of the men said.

"God knows already."

Mohammed wasn't religious, but he invoked God to undercut one of the core arguments of his enemy: that the Iraqi soldiers were heretics. Mohammed believed that few of the local tribesmen who invoked the Koran had true Islamic faith. The Americans referred to Anbar as complex religious insurgency, where deep spiritual beliefs emboldened mujahideen. Mohammed believed that if the typical Khalidiya terrorist was too stupid to understand that the Shiites constituted the majority of Iraq's people, he wouldn't know the difference between sharia law as preached by Moqtada al Sadr—the country's leading Shiite firebrand imam—and the Wahabi-inspired rants of the Sunni terrorist kingpin Zarqawi.

In Khalidiya, the guerrillas followed their tribes, and tribal leaders were like politicians who counted on a complacent constituency. The Americans wanted to give everyone a vote, thinking that democracy would change their whole outlook. But Mohammed didn't believe it. The sheikhs were in charge, not the voting booths. Sheikhs could end the insurgency overnight—but for two years they had been allowed to play both sides. They blamed the Americans for the nonstop violence on the streets even as they assigned some of their sons to AQI as day laborers, digging in mines or dropping mortars into an unsteady tube. Others ran the black market fuel convoys even as they bid on lucrative American contract trucking jobs.

Now that the New Iraqi Army was allegedly taking over the war, Mohammed wanted to end the naïveté. It was time for the sheikhs to choose sides. If they wanted to retain power, they had better rein in their people. Unfortunately, the Americans seemed determined to continue to do everything themselves, as they had for two years without success. To Mohammed, the country that put men on the moon was ruling as if they were still up there.

The insurgents he despised were flat out beating the Americans using crude mine warfare, planting bombs in full view of gawking locals without fear of exposure. U.S. soldiers in the big units like TF Panther made it even easier for the tribal knuckleheads to kill them because they drove everywhere. Patrolling in buttoned-up trucks gave the insurgents easy targets that could not immediately retaliate.

The Americans' reaction to the discovery of a roadside bomb was another example, in Mohammed's mind, of their flawed thinking. Their standard operating procedure was to quickly encircle every possible mine, evacuate the area, and neutralize the bomb. Mohammed thought they should leave the bombs in place for a few days. The locals tolerated the bombs because the Americans generally removed them within twenty-four hours, and the bombers rarely seeded the same doorstep twice. If, however, the Americans weren't so quick to dig up every IED, Mohammed claimed, the locals, driven mad by the fear of a random detonation, would put pressure on their tribal leaders to stop supporting the insurgency. The sheikhs would be forced to choose, and Mohammed believed many would turn.

Boz interrupted Mohammed's thoughts. He wanted to look inside the rice bag, too. He used a red-lens flashlight to view the artillery shell, then returned to the Humvee where he called for the four-man Marine Explosive Ordnance Disposal, or EOD, team based in Camp Habbaniyah and settled in for a long wait. Battalion 3/3–1's patrol schedule had increased the workload not only of the insurgents but also of their U.S. partners—the insurgents planted more bombs, Iraqis like Major Mohammed were getting more tips, and demand for EOD services quickly tripled. If any unit had a schedule as hectic as that of the advisors, it was EOD.

EOD arrived in a blacked-out Humvee, escorted by a security element from TF Panther. "What have you got?" asked Gunnery Sergeant Darrell Boatman, 38, the bomb killers' leader.

"It's in a rice bag on the edge of Michigan," said Boz.

"Sorry about the delay," said Boatman. "This is our third IED call tonight. How'd you find it?"

"Local tip," said Boz.

"They probably got paid for putting it in, then told you so it'd be removed, and they'll be paid for planting another," said Boatman.

Planting a mine required four or more people. The bomb maker was typically unknown to the digger, who often was just an expendable day laborer. The planter needed only a superficial knowledge of circuits to seed the bomb and run the wires, so he sometimes didn't know the weapon's maker. Then a triggerman took over, digital video camera in one hand, radio transmitter in another, his gig typically limited only by battery life. Most mines in Khalidiya had radio-controlled firing mechanisms; no insurgent wanted to be caught sitting at the end of a hard wire. So the blast initiators were stuffed into the nose cones of artillery shells and nail-packed, gasoline-topped paint cans, which were connected by wire back to a radio base station like a cell phone, mobile phone antenna, garage door opener, or remote control toy. When the triggerman dialed the phone, the closed circuit detonated the bomb, but it worked only as long as the system had power. The bigger and better the bomb, the more likely it had a big battery to keep the detonator juiced.

With their jammers on, advisors usually took point on Iraqi patrols. The insurgents responded by moving base stations farther from the bombs to get clean signals. But this required more digging and decreased the bomb's reliability.

Triggermen had to move back, too. So the insurgents started using elaborate explosive webs to defeat the technology, including decoys, trip wires, and pressure plates that never needed electronics to detonate, only a heavy vehicle that pressed metal sides together, igniting the explosives. The centuries-old race between arrow and armor always ended the same way: Offensive weapons were innovative, defenses improved accordingly.

When they were discovered, most mines were destroyed in place by explosive charges. But if Boatman thought he could deactivate a bomb by hand, he went to work with a knife and wire cutters, then simply dug it up. The advisors thought Boatman and his men were the craziest in Iraq. They didn't drive a massive antimine vehicle or wear blast suits like spacemen. Marine EOD used a flimsy high-backed Humvee and wore the same body armor as everyone else.

Boatman thought the advisors were just as crazy to live with the Iraqis.

"What happened on your other calls tonight?" Boz asked.

"The others were false alarms," Boatman said, exhausted.

Half his calls led to mere trash, but that didn't make those investigations any easier on the nerves.

Boatman pulled a robot with treads like a minitank out of his Humvee. It looked like an oversize child's toy to Boz, but to the EOD Marines, "Napoleon" was a team member. When a robot died, EOD leaders delivered a eulogy.

They used a remote control to steer Napoleon to the suspect bomb while Boatman watched a video monitor. The robot had a camera for an eye and a steel claw for an arm. It poked around the bomb.

"Looks like a big one," said Boatman. "Wait here."

"Not to worry," said Boz.

As Boatman approached the bomb, he sank lower and lower until he was on his belly, wiggling up to the bag. A few minutes later he returned with a large artillery shell on his shoulder, smiling like a hunter carrying a trophy kill. He dumped a cordless telephone base station and a washing machine timer in his truck.

"Whoever buried that one was nervous," said Boatman, still smiling. "They use the washing machine timers to give them a few minutes before the bomb is armed."

"Can you tell who's building certain bombs?"

"Not yet. Most have the same basic design," said Boatman. "But even if you don't respect the insurgent, always respect the bomb."

★

The advisors heard Boatman repeat his mantra many more times. Battalion 3/3–1 called for EOD on seven patrols in a row. Twice, the 3/3–1 advisors called in false alarms after midnight. They had no choice—policy was to call the experts at EOD to deal with every explosive, period. With just four men, EOD was too short-handed for rotations. The entire team was always on call. TF Panther rarely discovered IEDs at night, so Boatman enforced a strict sleep schedule to prep for endless stressful days outside the wire.

Now the Iraqis and their reservist escorts were calling at all hours, and crying wolf while they were at it. Boatman needed 3/3–1—and TF Panther—to cut down the number of bad tips. He wanted the Iraqis to get visual confirmation of the bomb before calling.

The advisors thought this was insane. The Iraqis were developing a fledgling network of sources. EOD needed to support this Iraqi effort by showing citizens that their tips brought results. Besides, the bombs weren't sitting out in the open. To confirm an IED, someone had to crawl to within inches of its hiding place. Neither the Iraqis nor their advisors had good optics, let alone robots.

The insurgents were angry, too. Following the successful discovery of five IEDs, on October 27 a bomber managed to detonate a massive bomb on Michigan. It exploded between a Bradley from TF Panther and one of its Humvees.

The lead Bradley skidded to a halt. To flee potential secondary explosions, the driver of the Humvee pressed the gas pedal to the floor and accelerated into the dust cloud caused by the detonation. The Humvee struck the Bradley, and several TF Panther soldiers inside got hurt in the crash. Out on patrol, 3rd Company, escorted by Huss and Roberson, rushed to secure the scene. Jundis quickly encircled the area, pushing the local audience back with rifle butts. A bystander nudged a jundi and whispered about a second IED buried nearby.

"Call EOD," Roberson told Huss.

"They're gonna want confirmation first, sir."

"Confirmation? I'll give 'em confirmation," Roberson said gruffly.

Roberson grabbed a few jundis and stormed off. The other advisors weren't sure how to read the new XO. Mostly they thought the man they had nicknamed "Ranger Danger" was tough but brooding, as if the city—or they—had wronged him in a previous life.

A jundi pointed at the corner of Market Street, then took his place in the file behind Roberson, who was so thick in the chest the Iraqis thought he wore double armor plating.

"Let me guess. Bomb somewhere in there, but you don't know where."

Roberson scanned the ground and noticed fresh dirt. He moved closer and knelt down. A wire was visible, but spent wire littered Khalidiya along with other debris. Hundreds of individual power lines covered the town like a giant cobweb, each one leaching off the others, and residents constantly snipped electrical lines for their homes.

Roberson scooted forward to get a better look and a sniper shot snapped overhead. He sprinted for the trucks, scattering the jundis like deer.

"You call EOD and tell them we got a bomb. Confirmed," Roberson told Huss. "That sniper was covering the site. We'll need to expand the cordon. And somebody chase down those jundis before they make it back to the ASP."

Five advisors—Huss, Roberson, Neary, Troster, and Boiko—supervised the security perimeter going up on rooftops and street corners. One by one, each man received a round from the sniper, who fired from five different locations, targeting only the Americans. The jundis noticed and now kept a safe distance from their mentors.

"At least the sniper's got some national pride," said Boiko.

Troster's radio beeped. It was the EOD security team from TF Panther that protected Boatmen's Marines, call sign Cougar. Their bomb removal convoy was idling outside the perimeter.

Dagger, this is Cougar. Need to confirm the site is secure before we come in. Over.

The shooting stopped an hour ago. Over, Troster said into the radio.

I see some Iraqi soldiers on the roofs, said the anonymous Panther radio operator. *Can you tell 'em to come down? Over.*

Those are my jundis, said Troster. *They're protecting you.*

I'm worried some of my guys might think they're bad guys. Over.

Since when do insurgents wear helmets! Troster barked into the radio.

It was hot. The advisors had been out for hours. Everyone on the street risked a sniper shot. The mine was eventually removed by Boatman's EOD team, but neither the guardsmen accompanying Boatman nor the advisors thanked the other.

Roberson was so angry with the dithering by EOD that he patrolled until 0100, slept four hours, and joined an early morning foot patrol with Lieutenant Khalid. A local man who was sweeping his stoop murmured something to Khalid, who did not stop to expose the man.

"Bomb up ahead," said Khalid after a few minutes.

The tip had been delivered so quickly that Roberson had missed it. The sweeper didn't want to be seen talking to Iraqi soldiers, but also didn't want kids to get killed by insurgent mines.

Roberson saw a red fire extinguisher that he didn't remember from his last pass. It was too obvious to be a bomb. He dug along the curb with the heel of his boot looking for wire.

"Bring the Humvee up here," Roberson told Rivera, his patrol partner. "It looks fake. I'm gonna use the truck as a shield. We need to get closer."

Rivera, who was driving, inched the Humvee forward toward the trash. He stopped fifty meters short of the suspected bomb and opened his blast door, hoping Roberson would take shelter behind the wing. Roberson stayed tucked next to the engine block. He peered over the hood and ducked again.

"Keep going," said Roberson. "I can't see for sure."

To Rivera, it was a good way to get killed. He thought the advisor operational tempo was too high at two or three patrols per man per day. Even Ranger Danger, with his Ranger School sleep deprivation training, was exhausted. An active day without sleep had the same effect on decision making as five beers.

As the senior NCO, Rivera felt torn. It was his duty to look after the men, but he couldn't cut back patrols. In combat, it was mission over men, Troster had made a promise, and 3/3–1 finally had momentum. But they were down to six men. Gentile was aiding the brigade, Lieutenant Bennett had been tapped to help build a base in Ramadi for a few weeks, Boz had gone home for his three weeks of leave, and Huss had gone to escort the Iraqi leave convoy to Baghdad for three days.

"Sir, this is a job for EOD," said Rivera. "Let's stay here."

"EOD will only come if they hear the tapping of a Leatherman on a bomb," said Roberson.

"That's crazy," said Rivera.

"Watch this."

Roberson snatched the radio handset and got into a long argument with the radio operator at the TF Panther who screened EOD calls. The team was busy on another call, and he wanted Roberson to assure him it was a bomb.

"See that?" Roberson told Rivera. "Now move the truck closer. I have a 4th Company patrol to go on in an hour and I'll disarm it myself."

"I can take your place, sir."

"No one takes my place on patrol," said Roberson.

Years before, as an active-duty soldier, Rivera had been infantry. He understood the XO better than any of the other enlisted men on the team. Some officers had no confidence and depended on advice, some were open to suggestion, and some, like Roberson, you couldn't debate because they didn't accept the concept of plurality. In combat that wasn't a bad thing. If you wanted to give input to an officer like Roberson, you had better have the rule book on your side and a strong approach.

"Sir, if you want to live, we wait for EOD. That's the SOP. No arguing."

"Fine," said Roberson grudgingly. "Over-under until they show up is two hours."

Two hours later, EOD's escort platoon arrived to inspect the Iraqi cordon, taking positions around the field. Boatman came on over the radio criticizing the Iraqi defensive formation, and a guardsman began waving at a few confused jundis. Roberson stepped out of the Humvee and jogged to Boatman's Humvee. The Marine gunny might rule over these guardsmen, thought Roberson, but he needed an adjustment out here.

"Let's get a few things straight," said Roberson. "You're not in charge out here. We set the cordon, you disarm the bomb. Tell your people the next time they try to move one of our jundis I'm going to field-dress him right here on the streets."

Boatman was shocked. No guard officer on Camp Habbaniyah would dare talk to him that way. Boatman took full measure of Roberson and his old school camouflage—Roberson still refused to wear the new blue digital uniform—before he spoke.

"Sir, you don't have to explain my job to me. I've been in for twenty years and we've reduced close to a hundred bombs since we got here. I'm trying to keep my team safe and I'm trying to keep you and your Iraqis safe."

"Then stop questioning us when we call," said Roberson. "If we say there's an IED, there's a pretty goddamn good chance it's an IED. All the arguing is ruining my patrol schedule. You want us to walk right up to a bomb with two Americans and ten Iraqis and no equipment, when you use a robot and an entire security platoon. Gunny, you take a lot of risk, but you're not the only one. We understand each other?"

"I understand you, sir, but I'm not sure you understand us. We have three Marines policing every IED in this sector. We're running on empty."

"Well, so are we," said Roberson.

One of the Marine engineers guided the robot to the fire extinguisher. The bomb exploded. A shot of shrapnel skipped off the ground, burned through Roberson's holster, and then bounced off his hand, leaving a pink dent like a ruler rap.

When the rocks stopped plunking, a Marine dragged a piece of the shattered robot behind the truck.

"They got Napoleon!" he despaired.

Roberson said nothing. He walked back to his truck, signaled Rivera to return to base, and collapsed in the command seat. The two most reticent men on the team drove back to the ASP in silence except for the prayers of the jundi in the turret. They stopped outside the ASP, where 4th Company idled in Nissan trucks, awaiting escort. The jundis swapped out turret duty, and Boiko took Rivera's place as driver.

"Guess it was an IED after all," Roberson said to Rivera.

"Yes it was, sir."

"Good thing I listened to you."

"Yes, sir."

Boiko settled into the cockpit, checked the jamming system, and pulled the Humvee into the convoy lead.

"How you doin', sir?" Boiko asked Roberson. "You look beat."

"You ready to go?"

"Yes, sir."

"All right, then."

★

Days later, Roberson was out with 2nd Company when they saw a lumpy burlap bag cooking like road kill in the dead heat. Roberson called for EOD, and Boatman arrived in minutes.

"Good morning, Major," said Boatman. The Marine had an infectious smile that everyone noticed, though Roberson's immunity was higher than most.

"It's afternoon," said Roberson.

"Morning in America, though, right? My kids are probably still asleep. You got kids?"

Roberson tossed his head at the jundis. "Yeah. About five hundred of 'em."

Boatman and his two Marines drove their Humvee to the spot where Roberson had been shot at days earlier. They sent Napoleon's replacement forward to tug on the bag while Boatman probed the ground for an initiating wire. The rumors in town were that a slain advisor was worth $200 and an EOD engineer $500—highest among all Americans in the al Qaeda dead pool but still a distant second to Major Mohammed's corpse, which was worth $1,000 in Khalidiya, an indication of his steady inroads with the locals, which threatened the insurgents.

Watching EOD work, Roberson was reminded of the motto advisors around the country had adopted, *Alone and Unafraid*. His motto was *Rangers*

Lead the Way. Roberson didn't know that Boatman's father, Roy, had been a famous Ranger, serving four tours in Vietnam before disobeying a standing order by attempting to rescue a wounded comrade in a minefield. He lost his foot and became one of the only Rangers to stay on active duty with a prosthetic, forced out only after he shattered a leg in a parachute jump.

Boatman the younger was genuinely overjoyed to serve like his father in combat. The Marine was known to showcase dance moves after successful missions, including a riverdance in downtown Khalidiya that went viral on YouTube.

Roberson knew he and Boatman were going to get along fine from now on. They had come to an understanding, and though it wasn't in Roberson's nature to chitchat, especially in the field, he promised himself to be friendlier on the next bomb call. Maybe he'd even ask Boatman about his family. Or something.

The following day, November 2, Roberson overheard some advisors cursing the radios in Troster's room. Boatman had been tricked into an elaborate insurgent minefield targeting his team and had taken shrapnel in the head. He wasn't going to make it.

The news tore at Roberson. Boatman was a kindred spirit, a professional warrior who did his job better than just about any other man in the world, and some amateur had killed him. Roberson walked outside the bunker so he could be alone.

Suddenly a massive bomb went off in Khalidiya, with a shock wave so powerful it felt like wind on his face. A column of smoke shot up between Market Street and the 611 Bridge. Watson and Bozovich were out on patrol. The despairing XO could tell from the acrid black smoke rising skyward that a vehicle had been hit.

An Iraqi Leyland had struck a massive bomb on Michigan. The two-ton vehicle levitated, rising a story high before gravity grabbed it back, its entire front end severed.

Skidding to a stop behind the crippled vehicle, Watson in his Humvee watched the three-hundred-pound engine block tumbling through the air toward him. The jundi in the turret screamed. Boz yelled to back up but there wasn't enough time.

The engine block tumbled past the Humvee like a flaming boulder. Burning hail-size asphalt thudded inside the Humvee. Five jundis in the Leyland had been wounded, one critically.

★

It was a long evening at the shock trauma station on TQ air base. Boz sat on the hood of the Humvee near the helicopter pad. When a bird came in you could catch a nice breeze. Helicopters didn't fly during the day, but soon the sun would drop into Lake Habbaniyah. Some siren went off and Fobbits sprinted for cover as if attacked by a dragon.

"We got rockets incoming!" one shouted. "Get to a bunker."

Boz and Watson laughed bitterly, then they returned to ASP Hill with the hot plates they'd cuffed from TQ for which U.S. taxpayers had paid $25 each. It was Ramadan. The jundis were going hungry each day. After sunset, the advisors sat in the courtyard watching their charges hunched over their meals like wolves.

Huss and Neary had the next patrol, but it was Boiko who spoke for the rattled group.

"I can't believe they got Boatman," he said. "He always said to 'respect the bomb.'"

"You can only be so careful," said Huss.

"That's my point," said Boiko. "You felt the explosion that almost nailed Boz and Watson. My point is, it's lethal out there and it's not getting better."

Rivera chimed in. "We knew it was going to get worse before it gets better. The IA need to keep up the presence patrols in town and things will change. That's the plan."

"I'm all for fighting. I just wish someone could tell me when, exactly, the assholes down there are going to change their minds and stop bombing their own countrymen," said Boiko.

"You forgot sniping," said Neary.

"Sniping, too," Boiko agreed.

"The IA say the people are coming over to their side," said Rivera.

"Could be any minute now," Watson drawled.

They laughed.

For some reason, the Iraqis had placed ASP Hill's dump just outside the Horseshoe. Three times a week they doused it in benzene and lit a match. If the wind blew west, the advisors' rooms filled with smoke and stink, so any clean-burning fuel—ammo crates, newspaper clippings from Grandma, paper plates—went into the courtyard fire pit to serve as a countervailing air freshener.

Roberson emerged from his room, watching the team around the pit. He believed that subordinates needed time to vent, even in small teams, and he didn't like eating with the Iraqi officers, so he usually ate alone. But now the time had come for him to tell Boiko and Watson to move out of Troster and Rivera's crowded radio room.

"Are you serious, Major?" said Boiko.

"Listen, I get it. It's hot. We're in contact every day. It sucks. I'm living in a sweatbox, too. But you need to move."

Watson and Boiko packed up with no further argument.

Later, Rivera and Troster unpacked duffel bags that hadn't been emptied in two months. Two men lighter, the four-by-four-meter concrete room felt like a chateau. They relaxed in their oily mattresses, listening to the radio transmissions from the patrol.

Eventually Rivera said, "Sir, it feels like just a matter of time before we lose somebody. We're running ragged."

"A month ago the only way we were finding IEDs was running over them. Now tips are starting to trickle in," said Troster. "Look, they'll break before we do. But it's going to take some time yet."

With eight men to work with, Rivera wasn't sure. If even one pair of advisors were hurt or killed, the team might become combat ineffective.

Rivera said, "One thing's for certain. We have an XO now."

"It's a beautiful thing," said Troster.

The Iraqi celebration of Eid al-Fitr on November 3, marking the end of the holy month of Ramadan, would have gone unnoticed by the advisors if GQ hadn't asked permission to ravage the Pepperidge Farm cookies from one of the care packages sent from home. As operations officer, Aamr had adopted the American infantry's habit of celebrating holidays when there was time, and there wasn't time. On Eid, he sent seven three-hour patrols into Khalidiya.

Exiting the HQ building after a brief, one of the advisors asked Aamr if the insurgents would relax now that Ramadan had ended. For the last two years, attacks had crested during Ramadan.

"The terrorists are not Islam. Every true Muslim knows this," Aamr told the advisor. "It is the Americans who talk like this, not us."

"The insurgents talk about it, too," said the advisor.

"They lie," said Aamr. "Was the American bomber terrorist, Timothy McVeigh, in the Army? All American soldiers are terrorists, with this thinking."

The advisor smiled. "You were ready for that one."

Aamr clapped the advisor on the shoulder. "This is what you teach. Be prepared!"

The Iraqi major was always in a good mood, which was difficult considering the circumstances. One of the 3/3–1 captains had organized a minor rebellion at the end of Ramadan. Khalidiya was too dangerous to patrol in pickup trucks, he said, and if enough Iraqi officers refused to leave the wire, the battalion might finally get proper equipment.

The furious 3/3–1 staff kept the mutiny hidden from the Americans. Falah rounded up his junior officers and solicited resignations; any officer who wasn't man enough to patrol could quit right then. The ringleader was the only man to raise his hand. He was cut without fanfare. The insurgents in Khalidiya celebrated the end of Ramadan by blowing up a Humvee from TF Panther on Route Michigan, killing a soldier.

Huss and Neary assisted the evacuation. When they returned to the ASP, Huss pulled Troster aside. "Sir, it was ugly down there today. We gotta keep our eyes on Neary. He's seen some terrible things in the past month. I'm worried about him."

"You've seen the same things, Huss," said Troster.

"I'm old. I already know the world is cruel, especially the third world."

Troster paired Roberson with Neary to keep an eye on him when Huss was on a different rotation. The jundis from Unlucky Company discovered four IEDs on the pair's first patrol together, and they were hit by RPGs and small-arms fire both going in and coming out. The next day the attacks were repeated. Unlucky Company discovered two large IEDs; EOD blew them. Then an hour later, a tip came in and the advisors called the bomb techs. The trashy edge of the soccer field had been mined again.

Roberson hailed the EOD Humvee. A Panther tank rumbled in the background, pulling escort duty. An RPG boomed just feet from Roberson's head, sailing over the hood of the Humvee. It skipped across the field and exploded against a stone wall. Roberson raised his rifle and tried to use the Humvee hood as a parapet. It was already moving in reverse. He tumbled onto his stomach. A burst of enemy machine gun fire rattled overhead. He didn't know where it was coming from and he didn't have time to look.

Roberson chased the tank into Khalidiya. Its commander had seen the enemy firing point. The opposing sides were two hundred meters apart in downtown Khalidiya, separated by two dozen apartments and a hundred gawking civilians. The tank couldn't fire its main gun without harming the civilians, and the insurgents couldn't destroy the tank. An Opel car drove to where the shooting had been and then disappeared into the city.

Roberson gave chase. He keyed the handset as he ran. *Dagger November, this is Dagger Five. I'm on foot. Got a black Opel headed toward Market. Tell the jundis to get to 20th Street, set a roadblock, and work their way back.*

Dagger Five, hold up. It's gonna take a few mikes to translate and move. Over.

It's over in five minutes, Roberson transmitted.

Roberson looked over his sights, but the car was gone. No jundi had followed him. His adrenaline drained, and he realized he was winded and alone somewhere in K-Town, an alien curiosity for the local men who were returning to their stoops.

"*Wain* Takfiri? *Wain* irhabi?" Roberson asked the gathering crowd. Where's the terrorist?

"No irhabi Khalidiya."

Dagger Five. Posrep? Over, Neary asked via radio, asking for the XO's position.

I'm headed back to your pos right now, Roberson responded.

Roberson popped the nipple from his CamelBak into his mouth, sucked and spat the warm tube water, and then pulled a long drink from the bladder. He looked over the crowd for an edgy character who might have been involved. Each man looked like the next.

The patrol had missed a good chance to kill insurgents. You didn't get many chances. It was clear to Roberson that the jundis lacked the killer instinct, but some U.S. Rangers didn't have it, either.

After the third bomb of the day was destroyed by EOD, the Iraqi patrol found a fourth mine on the road home. EOD had just returned to Camp Habbaniyah. They returned to Khalidiya.

"Can you guys get home already?" one of the tired Marines told Roberson.

"We're trying," said Roberson. "Whole city's a minefield."

A sniper shot split the air above them. A jundi returned fire with his PKM machine gun, and every jundi quickly fired a short AK-47 string back into the city. The EOD Marine and Roberson were lying on their sides facing each other like an old couple, protecting their open magazine pouches from the dirt.

"I hate this place," said the Marine.

"This place hates you back," said Roberson.

Two kilometers away, Camp Habbaniyah was being mortared from Jazeera. Troster and Boz were on base to grab emails, hot plates, and thirty minutes of R&R in the row of Porta-Johns by the airstrip. Troster hadn't used a potty seat in weeks. It seemed strangely peaceful. On ASP Hill they used gallon-size bags as toilets and then burned their waste.

The first mortar round didn't rumble; it cracked, like a close lightning strike. Troster put his head between his knees. The next shell exploded ten meters away. The shock wave pounded the plastic door of the Porta-John and a fan of shrapnel whistled high, shredding a palm. When the volley stopped, Troster took his time filling his shaking hands with alcohol gel from the broken dispenser, leisurely scrubbing until his heart rate dropped.

"You're awful sweaty, sir," said Boz.

"Hot as hell in there," said Troster.

Boz laughed. "Yeah, that must be it."

They told the story over dinner and Boiko laughed so hard he complained about his aching back. Troster and Rivera had noticed his hunch. They made him walk back and forth like a drunk on a sobriety test, then Troster grabbed his hip and pulled. Boiko screamed in pain.

When a day of rest brought no change to Boiko's back, Troster sent him to shock trauma at TQ, where he found out that one of his discs had been shattered in the previous month's IED strike.

"How soon will I be back with the unit?" Boiko asked.

"Sergeant, you're going to need months of bed rest in a stateside hospital," the doctor told him. "Your war's over."

Boiko cried. He had been on thirty-two combat patrols since being wounded, each one with more than sixty pounds of kit on his shoulders. Still, he'd let the team down and no one could tell him different. A week later he was hospitalized in the United States. Boiko wanted to rehab in California, close to his family, but the Army placed him in the facility closest to his mobilization site, in Indiana. Living on a tight budget, his family was able to visit him only twice during his four-month stay before he was discharged, declared unfit for further duty.

★

Khalidiya had the reputation as a sniper training center. Neighbors were beginning to point out mines, but still no one talked about the snipers. Direct inquiries in this regard killed conversations. Whether it was a lone sniper or a team of sharpshooters was intensely debated in the Iraqi ranks.

In Mosul, the Iraqi 3rd Brigade had lost several men to sniper fire, and the jundis believed it had been one man, a Chechen. In Khalidiya, they were convinced a team of local brothers armed, housed, and trained foreign snipers coming down the rat lines from Syria.

Troster's instincts told him the jundis were correct about the outside expertise, though the extent of local support was unclear. Snipers were differentiated by accuracy and personality. The most persistent was the shooter who had targeted the advisors in the aftermath of the car bomb and the traffic accident, firing more than ten shots in each case, ten minutes apart. He was opportunistic, wary of the jundis, and incompetent, a local who couldn't shoot.

Troster knew that one day a sniper who was patient and accurate would visit Khalidiya, and the Iraqi soldiers didn't have the snitches to hunt him down.

That day was November 10. An accurate sniper attacked TF Panther from a hilly little Khalidiya neighborhood named Sadiqiya just west of the 611 Bridge, which spanned the Euphrates into Jazeera. The Americans called Sadiqiya "Sad City" because nothing good happened there. Staff Sergeant Michael Parrot, a 49-year-old Colorado guardsman, was shot and killed in the open hatch of his tank. Parrot had joined TF Panther as an individual volunteer. Though he wasn't in favor of the Iraq War, he believed soldiers belonged in combat. It was his second tour.

Staff Sergeant Joshua Terando, a member of the TF Panther quick reaction unit, rushed to do the medevac. Terando placed his soldiers in a defensive overwatch and inspected the position. Then he was killed by a single shot.

The 3/3–1 jundis immediately nicknamed the shooter the "Sadiqiya Sniper." They used English because there was no good Arabic translation for snipers, mystery men who stalked human beings like big-game hunters, an exotic notion that fit their conspiratorial view of a war controlled on both sides by foreigners.

★

"If we want to catch him," said Major Mohammed at dinner a few days after the shootings, "we have to have many more local informants."

When Troster heard the translation, he sat up. "Major, I have been thinking the same thing. We've had a long, tough month of constant patrolling. Choosing to support the insurgents is more difficult now that they have seen the best of the Iraqi Army."

Mohammed clucked his tongue against his teeth, a friendly scolding. "Colonel Troster, you have children. To raise them right, you have to show both love and anger. Khalidiya has not seen the worst of us. Without fear, there is no respect."

Troster did not disagree about respect, but firm dealings with the locals needed to be augmented with carrots like public works improvements to inspire cooperation. Troster had no access to such funds. He and his men had trouble enough improving conditions on ASP Hill.

★

ASP Hill had not changed much in two months. The jundis took turns chipping holes in the bunkers like convicts so they could light fires at night to fend off the incoming cold. Battalion 3/3–1's medical facility, a tiny room whose examining table doubled as a barber chair when there was power, was in shambles. Gauze was sometimes used as a tea bag, reflecting the prioritization on rainy nights. Battalion 3/3–1 inflated its personnel numbers because it was poorly supported by the Ministry of Defense (MoD), which provided a minimum ration of food and equipment per man. The MoD knew that its units were inflating their numbers to get more supplies, so it reduced the deliveries and expected the Americans to make up the difference. Every battalion was severely undermanned, including 3/3–1. Recruits were always coming next month. If battalions recruited their own jundis, they would go without pay. There were a few jundis like this in 3rd Battalion, men who had followed brothers or friends back to ASP Hill on returning leave convoys.

The promise of shelter, American socks, and a rifle was a difficult sell, but sometimes it worked if a man was on the run.

Lieutenant Bennett, the supply advisor, a former MP, was having enough difficulty supporting his own isolated team. Advisors in Iraq were expected to beg, borrow, and steal gear. Bennett preferred the procurement system, and equipment upgrades took weeks. Thus was each item precious.

In early November, Troster had suited up for a patrol and waddled out to the Humvee. He noticed the new tow straps weren't affixed to the hood where they could be quickly rigged to pull a damaged vehicle out of an ambush zone

"They're still in the supply room, sir," said Bennett. "I didn't want anyone to steal them. I signed for them."

"What good are they in there?"

"It's a precaution."

A week later, Troster returned to a Humvee after a foot patrol to find the interior coated in rivulets of white, sticky fire extinguisher foam. Bennett had accidentally fired a signal flare inside the vehicle, setting fire to the rear seats. Troster bit his lip to keep from chuckling.

"I signed for this vehicle," said Bennett. "What happens now, sir?"

"What happens now is you use those interpersonal skills you're honing. Grab some jundis and clean the Humvee. That's what happens."

"I mean about reporting the damage, sir," Bennett said.

"We're at war, Lieutenant," said Troster. "A Humvee gets hit every week. Who's gonna care about smoke residue?"

But of course Troster knew the answer to his own question. Bennett cared.

One day in mid-November a large engineering team from TF Panther arrived at ASP Hill escorted by a security platoon. An enormous crane unhooked the main generator TF Panther had left behind, pulled it free of its home next to the Horseshoe, and loaded it on the back of a heavy truck. That left just a small generator to power the radios, and no air-conditioning for ASP Hill's human occupants.

"Hey, men. This is the first we've heard of this. Give me a week to sort it out with your boss," said Troster.

"Sorry, sir," said a guardsman. "It's orders. It's our generator, and it was only on loan. The Iraqis need to get their own."

The Iraqis and the advisors lined up as if watching a funeral procession.

"It's kind of like a reverse graduation present," said Boz. "The Iraqis are getting their independence, and the Americans are pulling the rug out."

Troster snorted.

The 3rd Iraqi Brigade, of which 3/3–1 was a part, was scheduled to become the first Iraqi unit in country given independent battle space. It was a huge step. A press junket was planned where an American general would announce that this unit had progressed enough to patrol without U.S. permission or integration. For 3/3–1, nothing was going to change. As far as Troster was concerned, they'd been operating independently since the move to ASP Hill.

"I was at brigade headquarters yesterday," said GQ, lamenting the loss of the power source for his hair clippers. "There are two generators just sitting there."

The advisors took a Humvee and an Iraqi flatbed to Camp Habbaniyah, where a startled jundi told them that the Iraqi brigade commander was taking a nap.

"When he wakes up," said Troster, "tell him we took a generator."

The Iraqi officers, who never acted without permission, were thrilled. Troster told them that in the U.S. military, it was often better to beg forgiveness later than to ask permission first. GQ hissed at that one. That was too much to contemplate.

★

The Khalidiya insurgents continued their attacks throughout November. On November 17, a jundi from 4th Company was burned alive by a gasoline bomb. Major Mohammed, who never wore armor, was quickest to smother the flames with his shirt. He rolled his screaming troop across the ground until the fire was out. The other jundis poured water over the scalded soldier. Mohammed gently patted his head until the ambulance whisked the jundi away, then he stood up and surveyed the crowd of bystanders, which had swelled to over a hundred.

"Get me my rifle," Mohammed told a nearby jundi.

AK-47 in hand, Mohammed strode toward the thick part of the crowd. Fearing retribution, Roberson shadowed him. Mohammed grabbed a roadside merchant who was dispensing black market kerosene with a cut two-liter plastic bottle scoop and a funnel. Behind him, the line for fuel was re-forming in the aftermath of the explosion. People argued over where they had stood before the explosion sent them scurrying.

"You have a license to sell fuel?" Mohammed asked.

"You know I have no license, sir," the man said.

"Who supplied the fuel for that bomb?"

"In the name of God I swear do not know, sir."

Mohammed turned to the crowd. Some sensed the coming storm and left, but most remained, determined to hold their places in line. They needed fuel, beating or no beating. The average Khalidiya family burned four liters of kerosene and one liter of diesel per day in the winter, and one liter of kerosene and five liters of diesel in the summer when their personal generators filled the persistent gaps in the government power supply.

In the old days, Saddam regularly shipped fuel to the two government filling stations in Habbaniyah, and the sheikhs worked out a reasonable apportionment. Now AQI ran the single government station, and they gave each family just one hundred liters of kerosene for the entire winter. To heat their homes and cook their food, Khalidiya locals turned to the black market.

"You want to help the Iraqi Army?" Major Mohammed asked his audience.

"It is a good thing to help the Iraqi Army," said one man.

"Then tell me who did this to my soldier."

"W'allah ma'aruf." I swear to God I do not know.

Mohammed put his arm around the man's shoulders. "That's too much to ask, isn't it? Come. Help me dump this container instead." He placed the man's foot on the edge of the container and together they tipped the fuel drum. Hundreds of gallons of kerosene spilled out across the street into the gutter. A few men tried to scoop it up. They fanned out with empty detergent bottles, chasing the thinning wave of yellowish crud. Mohammed sat on the curb smoking his cigarette.

"You might want to put that out," said Roberson.

Mohammed slapped his head as if to apologize for his rudeness and offered Roberson a cigarette. It took a moment for the joke to translate. The pair shared an overdue laugh. Mohammed and Roberson didn't speak much. Each man considered himself the toughest in the battalion, and they avoided the nightly bull sessions in the courtyard, where their unpolished personal skills drew laughter from both Iraqis and Americans.

Mohammed stubbed out his cigarette. He took the black marketer's hand and walked him around the Humvee. "You know who I am supporting? Iraq. I know who you are supporting. Terrorists. If they hurt another one of my soldiers, there will be no more fuel in Khalidiya. And it will be a cold winter."

But week later, on November 26, an IED shattered a 4th Company Nissan pickup on Route Michigan, blasting the driver into the roof, knocking him out. Mohammed didn't follow the ambulance back to TQ. He and a few of his crack soldiers spread out and began knocking on doors.

Roberson kept his distance while Mohammed and his group interviewed occupants who were so nervous that several started sobbing. Some of the Iraqi officers were still strangers in Khalidiya, but not Mohammed, who had developed a fearsome reputation. An hour later the jundis conferred in the center of the street. The richest homes and the largest apartment buildings stored fresh water in rooftop tanks. The jundis fired their AK-47s until water spilled over the rooftops and children splashed excitedly under the sudden spigots.

"Guess he didn't get any names," Roberson said to GW.

"But he did, sir. Many."

"Well, why'd they shoot up the neighborhood, then?"

"Major Mohammed must protect his sources or they will be killed. So he appears to be angry. Also, he must teach a lesson to the people."

"Remind me when we get back to ask Major Mohammed if property damage is the key to the population's heart," said Roberson.

"It is the Iraqi way," said GW.

Roberson wanted to tell GW that it wasn't the American way, but he wasn't prepared to answer the follow-up question: What *is* the American way of war? He didn't say anything, but the incident bothered him. It wasn't that the jundis had lit up a few water tanks. It was the maddening feeling that Major Mohammed, whom he was supposed to advise, had a clear, effective streetwise philosophy that the Americans running the war did not.

Like Mohammed, Roberson believed popular participation was the key to cracking the insurgency. Rough tactics alienated the people. Or did they? Mohammed never inflicted physical pain. But he believed the IEDs and sniper shots in Khalidiya would continue until the town decided Battalion 3/3–1 was stronger than the local insurgency. To turn the flock, you needed to demonstrate a willingness to use the stick, lest the residents continue on the path of least resistance, planting mines for spending money while seeking services from the coalition.

That night, Roberson discussed the Iraqi major's tactics with Troster. If Mohammed was forced to comply with the battlefield philosophy of the Americans, the advisors better be prepared to define what exactly it was. Right now they were going on feel.

"The key is developing a local network of sources. We've demonstrated grit, now we need to recruit top informants. It could take a while before good information flows," said Troster.

"How long, sir?" Roberson asked.

"In the DEA it took a year or more to penetrate gangs."

"A year? How do we speed it up?"

"The prescription is pretty clear," said Troster. "Most units are just afraid to follow it. We need to break the battalion down and live in platoon-size outposts downtown. We've got round-the-clock coverage in K-Town for the first time since the invasion, but we're still sleeping here at night."

"The Iraqis aren't ready for that," said Roberson. "Hell, no American unit

I know is even doing it. What we need, boss, is to get Panther involved in this mentorship. Go in heavy and smother the town."

"Panther?" Troster replied, stunned. "When we got here, I asked Panther if they wanted to integrate platoons or even companies. They looked at me the same way they look at the jundis. Like I was a freaking space alien. They said I'd 'gone native.' We've been going it alone since day one, Walt."

"I don't mind Mohammed being tough on those assholes in town," said Roberson. "I'm just not sure it's going to work without big war machines and big dollars, is all."

"This could be a case where Mohammed knows a lot better than us," said Troster. "We just can't say that out loud or we'll be brought up on war crimes. The American philosophy is to win a popularity contest by being friendlier and richer than the insurgents. Mohammed wants to be tougher. Who knows, Walt, it may work."

★

In December 2005, two violent months after tripling patrols into Khalidiya, Iraqi Battalion 3/3–1 suddenly entered a period of relative peace. In October and November, they had been hit by twenty-one exploding mines. They discovered an additional eleven bombs. And they took small arms or RPG fire more than four times a week.

But in December and January, the battalion got hit by only six explosions, and uncovered an additional six bombs located by tipsters. The 50 percent discovery rate was about average for coalition forces countrywide but seemed extraordinary in Khalidiya, where tips were once as rare as insurgent confessions. Small-arms attacks averaged fewer than one per week, mostly single sniper shots of varying accuracy. There were no RPG or SVBIED attacks.

One 3/3–1 jundi was lost. On December 23, a big mine exploded only three meters from a foot patrol Troster and Boz accompanied. Shrapnel sliced into the jundi's head. The casualties would have been much higher had the bomb been properly buried.

Troster pronounced the soldier KIA. Some jundis knelt along with Troster to pay their respects. The dead jundi's last breath escaped as fog in the morning chill. His comrades gasped and prodded Troster for an explanation, but he had none.

Three hours later, Lieutenant Khalid led a patrol to find the bomber. He fingered a suspect and threatened to kill the man. He settled for information instead. The patrol raced down 20th Street and encircled five men loitering near a bridal shop that had been closed for two years. Khalid questioned the men and one of them laughed about the bombing. The tiny jundi called

Private Crazy wrestled the big local to the ground and scrubbed off his smirk with the pavement. When the man stopped struggling, Private Crazy patted him down. He found a live grenade. The men were taken to the TF Panther detention facility.

On Christmas Eve, the Sadiqiya Sniper chased a foot patrol out of northern Khalidiya by firing two rounds that just missed Boz and Staff Sergeant Richard Blakley, 34, a medic from the Indiana National Guard who had joined the advisor team as Boiko's replacement. Blakley fit right into the shorthanded team because he was determined to get outside the wire as much as possible. Troster wanted the new medic to focus on building a sustainable Iraqi battalion medical aid station on ASP Hill; combat patrolling was a secondary duty. The other exhausted advisors, however, welcomed Blakley's endless attempts to get on the patrol roster. There were no Sundays on ASP Hill. Every day they went out, including holidays.

On Christmas, Troster surprised the team by announcing a group trip to the cavernous mess hall on TQ air base between patrols. The advisor team arrived in two U.S. Humvees with room to spare. Tacked to the bulletin board at the mess hall entrance were flyers for yoga classes and movie night. A *Die Hard* marathon was playing on a big screen on base somewhere. The advisors heaped spaghetti on top of their turkey dinners and stacked rolls on top of the spaghetti mounds.

"Merry Christmas, men," Troster said, hoisting an icy soda.

The advisors returned the salutation, but the conversation soon devolved. Several of them felt uncomfortable eating among the Fobbits, who seemed to be staring. Troster could not tell what was imagined and what was real, but it didn't matter. He had his own little family to protect.

"Grab your trays and get the meals wrapped up," said Troster. "We're outta here."

The day after Christmas, the Sadiqiya Sniper struck again, killing a guardsman from TF Panther. Whether it was one man or a team was indeterminable and, to the advisors, inconsequential. The jundis believed it was one cunning sniper, and the advisors accepted the theory instead of instilling fear of infestation.

The sniper struck again three weeks later. On January 16, 2006, Blakley was walking down 20th Street when he felt a dull thud in his trapezius muscle above his collarbone. *Some kid hit me with a rock,* thought Doc. *Odd. Most kids like me.*

"My back's wet," Blakley said.

"You've been shot!" said Lieutenant Bennett.

The jundis believed it was the Sadiqiya Sniper again. The advisors doubted it was the same man, but the target and the shot location worried them. Blakley engaged the locals with as much as enthusiasm as Neary, asking for Pop Rocks in his letters home so he could pass them out to delighted kids. All the Khalidiya kids knew Blakley and his bag of medical magic tricks. On a street full of jundis, the shooter chose the American medic. Worse, the sniper almost "turtled" the advisor, aiming for the narrow slot between his armored back plate and helmet.

The shot passed clean through Doc's trapezius. Blakley treated himself but Troster forced him to also be examined by the shock trauma medical unit at TQ air base. A ten-day hospitalization was recommended to avoid infection, followed by another month inside the wire to give the muscle time to heal. Blakley was retrieved by the team that same afternoon when he called to say he was fine. On ASP Hill that night, the jundis crowded around to watch him stick a Bacitracin-laden Q-tip through the wound when he was dressing it. They clucked their tongues when he pretended to faint. Troster told Blakley that spending a month inside the wire training jundi medics was reasonable rehab.

Two weeks later, Troster went home on annual leave and Blakley put himself back into the patrol rotation.

★

Troster took his three-week leave on January 28. The winter dust storms had begun, and his flight out of Iraq was delayed, giving him some time to decompress and think. After a tough three months in Khalidiya, enemy attacks had abruptly dwindled throughout December and were a rarity in January. Other members of the team pointed to the heavy-handed tactics of Major Mohammed that directly preceded the calming, but Troster suspected that 3/3–1 was simply enjoying a lull, not that the insurgency had been broken or even badly damaged.

The White House, though, had released a "National Strategy for Victory in Iraq," placing the war's outcome in Iraqi hands:

> As Iraqis take on more responsibility for security, Coalition forces will increasingly move to supporting roles in most areas. The mission of our forces will change . . . As security conditions improve and as Iraqi Security Forces become increasingly capable of securing their own country, our forces will increasingly move out . . . [1]

But Troster knew the shift in focus was premature. He believed that 3/3–1 was at least a year away from logistical independence. Falah's jundis were undermanned, poorly equipped, and ignored by their own government. The Americans provided ammo, fuel, medicine, water, equipment, signal flares, trucks, and even boots. The Ministry of Defense contributed dozens of chickens, some bags of rice, and several live sheep each month, and told Falah to feed his men as best he could. The sheep had nothing to eat and there was no freezer on camp, so the sheep were slaughtered right away and stuffed into the stomachs of the jundis.

To effect Iraqi independence, the Strategy for Victory called for a pacification tactic known as "clear, hold, and build."[2] Together American and Iraqi forces were supposed to wrest cities out of enemy control (clear), then install local government control (hold), and finally advance the local standard of living (build).

Troster doubted its authors understood urban combat. There were two ways to "clear" a city. The "hard" clearing done in Fallujah, where the insurgents stood and fought, had resulted in the destruction of the city. "Soft" clearing required intelligence. It took a year to develop a moderate informant network and probably much longer to recruit senior Sunni tribesman. Despite improving leadership, the jundis of 3/3–1 were still strangers in Khalidiya, and its officers had made no contacts with local sheikhs, assuming there were any left who would even speak to them. In 2005, several sheikhs in the Ramadi-Habbaniyah-Fallujah corridor had formed a "People's Council" to fight al Qaeda and reclaim power. By February 2006, half of them had been assassinated and the others fled the country.

The Iraqi clearing method was a mix of hard and soft tactics that made Americans uncomfortable. General David Petraeus had warned about conduct that would antagonize the people: "Setting the right tone ethically is another hugely important task. If leaders fail to get this right, winking at the mistreatment of detainees or at the manhandling of citizens, for example, the result can be a sense in the unit that 'anything goes.' Nothing can be more destructive."[3]

Troster knew what Petraeus meant but, embedded in the Iraqi Army, he allowed for cultural differences. The jundi Private Crazy waved merrily to locals. Yet he had surprised the advisors by suddenly attacking a suspect and dislodging a grenade hidden in his pocket. Major Mohammed, who lobbied to get medical care for women and children, also tipped over fuel drums, smashed up tea tables, and destroyed water tanks. Iraqi officers routinely slapped locals, as they in turn had been hit by their fathers and senior officers. Troster and his men understood humanitarianism, but they couldn't intervene to stop every beating in "Darwin's Playground," as Troster called Khalidiya.

Troster needed a plan that was both militarily sound and culturally relevant to steadily win over the local community. As an advisor to Iraqis, he saw the current U.S. model as confused. Beginning in December 2005, U.S.

headquarters in Iraq required all incoming U.S. commanders to attend a weeklong counterinsurgency course. Every American commander was taught to focus on the people and protect them. The enemy was secondary, the instructors asserted, and the best course of action was often to ignore them. Statistical indicators like body counts were dismissed as Vietnam-era relics of conventional tactics that caused more harm than good in Iraq.

Troster saw two glaring inconsistencies in the U.S. teachings. First, protecting the people meant living among them, but the generals and the White House were calling for a pullback to supporting roles on bases. Even without the pressure from the top to consolidate, it was extremely rare for a unit like TF Panther to break down into small units mixed with Iraqi soldiers and scatter among the people in the cities. Army battalion commanders, schooled to employ firepower at the company level, rebelled against such combined distributed operations.

The other problem with the counterinsurgency-school prescription was countercultural. American soldiers focused on the enemy, even in Iraq. The classified intranet sites, the intelligence summaries, and the nightly situation reports were overwhelmingly dominated by enemy activities. Each IED detonation required a two-page brief. Each exchange of small-arms fire was supposed to trigger a SIGACT, a significant action report. Civilians remained unknown. In the confused culture of the Army, generals claimed not to care about body counts, but every unit kept score.

To Troster, a ruthless enemy focus was a natural instinct of soldiering that should not be stifled. His team had used combat patrolling to gain influence among the Iraqi soldiers and to foster an aggressive warfighting spirit in 3/3–1, something Troster firmly believed in, though he had never seen it listed as a goal of advising. It was true that to get at the enemy in Khalidiya, 3/3–1 had to go through the people. But protecting them or winning their approval was not the right way to articulate the mission to his young advisors and Iraqi soldiers; it muted the underlying purpose of soldiering, which was winning in combat, and put them in position to fail. In this sense, Major Mohammed was right. Before benevolence, the combined team had to appear as winners.

Anyway, Troster did not have enough advisors and jundis to watch every city block every hour, nor could they strip off their uniforms and blend in as locals. "Protecting" was a passive strategy that by definition ceded initiative to the enemy. Instead, having demonstrated grit in the city, 3/3–1 needed to develop a source network so the jundis could spotlight and then shatter the enemy. Troster's advisors had a big role to play in instilling the battlefield confidence 3/3–1 would need to complete this mission, but recruiting reliable locals in Khalidiya was up to the Iraqi soldiers.

9

Outcast

February–March 2006

On the morning of February 1, a group of jundis huddled together for warmth while they listened to a patrol brief by Captain Dhafer. Winter in Khalidiya brought low temperatures in the high 30s. Many jundis lacked jackets, gloves, and hats, having sold nonessential gear in Baghdad markets for extra money in the fall. Now they needed warm clothing. Prior to each morning patrol in the winter, before the sun heated the desert, there was a scramble to borrow larger uniforms they could fit atop their own to supplement wool hats donated by their advisors.

The biggest jundi in the battalion was a Shiite named Haider, who stood six three and was built like a tight end. The advisors called him "Irhabi Hater," or just "Hater," because he was determined to kill a terrorist. He loved fighting but joked that the calm January the battalion had just enjoyed, with a few explosions and sniper shots, hadn't bothered him too much because it had been cold. On cold days, Hater made money lending his XL uniforms as second layers.

Hater stood next to a few jundis in his five-man squad, who looked ridiculous in his giant fatigues. He was a natural leader, but he didn't have to remind his buddies to pay attention to the patrol brief. They were going into Abu Fleis, and his peers were fidgety. Abu Fleis was overrun by palms, neck-high reeds, and experienced insurgents. It was a tiny suburb that sat across Route Michigan from central Khalidiya, a peninsula that jutted out into the Euphrates like an enormous green thumb. It was a mixed community. The river fed long, lush tracts of farmland that were tilled by workers housed modestly along Route Michigan but owned by wealthy Baathist retirees who lived in isolated mansions farther up the peninsula surrounded by five-meter-high marble walls. The patriarchs who owned the big houses—tough-looking, well-dressed 60-year-old men—claimed to be farmers, but Abu Fleis was notorious for its population of former officers of Saddam's Mukhabarat that once had kept tabs on the tribes in Anbar Province. When the Americans invaded in 2003, the secret police moved off Saddam's payroll and onto AQI's.

TF Panther had handed Abu Fleis over to Iraqi Battalion 3/3–1 in January, and the Iraqi officer who had since made the most progress with the local citizens was Captain Dhafer, who had been promoted to 2nd Company commander. The February 1 patrol marked Dhafer's tenth trip into Abu Fleis.

Dhafer wrapped up his patrol brief and pulled a cigarette from the pack he kept tucked in his helmet band. He looked over the shivering jundis and calmly lit the cigarette, projecting confidence to his men, as advisors like Roberson and Huss had done for him. Dhafer saw himself as aloof and self-contained, like Major Mohammed, but deep down he coveted the advisors' approval. Keeping the cigarettes in his helmet signaled to the advisors that he had been there, done that, like their fathers in Vietnam. He had watched *Platoon* several times.

"The brief is complete," Dhafer told Bennett, who today was paired with Neary.

"Let's roll, then," said Bennett.

"I will lead the whole way," said Dhafer. "The people know me."

A single narrow road formed the spine of Abu Fleis, running from an intersection on Route Michigan north for two kilometers. Dhafer stopped his truck at the foot of town, near a series of auto-body shops. He knew better than to order a patrol to burst into one of the mansions in the wealthy area in the northern part of the peninsula. That was a job for the Navy SEALs at nighttime. A young Iraqi captain who harassed a rich family during the day would not live to see the next leave convoy to Baghdad, so precise was the insurgent network of information in Abu Fleis.

Dhafer was trying to build his own source network. He couldn't compete with the Mukhabarat, so he was targeting their workers. When you didn't have bribery money, which was the American recruiting tool, you started not at the top but at the bottom, where a favor went a long way.

Dhafer was first out of the vehicles. Theatrics were effective for both the locals and his own jundis. He stared down the crowd of men hanging around the crowded roadside entrance to Abu Fleis, which served as the local market, then clicked on his radio and shouted an order. The jundis leaped from their trucks and fanned out. One of the benefits of the cold, thought Dhafer, was its ability to speed up shivering jundis.

The captain knew his NATO hand and arm signals, and silently called for a column patrol formation with a series of arm motions, but the only man responding to his gestures was Neary, the young advisor walking near the back of the file.

"Follow me!" Dhafer yelled in Arabic.

Instead of putting a junior jundi in the risky point position, Dhafer took the lead. He always did. In hostile neighborhoods like Abu Fleis and Khalidiya, it was important to send a message that he and his soldiers were not intimidated. He strolled into the parting crowd, looking for familiar faces. Dhafer believed that building an informant network among the skeptical Sunnis hinged on a series of small acts of power and kindness.

"Spread out," Dhafer told his jundis. "You may shop if you like."

The jundis slung their rifles and waded into the small vegetable market marked by wooden stands topped with bright-colored umbrellas. Jundis earned $350 every month, a very high wage in Iraq. They pooled some dinars and were soon laden with plastic bags filled with fruits and sodas. Neary traded greetings with a vendor and ordered some samoon bread in Arabic, attracting a group of curious eavesdroppers. While everyone in Khalidiya knew Yusef the Amerikee, he was an alien across the street in Abu Fleis, which was like the Upper West Side to Khalidiya's Harlem.

When Dhafer had first patrolled into Abu Fleis, it was a ghost town. Few shops were open. No man would sell Dhafer a cigarette. Now, a month later, jundi dinars were a part of the small souk economy, and a raw materials warehouse had reopened in hopes of attracting the interest of the Iraqi battalion on the hill. Some of the advisors thought Dhafer was wasting time in the market. On a recent patrol with the captain, Major Roberson had complained, "They'd rather be shopping than shooting." This hurt Dhafer, because the XO, whom he admired, was implying his jundis were lazy, a slur the advisors tossed on the Iraqis too casually.

But Dhafer knew what he was doing in Abu Fleis. By inserting his men into the village's daily economy, he was building familiarity. The local Sunni hatred of the Shiite soldiers had shocked him at first. A month spent haggling about prices had slowly but steadily migrated to local gossip, which Dhafer nightly recorded in his camouflaged all-weather notebook.

The captain ducked into a garage heaped with scrap metal. He recognized the owner, a casual source named Kamel who had so far limited his conversations to improving the sandy intersection at Route Michigan that had been chewed up by years of explosions. Dhafer fingered some of the steel in Kamel's shop and sniffed the air for gunpowder.

"God's peace be upon you," said Dhafer.

"Peace," said Kamel.

"How is your business?"

"Terrible. And yours?"

"Ha. It is too good. By God the most merciful perhaps we can help each other," said Dhafer. "Anyone bothering you?"

"You mean besides the Americans?" said Kamel.

"You know who I mean. Those who steal scrap metal from your shop. They use it to hurt my soldiers. They hurt us both."

"If I told you, my family would be in danger."

"I'll keep you out of it," said Dhafer.

"If I tell you, what will you do?"

"Put them in an American jail for a few days," said Dhafer. "They will not bother anyone again. They will be scared. Maybe they will move."

"No. They live here," said Kamel. "How do I know you will take them to jail?"

"This is a promise. The New Iraqi Army keeps promises."

Kamel peeked from his window. He stared vacantly at the makeshift souk. Finally he pointed at two young men dressed in sandals and sweatpants. "Those two are insurgents," he told Dhafer. "Very bad men."

Dhafer doubted it. The finger-pointing had come too easily. He tried to determine Kamel's intentions. There were three types of sources: those with petty vendettas who wanted to get a neighbor in trouble for things like property disputes, those who needed money, and those who hated al Qaeda and wanted to remove them from the community. It was tough to differentiate at the outset—new sources wanted to test the Iraq soldiers' handling of intelligence before revealing information that might get them killed, like the identity of an AQI bomber.

Dhafer scribbled down the information so Kamel would feel important. He had no intention of sharing it with his fellow company commanders or even Captain Zahir, the Battalion 3/3–1 intelligence officer. In the Iraqi Army there was little mutual trust. Senior officers robbed juniors of their best ideas and took credit for their most successful operations. If a major or a colonel learned of a good informant, every time a patrol was dispatched to Abu Fleis they'd demand an update from that source. After a few days of this, the informant's head would roll down Michigan along with the trash kicked up by the American benzene guzzlers.

Lieutenants and captains competed for promotions in the Iraqi Army with money, family connections, and—depending on how much power their advisors had—performance in combat. In 3rd Battalion, the Iraqis had watched advisors scuttle their commanding officer, replacing him in Mosul with Falah. Dhafer was better off hoarding intelligence so he could exploit it on his own terms and impress them. If Dhafer gave his notebook to Zahir, the intelligence officer might leak it to Lieutenant Falah to curry favor, and every lieutenant assigned to Abu Fleis would be knocking on the doors of his best sources until the insurgents wised up and killed them.

In Khalidiya, Dhafer had helped recruit a young informant called Zoro. Some of the Iraqi officers had made the mistake of paying him for information on IEDs. Now the kid bounded up to every patrol like a hungry stray. Dhafer told him the next time he did it, he'd shoot him before the terrorists could.

Dhafer walked out into the sunlight and talked to a dozen more neighbors, then walked back to the market, where a crowd of shoppers was critiquing Neary's Arabic. Dhafer needed a foil. He settled on a surly 50-year-old man who was clearly irritated by the jundis. He wore a dark leather jacket and an expensive watch.

"You haven't looked at me once," Dhafer said loudly. The man turned his head, glanced at Dhafer, and turned back to the murmuring crowd. The captain moved closer. "I hear the bombs are coming again."

"I don't know anything about bombs," the man said, turning away.

"What are you looking at? Are you signaling someone?" Dhafer asked with feigned interest. He squinted for effect. Then he pointed at the two men Kamel had identified. "That man nodded at you. Who is he?"

"What man?"

"The man you are looking at!" Dhafer shouted. "What is his name?"

The crowd went quiet. Neary backed up until a wall was on his back, his hand wrapped around his rifle's grip. Sensing trouble, the jundis tossed their bags of fruit in the back of the pickup truck and formed a perimeter around the market. They were as confused as the vendors. Dhafer walked over to one of the startled young men and grabbed the collar of his sweatshirt. "This man!" Dhafer shouted at the 50-year-old. "I ask you, do you know him?"

The man in the leather jacket blanched. He knew he was being set up. "I know him," the well-dressed man muttered. "He is Jassim. Everyone here knows him. He is a good boy who goes with God."

"Your eyes tell me different," said Dhafer.

The jundis seized the two young men and pulled from their pockets a few anti-American leaflets. It was the standard stuff churned out by a local imam in the Farooq Mosque, a Takfiri haven five hundred meters up the road in northern Abu Fleis. The young men were arrested for possession of propaganda, a flimsy charge.

The boys were released from the TF Panther jail after two days, but Dhafer's instinct to follow through with Kamel was sound. Empowered by just a few sentences, Kamel became a regular source, and his information steadily improved.

★

The following day, February 2, Dhafer was leading a patrol in Khalidiya when a local boy tossed a plastic bottle at his truck. Dhafer was a bit overweight. He chased the boy on foot, just intending to demonstrate aggression for his jundis. He was surprised to run down the boy in twenty meters.

"There are two bombs ahead," whispered the boy when Dhafer wrestled him onto his belly. "Marked by a blue soap bottle so the children can avoid them."

Dhafer whispered his thanks before dragging the boy roughly back to the truck and kicking him in his ass. "Next time, it will be a bullet!"

Dhafer was surprised that the boy had chosen to warn him so brazenly. An hour later, the Marine EOD team arrived. Two pristine 160mm artillery rounds were pulled out of 20th Street like enormous splinters. This worried Dhafer. Most bombs were improvised—soap shavings, Vaseline, and benzene stuffed into ancient, rusty shells and sprinkled with nuts and bolts. Only AQI had access to expensive new rounds smuggled from places like Syria.

To the captain, it was troubling evidence that AQI was going to counterpunch after four months of 3/3–1 saturation patrolling had steadily ground down insurgent attacks. Further, the two other Iraqi battalions in the 3rd Brigade, which were advised by active-duty Marine teams, had recently pushed out of Camp Habbaniyah and established combat outposts north of the Euphrates in the untamed territory of Jazeera. No friendly unit had ever camped in the twenty-square-kilometer patch of farmland that was infamous for its mortar teams, ammunition caches, and torture houses—let alone built outposts there. AQI must be responding to the surge, thought Dhafer. *The fight is back on.*

★

Three hours later, Rivera and Watson escorted the next patrol from ASP Hill, led by a 4th Company lieutenant named Abbas who had not been briefed by Dhafer. Abbas was more eager to go deeper into Abu Fleis than were his rivals in the other companies, who so far had focused on the crowded neighborhood along Route Michigan.

The three-vehicle patrol roared down Michigan and wheeled a hard right onto Abu Fleis Road, blowing past the automotive shops and heading north into the farming plots. Locals sat on red-and-white plastic chairs lining the street like concertgoers awaiting a show in the park.

When the patrol approached the first bend in Abu Fleis Road, five hundred meters north of Michigan, the crowd scattered. Rivera immediately swerved the Humvee, frustrating the triggerman who detonated the roadside bomb too late. Watson, who was standing in the turret, felt the shock wave slap the back of his neck like a flyswatter. People returned to gawk at the unscathed vehicle that emerged from the dust cloud, then the street started bustling again. Rivera grinned crazily at the mob.

"I get the feeling they knew about that one," said Watson.

"How'd you guess?" Rivera asked.

"I think Watson is correct," confirmed "Joe," a new 50-year-old Iraqi interpreter who had not yet developed an ear for sarcasm. Joe was bald, and he looked like a professor. He rarely wore armor plates because it aggravated an old shoulder injury he'd sustained lifting his child.

★

Two days after the close call, Rivera, Watson, and Joe followed Unlucky Company back into Abu Fleis. An Iraqi ambulance took the rear of the file because the Iraqis were nervous about a rumored alliance. The Hazim tribe on the north side of the Euphrates had supposedly partnered with the Khalifah tribe controlling Abu Fleis. In the old days, the tribes haggled about crossing rights for the small fishing boats based in Abu Fleis or the prices for crops. Now they agreed to join forces in resisting the demeaning encroachment of the Iraqi 3rd Brigade into Jazeera, Khalidiya, and Abu Fleis. Offering assistance were both AQI and the 1920 Revolutionary Brigade, a tough Sunni insurgent militia led by former officers in Saddam's army who claimed a nationalist goal: to rid Iraq of its colonial occupiers and return to a liberated state run by Sunnis.

AQI and the 1920s had a tenuous understanding. AQI insisted on establishing a strict Islamic state that was in contrast to the desired end states of nationalist groups like the 1920s who wanted many of the Western freedoms Iraqis had enjoyed under Saddam. The tribesmen around Khalidiya tolerated AQI because they had no choice, so rich, powerful, and ruthless were its ranks. This cooperation usually took the form of information and low-level workers in exchange for payoffs. In terms of active fighting, many tribes instead joined the local branch of the 1920s, which was supposedly headquartered in Abu Fleis.

Dhafer and Mohammed didn't believe the widespread rumors of alliance, which were all over town. It was counterintuitive to the advisors, but more tips usually led to less accurate information. When everyone had the same tale, the townspeople embellished to increase their stature, forcing others to follow suit, including the original source who knew the rest were lies. Still, Unlucky Company sent the ambulance along on the patrol into Abu Fleis, just in case the alliance wanted to kick-start their resistance campaign with a bang.

Unlucky Company's patrol halted at the market at the intersection of Route Michigan and Abu Fleis Road, next to the auto-body shops. Rivera was in the advisor Humvee's turret. As Captain Walid and the jundis spread out among the shoppers, a tactic most Iraqi soldiers now used in dangerous areas, Rivera swiveled his machine gun until it faced the sinister line of open garage bays. Bombs rarely exploded in a crowd of civilians and sometimes there was a tip to be had.

"The jundis say there's an IED in a garbage can around here somewhere!" Joe shouted from the passenger seat.

"Can they be more specific?" Rivera asked from the turret.

"That's all they know," said Joe, listening to his radio. "Captain Walid wants to leave the IED. Too dangerous."

"The hell we're going to leave an IED. You tell him no one in this battalion leaves an IED. Not ever. What happens when 4th Company comes in after us?" said Watson. "Get out of the truck, Joe. The Warlock didn't work the other day, remember? If they got some new frequency, we're gonna get hit. You might as well avoid it."

Joe was out before Watson had finished speaking. Walid pulled the jundis back. He pointed to a dozen cans in the market, mostly full of water and trash. The locals backed off to watch the show. Watson looked again at his Warlock. *Please work.*

Looking over his gunsights, Rivera couldn't see anything unusual. He didn't want any jundis killed while peeking into cans with bombs the advisors could jam with the Warlock. He considered asking the shopkeepers to tip each container over, but if they got clipped he'd never forgive himself. *Win their hearts and minds,* he told himself.

"Take it slow. I'll spot from up here. We may have to bump a few," said Rivera.

Watson put the Humvee in drive and tapped the brake. The armored hulk crept toward a trash can like a rhinoceros sniffing at a strange plant. Rivera ducked inside the vehicle. Watson released the brake and rammed the can. Rivera and Watson exhaled.

"Only five to go," said Watson.

He repositioned the Humvee.

Rivera popped up to scan. "All clear."

A monstrous explosion shredded the steel beneath Watson's seat, crumpling the thick armor like aluminum foil. The blast lifted Watson out of the vehicle, dragged him across the roof, and then hurled him toward the cringing crowd, on fire, a chunk of his leg smoldering. Two antitank mines placed on top of each other, called a "double stack," had been buried in the sand next to the can.

Shards of metal and hot fabric from Watson's seat lanced Rivera's legs. The gun fell from his hands. He slumped into the gut of the smoking Humvee, where the steel glowed red. He looked outside at Watson's charred body. He reached for the handset. The radio was shattered. "Joe, get the ambulance up here!"

Both his ankles broken, Watson clawed himself to a low wall, carbine dragging between his legs, gloves filling with sand, wet and sticky with blood. He didn't want kidnappers to snatch him. *We're all alone out here.*

He crawled. There was an unconscious civilian, his leg sawed off by shrapnel. The blast had melted bits of Watson's cotton and nylon uniform into his largest wounds, keeping him from bleeding out. Neighbors approached.

He crawled away from them. The shrapnel in his eye made them all look hazy.

Who are they? Kidnappers?

He raised his rifle. "Get away from me!"

"You okay?" shouted Rivera from the Humvee.

"I'm hurt pretty bad, man."

Joe was the first to reach Watson. He held him while Rivera, ignoring his own stinging legs, wrapped Watson's wounds in gauze and helped him into the ambulance. There was no shooting. Just a hundred curious men from Abu Fleis crowding around to watch an American die.

Watson came out of his haze in Fort Knox, Kentucky. It was only a matter of hours before Boiko appeared at his hospital door, ecstatic to see his buddy. At first they plotted an adventurous return to the ASP. Maybe they'd type up some fake orders and grab the next hop back to Baghdad International. But Watson's wounds were far too severe.

Boiko held Watson's elbow during his daily rehab walks, always with a smile, but at night he lay in bed praying for his buddy's recovery. Watson never cried, so Boiko cried for him.

Between the braces and the bandages, Watson fumbled a lot of things. The floor was linoleum, sanitized with cheap military suds that made your eyes water whenever janitors slopped the hallways. He broke glassware and electronics. A week after Boiko transferred to Walter Reed Army Medical Center in Washington, D.C., Watson received a $500 digital camera. "I bet you've broken your camera by now," Boiko wrote on the card he enclosed with the camera.

He had.

A week after the explosion, Rivera reached Watson by phone.

"Are you going to be able to police again?" Rivera asked.

"I'm just fixing to walk again on my own, man."

"Colonel Newell wants to burn me," said Rivera. "He's been telling people it's all my fault, driving around bumping into trash cans."

"We were doing our job."

Rivera didn't say anything for a long time. Watson could hear his pained, shallow breathing ten thousand kilometers away.

"Hey, Eliezer," said Watson. "I'd rather live like this than live with the thought of another soldier dying in my place."

★

A few hours after Rivera and Watson were wounded on February 4, a rainstorm swept over Khalidiya. Rivers formed in the long cracks of baked earth. ASP Hill quickly turned to mud. The advisors raced to the motor pool, situated in a depression that was forming a pond. They helped the jundis tow the Iraqi Nissans through the slop toward the front gate to stage for the next patrol so they would not be marooned.

The sun set and the temperature plummeted. Still it rained. The jundis guarding the front gate were coughing so loudly that Doc Blakley braved the downpour to check on them, bringing cough suppressants and a water bottle filled with hot tea. At dinnertime, the Iraqi officers and the advisors donned ponchos and trudged across the mud pit separating the Horseshoe from the small mess hall, punching deep, sucking holes in the ground with their flip-flops.

Roberson stayed behind to munch potato chips by himself. He was a loner who rarely ate with the Iraqis, and tonight he needed to get his thoughts in order. The advisor team was down to six men. Troster was gone on leave, Gentile was still working with the brigade team, and Rivera and Watson were wounded. They had a single operable Humvee. Additionally, half of Battalion 3/3–1 had gone home on a ten-day leave starting February 2, leaving only two hundred Iraqi soldiers behind. The combined team on ASP Hill was at a low point; meanwhile, hard-core insurgents in town had supposedly joined forces to reassert themselves. Roberson wanted to take the enemy head-on.

Roberson decided to renew the push for combined operations with TF Panther. Troster had rarely mentioned Panther except to vent, most recently about a Panther tank in mid-January that had used its powerful machine gun to shoot at a suspected mine along Michigan instead of calling for EOD, sending screeching ricochets all over Khalidiya that had terrified and enraged the locals. TF Panther just wasn't part of Troster's vision to pacify Khalidiya and Abu Fleis.

Roberson wasn't overly impressed with Panther's operational conduct either, and he did not know their officers well. Although ASP Hill was directly across Route Michigan from Camp Habbaniyah, the TF Panther commanding officer had visited his Iraqi Battalion 3/3–1 partner only one time in four months that Roberson could remember, and even then he brought along his personal security detachment—three National Guardsmen who remained in full battle dress throughout the meeting.

"Does he think we're going to assassinate him?" Aamr had joked in Arabic.

Troster had asked the Panther commander, a fellow lieutenant colonel, why he came loaded for bear. "It's just what we do," said the commander. "Don't take offense."

But the Iraqis did take offense.

Roberson didn't care about hurt feelings. What mattered now was responding in force to the bombing that had taken out two advisors and shattered their Humvee. TF Panther had manpower and a slew of armored vehicles. Battalion 3/3–1 had improved its standing among the locals to the point where tips were trickling in. If they worked together, TF Panther could provide an umbrella of security that would not only signal fortitude in town but also provide the Iraqi soldiers with breathing room to focus on recruiting informants from the populace, instead of wading into sewers in search of telltale signs of bombs. Plus, TF Panther had money available for civic projects. Roberson hoped a reinvigorated relationship with Panther might land 3/3–1 some recruiting funds.

The timing within 3/3–1 was good—Lieutenant Colonel Falah had gone home on leave with most of the battalion. The advisors set their goals by the leave roster, with a third of the battalion rotating home every eight to ten days. When a strong set of officers gave way to weak ones, the advisors referred to it as the "dark side of the moon." That meant delaying dangerous missions or shifting company responsibilities until the return of commanders like Major Mohammed and Captain Dhafer and lieutenants like Khalid and GQ.

Roberson saw Falah's absence as a bonus. While he didn't really connect with any of the Iraqis—Troster had once covered for one of Roberson's fuming walkouts during a meeting with the Iraqi staff officers by saying, "It's just his way of telling you he cares"—the XO was especially disillusioned by Falah, whom he considered a military dilettante. But Roberson liked Falah's second in command, the XO Lieutenant Colonel Fareed, who took charge when Falah went on leave. A former instructor in Iraq's military college, Fareed was a smart soldier and a savvy politician who knew how to execute military operations without upsetting the Iraqi military hierarchy. If Falah asked why Fareed had suddenly embarked on joint operations with Panther while he was away, Fareed could always say Roberson forced him.

Roberson hitched a ride down to TF Panther HQ on a patrol that left after supper. He found the TF Panther OpsO fixated on a giant spreadsheet that depicted the scheduled deployment of his various units for the upcoming week. Roberson offered 3/3–1's assistance on the Budimnah peninsula, which was Panther battle space. "My Iraqi soldiers will help you break through with the locals on Budimnah and give them a glimpse of the future," explained Roberson. "Then you guys can return the favor in a few days by coming into Abu Fleis hard, side by side with us. I want to conduct a weapons sweep of the entire town."

The Panther OpsO thought it was a good plan. "How many Iraqis can you provide in Budimnah?"

"About fifty. That maxes us out without leaving Khalidiya and Abu Fleis unpatrolled," said Roberson. "I'll be going with them."

"How many other advisors?" the OpsO asked.

"Just me."

"Just you?"

"Just me," said Roberson. "We lost two guys this morning."

★

The following morning, Roberson accompanied 1st and 2nd companies into Budimnah with TF Panther. The rain had stopped overnight and the ground had dried in waves, like a frozen sand dune. Roberson was riding in Captain Dhafer's Nissan truck so the rest of the advisors could use the Humvee to escort other patrols. It was a bone-rattling movement.

At the entrance to Budimnah, which was a kilometer west of Khalidiya, two sixty-ton tanks belonging to Panther pulled into the lead of the Iraqi patrol convoy, their treads flattening the ground. The Nissan swerved into the tracks of the tank to avoid tripping a mine. Suddenly the ride was smooth.

"This is more like it," said Roberson, relaxing the death grip on the glove compartment he had used to steady himself.

"I like tanks very much!" said Dhafer.

An hour into the Budimnah operation, jundis solicited a local tip about weapons hidden inside a car. TF Panther guardsmen swiftly surrounded the suspect vehicle, arresting two men and recovering several AK-47s, a PKM machine gun, and a rocket-propelled grenade launcher.

"That was good work," Roberson told Dhafer in the truck on their way back to ASP Hill after the operation. "Now Panther will return the favor in Abu Fleis."

Dhafer smiled and tilted his head in the direction of the tank rumbling in the lead of the vehicle column, its turbine engines putting a tremor into the ground that could be felt in the truck, like an earthquake aftershock.

"I think if we use tanks, the insurgents will run away," said Dhafer. "I feel fear, and I am a good guy!"

★

Rivera made it back to the team a week after he was wounded. Still sore from the antitank mine blast, he convinced the doctors at the TQ trauma ward to let him convalesce on ASP Hill, where he promised to remain sedentary for a month so his stitches could dissolve. He was hobbling about after a few days on the hill and scribbled his name on the February 13 patrol roster. That night, after the patrol, Blakley, the medic, squirted Betadine into Rivera's reopened wounds, topped them with Neosporin, and slapped on adhesive dressings.

"Don't say anything. You did the same thing when you were shot," said Rivera.

"You hear me talking?" asked Blakley.

★

The joint weapons sweep operation with TF Panther into Abu Fleis took place on February 18. A pair of TF Panther tanks sealed the southern entrance to the peninsula on Route Michigan, and another pair cordoned the northern turnaround, where Sergeant Dunlap had been killed five months earlier. Platoons of guardsmen in armored Humvees moved down the side streets, securing the perimeter so the 3/3–1 jundis could work their way down Abu Fleis Road, searching cars and pulling aside assorted groups of residents for questioning.

Major Mohammed's 4th Company soon discovered two bombs wrapped in a plastic tarp and buried under a pile of straw for future use. No local recognized the donkeys that were munching on the straw.

"If these donkeys have no owners," Mohammed told a group of nearby farmers, "I will take them back to the ASP."

Mohammed tugged at one animal's bridle, but it would not budge. Mohammed returned to his truck, irritated that one of the advisors had tried to take his picture with a donkey. Two young men pounded on his door. "Esam and Hamed are right up there!" They described the suspects, two young thugs notorious for their cruelty.

"Am I supposed to know these men?" Mohammed said.

"They are robbing fuel trucks and stealing money!"

Mohammed brushed the tipsters away. Esam and Hamed were apparently thieves, not insurgents, and Mohammed did not want to expose them to a broken justice system.

The American soldiers treated major criminals better than they did low-level insurgents. The tribal justice system had been shattered during the war. There were no courts in Anbar except the American military version, which focused solely on insurgents. But to Mohammed, the line between insurgent and criminal was gossamer thin—in the chaos of war, thieves intertwined with insurgents to pillage the city. He and his fellow Iraqi officers wanted to restore order as well as security, but the Americans refused to allow the traditional Iraqi form of swift justice, which ranged from fuel allotments handed over to the aggrieved party to public humiliation.

"Who will stop these men?" the tipsters persisted.

"It would be better if they stole an American antenna from a Humvee," said Mohammed. "Then these American soldiers might shoot them."

The local boys turned to the advisors and pounded on their Humvee window screaming, "Ali Baba! Ali Baba!"—slang for thieves. Inside, Mark Gentile's toes curled in his boots, awaiting an explosion. The mechanic, who had been assigned to Newell's brigade team soon after arriving in Habbaniyah, had returned to the 3/3–1 team as a replacement for Watson. He had forgotten how crazy this life was.

"Ali Baba? We chasing thieves now?" Gentile asked.

The young men turned back to Major Mohammed's truck and leaned inside the window, talking privately. The truck suddenly leaped forward, tearing down a side street and popping back out behind a group of loiterers. By the time Gentile arrived, two men were on their bellies shaking their heads in protest.

"What's going on?" he asked.

"These men planted the IED in Abu Fleis that hurt Watson," said Joe.

I'll be damned! thought Gentile.

The jundis piled the suspects into the truck. On their way back to ASP Hill, the jundi guards kicked the men anytime the truck turned, mashing their boots into cheekbones and noses.

At the ASP, the suspects started screaming as they were dragged by their elbows into an interrogation room that doubled as the barbershop. The jundis ran to grab tape, water, and blankets. In Mosul, they had watched one Marine advisor demonstrate waterboarding on a suspect. The Marine had been relieved of duty, but the effectiveness of the interrogation technique was not lost on the jundis.

Huss heard that the men who allegedly hurt Watson were in custody. As he accompanied Major Mohammed to the interrogation shop, his head was tingling. It was dark in the bunker, and it smelled like urine. The light danced on a pool of water. One of the suspects was so scared he wept. Major Mohammed squatted beside him, breathing through a lit cigarette, and they had a short conversation. Then he tipped back the suspect's metal fold-up chair, and the suspect ripped through a few fast, desperate sentences.

Mohammed shrugged at Huss. The men weren't stupid enough to admit to having buried the mine. Watson was an American, so in the end it was up to Huss how far this went. The jundis were agitated. "Let us get the information right now," a jundi told Huss, "or you'll never know."

Huss faced a dilemma common to advisors in Iraq. Each battalion in the brigade had incidents of prisoner abuse. The advisors curtailed the rough stuff, but the point of intervention during questioning was blurry. Huss had heard that Watson was going to lose a leg. It was wrong that Watson had come halfway around the world to help these people only to be crippled by these two. The sharp crack of an open-handed slap brought the advisor back.

"Stop it," said the advisor.

"Finish?" asked Mohammed.

"Finished."

Major Mohammed gave some terse orders to the disappointed jundis. The suspects were taken to the TF Panther detention facility on Habbani-yah for questioning by American intelligence officers working within strict limits, including a ban on any line of questioning that greatly shamed the suspects. Walking back to the Horseshoe, Mohammed put his arm around Huss. It was the most intimate thing he had done in the six months they had worked together. The advisor held on long enough to make it to the festering latrine, where he turned the sink and the shower pipe up full blast.

Returning from his three-week leave on February 21, Troster studied the patrol logs. The Iraqis of 3/3–1 had captured nineteen suspects and run four large-scale joint missions with TF Panther. "Walt, you've been busy," Troster said to his XO. "How'd you pull off the joint ops with Panther?"

"Assholes think alike," said Roberson.

"I'm going on the next patrol. I have to see this for myself."

"You're requested at Camp Hab first," said the XO. "The new brigade advisor is on deck and Newell wants to say good-bye."

At Camp Habbaniyah, Colonel Newell introduced Troster to the lead-ers of the incoming advisor team replacing Newell's at the Iraqi brigade HQ. The team was all Marine, predominantly active-duty grunts, and sev-eral advisors had impressive combat records. Newell's replacement as team leader—and Troster's new boss—was Lieutenant Colonel Jim Zientek, an active-duty Marine infantry officer on his second tour. Zientek's operations advisor, Captain Drew McNulty, earned the Bronze Star as a company commander in the Second Battle of Fallujah. He had stabbed an insurgent in the heart while fighting house to house. Both Marines were physically fit and wore short flat-top haircuts with minimal hair on the sides. They looked him dead in the eye upon introduction, as if searching for something. Troster had the feeling that the Marine Corps took its advisor teams more seriously than the Army did.

"You hear about your guys' attempt to win the Darwin award?" Newell asked.

Troster was stunned. Here he was meeting the new boss, and his credibility—all the hard work his team had done—was evaporating.

"The people rely on us to remove the bombs. We both know EOD won't show up on a hunch," said Troster.

"Bumping into trash cans with a Humvee is outright stupid. Rivera was the senior man. He should have known better," said Newell.

"He knows."

"Does he get it?"

"I've talked to him," Troster said. "He gets it."

Troster was steaming when he left the room. He knew his boys were once again seen as shaky army reservists. They had to prove themselves to the Marines all over again, and that hurt.

When he returned to the ASP, Roberson told him they needed a new call sign. "Dagger" was being used by the new Marine route clearance team.

"That's easy," said Troster. "Outcast."

★

Troster spent the next day going over 3/3–1's operations schedule with Roberson and Major Aamr. There were several company-size joint patrols with TF Panther planned.

"They're suddenly willing to work with us?" a skeptical Troster asked.

Aamr shrugged halfheartedly.

Roberson quickly said, "Having that heavy footprint has been nice, boss. The jundis love the tanks."

"It's not the tanks I'm worried about, Walt," said Troster. "We've got no relationship to fall back on if something goes bad."

"Men bond under fire," said Roberson.

Troster excused himself, put his heavy equipment on, and caught up to a patrol that was just about to depart ASP Hill.

"Mind if I join you?" Troster asked Bozovich. "Need to get my head out of the paperwork."

"Just don't wave a white flag, sir. Panther will shoot you because of it."

"What's up?"

"Freaking Panther snipers just whacked a local dude who was building a house in K-Town. Had a white 'don't-shoot-me-I'm-working' flag and everything. He picked up a PVC tube to lay some plumbing and they popped him. Then when he was lying there they shot him again to dead-check him, but they denied it. It sucks."

"Don't jump to conclusions," said Troster. "I've seen a lot of 'bad shoots' that turned out to be righteous. Look at it from the sniper's point of view. Remember that IED digger they nailed? That PVC probably looked similar."

Troster had returned to Iraq intent to start fresh with TF Panther. And as a DEA agent, he was sensitive when outsiders judged a shooter. But he and Roberson had a history with the TF Panther snipers. One time in January, the snipers saw a "suspicious man" on a roof and alerted the advisors. Troster and a platoon of jundis shattered a courtyard lock and raced into the house. It turned out to be an old woman hanging laundry. A younger lady cornered the embarrassed group.

"What are you doing in our house?" she said in English.

"Uh, you speak English?" said Troster.

"I lived most of my life in Chicago," she said. "You give America a bad name."

Troster had bit his tongue and left.

Every soldier's imagination expands in combat. They see detonation cords instead of power lines. They see grateful children instead of seasoned cons. And they see the enemy in everyone. Troster liked snipers because they were hunters, trained observers with advanced optics who typically gave the best battlefield reports, but their recent mistakes shook him.

"I did look at it from the sniper's perspective, sir," Boz replied. "But why the hell would this dude dig in a four-meter PVC bomb at high noon? His brother approached us. All we could say was, 'Go to the front gate to collect your pay.' It was wrong."

"I'm just saying, those guys are out there protecting us," Troster said weakly. "Let's get going."

The patrol went without incident, but Troster had trouble focusing, distracted by the challenge of working with TF Panther, as Roberson had managed to do, without losing his cool over incidents like the ones Boz had described.

★

On Camp Habbaniyah that night, the new brigade advisors were struggling with similar feelings. The day's sniper shoot required that a significant action report be sent up the advisor chain of command, since the 3/3–1 advisors had been involved. They didn't want to get TF Panther in trouble, or stir any controversy on their first few days, but they didn't want to sanitize the report, either.

Captain McNulty, the veteran of house-to-house fighting who understood snap decision making, took charge. He refused to pull punches in his report, which indicated that the man shouldn't have been shot.

★

By March 2006, every advisor in Team Outcast had been shot at or bombed near the abandoned hospital in Khalidiya, which was located on the corner of 20th and Market streets.

There were no doctors in K-Town, none foolish enough to identify himself, anyway—the insurgents might demand his services in some torture house that could be destroyed at any moment and the Americans might arrest him for treating insurgents. In K-Town, a doctor might sell you a chicken, but if you asked him to carve it he'd tell you blood made him faint.

The Iraqi soldiers thought the U.S. military should donate an ambulance to Khalidiya, if only to allow pregnant women safer passage to the Iraqi hospital in Fallujah. There had been several shooting incidents involving frantic fathers-to-be who were trying to drive their wives in labor to hospitals after curfew.

The advisors of Team Outcast were concerned that the insurgents would turn the ambulance into a VBIED. Why couldn't they simply call the local midwife? To the Iraqis, this response was another example of the cultural gap. Would an American want his wife to deliver her baby at home while SEALs kicked in the neighbor's door? Or would he want her in a proper hospital?

The Iraqi soldiers won their argument. On Panther's orders, contractors who ran the scrap yard on Camp Habbaniyah refurbished an antiquated, unarmored Humvee left over from a past U.S. unit. On March 7, TF Panther's civil affairs unit was to deliver the "ambulance" to a group of Khalidiya locals in a minor ceremony organized by 3rd Company's Captain Walid.

A few minutes before the scheduled handover, the jundis spread out along Market Street, inviting folks to witness the gift. Two jundis with sledgehammers rushed up to the hospital gate but could not fracture the lock. Watching them, Boz's patience evaporated in the heat. He grabbed a hammer, carved an arc in the air, and the gate flew open. The jundis exhaled as if they'd just seen a man dunk a basketball.

The TF Panther civil affairs platoon delivering the vehicle was late. The sun climbed slowly until it was too bright to locate in the blinding haze. Winter was behind them. The sweaty jundis followed the shadows until they disappeared. They asked the advisors for water. Boz brought dripping bottles to Unlucky Company and tried to calm them, but half of the jundis had begun tugging on prayer beads.

"Where is the ambulance?" Walid asked Tiger, a new interpreter. "It is now two hours late!"

Huss didn't like Walid, who was a shirker, but the Iraqi was right. Loitering for two hours on Market Street was never a good idea.

A single high-pitched snap, then a jundi fell on his belly, gurgling blood and saliva from a gaping hole in his neck.

"Sniper!" shouted Boz. "Watch for the next muzzle flash."

The jundis fired out their magazines and screamed about the Sadiqiya Sniper instead.

In the turret, Huss fired carefully aimed bursts along the city's roofline so the sniper wouldn't realize the jundis were just shooting randomly out of fear and rage, an emotional release more than an attempt to drive the sniper from his hiding place.

The well-aimed round had pierced the fallen jundi at the base of his neck, just above his back plate. He still held a pink plastic bag full of fresh fruit. A half-eaten falafel had spilled from his mouth onto the street.

Boz dragged him to the Humvee. The jundis shouted prayers. Tiger dove into the armored vehicle and straddled the backseat. Boz struggled alone to get the fallen man inside.

"Get out here and help me," Boz told Tiger.

"Don't do it, Bozovich!" the terp shouted. "We could die!"

"Shut your freaking mouth and move your ass, Tiger," Boz hissed.

Boz plopped the shot boy in the backseat, grabbed Tiger's wrist, and placed the crying terp's hand on top of the wet gauze. "You hold that tight, you pussy."

"We have to get to the aid station right now or he's gone," Huss shouted at a soldier from TF Panther's Pyro platoon who had driven the jundis into position. "You stay here with the rest of the patrol. Don't leave the Iraqis, man!"

The advisor Humvee ripped alone down Route Michigan, swerved through the serpentine barrier outside Camp Habbaniyah's west gate, and accelerated down the muddy hill onto the airstrip. The engine was roaring and still they could hear the jundi's bubbling death rattle.

"Tell him to hold on, Tiger," said Boz. "Jesus, look at this!"

A group of TF Panther soldiers was playing touch football at the edge of the mirage, on the east end of the hot runway. Boz tried the horn, but it was broken. He stomped on the accelerator, released it, and stomped on it again to warn them. Huss screamed.

The shimmering image of the soldiers gave way to angry shirtless men who parted only at the last second. One of them threw the football at the Humvee and swore. The ball struck the windshield with a thump and bounced high.

Huss cursed the soldiers all the way into the field hospital compound. But he was really cursing the sniper, their lousy mission, and the realization that the young jundi was already gone.

Unlucky Third.

The doctor at the field hospital cut the jundi open and tried to tube him. The big attendant who had calmed Boiko after the car bomb leaned into his chest and pumped. On the operating table, the body shifted loosely, like a puppet cut free of its strings.

"He's dead," said the doctor.

"Yeah, I figured that," said Huss. "Thanks, anyway."

Huss and Boz told Tiger they were going to look for the football players. One way or another they'd be back at the hospital, so he should wait there. They walked out into the heat in search of someone to fight.

But the football players had gone home.

They drove back to Market Street to deliver the bad news. The trucks from Pyro were still there, but the jundis were gone.

"Where the hell is 3rd Company?" Huss shouted at one of the truck drivers. "I thought you were going to stay with them."

"They're in town somewhere. We called our HQ but they said we had to hold in position. Sorry."

Huss wheeled down 20th Street. The jundis were pulling local men from shops and houses, dragging them into the center of the street. Walid had about fifty suspects facedown on the hot asphalt. The jundis were casually booting them. There were too many busted doors to count and several broken car windshields.

"Captain, stop right there," said Huss.

"He is dead?" Walid asked.

"*Nam,*" said Huss. Yes.

The news moved electrically through the furious school of jundis.

"Hey! You can't take them all," said Huss. "Let's wrap this up."

"We must get the information," Walid said dismissively.

"Captain Walid, take the best suspects and get back to the ASP. Now!"

Walid could have ignored Huss. He was a captain, after all, and Huss was enlisted. Iraqi officership was a privilege. Enlisted workhorses were treated a bit better than pack mules. For jundis, shouting orders to an officer resulted in instant dismissal. Depending on the affront and the officer's connections, slander could result in a gunshot. But most Iraqi officers were more political than honor bound, and Walid was uncertain about the fallout if he tangled with Huss. The American officers protected their enlisted personnel. Plus, Huss had a quick temper and was thickly built. Walid had once seen Huss's strength during a patrol to snatch mattresses from a blown-up building for use on ASP Hill, when a raging Huss had tossed them like cardboard to demonstrate work ethic.

Back at the ASP, Walid's sniper suspects were tied together like fish on a stringer but interrogated without violence. Huss trudged to the Horseshoe. The Pyro transport trucks were still idling inside the wire.

"Why are you still here?" Huss asked a Pyro guardsman.

"Got a jundi back there who won't come out. Been in there crying for an hour."

Huss climbed into the back of the truck. It was well over 100°. A jundi he recognized as Bassim, a young kid who couldn't have been more than seventeen, sat crouched in the dark, hugging his shins. He wasn't yet cried out. Huss sat next to him and pulled the jundi tight. He met no resistance.

"It's okay, Bassim. It's gonna be okay."

When the jundi found his voice, he thanked Huss and walked back to the bunker without any shame that Huss could see. Walid, who had cooled off, approached Huss.

"When do you want to deliver the ambulance?" Huss asked.

"Khalidiya deserves no ambulance," said Walid.

Two days later, Walid stood in the middle of 20th Street during a patrol and dared the sniper to shoot him. Huss joined him. They walked alone ahead of the vehicles with their weapons slung and their arms held toward the sky shouting, "Show yourself if you have courage," in Arabic. It wasn't a tactic Huss had learned at Camp Atterbury.

A man in a dirty dishdasha hailed the two soldiers. He claimed to know the jundi's killer: It was a sniper team, headed by an insurgent called Abu Roma who had configured his car so the shooters could fire from a hidden compartment in the trunk, a design made famous by the father-son tandem who had murdered people in the Washington, D.C., area in 2002.

"How do you know Abu Roma?" Walid asked the man.

"The whole city knows Abu Roma. He is death."

Walid confiscated a car, but Huss thought it was just a show to calm the jundis, who were still simmering after the sniper attack. For a few days the car was used as a shuttle between the bunkers on the ASP and then it was placed in the vehicle graveyard on Camp Habbaniyah to be stripped night after night by Filipino mechanics contracted to fix Iraqi trucks, until it vanished altogether.

★

In the week following the shooting, the Iraqi soldiers searched hundreds of houses. They were like police hammering to find a cop killer. The apartments of uncooperative citizens were tossed. More names of suspects were whispered to the jundis in alleys. Seven suspects were sent to the detention center on Camp Habbaniyah with charges of sniping, including a man who drove his car up to the ASP gate and turned himself in when he heard his name was on the wanted list. He demanded to be put in the American prison for fear of being slowly drowned by jundis in Lake Habbaniyah, which was the current local rumor about what happened to suspects in Iraqi custody.

After thirty months of occupation, every man in Khalidiya and Abu Fleis knew someone who had been arrested. Since the arrival of American forces in 2003, five thousand fighting-age males between the ages of 18 and 55 were detained in Khalidiya and its tiny suburbs, about one out of every three. Most had been quickly released. Even those who had been twice recommended for imprisonment after being screened by U.S. battalion and brigade lawyers averaged fewer than nine months behind bars. Iraqi and American soldiers called it "catch and release."

Troster knew what the problem was. U.S. military lawyers had imposed high evidentiary thresholds for incarceration that in his opinion had no place on the battlefield. In war you had to rely on circumstantial evidence and witness statements. The lawyers wanted fingerprints and confessions. In the end, for a hard-core insurgent, an arrest by the Americans was just the cost of doing business.

Advisors felt pinched between a failing U.S. military justice system on one hand and a lawless Iraq on the other. Iraqi society had grown almost comfortable in conflict, and the jundis were willing to take a prisoner's honor if they weren't given information. Slapping a Sunni around was a minor transfer of power for a young Shiite.

The advisors' morality sometimes rankled Iraqis who grew up in a police state, where violence was a constant element of life. An open-handed slap had a deterrent benefit. The red handprint on a local's cheek, if there was one, quickly disappeared. Innocent suspects who wore no physical stamp when they returned home retained their honor. But there was no hiding a wrongful arrest, no matter how the prisoner was treated. Jailings brought shame on the family. Upon release, there was pressure from peers, imams, and even family members to avenge the family honor, which typically took the form of a few potshots fired at American vehicles.

Khalidiyans considered the American brig a joke. But a layover at an Iraqi outpost filled with raving Shiite lunatics was a horrifying thought. Rumors of torture spread through Khalidiya, from electric shocks with car batteries to drownings in Lake Habbaniyah.

Insurgents knew the American system cold, including to the hour when prisoners would be released, which meant that any threats by U.S. guards were considered empty. A visit to an ASP controlled by Shiite jundis became an exercise in terror, even if the advisors would never allow detainees to be abused.

★

During the second and third weeks of March, insurgents steadily ratcheted up the pressure, attacking almost every day. Huss and Bozovich were paired up during that period, and their patrols got smacked with AK fire for fourteen consecutive days.

The advisors believed that mines were the single best barometer for measuring AQI infestation. Each find was reported in detail to headquarters and then sent up the chain of command to the Pentagon as SIGACTs to be analyzed by an anti-IED task force that recommended modifications to armored trucks, steering procedures, and equipment. But sporadic gunfire—called potshots by the advisors—was considered the best barometer of local sentiment. Subjected to constant potshots outside the wire, beginning in October the advisors decided not to write normal gunplay up as SIGACTs unless there was a casualty, even though the SIGACT website was filled with small-arms fire taken by other units.

Unlike with mines, there was nothing a general in the Pentagon could do to prevent an angry civilian from popping a few rounds at a passing patrol. Every Iraqi household was permitted to have an automatic rifle for protection, so it was impossible to eradicate random gunfire from the urban battlefield.

As former football players, Huss and Boz began to think of the random bullets as equivalent to the roar of a hostile crowd. Only your team could shut them up.

But the team was shrinking again. Roberson had gone on leave on March 15, doubling Troster's administrative duties. Blakley went on patrol as much as possible, but every morning a gaggle of ailing jundis awaiting treatment stood outside his door.

That left six men on the full-time rotation to accompany every Iraqi patrol. Troster considered pulling the advisors out of a few, but the Iraqis were not yet ready for independence and, anyway, he had made a promise to Falah back in October to accompany every patrol.

The promise paid off one night in mid-March when eight men masquerading as jundis burst into the Abu Fleis home of a shopkeeper. They were dressed in chocolate chip camouflage uniforms, Iraqi body armor, even authentic helmets. There was no resistance. The patriarch was handcuffed, interrogated about his social contacts, and executed in front of his family. One of the killers kicked the corpse and issued an official warning from the Iraqi military.

Dhafer noticed the crowd outside the house the next morning and diverted his patrol. When he heard the horrifying story, he asked how the people knew the assassins were imposters.

"We knew they weren't Iraqi soldiers," said a neighbor. "They had no advisors."

★

So short-handed was the advisor team that some men remained in the same uniform for days, sleeping in restless four-hour bursts interrupted by sharp bangs on their aluminum doors or, worse, deep bangs in town. Life devolved to an endless patrol. The rigorous schedule eroded politeness. Advisors became curt, jundis distracted. The Iraqi officers grew dismissive, and the reliable interpreter GW asked Troster if he could move to a unit surrounded by less violence.

"Request approved," said Troster. "You've done your time, GW."

For all their quirks, it was clear by then that the jundis who remained in 3/3–1 knew how to suffer. And the advisors knew that they had to outwork the jundis, or they would lose respect for the Americans.

The advisors of Team Outcast were out of fumes. Huss was so tired he once fell asleep on his feet in the heart of K-Town. Another time he spent an hour trying to remember where he'd put his rifle. Gentile had spent the first few weeks back with the team imagining every possible IED. Now his eyes were too tired and his neck was too stiff to care. All of the advisors felt the nauseating effects of long-term sleep deprivation except Neary, who was the youngest soldier and had a constitution apparently forged in the dives he played as a rock guitarist.

On the night of March 18, Troster was driving a Humvee down Abu Fleis Road. Lieutenant Khalid pulled his trucks to the side of the road. Assuming Khalid wanted the Warlock jammer in the lead, Troster pulled ahead, squinting at the sparkling pixilation in his night-vision goggles. Driving without goggles without heavy moonlight required focused intensity, and even then it was 30 percent luck. A Russian antitank mine as fat as a wedding cake appeared in the electric green froth of Troster's night-vision lens. He was going too fast to stop, so he straddled the mine. If there was a tilt-rod trigger, a one-meter-high vertical stick that would detonate the mine when struck, they were dead.

The Humvee chassis cleared the mine. Troster wheeled a tight U-turn to warn the Iraqis following in trace, but they were still idling where Khalid had pulled off the road. Troster hopped out to tell Khalid about the mine he'd seen.

"We saw this mine earlier tonight," Khalid told Troster.

Troster was so infuriated he almost snatched a burning cigarette from a jundi's lips to extinguish it in Khalid's eyeball. "We could have been killed!"

"We stopped but you kept going."

"We kept going because we thought you wanted us in the lead!"

"No, I lead my patrols," said Khalid.

"Lieutenant Khalid, you are a good officer," said Troster. "But if you ever again leave a mine on a busy road for three hours I'll make you eat it."

On their way home after EOD removed the antitank mine, Troster and Rivera hit a different mine that blew up the Humvee's front tires, leaving them shaken but uninjured. Luck of the draw. And Troster couldn't blame Khalid for that one.

A few days later, on March 21, Huss and Boz bounced along behind one of Dhafer's vehicles on a narrow street that doubled as a garbage chute in K-Town. They tripped a mine. Most of the shrapnel sailed wide, and the Humvee's armor skeleton absorbed the rest.

"Is that all you got!" screamed Huss from the turret.

He plucked one of the blackened ceramic marble shrapnel from the skin of his Humvee and brought it back to the EOD team. The Marine studied it with one eye like a diamond dealer. "Cool! You found an Italian mine," he said. "We gotta report this one."

The near misses made it clear: AQI or the 1920 Revolutionary Brigade or both had planted an expensive crop and it was blossoming. What bothered Troster wasn't the determination the enemy had shown in February and March in response to increased patrols. What bothered him was the battalion's inability to crack the insurgent network.

★

On the morning of March 23, Staff Sergeant Brock Beery steered a hulking armored transport truck up ASP Hill. Beery had just been transferred into TF Panther's Pyro platoon after a squabble with a senior NCO, and he immediately volunteered to get outside the Camp Habbaniyah wire as a driver. That was fine with Lieutenant Fonseca, the platoon leader who on this day rode shotgun next to Beery. Behind them, a second transport truck lumbered in trace.

"The plan is usually the same," Fonseca told Beery. "We pick up about thirty jundis at ASP Hill and follow their advisors into Khalidiya or Abu Fleis, where they get dropped off. After their foot patrol, we come back to get 'em, and of course if they call for help we're always ready."

"That's where I come in," shouted Specialist Edward Fisher from above, who manned the machine gun in the turret.

"It's the best mission we have," added Fonseca.

The last winter rainstorm had come overnight. The armored transport trucks carved muddy arcs at the entrance to ASP Hill and took their place in the patrol formation behind the advisors' Humvee idling near the gate.

"Lovely day for a patrol, sir, " Boz joked.

"Wouldn't miss it," Fonseca replied, leaning out his door, which was two and a half meters aboveground.

Two lines of reluctant jundis stepped into the tire tracks where the ground still had some crust and walked gingerly toward the vehicles in hopes of keeping their boots dry. Jundis hated mud almost as much as they hated walking. Lake Habbaniyah was just two klicks south of the bunkers; that was a long walk in Iraq. Instead of washing it off, they would let the mud cake dry in the sun and stomp it out in the evening.

A jundi leaned back on the handhold of the second armored transport and stepped onto the grated ladder. Specialist Carl Prine, another Pyro soldier, emerged from the shadow of the troop hold. He extended his hand and yanked the jundi into the back of the truck, then turned to help the next man. The jundis knew him well.

Pyro was a motley crew, but Prine, a 39-year-old junior enlistee, was strange by any measure. A former Marine NCO grunt turned war correspondent, he had lived with and studied guerrillas in the brutal West African wars of the 1990s. He also had broken the story on lax security measures at American chemical plants in the wake of 9/11. Called by a recruiter looking for prior service volunteers, Prine had joined the Pennsylvania Army National Guard in the summer of 2005 and was shipped to Habbaniyah as an individual augmentee in December.

Keenly interested in guerrilla warfare, Prine corresponded with the best American and French counterinsurgency veterans and openly critiqued his battalion's tactics, using terms like "center of gravity," "cultural topography," and "deterritorialized foreign fighters"—discussions befitting a military strategy wonk—to blueprint the various insurgent undergrounds in K-Town and their motivations.

He believed TF Panther's effort to minimize casualties by centralizing in heavily fortified Camp Habbaniyah got decent men killed and prolonged the savage combat in Habbaniyah by making it easy for insurgents to prey on them by planting mines at will. So he volunteered to go into Khalidiya daily with the jundis as an extra infantryman for Pyro.

Prine wasn't alone in his critique. In March 2006, an email listing counterinsurgency best practices was spreading rapidly throughout the U.S. Army and Marine Corps. "Twenty-Eight Articles: Fundamentals of Company-level Counterinsurgency," written by Dr. David Kilcullen, a former Australian army officer with experience in East Timor who researched the Iraq War for the State Department, captured the growing frustrations felt by many American junior officers and NCOs who had come to question the conventional tactics mandated by the top brass. Kilcullen's most stinging advice to the U.S. military: "Rank is nothing: talent is everything. Not everyone is good at counterinsurgency . . . but a few 'naturals' do exist . . . Put them into positions where they can make a difference."[1]

Prine was one of those naturals—an enlisted man of minimal rank who instinctively understood counterinsurgency as it was playing out in Khalidiya. He was full of good ideas. Prine ran a program soliciting school supplies, toys, and candy from Pittsburgh Marine Corps League chapters for distribution in Iraq. But he and the jundis didn't toss the gifts from their trucks just to make nice with the locals. Prine used them to ward off local insurgents who would never hit the patrol when there were kids around. It also gave the jundis an opening to develop the children's parents as informants.

The problem was, notwithstanding Kilcullen's instruction to choose talent over rank, that the American military did not accept that advice. On Camp Habbaniyah, rank was everything. The American military is built to thrive despite the constant personnel turnover of combat; the chain of command insists upon rank as the determining measure rather than individual talent, so that privates, lieutenants, even entire units can be seamlessly shifted back and forth on the battlefield with minimal disruption. All you have to do is follow the man who outranks you.

In TF Panther, Prine was assigned to Pyro as a turret gunner. He was to remain atop the truck manning the gun, three meters above the foot soldiers. But Prine lobbied Fonseca to employ his own peculiar method of fighting the insurgents on the ground. Like Lieutenant Fonseca and the 3/3–1 advisors, Prine believed the key to Khalidiya was empowering trained jundis, but he took this concept a step further. When he patrolled with the Iraqis, he inserted himself in their formations as an American jundi, looking to take orders from any Iraqi officer or NCO.

He knew just enough Arabic to pull it off. The Iraqi officers relished the opportunity to give direction to an American soldier, and the elders in town noticed. When Prine encountered a particularly recalcitrant group of civilians, usually hanging around one of the seven mosques in K-Town and Abu Fleis, he played the part with gusto. Imams referred to Iraqi soldiers as "American puppets," but with Prine visibly taking orders from Iraqi officers and NCOs, that was no longer convincing.

Fonseca was happy to have Prine's steady influence and expert rifle, but his constant input on how to win the war made the lieutenant's life diffi-cult. In late February, a few 3/3–1 jundis had shown Prine some handwritten threats the 1920 Revolutionary Brigade had posted on the doors of the few Shiites who lived in Khalidiya. Prine reported the threats to the TF Panther intelligence officer.

"Brigade hasn't said anything about that," said the officer.

"Sir, how would Brigade know what goes on in Khalidiya? They're in Ramadi," Prine said. "I think we should track the Shia, Kurds, and Christians in town."

"Like I said, Brigade is reporting no religious issues in our AO [area of operations]. Who are you again, Specialist?"

In early March, Prine had been encouraged by fellow Panther soldiers to take a "drop gun" on his missions. The practice illustrated that Iraq was a police war: If there was a questionable kill outside the wire, a civilian instantly became an insurgent when a spare AK-47 got placed near his body. Prine did not know of anyone who had covered up a wrongful shoot with spare weap-ons, but in his mind drop guns sent a message to the troops that it was okay to get careless.

Prine went to Fonseca with his concerns. "Those weapons trash the rules of engagement, sir. I'm told it's common practice in other companies."

"My focus is on this platoon," said Fonseca.

"Battalion sets the tone. This should be investigated. Right now Panther is fighting a tribal-religious insurgency like it's a bad '70s cop show. "

"I was born in 1982," joked Fonseca. "Look, Prine, let's just do our jobs in Pyro. We both agree that helping the jundis is the best thing we can do in this war."

★

The patrol on March 23 was about Prine's twentieth time accompanying the jundis. Packing themselves inside the armored truck next to Prine, most of them asked for candy.

"That's for the children," Prine said. "Not you."

Prine squeezed onto the bench and held a tutorial on weapons safety. A careless jundi had recently fired his machine gun inside an LMTV, an armored truck, injuring three. One of them once put a stray machine gun round into Prine's turret plate while the troops were dismounting in K-Town.

Huss, Boz, and Bennett took out the patrol with 3rd Company, their first with Unlucky since the jundi had been shot dead during the ambu-lance mission a month earlier. They were glad to have Pyro riding along. The guardsmen brought two monster trucks, two .50-caliber machine guns, good communications, some brave men, some strange men, and Prine, who was both brave and strange.

Huss sat inside the Humvee on the greasy turret strap that was supposed to tether the up-gunner to the vehicle if it exploded. But no one wore the belt—they used it as a seat. Boz, who was driving, switched on the jammer and inspected the light display.

"Unlucky Third," said Boz.

"Tighten your chin strap," said Huss.

The advisors took point into Abu Fleis, followed by Beery's LMTV with Fonseca and Fisher. The second Pyro transport was controlled by a similar three-man crew and carried Prine in the uncovered back with the jundis. The plan called for the jundis to patrol Khalidiya and then meet up in the afternoon to run another sweep with TF Panther's Alpha Company.

An LMTV got stuck in the mud in Khalidiya near the soccer field. The jundis kept the crowds at bay by tossing stuffed animals at them that Prine had brought along while Fonseca organized the tow. It took fifteen minutes to free the truck.

"We've been here too long," said Huss. "Let's swing into the lead and take the back road to mix it up."

In the lead, Boz kept a steady pace so one of the kids wasn't chewed up by an armored truck. If you slowed down, the trailing vehicles moved in tight, like an accordion, and kids thought it was safe to dart between them. A sudden acceleration had the opposite effect. The patrol entered the backside of town where there was no pavement. The dirt road was abnormally quiet. It was noon and the tide of garbage caked the choppy mud. Boz accelerated to throw off any lurking triggermen.

In the rear, Prine and the jundis noticed that the children had abandoned the chase—always the sign of an impending attack. But would it be an explosion or a sniper?

Before he could react, Boz ran over a cardboard box top, the tell of a pressure-plate mine—a surface-laid mine detonated by applying pressure on a metal plate, completing a firing circuit. Boz jerked the wheel and cursed. The Humvee seemed to float over the rectangle as if in a sickly spin on an icy highway. All Boz could do was cringe. The tires missed the cardboard. Over the hump in an instant, Boz screamed, "IED!" into the radio handset and stomped the brake.

Too late. Beery's LMTV hit the cardboard and, below it, the pressure-plate detonator. Three artillery shells erupted like a molten geyser. Overpressure caused by the explosion's shock wave filled the cab with scalding water, washing over Fonseca and Fisher and shaking their organs. Through the flames and smoke, the lieutenant called for his driver. He reached to grab his arm but could find no purchase.

"Beery! Beery!"

Fisher had been blown out of the turret. As he hung on the crumpled steel, bullets zipped overhead. Others pinged into the trucks or struck rocks, the ricochets twanging through the kill zone.

Huss had taken a random route to outfox the enemy and walked into a coordinated ambush. Jundis fought their way out of the kill zone as the bullets poured in.

Huss cranked the turret grinder and hosed a suspect building with his machine gun to suppress the enemy fire.

Inside the second transport, Prine took control and pushed the remaining jundis over the sides of the truck like a jumpmaster tossing paratroopers off a burning plane. He hit the ground hard and rolled. Jundis fired like mad in all directions. One of them spotted an enemy muzzle flash, and Pyro's lone surviving .50-cal opened up alongside Huss to suppress the ambush.

Prine sprinted to the burning LMTV. The front left tire was gone and the truck listed face-first into the deep crater, slathered in oil and blood. The driver's heavy blast door was hanging by a single twisted hinge. Prine jumped to the steering wheel. There was nothing left of Beery.

A fine white silt sprinkled over the red gore, as if the three guardsmen inside had been dusted in lime. Prine heard Fisher, known as "Fish," screaming in anger. He called out for Fonseca.

No response. Just mumbles heard between blasts of enemy and Pyro gunfire.

He rushed to the passenger side, called to some nearby jundis, and together they shuffled through the piles of garbage looking for daisy-chained secondary IEDs to make the spot safe for Fisher and his lieutenant when they exited.

Prine clambered onto the running board. The cab cantered forty-five degrees into the crater, with Fonseca's locked hatch up in the air. Slinging his rifle on his back, Prine yanked the door open.

A severed leg fell on him.

Fish slumped back in the turret and begged Fonseca for his rifle to return the gunfire blasting at him. Prine thought Fish had a concussion but handed it up through a turret hole now smoking like a chimney. They needed every available gun in the fight.

Fonseca was mumbling into the radio for backup. Prine saw that the spiraled line connecting the hand mike to the radio had been severed by the blast. Fonseca was carrying on a conversation alone.

"Sir, are you ambulatory?" Prine asked.

"Yes," Fonseca whispered, but Prine didn't believe him. The severed leg was sliding off his body armor into the cab. Prine pulled his lieutenant out of the truck, cradling him. The limb belonged to Beery.

Fish fired out his magazine to keep the enemy down, then Prine and the jundis carried him and Fonseca through the piles of spent brass casings from Huss's gun. They set them side by side inside the advisor Humvee.

"You know I ain't staying in here, right?" said Fisher.

Huss looked down through the hatch. He was immensely fond of Fonseca and his men. They shared the risks; in the last two months, every able-bodied guardsman in Pyro had been smacked by a roadside bomb while helping the jundis.

Huss tapped the young lieutenant on the shoulder with the toe of his boot. "How you doin', sir?"

Fonseca mumbled. He stared out the windshield. Huss remembered his own migraine after the car bomb. He scanned the south side of Khalidiya, hoping to see one bad guy running with a rifle, just one, so he could tie the score.

The Iraqi officer GQ organized a defensive ring around the burning gun truck. Troster arrived on scene accompanying the quick reaction force of jundis.

"What've we got?" Troster asked.

"Fire coming from that cluster there," said Huss.

"We're going to clear those buildings," GQ told his men. "Prine, up here."

Prine and the jundis gathered for an assault on the cluster of suspect buildings. Prine checked his rifle chamber and took point on the single-wing formation as the odd duck, still taking orders in public from Iraqi leaders.

They charged together.

"Y'alla!" shouted GQ. Let's go.

"Y'alla!" Prine and the jundis replied.

They went house to house under covering crossfire from Huss and Pyro, leaving countersnipers in the top floors and then snaking through buildings, chasing the insurgents away.

Troster was surveying the scene—the red-splattered windshield, the dripping bumper, the acrid smell of diesel and burning rubber and wet garbage, enemy bullet holes that were still steaming in the cement walls of nearby apartment buildings—when soldiers from TF Panther rolled up to assist.

The first soldier out was carrying a video camera instead of a rifle.

"If you don't put that goddamn thing away right now I'm going to break your teeth with it," Troster told the soldier. "Go earn your own war porn."

Troster turned his attention back to the assault squad. He was impressed with both Pyro and 3rd Company. They'd taken a hard jab and counterpunched. The jundis were aggressive. GQ was thinking a step ahead. The Iraqi NCOs took control: They cornered three men who had remained in the buildings and arrested them without manhandling them, a sign the jundis considered them stupid but innocent.

Two hours later, after the children had picked over the kill zone for wartime souvenirs, the only evidence of the fight was a dwindling crater lake of blood and oil, one of dozens like it in Khalidiya.

When Troster returned to the ASP, the TF Panther executive officer was waiting for him. Troster was angry the man hadn't gone to the battle scene. He told the XO that Beery had been brave to volunteer.

"Actually, Beery was kind of an asshole," said the XO, explaining that he was under investigation for theft.

Troster was disgusted. The XO kept talking, but Troster didn't hear a word until he was asked if the joint patrol was going to leave as scheduled that afternoon.

"Of course it is," said Troster. "We need to get right back out."

"I agree," said the XO. "And I'm going along to show leadership."

Two hours later, a truckload of jundis from 1st Company joined Alpha Company/TF Panther for a sweep of Mudiq, an isolated community two kilometers west of Khalidiya, next to Sadiqiya. Thirty minutes into the mission, a single shot rang out. Sergeant First Class Randy McCaulley, 44, a popular twenty-five-year veteran of the Pennsylvania Army National Guard, was killed. The jundis suspected the Sadiqiya Sniper.

TF Panther mourned one of their most beloved soldiers. He was the first KIA from the 1–110th Infantry. After that terrible day, joint patrols between Panther and 3/3–1 faded away.

That night, Troster visited the Pyro team. "It was tough out there today. In the jundis' eyes, you guys are like big brothers. We're proud to serve with you. We'd love it if you'd move up to ASP Hill, but you know better than anyone here that we don't have much to offer up there."

The men chuckled and Troster turned to leave.

"Hey, sir," said Fonseca, whose head was still ringing. "I know I speak for all of us when I say thanks for coming down. You're the only senior officer who's come by."

10

The Terp

★ ★ ★

March 2006

At Camp Victory, a massive U.S. base located at the Baghdad International Airport, a long line of young Iraqis stretched around the corner of a building housing an American contracting firm that charged the U.S. military for sourcing interpreters. Among the prospective terps was Ahmed Yasin, a 20-year-old boy who had learned English by taking small jobs on several bases. On his hand he had tattooed the name of a 40-year-old American contractor—a love affair that ended when she returned to Alabama.

Ahmed and two other Iraqis were suddenly pulled to the head of the line. They were the only ones who said they'd deploy anywhere in Iraq.

"So you'll go to Anbar?" the American contractor asked Ahmed. "You won't quit or ask for another province?"

"I go to the action in Anbar."

"You'll get action, all right. Pick a name."

"I am Ahmed Yasin, buddy."

Ahmed had bluffed his way through interpreter screening. He'd never had an English class, but his soldierspeak—profanity used by American servicemen and -women—was superb.

"A new name," the American contractor said. "One that's easy for American soldiers to say."

Ahmed studied the flyers posted on the bulletin board.

"My name will be Alex," he said.

"Anbar Alex," said the contractor.

"Anbar Alex!"

In mid-March 2006, Alex boarded an old Marine CH-46 helicopter, wiped the hydraulic fluid from the seat, and gave the gunner a happy thumbs-up as he faked fastening the strange buckle. The Marines onboard stared at him. They hated riding in the dreaded bird, a relic built in 1964. Alex was excited to be riding in a helicopter that leaked oil over every passenger. Wasting oil was a sign of wealth and power.

Once at Camp Habbaniyah, a Marine sergeant drove him to an abandoned barracks.

"I want to see the action," Alex told him.

"You want action, huh? Stay here for now," the Marine said. "There's MREs if you need 'em."

Alex stuffed his belongings into a plastic sack, a makeshift pillow and temporary ruse against thieves. He waited alone. He had nowhere else to go. No one in Iraq risked as much as combat interpreters. They were hated by the insurgents because they were the face of interrogations, considered traitors by their countrymen, resented by the jundis for their high pay, and ostracized by their own families for exposing them to retribution.

Back in Baghdad, Alex's father had attacked him with a sword for reading American magazines, inflicting a deep cut on his head. His older brother berated him for running from his family responsibilities. Only his younger brother understood that he was built differently and wanted desperately to help the U.S. military.

What Alex admired most about the Americans was their personalities. They dressed alike, like jundis, but they joked, cursed, smiled, and played games openly, without fear of reprimand. They were relaxed and funny. They were free.

After five days in Habbaniyah, Alex was told he was going to Team Outcast on ASP Hill as a replacement for the gun-shy terp Tiger, who could no longer handle combat. He waved at the approaching Humvee, excited to finally join an American military unit, and expertly tossed his duffel inside when it rolled to a halt.

"Is there action up there?" Alex asked the turret gunner, a U.S. soldier.

"You the new terp? You seem too full of it to have done this for long," said the gunner. "Just hope you last longer than the last guy,"

"Yes. But you're not a Marine."

"Do I look like I had my brain sucked out my nose?"

"I'm not sure," said Alex. "What kind of man is the advisor commander, Lieutenant Colonel Troster?"

"A real asshole. He's fired twenty terps. Good looking, though."

Alex nodded uneasily. The Americans mixed too much sarcasm into everyday conversation. The Humvee sped across Michigan and up ASP Hill to the Horseshoe. The gunner detached the machine gun and handed it down. Alex loved the feel of power.

"Can you introduce me to this asshole?" Alex asked.

"You're looking at him. I'm Troster."

Alex was mortified. "I have to apologize, sir."

"Alex, right?" asked Troster. "You need to understand something. None of us can do anything without our terps. You make the whole thing work. Just translate what the Iraqis say exactly and what I say exactly, and never forget that you're our eyes and ears. Welcome to 3rd Battalion. Everybody fights."

The Horseshoe was a small but strange community that could have been the space station as far as Alex was concerned. Neary greeted him in impressive Arabic and pointed to the interpreter room, which looked like an American college dorm room from the movies.

"Don't go into the American rooms without knocking," said Reyes, a former jundi turned terp. "They sleep with pistols under their pillows."

"Afraid of the jundis?"

"No, any jundi could kill them easily. They're waiting for an attack on the outpost. The major across the hall is hoping for it. Stay out of his room."

"What's his name?"

"Roberson."

In one corner of the courtyard, two Iraqi officers were complaining to Joe, a fellow interpreter, about a dog the Americans had adopted. "Pyro" was a smelly stray that Roberson had taken into his room, sparking rumors that he might have feelings after all. Alex later realized that Roberson enjoyed Pyro for more than easy company. The Iraqis hated dogs and there was no better firewall for a begging jundi than a drooling mutt with the same wanting stare.

As Alex overheard the conversation that first night, one officer was particularly despondent about the animal's presence. He believed that by licking a man, Pyro was intent on stealing his soul. The Iraqi officers left Joe to deliver the message.

"I will not reveal him," Joe told Roberson a few minutes later. "But if that animal sneaks into this particular officer's room, it could die."

"If someone kills my dog it won't be the only thing dying," said Roberson.

Joe returned to the interpreter room, having decided no good could come of further interaction with either party. It was Alex's first lesson in interpreting.

★

As a terp, Alex soon felt caught among the competing interests of the locals, jundis, Iraqi officers, and American advisors. The Iraqis tested his loyalty but he said little. He'd been told to observe, so that's what he did.

Troster's relationship with Colonel Falah (who had been promoted) was strained, and Alex tried to figure out why. The Iraqi company commanders told Alex that Falah was better than the previous battalion commander, but he was a snob. On his desk, Falah kept digital cameras the Americans had purchased for evidence collection. The row of cameras was his way of signifying authority. To borrow one, the company commanders had to genuflect.

In the old Iraqi Army, snobbery was acceptable. But the advisors' democratic approach to battlefield toil had affected the Iraqi junior officers. Company commanders saw themselves in Troster, who led from the front.

But to them the American colonel also had a glaring flaw. He solicited opinions from enlisted men with little regard for rank, let American NCOs run patrols, and boosted their egos. The American sergeants ate in the Iraqi officers' mess and felt they could speak up when they chose. Soon Iraqi NCOs would be speaking up, too, and that was seen as deteriorative. Several Iraqi officers kept their distance from the jundis so their decisions weren't questioned. They followed the model set by the Army Ranger Roberson.

Alex asked Neary if Roberson stayed apart from enlisted men.

"He doesn't talk to me much," said Neary. "But he doesn't talk to anybody, including the Iraqis. Troster is his interpreter."

"He speaks another language?" asked Alex.

"Not that I know of."

Alex quickly discovered that Colonel Falah expected to use him as a supplicant. Complaining of stomach pain, Falah insisted that Alex tell Troster to take him to the shock trauma unit at TQ. "This is part of our good relationship," Falah told Alex.

"Tell him he has his own doctor at brigade," Troster said when Alex delivered the message. "You can't go to TQ for a stomach cramp."

Falah countered that he was deathly ill. His health dominated the morning staff meeting. Chai Boy was in tears. There were rumors of poisoning. So Troster drove him to shock trauma, where a female doctor was on duty.

"I cannot see her," Falah protested. "It is . . . different. Not for a lady."

"Whatever it is, she's the only doctor on duty, Colonel," said Troster.

Thirty minutes later, Falah shuffled out. He looked miserable but pronounced himself cured, flashing a tube of medicine. Troster went inside to fill out the paperwork. "What'd you do to him? Remove a kidney?" Troster asked the doctor.

"It wasn't his stomach. He had inflammation of the scrotum, epididymis. All that scratching had bruised his testicles. I gave him some topical cream."

Troster laughed. "Give him anything else along the way?"

"I had to rule out prostate cancer," she said, smiling. "We're professionals here."

★

Alex was surprised by the austere supply situation on ASP Hill. Iraqi jundis had always lived hard. Alex knew that from his neighborhood stories about the decade-long Iran-Iraq War. But he expected that the Americans, if they did not like to use Route Michigan to deliver daily supplies, would at least fly in pallets of food, drink, and clothing by helicopter to care for their advisors.

Instead, the advisors ate as Iraqis, supplemented by care packages from home. The Iraqis ate poorly. Ministry of Defense deliveries to ASP Hill were also infrequent. Twelve live sheep had recently been dropped off, the entire battalion's monthly allotment. There was no vegetation on ASP Hill and the finicky sheep refused to eat discarded meals. Battalion 3/3–1 was forced to slaughter them before they lost muscle weight, but in the interim, three sheep had fled downhill to Khalidiya. Alex noticed that the rest were spray-painted blue. If a local had a blue sheep, he was stealing a hungry jundi's meal.

The battalion's logistics advisor was Lieutenant Bennett, a capable logistician who knew the book. The other advisors had no logistical training or scruples about regulations. Whenever they drove to TQ air base, Bennett's teammates scrounged for anything that wasn't bolted down and could be smuggled out without attracting the attention of the military police.

Bennett didn't have the personality to wheedle goodies, so he borrowed higher authority. On March 1, Marine Major General Richard Zilmer and his 1st Marine Expeditionary Force (I MEF) had taken command of all units in Anbar Province. Zilmer had immediately made his intent clear: All U.S. units were to devote their deployments to advancing Iraqi forces. Bennett found a memo on the I MEF website where Major General Zilmer had declared that Iraqi battalions and their training teams were his "focus of effort." Bennett downloaded the pertinent sentences, with Zilmer's name in bold font below the I MEF letterhead. In mid-March, Bennett had printed out a dozen copies on heavy paper, giving one to each advisor.

Flourishing under their newly assumed authority, the Outcasts secured passes for take-out food from the sumptuous TQ mess halls. Soon they were hauling pieces of furniture, small air conditioners, and even a refrigerator back to ASP. Bolt-on armor was requisitioned for their damaged Humvees. Bennett even located some funds to spend on the Iraqi battalion, purchasing office equipment in downtown Khalidiya, pleasing the Iraqi officers and merchants alike. The jundis were outfitted with cooling fans, coffeemakers, even new uniform sets.

But Bennett's biggest coup was the delivery of six refurbished armored Humvees to the Iraqis. Detailed with desert chocolate chip camouflage patterns, and richly colored Iraqi flag decals glued on their blast doors, the glistening Humvees drew wild cheers from the Iraqi soldiers as they rumbled slowly past the ASP headquarters building toward the motor pool. The days of patrolling in aluminum Nissan pickup trucks were over.

"Thank God for *Mulazim* TV!" GQ said, poking fun at Bennett's thick glasses. "He sees more problems with his big eyes."

★

On his first patrol, on March 24, Alex expected the hundreds of loiterers to suddenly turn into crazed zombies like he had seen in movies. Instead, the young soldier Neary paraded through a fawning crowd. All the locals knew exotic Yusef, whose Arabic was so good the rumor was he hailed from Kirkuk.

Major Mohammed rolled his eyes at the scene. But then he said seriously, "It was not like this even two months ago. The people know us by name, and they know what we do."

A shaken old woman approached Mohammed. "My son is missing!" she said.

"I will find him, Mother, if it is God's wish," Mohammed told her.

"He is my only boy, *saydi*. He must come back to me," the woman replied.

Mohammed formed the patrol into search teams to find the boy. Alex asked him if he had permission from the Americans to change the original plan, which was to look for IEDs. He thought Mohammed would extinguish his cigarette on his tongue.

"This is more important than finding another IED," Mohammed said, cutting him short. "And never again question me, child."

A jundi found the missing boy playing in the Christian neighborhood. Major Mohammed walked the most densely populated route back to the child's house for maximum effect, and after a gentle scolding delivered him to his mother, who was waiting on the street. A bystander warned Mohammed not to take the same route back to the ASP, because an ambush awaited. Other men gave similar warnings and pointed out a specific house. Mohammed tapped his chest as a sign of sincere thanks and charged into the house with his men.

A young man made a dash for the back door. He was corralled by the jundis, who dragged the suspect across the marble foyer and propped his chin on a cement step. Another jundi handed Mohammed a video camera and a box of fresh shotgun shells. Mohammed sucked the back of his teeth and pressed Rewind. On the tiny video screen were three men, including the suspect, ranting about Shiites.

The jundi charged with guarding the front door leaned back inside the house to catch a glimpse of the video. Boz grabbed his shoulder and cursed the jundi until he was down on one knee. Alex was stunned by the American's profanity, unsure what to translate. Mohammed rendered his dilemma moot by slapping the jundi.

"Maybe they'll figure out how to pull proper security if we stick 'em in the guard towers when they're not out patrolling," Boz suggested as punishment.

"The vehicles have made them lazy," said Mohammed. "We'll walk home."

Boz laughed. "That's even better."

The column plodded up ASP Hill even as the prisoner rode in the Humvee's backseat, guarded by Alex. The weakest jundis fell back near the crest of the hill, where the wind didn't blow and the dust was thickest. Boz and Mohammed could be heard cheering on the hacking laggards like sheepdogs.

"You ever hear of good cop, bad cop?" Huss asked Alex. "It's a game American police play where one cop acts mean to drive the bad guy into the arms of the good cop. Boz and Mohammed are good at it."

"They do good cop, bad cop?"

"Bad cop, bad cop," said Huss.

Mohammed, Boz, and Alex talked to the suspected jihadist for an hour before setting him free, having decided he was just a young kid caught up in all the hate, with no charges that would stick when reviewed by American lawyers.

"Certainly lawyers do not know better than you who is guilty!" exclaimed Alex in Arabic.

Mohammed had him translate that for Boz, to include him, then smiled mischievously. "But, Alex, do you not know that this entire war is to enrich American lawyers? They cannot convict or they will have no job. Ask any jundi!"

★

The day after Mohammed made 4th Company walk home, his deputy, Lieutenant Abbas, lingered at the front gate, late for patrol. He wasn't wearing his body armor and Huss wasn't in the mood for private admonishment.

"Alex, tell this officer he has five minutes to find some armor or I'm going to lose my temper," Huss said, suppressing his rising anger.

Embarrassed to be called out in front of his men, Abbas addressed Huss directly. "Major Mohammed does not patrol in armor."

Huss said, "You couldn't fill Major Mohammed's jock, let alone his uniform."

Alex was unfamiliar with the men and softened each verbal blow. He translated: "You are not Major Mohammed and that is not his uniform."

"You are not in charge of me," said Abbas.

"Keep pushing me and you'll find out who's in charge, Lieutenant, Darwin style. You're supposed to be setting an example. You're about to become the example."

Huss stormed off and completed his radio checks. He returned to the huddle to find Abbas strapping on armor he'd taken from a jundi in his patrol formation. It was the most blatantly selfish thing he'd ever seen an officer do.

"We have a patrol to do, God willing," said Abbas.

Huss exploded. He chased the terrified lieutenant all the way back to his room, screaming so loudly that the men in the Horseshoe rushed to man the perimeter defense in T-shirts and boxers, convinced insurgents were finally attacking.

Huss triggered one emotion in the young terp Alex: fear. When he translated something unpleasant for Huss, it was like gingerly cutting the wire of an IED. In Alex's mind, Roberson fell into the same general category, but Huss was touchy-feely by comparison. The XO was a man apart. He rarely exchanged pleasantries with the Iraqis to solidify a bond. He appeared to have an entirely different hierarchy of needs from the others. As Neary once said, "When they built Roberson, they left out a chip."

On Alex's second patrol with Roberson, the brooding American noticed a tank rumbling along Route Michigan. He jogged after it and fell in behind as if on a morning formation run. Alex knew his job was to shadow the senior advisor on patrol, but this was too much, even for someone who was desperate to prove himself in a scrap. The rest of the patrol halted in their tracks, staring after the XO as he disappeared in the mirage.

"Should I follow him?" Alex asked.

"Not unless you want to die," GQ said.

"Where is he going?"

"That is a question for God," GQ replied.

Roberson ran alone for more than two kilometers, waving good-bye to the tank driver when he reached the 611 Bridge. He took in his dangerous surroundings. In front of him, Sadiqiya loomed, home to the best sniper in the area. On Route Michigan, he could see the noses of civilian cars inching back onto the road to check if the monster tank had passed. It was a little over two kilometers back to the friendly patrol. Temperatures approached 100° in the shade and hundreds of curious townsfolk were staring at him—a short adventure befitting a warrior king. Hooah.

When Roberson jogged back to the waiting patrol, Alex offered him a two-liter bottle that was splashed across his face then inhaled in great sucking gulps and tossed into the Humvee where it rattled, empty.

"Ready to roll?" said Roberson.

"GQ and his men are ready, sir," said Alex. "How far did you go?"

"Down to the 611. Nice this time of year."

Joining the patrol file behind Roberson and GQ, Alex was left to ponder his own fortitude. It was like being called up from a neighborhood soccer team to the national squad. How could he steel himself to act as did these men? Alex later learned that in combat you had to believe you were the toughest son of a bitch on the battlefield, that every other man relied on your sword and smarts, so you couldn't let them down . . . while also counting on someone tougher always being on your side.

Alex was glad Roberson was on his side.

The younger advisors themselves thought that Ranger Danger was reckless. Roberson sometimes patrolled the perimeter wire alone at night, setting trip flares and sitting on the hill overlooking the sleeping city like a wolf for hours at a time. Troster was known to do the same thing, but it was understood the commander did it to clear his head.

Roberson puzzled the younger advisors, but the older soldiers accepted the XO's peculiar behavior. Huss told Alex that on one patrol, while waiting for EOD, Roberson had stripped off his armor kit and reclined on the hood of the Humvee.

"Why does he do these things?" asked Alex.

"I think he does 'em partly to send messages the best way he knows how," said Huss. "But mostly he does it because he can."

"I do not understand."

"Alex, I've been in the Army for thirteen years, about the same as Roberson," said Huss. "He does it because up here, he's free."

★

If Roberson represented America's savage and unrelenting power, then Blakley, like most medics, stood for its conscience. For protection he carried an

M-4 carbine—but like Major Mohammed always said, Doc's real weapon was a medical kit.

Blakley was easily the most popular man in the team. The Iraqi officers sought his advice in their own subtle way, like drunken guests approaching a surgeon at a cocktail party. But the jundis approached Doc at all hours, queuing in front of his door morning and night as if waiting for an autograph. They raised their shirts, and hacked, and held their eyelids open even as Blakley trudged back to the Horseshoe after an exhausting patrol. One fragile jundi the advisors called "Mr. Jeebs"—who looked either fifteen or fifty, depending on the light—grew dependent on Doc Blakley, complaining of daily migraines that Doc eventually cured with Tic Tacs.

"You are like my father, Blakley," said Mr. Jeebs.

"But you are older than I am," said Blakley.

"A father in my heart, I mean."

The other advisors ribbed Doc, but with respect because he constantly sought to go outside the wire. Troster needed him to reform the Iraqi battalion's broken medical operation and wanted Blakley to focus on training a solid staff of Iraqi medics who could treat their own jundis. But he understood better than anyone the feeling of inadequacy that came from watching teammates roll out on patrol twice as often as he did.

On patrol in late March, Alex noticed Blakley bent sideways, resting the lower edge of his torso armor on his hip. He hadn't yet regained all the strength in his trapezius from the sniper shot, and the heavy vest rubbed against the knobby wound.

Three boys approached and Doc waved them over, asking them their names in Arabic to take his mind off the throbbing pain building in his shoulder. He scanned their bodies and teeth while he chatted. Then he showered a handful of Cheerios into each of their cupped hands, tossed his meal packs, and stepped back to watch the joyful fireworks display.

A small crowd gathered. Everyone knew Doc by name. They asked him to visit a diabetic man on the verge of collapse. The Iraqi soldiers loved his particular brand of American counterinsurgency because Blakley provided something the insurgents could not. The patrol was diverted. Blakley stabilized his patient, but without insulin the prognosis was poor. So he paid for the drug himself, using an Internet mail-order company. Few advisors understood why. There were hundreds of ailing people in Khalidiya and Abu Fleis, and other ways to get the prescription, like the black market in Baghdad, but Doc dug into his own pocket.

Alex understood. In the same personal manner that Roberson chose to impart lessons, so too Blakley was signaling. What each member of the audience gleaned was up to him. To the jundis the XO was a silent, swaggering

American fighting man and Blakley was a brilliant scientist and an ambassador of decency to Khalidiya.

During a visit to his guardsmen in Anbar, Indiana governor Mitch Daniels asked to meet Blakley personally so he could present the Purple Heart to his fellow Hoosier. A photograph was taken for the Indiana papers.

Another soldier might have used the wound or the attention as a plane ticket home. But Blakley was embarrassed to receive the same award for a clean-through gunshot wound as Watson got for nearly dying. After the ceremony, Blakley shoved the medal in his sea bag and never spoke of it.

11

The Kidnappers Are American

★ ★ ★

March–May 2006

O nly the flies stirred on Market Street. It was March 28, and by noon the temperature in Khalidiya was over 85°. Winter seemed to have disappeared overnight. The suddenly hot sun drove most people into the houses of wealthy friends with air-conditioning. Springtime also meant sandstorms, called *shamals*—thirty-meter walls of dust and pebbles that came out of the desert northwest like airborne tidal waves and turned the city orange until the next hot, clean wind.

Major Mohammed was cautiously walking on a deserted section of 20th Street. Behind him, two brand-new Iraqi Humvees crept forward, surrounded on all sides by jundis who were sweeping for mines, determined to prevent any explosion that could damage their precious new vehicles. Several jundis had developed guttural coughs that echoed on the abandoned street. Doc Blakley had nicknamed the sickness the "Khalidiya krud," a flu that was embroiled in the shamal winds and exacerbated by unacclimatized bodies leaking sweat to fight the newly recharged heat.

Approaching Market Street, Mohammed halted the patrol by sticking his clenched fist into the air. He went forward to check the intersection. Over the past few weeks, several shops had reopened in Khalidiya. The most striking was the bridal store on the corner of 20th and Market, one of the most repeatedly mined corners in all of Iraq, with more than twenty explosions in the six months since 3/3–1's arrival. A dusty wedding dress stuffed with fabric twisted in the heat like a scarecrow.

"Look at that. A beautiful woman makes men careless. That is why I picked an ugly wife," Major Mohammed joked with Troster, who had

166

come forward to check his progress. "Still, good things are happening in Khalidiya."

There came a high-pitched whistle from deep inside a nearby bodega housed in a cement garage. Two young men were tucked back in its corners where it was cool. They tentatively moved out of the shadows to inspect the patrol.

"Major Mohammed, you have Humvees? Iraqi Humvees?" one of the men asked.

"They are giving me fighter planes next," said Mohammed, thumbing Troster.

"Is this true, Uncle?" the man asked Troster, smiling. By April, the curious locals knew 3rd Battalion well and had nicknames for many of the advisors. "When do we get Humvees?"

"You ask many questions, but you never give," said Mohammed, moving on.

"Wait, Major Mohammed!"

The young men pulled Mohammed into their store. Using a pencil on their shop wall, they outlined a supposed ambush awaiting the patrol just a hundred meters away.

"There are two bombs," they told Mohammed. "One in the sand and one in a white Volkswagen Passat. When it explodes, they will shoot."

"Who?" Mohammed pressed.

The boys looked at each other and shrugged.

Troster and Mohammed peeked around the corner of the garage onto Market Street. There was indeed a white Volkswagen parked in front of the abandoned hospital.

"No dust," said Troster. "Someone parked it recently."

"The people are coming forward," said Mohammed. He wheeled around and gave a series of hand and arm signals to the jundis, who crisply formed a perimeter encircling the Volkswagen at a safe distance. Mohammed and Troster found cover in a nearby garage.

Rivera, who was driving the advisor Humvee, turned off the jammer to get a clear radio signal to reach EOD. A large mine exploded in the sandy wash Troster and Mohammed had been standing on minutes before. The geyser squirted seven meters high. The bomb was the same triple artillery shell design that killed Beery. The men flopped facedown, tucking their extremities into their body armor like turtles in a hailstorm as the sand swirled across their necks and into their nostrils.

Their ambush blown, a group of distant insurgents fired off a few magazines toward the Market Street intersection and fled into Sadiqiya. The biggest jundi in the battalion, Hater, rallied a squad and chased the enemy on foot. Troster was impressed with their tactics. The jundis remained spread out, bounding in small groups. When they crested the hill at the top of Market Street, where you could see into Sadiqiya, a short firefight erupted.

"The jundis look good!" Troster commented.

"I'm going with them," Mohammed said. "You deal with EOD."

"My pleasure," Troster replied.

Troster jogged over to the advisor Humvee, which had remained parked fifty meters short of the intersection alongside the Iraqi Humvees. Rivera told him it would be about an hour until EOD showed up to check the Volkswagen for bombs. Across from the Humvee, the blue aluminum door of a garage shop clattered open. The jundis guarding the perimeter raised their weapons and shouted. A man came out of the garage with one hand in the air and the other holding a red plastic chair. He set it up in front of his shop and sat down, as if setting up for a school play held on a lawn. Soon others joined him.

"What are they doing?" Rivera asked Alex, who was also sitting in the Humvee.

"Guess they want to see the bomb explode," said Alex.

"Someone in that group of bystanders paid for it, and maybe even planted it. He just wants to get his money's worth now," Troster explained. "We're getting more and more intelligence, but we're still dealing with low-level snuffies. What we need is to get some bosses on the payroll. The higher you go, the better the information."

"You're talking sheikhs," Rivera commented.

"I would start with imams," said Alex. "The only sheikhs worth talking to are on the Khalidiya Tribal Council, and they are hidden. Many others call themselves 'sheikhs' because they have money, probably from the terrorists. They will not help us because they want to get paid. But imams have the power. If the people are showing respect, one might help us."

"You know a lot already."

"I am an observer," said Alex. "And you told me my job was to listen, sir."

"Find out what the company commanders think about approaching the imams and get back to me in a few days," Troster said. "It's time for a push."

Hater's band of exhausted jundis returned with Mohammed to the Humvees after an hour fruitlessly chasing ghosts across Sadiqiya. They accepted big water bottles and warm congratulations from Troster and Rivera for reacting so swiftly. The EOD team arrived from Camp Habbaniyah to the delight of the crowd, which was now lining both sides of the streets behind the Humvees, hoping to glimpse the action.

The Marine EOD chief asked Troster to shoot the windows out of the Volkswagen so his robot could peek inside with its telescoping remote camera. Troster and the other advisors were happy to oblige. It felt good to shoot. Their magazines were packed with tracer rounds at the top, which left hot red contrails to help guide the jundis onto targets. The thin rounds punched burning holes in the Plexiglas until it caved in.

"Sir," Alex interrupted, "Hater wants to shoot. Can he?"

Troster looked back at Hater, who was grinning. Getting replacement ammunition for the jundis was a paperwork nightmare.

"You can shoot, Hater," Troster told the jundi. "But promise me you'll find a weapons cache and replace your own ammo."

"I will get some!" shouted Hater, excitedly firing a string of bullets into the Volkswagen. The AK had a deeper report than the U.S. M-4 carbines, a rhythmic beat that the advisors could not help but cheer.

EOD's remote-controlled robot rolled up to the shattered Volkswagen, extended its camera neck, and peered inside. Four artillery rounds were wrapped in detonation cord. In September and October, IEDs were discovered only when they exploded. In April, thanks to local tips, the battalion found seven out of ten before they blew.

The robot dropped a chunk of plastic explosive into the car and the EOD Marines began the verbal countdown that the closest Iraqi bystanders mimicked, like spectators at a rocket launch. With ten seconds to go on the fuse, a large pack of dogs trotted happily through the patrol formation toward the Volkswagen. The Americans shouted and threw rocks to drive the dogs off. The jundis, who had no fondness for dogs, laughed. Sure enough, metal rain and clumps of hairy dog meat fell on Khalidiya. Children rushed from under awnings to snatch bits of hot aluminum. As the patrol left, teenage boys holding cell phones encircled and danced on the charred car, celebrating either insurgent bombing power, their participation in the bomb's demise, or another day survived in Khalidiya.

On the way back to ASP Hill, Alex hitched a ride with Major Mohammed to ask about recruiting high-level informants.

"The Khalidiya Tribal Council will approach us before we approach them," said Mohammed. "Finding them is like finding this country's soul. It may no longer exist."

"What about imams? I was talking to Colonel Troster—"

"You're a smart boy," interrupted Mohammed, "but do you think this is a new idea because it is the first the advisors have heard of it? Captain Dhafer and I have been working on Imam Mahish for three weeks now."

Mohammed's driver wheeled to the Bashir Mosque, located near a large Khalidiya elementary school off 20th Street. Mohammed popped out of the Humvee and led Alex to the rear courtyard of the mosque. A servant welcomed them inside. Mohammed hung his ammunition vest on a tree branch and left his AK-47 resting on a small cement bench on the clean slate patio.

"This is the polite thing to do," said Mohammed. "But Dhafer hates to come inside without his weapon. Mahish does not mind it because Dhafer has himself removed so many mines on the school grounds that the children call him 'Captain Bomb.'"

"Without EOD?" asked Alex.

"Yes. Dhafer knows what he's doing, but if he does not, he has promised me his boots and the stout American helmet he wears," joked Mohammed. "Assuming they are not destroyed in the explosion."

Imam Mahish appeared in the rear doorway. He wore a clean dishdasha and a gold watch. Mahish steadfastly preached against the American occupation but was gradually coming to accept the presence of Iraqi soldiers in Khalidiya. He was 3rd Battalion's first well-placed informant.

Mohammed embraced Mahish and tossed his head at Alex. "Tell this young interpreter what you think of me and my jundis."

"I don't like you," said Mahish. "But you are the enemy of my enemy."

This attitude was considered liberal in Khalidiya. Mohammed and Dhafer had wooed him by plucking bombs the insurgents planted on his block and encouraging their jundis to buy goods from the Bashir congregation. When Mahish's first tips trickled in, naming mine diggers but not the bomb makers, Mohammed and Dhafer swiftly arrested the accused. Mahish was impressed. He promised bigger fish in the future.

Upon his return to ASP Hill after the short visit, Alex briefed Troster, who brought Roberson into the conversation.

"Think Mahish is using us to settle scores?" Roberson asked.

"In the drug war, the best scoop comes from rival gangs," said Troster. "But Mahish has some *wasta*. If he becomes a true ally, we need to locate some dollars, give him a service contract or two, and expand his power base. That will lead to better tips."

★

The American military had other ideas. On April 2, five days after the encounter with the Volkswagen car bomb, Troster sat on his cot in the Horseshoe listening to radio traffic from Boz on patrol over the steady roar of the air conditioner, which by then was running at maximum fan at all hours.

Outcast Actual, this is Outcast Bravo. We got a big problem at the Bashir Mosque, Boz transmitted.

Troster hadn't heard explosions or gunfire. He asked for clarification.

We got a mini riot going down here on 20th Street. People claim that last night Sheikh Mahish, his sons, and maybe some other relatives were snatched from their home. Some people are saying he might be dead by now. They are highly pissed. Over.

Troster stomped his boot on the cement floor in anger. After Alex's visit with Mahish, all the Iraqi officers in the battalion knew about the superb source, and last week over dinner Troster had lectured them not to visit the mosque so often on patrol, tipping off the insurgents. Now Troster knew he'd been murdered.

Any information on the insurgents who took him? Over, Troster said.

Boz transmitted, *That's the thing. The kidnappers are American. Over.*

★

In Iraq, America's special operations forces roamed the country killing or snatching the most-wanted insurgents at night. These "Superfriends" executed the toughest missions. Coddled by high command and given the best resources, spec ops garnered coveted air cover anytime they left the wire, protection rarely provided to Troster's team and its battalion of Iraqi soldiers.

Air support from spec ops could mean one aircraft per infantryman, including Blackhawk transports, minibird command helicopters, Apache and AC-130 gunships, F-15 fighter-bombers, and Predator drones. Advisors joked that their "air cover" was a sleepy jundi sitting on the hood of a Nissan.

The advisors didn't care about the disparity in support so long as the Superfriends stayed out of Khalidiya. Several times over the past six months, however, U.S. high command had ordered 3/3–1 to abandon night patrols and withdraw to ASP Hill on short notice with no information. This greatly embarrassed the Iraqi officers. On the hill, the Iraqis and advisors sometimes gathered on the Horseshoe roof after receiving these orders. Together they listened to the breaching explosions when suspects' doors were blown open by the Superfriends and the heavy chopping as American helicopters whisked captives to Baghdad. But neither the advisors nor the Iraqi soldiers ever learned who was targeted in Khalidiya or why, and this hurt their credibility in town.

Hearing Boz's last transmission, Troster rushed to don his kit. Alex was always the first one dressed, and he was standing next to an idling U.S. Humvee.

"Captain Dhafer is heading down to calm the crowd, sir," said Alex.

Sliding into the driver's seat, Troster blurted, "General Zilmer's main effort in Anbar is Iraqi force development. So how the hell is 3rd Battalion brushed aside to capture one man we could have arrested ourselves?"

"Why would we arrest Imam Mahish?" asked Alex.

"That's my point. The men in black didn't know Khalidiya from KFC. They have no stake in the local fight. Now our boys have to clean up the mess."

"From what I have seen, sir, Khalidiya is too messy to clean," said Alex, who was still struggling with colloquialisms and imagined a group of U.S. soldiers going through town with trash bags.

Troster followed Captain Dhafer's Humvee into Khalidiya. The protest had grown in size, an angry anthill of men who pounded on the hoods of their Humvees demanding that Mahish be returned. People were prepping for a citywide strike. There was talk of rioting. Troster and Dhafer ducked inside the relative safety of the mosque courtyard where the imam's wife and daughters set upon them.

"Why did you take him! As God knows, you have no right!" they screamed.

Dhafer calmed the wailing family and touched his mustache as a sign of sincerity. "We will demand the immediate release of Imam Mahish, as is God's will. We will not rest until this son of Iraq is back home. This is our first mission now."

As they rushed back outside through the gauntlet toward the idling trucks, Dhafer said, "This is a great opportunity, sir."

"To get ourselves killed, you mean?" asked Troster.

"To demonstrate the power of 3rd Battalion to the people."

"What if we don't get him back?"

Dhafer smiled. "Then I am still a liar and you are still a bad guy."

★

Troster took the problem to the 3rd Iraqi Brigade advisors on Camp Habbaniyah. Lieutenant Colonel Zientek was busy battling his own fire. His brigade had television access and had awakened to reports that U.S. Special Forces killed Shiite worshippers during an overnight raid on a Baghdad mosque. The Iraqi brigade's officers were sulking, unable to focus.

Zientek added Troster's request to the list. "You have any idea why Mahish was snatched?"

"Probably a special operations source that wasn't properly vetted," said Troster. "Gangs snitching on rivals is nothing new. Could be another sheikh set Mahish up. I wouldn't be surprised if the snitch has insurgent ties."

"Who doesn't?" said Zientek.

Zientek sent a request to higher headquarters warning that if Imam Mahish was not immediately released, "irreparable damage will be done."

Troster did not expect a swift release, but two days later Mahish and his sons returned home via helicopter. The first 3rd Battalion patrol appearing in Khalidiya after Mahish returned was invited to an evening celebration in the mosque courtyard. That night, Troster, Dhafer, and Lieutenant Colonel Fareed, the battalion XO, drove down to the Bashir Mosque, where they were treated like kings.

A lamb was killed and roasted by giggling boys who looked as happy to eat fresh meat as they were to see the patriarch. Mahish warmly greeted the trio. "I am told that I must thank you for freeing me," said Mahish, taking the large plate of rice, raisins, and pistachio nuts Lieutenant Colonel Fareed had brought from ASP Hill.

"You are an important man," said Troster, who doubted he had anything to do with the release. Prisoners were snatched up and spit out every day in Iraq.

"In the name of God we were determined to free you," said Fareed.

"We are a team," said Dhafer. "We need more teammates."

"You have my thanks. You did this thing for me, Uncle?" Mahish asked Troster.

"As Lieutenant Colonel Fareed said, the 3rd Battalion wanted you free. Here you are."

"Under God's eyes it is most impressive, what you have done. We will remember this day when there was justice," said Mahish.

They broke bread and drank soda from small paper cups stenciled with flowers. In the corner of the courtyard, an old woman splashed the lamb with palm oil and the flames rose up and blackened the carcass while the boys danced in a clapping circle and the girls set the table. The crackling lamb was dumped on a giant clay tray coated in rice and served to Mahish.

"Did they say why they captured you?" Troster asked.

"They told me they picked the wrong man," said Mahish. "But I have never before been on a helicopter!"

★

After Mahish returned, the intelligence continued to improve. On April 6, there came a good lead from a member of Mahish's congregation. Two brothers, Nathim and Dahid Jfaal, well known to 3rd Battalion because they were notorious beggars, were identified as expert bomb emplacers. They were rumored to be visiting their mother in Abu Fleis. Dhafer quickly organized a patrol to capture and question them. An hour later, in full daylight, he burst into their house as the point man, as was his habit, followed by six jundis and Neary.

The boys had been napping on the marble floor of the foyer for a quick getaway. They awoke too late, with Dhafer's rifle barrel prodding through their cobwebs. Following Dhafer's sharp barks of instruction were a series of increasingly louder screams as their mother and sisters came running downstairs. Jundis warned the women to freeze. The cacophony of terror and anger filled the entryway.

Neary lurked in the corner of the foyer like a ghost. Troster didn't want advisors wrestling suspects or ripping apart their pillows and mattresses looking for contraband on raids. That was the jundis' job. As a result, advisors were sometimes viewed as ombudsmen by the frazzled suspects.

Suddenly out of the kitchen came a third man, armed with an AK-47. Dhafer wrestled him down, trying to work free from his utility belt a small wooden club he'd purchased from a Baghdad cop. In the confusion, the Jfaal brothers grabbed a startled jundi's rifle barrel, twisted it into his arm, and fired. The jundi went down screaming. Hater leveled the brothers with consecutive punches. They fell like puppets cut free of strings, but the third man escaped.

"You're mine now," said Hater, straddling Nathim, who was older.

"I want an American!" Nathim screamed, eyes darting around the room.

The jundis dragged the brothers outside onto Abu Fleis Road, where Neary calmed their mother in Arabic. The old woman clutched Neary's forearm and dragged him to her boys, who were facedown on the street surrounded by a circle of jundis and, beyond it, a ring of men who had rushed outside to witness the arrest. The jundi who was shot was resting his forehead on the hood of a nearby Iraqi Humvee, holding his bloody arm, while a buddy poured water across the back of his neck.

"Yusef!" Nathim shouted expectantly. "Help me, Yusef!"

Neary turned red with rage, then roughly planted a knee in the back of Nathim's swollen neck, zip-tying his wrists before shoving his face into the road.

"But, Yusef, why? Why, Yusef? I am your friend!" said Nathim.

"You're not my friend!" Neary shouted in Arabic, working over Dahid now. "You were never my friend. You're a terrorist. If I see you in Abu Fleis or Khalidiya again, I'll kill you!"

"Yusef!"

The Jfaals were sent to the TF Panther jail, and the evidence against them was strong enough that they were sent to jail in Ramadi, but after that they disappeared from the records. There was no system in place for Iraqi units to track the detainees they had captured.

★

The next day was Friday, the day of rest and prayer. Mahish delivered a sermon asking his congregation to compare the jundis to the insurgents, and judge intentions for themselves. The Sunni people of Khalidiya and Abu Fleis initially regarded the Shiite jundis as territorial invaders sent by George Bush to punish them for Saddam's sins. Their battlefield agents were the American advisors who, like all the other U.S. soldiers they had encountered, lusted for dominance. But after gawking at hundreds of patrols, the townspeople knew these uniformed men as well as they knew the insurgents who slept among them. Now Mahish was giving them permission to pick either side.

Lieutenant Bennett was in an overwatch position near the Bashir Mosque with a 3rd Company patrol waiting for Mahish to dismiss his flock after Salat al Zuhur, the noon prayer. Leading the patrol was a serious Iraqi captain named Haadi who had recently joined the battalion, replacing Walid as 3rd Company commander. Haadi was the most religious officer the advisors had encountered, a devout Shiite with little sense of humor but a strong nose for local undercurrents, especially religious. Haadi was new to Khalidiya but liked to hang around the mosques on Fridays because he considered them excellent social barometers. His instincts were good. In the fall and winter, 3rd Battalion patrols had taken the most incoming potshots on Fridays, after imams had stoked congregational rage.

"Here they come," said Haadi, spreading his jundis out as the crowd spilled from the mosque and moved up the street to where the patrol was holding.

Children raced out of nearby houses to greet their relatives. Bennett pulled a small soccer ball from his day pack and juggled it a few times. Delighted, the children surrounded him, each asking for a turn to show off, until finally Bennett gave the ball to the smallest boy.

An old Iraqi man stood watching this play out. "Why do you play as a child?"

"Because we are all God's children," said Bennett.

"You are Christian?" the man asked.

"Yes." Iraqis tolerated Christianity and loved to talk religion, which made the others uneasy but suited Bennett quite well. "Descendants of Abraham, you and I."

The man chuckled. "Advisors are different from the others," he said, referring to units past. "They kidnapped us and destroyed Khalidiya. You help the children."

"Don't forget about your countrymen!" Haadi joked, eavesdropping.

"No one does more for the children than Captain Bomb," the man said coolly, referring to Captain Dhafer. "He pulls the bombs from our neighborhood. Who are you?"

"My name is Haadi. I will tell you about myself if you tell me about you."

Haadi pulled from his satchel the source sheets the battalion intelligence officer, Captain Zahir, had recently designed, and asked the man for information so he could fill out the card. A typical tip read:

Name: *None given*
If no name, state reason: *I am afraid for my life and for my family.*
Tribe: *Al Fahdowi*
Describe the activity that took place: *XX has been seen placing IED on Michigan Rd. Also provides shelter at his house for the terrorist groups in Khalidiya and Abu Fleis. They use guided rockets, RPGs and place IEDs. Most especially Austrian shells. When we saw that, the people of the area had a meeting and we threatened the terrorists that we would go to the IA to report them and the IED. They removed it at 0700.*
Where: *An IED had been placed behind my house, which leads to Abu Fleis, for the Iraqi and American patrol.*
How: *They met at 0900 at XX's store to collect information about the patrols and convoys and to coordinate with each other. Around sunset they wear masks and ride their bikes and start placing IED's on Michigan Rd toward Abu Fleis. They make ambush on patrols.*
What other information do you have: *They shoot RPGs from Al Amin school. They use sand mounds and piles of construction materials on the service road to Abu Fleis.*

!ALL OFFICERS MUST RETURN THIS STATEMENT TO S-2
WHEN COMPLETE!

Captain Zahir, called the S-2, had undertaken the monumental task of centralizing all intelligence at the battalion. It was a difficult goal because the Iraqi officers did not trust one another. They kept their intel to themselves so that a hard-won source was not used by others. As a result, there was no standard model for exploiting tips. Some officers visited their sources primarily to get picky advisors off their backs, proving they had a connection with the people. These officers often saved their few arrests for the afternoon so they could impress Lieutenant Colonel Falah at the dinner table.

Captain Haadi was willing to help Captain Zahir because he believed his fellow captain was competent and would not trade source information for favors from other officers. When Haadi got to the battalion in early April, he was surprised they did not track detainees, or keep a map of human contacts. Haadi thought Zahir might finally build a coherent picture of the local enemy network, especially with well-connected informants like Mahish. Haadi jotted down the information the old man gave and then let Bennett play soccer for a few more minutes before calling an end to the patrol.

During his turnover, Captain Walid had told Haadi to beware the Americans' intentions, which were all over Khalidiya in the form of bullet holes. Watching Bennett, Haadi was sure that in their hearts they meant well.

"You and Blakley can start an orphanage, Lieutenant," Haadi said.

"I've thought about it," said Bennett, wiping sweat from his face before replacing his thick glasses. "Believe me, I have."

Back at the ASP after the patrol, Zahir took Haadi's informant tip sheet and studied it, deciding if any information belonged on the large poster board he was building. It reminded Troster of the murder-tracking whiteboards found in most homicide divisions of small U.S. police departments.

Zahir never got to build his board. He was fired by Falah within the week because of two bizarre incidents. On April 9, a drugged-out jundi hallucinated on a patrol, zigzagging across Khalidiya like a dying chicken. Troster examined the crazed soldier's dilated pupils and recognized hard-core narcotics use. The jundis drove their babbling peer back to ASP Hill, where Colonel Falah determined that he belonged in jail. In the New Iraqi Army there was no such thing as an enlistment contract or a military justice code. So Falah caged the man for a few days in a bunker and released him on Route Michigan to find his way back into civilian life.

On April 10, another jundi who had been complaining of stress and nightmares sprinted out of his ASP bunker, ducked under the barbed wire, and ran into Khalidiya. He disappeared. The Iraqis chased him on foot and in Humvees for hours, calling his name like a search party looking for a lost child in the woods. No local admitted seeing the soldier. Within days, a DVD of his execution by AQI was distributed throughout Khalidiya. On the video, the torturers demanded the names of Major Mohammed's sons and father, his military background, and his patrol schedule. Then they drove nails into the jundi's head and cut off his genitals.

"They're trying to kill you!" Alex warned Mohammed.

"It is war, and everybody is trying to kill everybody," said Mohammed. "The real lesson is that the enemy is scared."

Falah called Troster into his office and announced he was firing Zahir, who was a favorite of the advisors because of his intentions of diagramming the insurgent network. "Why are you firing him?" asked a stunned Troster.

"I fired Captain Zahir because he wasn't doing his job," said Falah. "Same as when you fired your first XO."

"Zahir was trying to wrestle the information out of the company commanders and centralize it in the intelligence shop, where it belongs. What you really mean is that the company commanders didn't like it. So you fired him."

"No, this is not the case. After the first jundi was using the drugs, I gave Captain Zahir a warning. Then another jundi goes crazy. He knew nothing about this problem, yet he called himself the intelligence officer? Where is the intelligence?"

Troster wanted to punch Falah. "I've been fighting drugs for two decades. This battalion does not have a drug problem. But let me understand something. Colonel, are you saying the job of the battalion intelligence officer is to spy on the jundis instead of spy on the insurgents?"

"I am saying Captain Zahir didn't do his job."

★

Fortunately, Zahir's dismissal did not interrupt the trending information flow. On April 11, with their newfound tips, jundis arrested a pair of suspects on three consecutive patrols, a feat Major Mohammed labeled an "irhabi kebab." Even the advisors were receiving tips. During a roadside interrogation of the driver of a suspicious van by Captain Haadi, a bystander sidled over to Roberson, who was alone watching an alley. The man began intimately toeing Roberson's calf.

The XO grunted and joined Haadi as he searched the van's trunk. The strange man followed, popped a hairy foot out of his sandal, and again tried to play footsie with the Ranger. Roberson wagged his finger in irritation.

The man giggled and chanced a quick brush with his fingers. Roberson blanched and called for Alex. "Tell this freak to stop touching me or it will end badly."

"Sir, he signals you. He has some information on bad guys."

Roberson growled, knowing how close he'd come to hitting the man and losing the tip. "Tell him to take it to the jundis next time. I almost caved in his face."

The tip was a good one. A mine was located and removed by hand by Major Mohammed, to shouts of encouragement from a group of local men. Seeking solitude, Roberson returned to his outpost at the alley entrance but soon got dragged into an argument between an overheated jundi and a sharp-tongued local man who was joking about the Sadiqiya Sniper. Sensing escalation, as Roberson jogged over to the angry jundi he raised his AK-47 high over his head like an axe. Roberson punched the jundi in the chest plate, sending him sprawling.

The talkative citizen stood over the winded jundi to add a final insult. But Roberson grabbed the man by the neck and sent him flying, too. Both men looked up at the big U.S. soldier from the ground, furious at each other and at him.

"Warriors do not use weapons on unarmed men," Roberson told the jundi. He reached out and helped the jundi to his feet, waiting until Alex finished the translation. "You are more powerful than him. You must show mercy."

He held the embarrassed jundi tight around the shoulders and wheeled to face the local man dusting himself off.

"Take a good look at this soldier," Roberson told the man. "He has the courage to defend this country so you can speak carelessly. Next time, keep your mouth shut."

★

On April 14, a faulty roadside bomb destroyed the water main in downtown Khalidiya. It was the first detonation in three weeks, the longest continuous stretch of unexplosive calm since 3/3–1 had arrived in Habbaniyah. GQ diverted his patrol to the blast site. Large bubbles of crud were forming as if in a volcanic pool. GQ waded into the soupy mess, feeling along the pipe until he found a valve. When the bubbles stopped, children in the crowd banged on pots with rocks to show their appreciation.

"Form a line, and we will give you the water from our bottles and canteens," said GQ, who had come to think of the locals as confused cousins for whom he was responsible. "We'll get this pipe fixed in a few days."

The crowd parted and a short, fit Iraqi man of about 45 in an expensive leather jacket talked his way past the jundis. GQ climbed out of the sludge to greet the man and noticed his well-trimmed beard and hair.

"Peace be upon you," said the man. "I am abu Yusef, and these are my people."

GQ recognized the name immediately. He couldn't believe it. Here stood the leader of Khalidiya's Tribal Council, a mysterious sheikh known in the community as Abbas and whom many officers considered a myth. Nothing happened in Khalidiya without the blessing of Sheikh Abbas, tacit or not. GQ was mortified to notice that on this momentous occasion his uniform was coated in mud. "I could do more if I knew who planted the bomb," he said.

Abbas helped GQ out of the pit and led him by the arm behind a house.

Three bodyguards in heavy coats followed them, immediately attracting a squad of jundis who started to frisk them.

"We have different protectors," said Sheikh Abbas. "But we are the same."

Abbas smoothly flicked his hand and the bodyguards faded back into the crowd. GQ smiled, and his jundis backed off, leaving the pair to talk in private.

"God does not want his people to live like this any longer. I would like to meet with the leader of the 3rd Battalion. Together we will bring security for the people, as is the wish of God the most merciful," said Sheikh Abbas.

GQ was astonished. Many of the shots and bombs he and his jundis endured had been triggered by Abbas's tribesmen, who did not espouse the radical views of AQI but had been sucked into its murderous wake. Now here was Abbas asking for a meeting!

GQ took a moment to compose himself. He was just a lieutenant, and he knew that if he said the wrong thing the consequences might be irreparable, but he was as close to the insurgency's senseless killing as anyone else in the battalion.

"To end it we need names," said GQ. "Not just promises."

"We will give you more than names. We will give you the terrorists," said Abbas.

"They are your men?"

Abbas smiled coldly. "Younger brother, tell your colonel that if I hear talk like this during our meeting, I will be insulted. When I say we will give you terrorists, as God instructs us to do, I mean we will hunt them down together. We know who they are. You do not."

Abbas disappeared into a group of well-heeled men who whisked him away in a nondescript Opel. Then several bystanders broke from the crowd to give information, one-upping each other in an attempt to deliver the toothiest rumors. GQ had never seen such a bold public display of allegiance. He and his jundis spent thirty minutes writing furiously, then sped back to ASP Hill where an emergency meeting of the Iraqi officers was called.

"This is the most important event in our time here," said Major Aamr. "We must listen to what Sheikh Abbas offers but be firm in our vision. We cannot hand Khalidiya and Abu Fleis from one enemy of Iraq to another."

"Imam Mahish vouches for him," said Dhafer. "He is willing to switch sides."

"Without conditions?" Aamr asked.

"Conditions will be better if we kill the al Qaeda terrorists," said Major Mohammed. "The tribes want their old life back. We guarantee nothing until there is security for the people. Remember, it is the people who pushed this thing, not the sheikh."

A meeting was arranged through Imam Mahish. For two days, the Iraqi soldiers rationed their food to save for the planned feast. Rumors swirled over the number of tribesmen under Sheikh Abbas's command, from a few dozen fighting-age men to several hundred.

Just after midnight on April 17, the day of the meeting, U.S. special ops raided Khalidiya by helicopter. A team of elite soldiers wearing night-vision goggles used explosives to blow down the courtyard gate and door of a house, but it turned out to be the wrong one. The raiding party embarrassed an elderly patriarch by rifling through his personal effects and shining bright flashlights in his eyes while he was pinned on his back before realizing their error. They took his household AK-47, permitted for personal protection, but offered no payment for the bungled raid. Moving swiftly to an alternate target, the Superfriends shotgunned the hinges of the back door and dragged a screaming 16-year-old-boy from his father's arms. They blindfolded the boy and shuttled him to the waiting helicopter, which roared over ASP Hill on its way to a secret location in Baghdad.

Several men in the Horseshoe were awakened, and they stood there in the darkness peering out into space as the beats of the rotor blades faded.

"You gotta be kidding me," said Troster. "Let's go get a damage report."

Lieutenant Khalid, Boz, and Huss suited up for the next patrol, which departed ASP Hill for Khalidiya at 0100 hours. As with the abduction of Imam Mahish, the streets were crowded with seething townspeople waving flashlights and homemade lanterns. After a few minutes of interaction, the Humvees were in danger of being surrounded. Thinking quickly, Khalid's driver, Private Crazy, cut down a side street and accelerated onto Route Michigan, where the crowd was reluctant to follow.

Outcast Six, it's bad down here, Huss radioed.

What are the people saying? Troster asked.

Superfriends kidnapped some high school kid named Mohamad. Beyond that, Alex says they're too pissed off to make any sense.

When the sun came up, Roberson accompanied Captain Haadi into Khalidiya to check on the atmosphere. Rocks were thrown at the Humvees from the school near the Bashir Mosque. Haadi parked the Humvees near Michigan, in case of emergency, and led Roberson and a few jundis on a stealthy track on foot to the mosque. Haadi had to beg his way inside to visit with Imam Mahish and emerged only minutes later.

"It is a disaster," Haadi told Roberson. "Mahish will not speak to us until Mohamad is returned, and even then he told me he doubts our ability to control Khalidiya."

At ASP Hill, Troster was furious when he got the full debrief. He wrote an official emergency request to be passed up the chain of command.

Whether his last memo even reached the special operations command in Iraq was doubtful. He considered hopping a flight to Baghdad where he would demand an audience with the commanding general, but he knew he was just one advisor of hundreds who struggled to come to terms with his increasingly sour view of his fellow U.S. forces. He drove down to Camp Habbaniyah, where he delivered the memo to Lieutenant Colonel Zientek.

"This is a huge problem, Jim. We're on the verge of a breakthrough," Troster told him. "Khalidiya and Abu Fleis have been cold for weeks as a result. I'm worried, if we don't get this kid back, and offer a big freaking apology, the zone will heat up again. Fast."

"You've been arresting quite a few suspects lately," Zientek said.

"All because the people are coming over. Now outsiders have jeopardized it. They haven't lived here for seven months. They have no loyalty toward the locals."

"I got it," Zientek replied. "And I agree."

Days passed but there was no sign of the 16-year-old Mohamad. Whether or not he was guilty, 3/3–1 was desperate to get him back to Khalidiya. His reputation on the streets had been scrubbed so clean he had become a saintly figure. His visage began to appear on posters and in chalk portraits on 20th Street. The high school headmaster started each day's lessons with a courtyard prayer for innocent Mohamad's return. The jundis had nothing on the kid to implicate him as a terrorist, so they were in no position to argue. Troster wasn't privy to special operations targeting intelligence.

Imam Mahish refused to speak to the Iraqi officers. The people of Khalidiya gave the passing patrols the silent treatment. Worse, Sheikh Abbas didn't appear at the scheduled meeting with the 3/3–1 officers, and no one in Khalidiya claimed to know him, let alone his location.

★

Three days after the special operations raid, the bombs returned. The new fleet of Iraqi Humvees was halved in under a week. On April 20, an explosion turned a Humvee on its side in Abu Fleis, wounding two jundis. On April 22, a bomb hidden under a flapping plastic tarp blew the front end off an Iraqi Humvee on ASP Road, fifty meters from the ASP gate. Miraculously, the jundi driver suffered only a bad case of hot foot. On the 26th, Troster and Roberson watched Major Mohammed's Humvee levitate after striking an antitank mine planted at the notorious intersection of 20th and Market. The planter had carelessly placed the mine on its side, so the blast acted like a propellant instead of a penetrating force, floating the Humvee on a cushion of air for a second before gravity slammed it back. Mohammed staggered out, and after checking on his dizzy jundis, kissed the Humvee.

Captain Dhafer managed to strong-arm a suspect name for the bombing from a savvy Market Street shoe vendor whose business had spiked during the calm period. An orphan had supposedly planted the big mine as revenge for the missing Mohamad, a classmate. When Dhafer arrested the orphan after school, he discovered a DVD. The boy and his friends were shown brazenly celebrating their achievement, digging in the fat mine as if pulling a classroom prank.

"Where did you get such an expensive mine?" Dhafer asked the orphan.

"It is not mine."

"I know it is not yours, you jackass," said Dhafer. "Who gave it to you?"

"I want to go to jail now," said the boy. "They will put my picture next to Mohamad's."

Dhafer shoved the boy into the eager hands of his jundis with instructions to treat him gently. The orphan was just a sheep. It was the wolves he was after, and he didn't know where to find them.

The bad times were back. It was popular again to take potshots at the jundis. During the last week of April, patrols took sporadic small-arms fire every day. The Iraqi officers responded by arresting suspects with minimal cause. Taking their cue, some jundis belittled the Khalidiya citizens and picked fights elsewhere. During a patrol in Sadiqiya, a jundi accused a TF Panther guardsman from Pyro of firing his rifle without provocation. The guardsman told him to shut his mouth. There was a brief scuffle and the guardsman got the upper hand, slapping and then twisting the teary-eyed jundi around and shoving him back into the arms of his comrades.

The fight didn't reflect 3/3–1's relationship with Pyro. Their patrols together had grown sporadic since the bombing that killed Beery—and the delivery of Iraqi Humvees, muting the need for armored transportation—but the jundis remained fond of the Pyro and its motley group of soldiers, like Specialist Prine who remained determined to patrol with their Iraqi partners. TF Panther seemed less enamored of its own transport unit.

In mid-April, Prine had accompanied a squad of jundis on a weapons cache sweep near Sadiqiya. A convoy from TF Panther arrived to reinforce the operation. One of their staff sergeants squinted at an American who was walking with a squad of Iraqis through a known ambush zone.

"Hey, who's that?" the staff sergeant asked Huss.

"That's Prine."

"I know it's Prine. How'd he get out here?" asked the staff sergeant.

"He rode out with 4th Company," said Huss.

"Fourth Company, as in the Iraqi 4th Company?"

"Today, yeah. He rotates."

"Well, how the hell did he get up to ASP Hill on his own?"

"Isn't that a question for you?" Huss asked.

After Prine gave evidence in the drop gun investigation, TF Panther punished the infantryman by removing him from Pyro and sticking the so-called media spy in the battalion operations center where they could keep an eye on him.

Prine did his job there but regularly went outside the wire with the Iraqis, determined to see combat. He was officially counseled and banned from participation on future Iraqi patrols, which his superiors told him were "too dangerous" because of the constant combat.

"You will go on patrols with U.S. soldiers and stay with the U.S. soldiers for the duration of the patrol," read the written reprimand in Prine's record book. "Concern for soldier welfare and safety is foremost responsibility for all NCOs and leaders in the Chain of Command."

"I reiterate my request to leave the TOC for duties more conducive to my abilities," Prine wrote in his response section, already plotting his next journey outside the wire.

★

In May, the bombs rolled in like thunderstorms. The motor pool on ASP Hill was overrun by shattered Humvees and Panhards that had been towed in from the field after explosions and dumped like bodies in a mass grave, streams of motor oil leaking in long strips of dusty gunk. Bits of Plexiglas twinkled in the sunlight. The temperatures were back up in the triple digits. Aided by Gentile, the Iraqi mechanics on the hill cobbled together broken drive shafts and patched incinerated floorboards with cardboard. When the Americans first bolted steel plates to their Humvees in 2004, they called it "hillbilly armor." It was lavish compared to what the Iraqis did to keep their vehicles on the road.

Still, when bombs detonated under Iraqi vehicles on May 9 and 10, Battalion 3/3–1 was down to a single operable armored Panhard. The other five were in the shop. All six Humvees were busted. New regulations barred the Iraqis from revisiting the wild days in their Nissan pickups. So GQ, who was leading a patrol the following night, planned for a foot patrol.

On the evening of May 11, jundis smoked and hugged each other for comfort as the sunset lost its color. A dozen jundis had been wounded by the bombs in the recent weeks. They asked Reyes, the terp who had once been a soldier like them, to wager the night's chances for enemy contact.

"We will be walking," said Reyes. "If you don't talk, they won't strike."

"Are you ready?" GQ asked Troster, who was escorting.

"It's your patrol," Troster replied. "We're ready when you're ready."

"I think it's good now," GQ declared.

GQ led his men into the darkness. Roberson was to walk with them; Troster drove the truck. As they navigated by moonlight, a huge firefight erupted across the Euphrates in 1st Battalion's sector in Jazeera, four kilometers away. The patrollers watched insurgent antiaircraft fire flickering above the river, coming toward them. The green tracer rounds seemed to close on them slowly, like glowing Frisbees. As they approached, the bullets appeared to suddenly accelerate, soaring overhead with sharp cracks as they zipped through the sound barrier. The patrollers dove for cover.

"What are they shooting at?" GQ asked.

"The moon," said Roberson.

"I think they shoot at me," said GQ, "because I'm better looking, even in the dark."

A swarm of outgoing red tracers from the 1st Battalion Marine advisors across the river answered the big insurgent gun, which was shooting at their base but hadn't found the proper elevation. Insurgents had launched a major attack against their brother Iraqi battalion. Roberson hopped to his feet and jogged back to the Humvee.

"All that firing may cover our movement," said Roberson.

"Walt, anyone tell you you're a glass-full kind of guy?" joked Troster.

"Nope."

Then everything went quiet.

The jundis moved quickly down the hill and across Route Michigan, then slowed their pace as they neared a school on Abu Fleis Road, a very dangerous area. Even the compression of the sand under their boot heels sounded loud. Roberson moved to the front of the patrol and Reyes the terp followed as if tethered to him.

A group of jundis switched on their flashlights to search for bombs along the levee. Roberson had an eerie premonition and strode over to the search party. Walking alongside his advisor, Reyes stepped over an antitank mine that was buried in the road.

In the dark, the insurgent spotter was a second late on the trigger. The explosion blew a steel penetrating plate, designed to rip through the underbelly of a tank, straight up in the air, but while it was too late to kill Reyes, the sharp droplets from the incinerated molten plastic mine casing shredded his arm. The blast wave sent him spinning in the air. Another jundi was blasted down Abu Fleis Road like a burning tumbleweed. Roberson suddenly felt like he was flying. He landed unhurt in a roadside culvert.

Talk to me, Walt, Roberson heard in his radio earpiece. It was Troster.

Assessing, radioed Roberson. He patted himself down but didn't feel any major holes. He was sure he'd been hit, but he didn't have time to pinpoint shrapnel wounds.

Two wounded. One jundi and Reyes, radioed Roberson. *That was an antitank mine. The Muj are up to their old tricks again.*

★

Roberson escorted Reyes and the badly bruised jundi to Troster's Humvee, and they raced to the hospital on TQ air base. The jundi needed a dozen stitches and Reyes was admitted for several surgeries on his burned arm. The advisors rubbed his hair and promised to visit as often as they could. In the hospital hallway, Roberson held his armor vest up to the fluorescent light, looking for leakage. Nothing.

The jundi's stitches were not high priority at the hospital. Roberson and Troster were told it was going to be about an hour, so they decided to sneak in a full meal before the TQ mess hall closed. They removed their fetid helmets and rolled their heads to work out the kinks of the day. Walking to the mess hall, they were intercepted by an irate Marine sergeant major yelling on the jog, "Stop right there, gentlemen! Where are your covers?"

Roberson immediately engaged. "About ten klicks up the road."

"Well, you have to have it when out of doors," said the sergeant major.

Roberson said, "Okay. Go get your body armor on, hop in the truck with me. We'll go up the road to where I live and you can show me how to wear a hat."

"Where do you live?" asked the sergeant major.

"On that hill. See that shadow on the skyline? It's nice. Come check it out."

The sergeant major demurred, but it wasn't the end of the TQ follies. The next day, Troster and Roberson returned to check on Reyes but were pulled over by MPs who chastised them for speeding and not wearing seat belts. It wasn't only difficult to stretch the nylon webbing across a full combat load but also potentially deadly if a gasoline bomb exploded.

Troster managed to wiggle out of any incident report by being friendly with the MP. Roberson sat there brooding.

"I'm starting to think it's me," said Roberson.

"It's not you. It's the difference between us and them," Troster replied.

"The thing I hate most about this war is the FOB. You see they had an Easter egg hunt a few weeks back? Good Lord, strike this madness down!"

Troster laughed. "Okay, Walt. Maybe it's a little bit you."

Roberson pulled out the waterproof notebook he kept in his uniform pocket. He jotted down a note on Reyes's condition and tallied the recent wounded in action.

"With all the injuries, the battalion's total strength has fallen big time. We're down in the four hundreds somewhere," Roberson concluded. "We need an infusion of replacements immediately."

In the nine months since arriving at Habbaniyah, Iraqi Battalion 3/3–1 had lost nearly a third of its soldiers to injury, death, and desertion. The leave block at any given time snared another 50 percent, leaving around two hundred jundis—about the size of a single U.S. infantry company—to patrol a combat zone befitting a fully staffed battalion.

"Anbar doesn't exactly make for recruiting poster material," Troster commented.

"We have to do something. According to this, 3rd Company has just twenty-two available jundis to patrol. As for vehicles, boss, we're fresh out, unless the jundi finds a magic carpet."

"We'll talk to Zientek and McNulty at the next brigade meeting on Camp Habbaniyah. You work the vehicles, I'll work the bodies," said Troster.

"Who'll work the miracles?" asked Roberson.

12

Running on Empty

★ ★ ★

May 2006

Lieutenant Colonel Jim Zientek was fighting three small wars that spring. As the senior advisor to the 3rd Iraqi Brigade, he supervised three battalion advisor teams, coached the Iraqi brigade commander, and acted as a bridge between the Iraqi and U.S. units. He felt like a new bouncer arriving at work to find multiple separate fights raging inside the bar.

In the farmlands of Jazeera, across the Euphrates, his 1st Battalion was mortared daily. Any patrol that ventured into the hinterland got ambushed. Insurgents regularly attacked the small Iraqi outpost. North of Camp Habbaniyah, his 2nd Battalion chased invisible ambushers around swampy palm groves that resembled Vietnam. On the south side of Route Michigan, his 3rd Battalion fought urban combat in Khalidiya and Abu Fleis. The 3rd Battalion had the most arrests of any battalion. Zientek was convinced that a local police force was needed to crack the insurgency in Khalidiya, but they had been driven out in the fall of 2003, when the police chief was assassinated and a car bomb leveled the Khalidiya station on Market Street, killing twenty-three cops and civilians.

The only police station left in the Habbaniyah zone sat a grenade's throw outside the east gate of Camp Habbaniyah on the edge of Coolie Camp. How many cops were in tiny Coolie Camp was undetermined because they never ventured into Khalidiya or Abu Fleis and they had no U.S. advisors. They were led by a corrupt chief named Shalal, a thickly built officer whose allegiance was suspect. After the police were pushed out of Khalidiya in 2003, a local Iraqi National Guard battalion was formed under Shalal and placed atop ASP Hill. One night in 2004, a flurry of gunfire erupted on the hill. When the firing subsided, Shalal showed up at Camp Habbaniyah in tears, claiming his guard force had fled after a heavy attack. The insurgents had stolen all of the battalion's weapons, provided by the Americans, including dozens of heavy machine guns. For his stout defense, Shalal was rewarded with the post of police chief for Habbaniyah District. As far as Zientek could tell, the only job Shalal had performed was staying alive.

Zientek had sent three separate memos requesting police presence in Khalidiya, but each time was met with nothing but commiseration from higher headquarters. There were no police in Khalidiya for the same reason that no man from the city had ever volunteered to become a jundi—the insurgents had such tight control that all the boys were either fighting for the other side or too terrified to oppose them.

Zientek and his advisor team's operations expert, Captain Drew McNulty, were in the 3rd Iraqi Brigade headquarters building on the morning of May 13 for the weekly brigade operations meeting, when representatives from the three Iraqi battalions and their advisors convened to discuss the state of affairs. The Iraqi brigade officers ostensibly ran the meeting, with advisors only occasionally weighing in, but in reality it was Zientek and McNulty's show.

Inside the brigade HQ sat a modest bank of Motorola radios that could have fit in the cab of an eighteen-wheeler. Across the room was a wooden vault stuffed with the encrypted electronics communications gear of the U.S. advisors. The Iraqi brigade radio operators only sporadically tracked the patrols of their subordinate Iraqi battalions, when patrol leaders bothered to tell them they were leaving the wire. To fill in the blind spots, McNulty and his operations team vetted every patrol ahead of time and required the U.S. advisors to send GPS location updates to ensure no patrol fell through the cracks. It may have been the Iraqis' ops center, but it was McNulty's house.

Zientek's decision to help run the Iraqi brigade instead of just advise it had come from within. When he and his team had arrived in Iraq four months earlier, they had been instructed by the advisor trainers at the Phoenix Academy to "work yourself out of a job" and "accept Iraqi solutions."

All of that collapsed in the reality of mentoring Iraqis in the middle of intense combat. Zientek doubted the Phoenix instructors understood just how ugly Iraqi solutions could be, especially when the Iraqis had no training by American advisors. Although battalion staffs like Troster's on ASP Hill remained fairly stable and built steadily upon a foundation of experience, at 3rd Brigade headquarters it was constant upheaval.

The 3rd Iraqi Brigade staff averaged a complete turnover every four months. By the end of their yearlong tour, the U.S. brigade advisors would have coached three separate brigade commanders, six intelligence officers, and seven operations officers. Part of the problem was that Iraqi officers paid for their promotions. Command of the 3rd Brigade came with a $10,000 price tag. Lesser promotions still cost several months of salary. At the top, Iraqi officers collected money from their families and friends, angled to move up into influential billets at every opportunity, and then repaid their debt once they consolidated power—and their own revenue stream. While the Ministry of Defense "screened" the newly promoted officers, a euphemism for running the payout tree from top to bottom, which took a couple of months, temporary officers were installed who were reluctant to issue any interim orders.

So Zientek's advisor team represented continuity in the face of continual upheaval driven by the corrupt Ministry of Defense. Zientek and McNulty chose to set the example, like instructor pilots with firm hands on the stick, rather than stand back and let Iraqis falter.

The meeting was starting soon. Zientek knew that Roberson and Troster wanted to talk about casualty replacements. Zientek walked into the U.S. vault and studied the 3rd Brigade casualty list from September 2005 to May 2006 on one of the computer workstations. The Iraqis kept their records on paper. Where the papers were was a mystery.

Every battalion was undermanned because the fighting had been hard and jundis did not sign enlistment contracts. They were free to come and go. Among the three battalions that composed the 3rd Brigade, the advisors estimated that over a hundred jundis had fled while on leave. For obvious reasons, casualties were highly correlated with desertions. The nine-month casualty figures were:

1st Battalion had 4 jundis KIA and 32 WIA
2nd Battalion had 6 KIA and over 20 WIA
3rd Battalion had 16 KIA and 34 WIA

Zientek had been asking U.S. training command for jundi combat replacements since his advisor team arrived in Habbaniyah in February 2006. After months of pestering, Zientek was told by Marine HQ in Fallujah to prepare for an influx of two hundred new jundi recruits on May 1. Sunni boys from western Anbar Province had been recruited as jundis and trained on Camp Habbaniyah. Zientek was thrilled to finally introduce Sunnis into the jundi ranks and thought they might better glean intelligence from the locals.

The U.S. training command considered the recruiting effort a monumental achievement and an indication that local sentiment was finally trending positively. Reporters were flown to the graduation on Camp Habbaniyah, including several Arab television news networks.

And then it all fell apart.

After the graduating on the morning of May 1, the recruits paraded past the reviewing stand, where an Iraqi officer read the duty assignments aloud. Two hundred of the new jundis were to remain in Habbaniyah with 3rd Brigade. The recruits rioted, having been led to believe they would return to their hometowns. Dozens ripped off their uniforms and stormed off the parade deck, a chaotic scene that was replayed for the next several days on Arab television.[1]

After the quitters arranged for transportation back to their villages, they went en masse for a final free meal at the Camp Habbaniyah mess hall. Several of them slandered the veteran Shiite jundi recruit training cadre eating in the corner with "their American masters." Hearing this, the jundis gathered outside the mess hall to teach a lesson in real combat. But their former recruits did not emerge. Inside, several recruits fell ill, and rumors of poisoning spread through the class. They ultimately called for an escort from U.S. advisors.

"I have bad news and good news, boss," Captain McNulty had told Zientek that night. "The bad news is, out of 200 Anbari recruits supposed to come to 3rd Brigade, 191 quit today. The good news is, 9 stayed."

"Nine? I was having a tough time dividing two hundred by three battalions. Now each gets three jundis and no one can bitch," said Zientek.

Iraqi replacements weren't the only problem. The advisor teams, which were too small to begin with, were undermanned as well. In the 1st Battalion team, five advisors had been wounded in action, including the team leader. The 2nd Battalion advisor team had two wounded advisors. And Troster's 3rd Battalion team had six wounded advisors, two of whom, Watson and Boiko, had been evacuated to the United States.

Zientek had sent a memo up the chain of command arguing that ten-man advisor teams were far too small for the job, and that when teams dipped down to six men they became "combat ineffective."

Troster and Roberson pulled up in their beaten-up Humvee for the meeting. Zientek remembered that Troster's team of reservists had twice dipped below seven advisors yet still patrolled constantly. But if Troster's team took just one more casualty, the remaining advisors would have to conduct twenty-one patrols every week, on top of radio watch, logistics runs, pre- and postpatrol maintenance, and six separate staff briefings. And that was running two-man advisor teams in a single Humvee, which was banned in most areas. Zientek let Troster slide because there was no choice. He didn't have enough people. Nobody did.

Troster stripped off fifty pounds of body armor so he didn't stink up the place, hung his rifle on a peg, and paired off with Lieutenant Colonel Zientek in one corner of the brigade HQ. Roberson pulled Captain McNulty aside to ask for a loaner Iraqi Humvee. He remained in full battle rattle. McNulty had interacted with Roberson more than a dozen times, but the Ranger remained an enigma.

"Why do I feel like you're going to return this vehicle with more than a few dents?" McNulty asked Roberson. "It belongs to the brigade commander's fleet."

Roberson said, "If it gets blown up, the Iraqi brigade commander, whoever he is this month, can tell everyone he's been to hell and back. A story's worth a promotion in this country."

"Ours too," McNulty reminded him. "I had a dozen Marines who fought their asses off in the Battle of Fallujah but were passed over for Bronze Stars in favor of staff officers."

"Hmph," was all Roberson said, but McNulty detected a hint of kinship.

They sat at the table in front of the large projector screen that displayed a digital map of the Habbaniyah area. McNulty chatted with the Iraqi officers taking their seats at the table. Roberson burrowed into his notebook, dismissing the brigade Chai Boy with the back of his hand.

Troster was wrapping up his discussion with Zientek. There were no available jundis, but Zientek was pushing for advisor replacements to lower the burden on Team Outcast. There was no prepared pipeline for advisor combat replacements—each augmentee was a back door arrangement, as Roberson had been.

"Aren't we supposed to have a police advisor team in Habbaniyah?" Troster asked.

"Before you have advisors, you need people to advise," said Zientek. "I've been asking for cops, Mike. If you guys arrest many more people, you won't need police."

"The jundis have become good infantrymen, but they don't have cops' instincts," said Troster. "I tell you, Jim, we were on the verge of something when the Superfriends kidnapped that kid. Now . . . guess we just keep fighting. If that's what we're doing. We don't have a confirmed kill yet. "

"Keep fighting. That's exactly right," said Zientek. "That's the message General Zilmer is sending, too."

A few weeks earlier, Major General Zilmer, who was in charge of all Anbar forces, and his pit bull deputy, Brigadier General Bob Neller, a stocky Marine who pulled no punches, had visited Zientek and McNulty on Camp Habbaniyah. They stressed that the advisors were the main effort in Anbar. Individual creativity was encouraged as long as it supported the main mission—relentlessly pushing the Iraqis forward.

"Keep the fire lit under the Iraqis," said Neller. "And if you see a nearby U.S. unit that's not cooperating, tell me, and I'll be the firestarter."

McNulty was tempted to bring up TF Panther, whose participation in joint operations with 3rd Battalion had regressed after the losses of Beery and McCaulley on the same terrible March day, but the guardsmen were departing in a month. In McNulty's experience, when a general mentioned fire, it meant whole forests, not a spark plug. So he had focused on growing Iraqi battle space. More kilometers of responsibility meant increased development. Zientek agreed. Shorthanded or not, the Iraqi battalions needed to be pushed.

When everyone was seated, the Iraqi brigade operations officer politely cleared his throat and said, "Third Battalion, the brigade commander is considering giving you responsibility for Route Michigan security when Task Force Panther leaves in two weeks."

The order blindsided Troster. He looked across the table at Major Aamr and Colonel Falah. They were dumbfounded as well. Securing Route Michigan was a huge task. Panther patrolled the highway with dozens of Humvees and Bradleys, plus seven main battle tanks. Although the four-lane road cut through 3rd Battalion's battle space, bisecting Abu Fleis and Khalidiya, the Iraqis would be hard-pressed to replace Panther.

Aamr and Falah had a terse exchange with the brigade staff officers that no terp in the room was willing to translate. All eyes fell on the Americans. Everyone knew that if Zientek and McNulty wanted it done, the Iraqi brigade commander would give the order. The four advisors excused themselves to huddle near the vault.

"We want 3rd Battalion to take a slice of Michigan," said McNulty.

"That's premature," said Troster. "Between K-Town and Abu Fleis, we're barely hanging on. Drew, we came here today to beg for bodies and trucks. Now you're giving us the toughest strip of territory in the valley?"

"Sir, it's got to happen eventually. General Neller will see to that," said the exasperated McNulty. "Everything takes months out here anyway. Let's just get the ball rolling."

"I'm here to tell you on behalf of 3rd Battalion that any such plan is premature," said Troster. "My position is no."

After the meeting broke up, Troster remained behind to speak with Zientek. "I know 3rd Battalion has to eventually guard Michigan," he said. "But we're short jundis and I have to back my Iraqis. Let's look for a workaround that enables them to save face."

"This isn't about you, Mike," said Zientek.

"Jim, the Iraqis know the advisors are running the show. Everything we do is high conspiracy. We have to transition that perception first."

"Fair enough. But change is coming, whether Falah embraces it or not," said Zientek. "Marine Battalion 3/5 is inbound to replace Panther. My hunch is that they'll be the partner the Iraqis have been asking for, but they're under the same orders to push as I am."

★

Back at ASP Hill that night, morale shot up. Troster had stuck up for 3rd Battalion. At dinner, Alex performed a skit retelling the staredown with higher headquarters—a routine discussion for the Americans but a feat considered supernatural by the überhierarchical Iraqis.

A small feast was prepared. A jundi had fished a fifty-pound carp from Lake Habbaniyah. The Iraqis slow-roasted the orange fish over a trash fire using a rifle-cleaning rod as a spit until the scales curled. They dug their fingers in through the skin and removed hunks of steaming meat for the advisors, who squatted to share a meal with their smiling comrades.

"In Iraq, you have not bonded until you pull goat," Alex told the advisors.

"Goat has to be better than this," said Boz.

"You don't like it?"

Boz considered his audience. "It is better than any meal except my mother's cooking. I'll get her to send you boys some cookies in a few weeks. Then we'll pull chocolate chips together. That's American bonding right there."

The jundis were pleased, and the group traded stories of combat deep into the night. Eight months into the mission, the advisors on ASP Hill were well respected by both the jundis and the officers, but every relationship suffers periodic mood swings. On an outpost in the middle of war-torn Anbar it was an emotional roller coaster.

In the Horseshoe courtyard, a rickety ladder led to the sandbagged rooftop observation post manned by napping jundis. In late May, the advisors accused the jundis of stealing hot water from the electric tank bolted to the roof. The Iraqi officers angrily defended the jundis, so Alex wrote an apology and went to Troster for approval.

"That sounds fine, Alex. Make sure the jundis know we were wrong," said Troster.

"Wrong for what you said or wrong about the water, sir?"

"Wrong about both," said Troster.

"Sir, the jundis did steal the water. They've been cooking and shaving with it for weeks. That's why it smells like rice," said Alex. "The Iraqi officers have been complaining."

"Why're they so pissed off?"

"Because you accused their men of stealing."

This first apology buoyed the Iraqis, but another was needed days later when Troster caught Lieutenant Baby Falcon Bez Boz using a cell phone on the roof of the Horseshoe, which was not allowed because it was an observation post.

Baby Falcon remained the worst officer in the battalion. Neary once had the misfortune of accompanying three of his patrols over two days. It was an unnerving experience. The lieutenant chose the most obvious routes. He sat inside his truck for long stretches, idly studying maps and gobbling yogurt while his jundis walked in circles. He refused to forge ties with the citizens. When Neary complained, Bez Boz accused him of lying. So Troster stole into Neary's Humvee at the last minute to observe a patrol, then stormed into Major Aamr's office to deliver the same critique.

"I will communicate this failure," said Aamr.

"Can we get rid of him?" Troster asked. "He's dangerous."

"No. It is impossible. He is rich. It is the Iraqi way, this thing."

On May 25, Troster caught Bez Boz sneaking up the ladder to use his cell phone again. "If I catch you with that phone, I'm going to shove it right up your ass!" shouted Troster.

"Careful, sir, he might like it," one of the advisors quipped.

Bez Boz complained to Colonel Falah about Troster's threat. Over dinner, the other Iraqi officers—who had been laughing at the exchange hours earlier—joined the ranks of the offended. They mashed their samoons into their chicken soup and conversed quietly in Arabic. Boz noticed the sullen mood at the table and asked Alex what was wrong.

"They say the advisors think they are gay," said Alex.

"That's not true," Boz protested.

"That does not matter."

That night Troster asked Chai Boy for a moment alone with Falah. Troster and Falah had grown tired of each other. Falah had recently complained to Lieutenant Colonel Zientek that Troster was undercutting his authority by visiting the jundis after patrols and hogging all the "good news."

"Lieutenant Mustafa [Bez Boz] tells me you wanted to shove his phone into his ass, and that he was a homosexual. Is this correct?" asked Falah.

"That was a figure of speech," said Troster. "The important thing is the policy."

Falah spoke good English but he used terps as foils. He spoke for a minute in Arabic. Alex translated, "Colonel Falah does not understand the difference in the speech. All Americans make fun of Iraqi men for being gay, and this hurts their honor. But it especially hurts when advisors do it."

Troster ignored Alex and spoke levelly to Falah. "Colonel, you and I both know that my men would die for your men and your men would die for mine. That incompetent lieutenant was wrong, so I lit him up. If you want to use the issue as a wedge between our units, that's on you. As for us, we'll be on the next patrol, warts and all."

★

On May 30, Captain Dhafer led a vehicle patrol into TF Panther's territory on the Budimnah peninsula to check some houses for weapons. The road into the peninsula was guarded by a small bridge that spanned a muddy canal. Approaching this choke point, Dhafer pulled his Iraqi Humvees to the roadside. Troster checked the radio jammer to ensure maximum electronic interference, passed the Iraqis, and parked in the middle of the bridge to stifle IED signals as they crossed. The Iraqi Humvees clattered across the wooden planks onto a road so littered with craters it looked like a moonscape. The Americans fell in trace, tailgating the Iraqis to push their electronic force field as far forward as possible.

Budimna was unusually quiet. Too quiet.

"Get ready," said Dhafer. "I think it is an ambush."

They felt on edge, but after two hours they still hadn't been hit. With the weapons sweep finished, Troster accelerated the Humvee into the lead and again parked on the bridge. The Iraqis passed. Troster's Humvee nosed forward, last in the file now.

A monstrous mine exploded behind them. Dirt clumps were still raining into the canal twenty seconds after the shock wave passed. Troster and Roberson dismounted to gawk at the huge crater. Dhafer and Hater came trotting back to look as well. The jammer had delayed the detonation just long enough.

"There's a defense contractor somewhere that deserves a kiss," said Troster, patting the jamming antenna like a pet dog.

"That's a little strong," Roberson replied.

A gray Opel rolled into the middle of a sandy intersection three hundred meters away. Passengers inside cracked their windows and fired clean their AK-47 magazines at the stunned group, who dove into a rancid irrigation ditch.

Troster and Roberson knelt up and in an instant had their rifle stocks tight against their cheeks. Mounted on their iron sights were ACOG four-power scopes they had borrowed from the brigade Marines. Troster shot first. Roberson's barrel followed the tracer path and he joined in. Their 5.56mm bullets flew under the high-flying enemy 7.62mm rounds and shattered the Opel's side windows. Captain Dhafer crawled to the lip of the gulley on his stomach and held back his trigger. The car slowly reversed down a gradual slope. Unwilling to give up their superior firing angle, the advisors stood bolt upright and continued the torrent of bullets.

The car lurched for safety behind a stand of date palm trees. Bullets followed like angry bees, sloughing the rear window. The car's spinning tires created a rooster tail of pebbles and dust. Then it was gone. The one-sided brawl was over in seconds.

The jundis formed a perimeter and shouted victorious catcalls into the deserted farmland. The only soldier who didn't celebrate was Hater, who couldn't believe the fight had ended before he was able to fire even one bullet. His safety had jammed.

He tugged at Troster's sleeve. "You shoot very good! Picture?"

The only soldiers who like pictures more than jundis are Marines, thought Troster. He took a few snapshots of the big jundi looking tough in the bottom of the crater. At six three, Hater was almost swallowed whole.

It was the battalion's first sustained gunfight—and probably its first enemy kill, though enemy casualties were unconfirmed. The advisors felt satisfied, but they didn't make too much of it to the jundis. On the road home, Troster said, "Your muzzle was right next to my ear when you opened up, Walt."

"Yeah, sorry about that, boss," said Roberson. "I was feeling it."

"I know what you mean. It's about time."

"Don't depress me," said Roberson. "We still have a few weeks to get some more."

"It's not about us. The key is developing the killer instinct in the jundis. But they're getting it, slowly but surely. They've come a long way."

"Unlike the Cowardly Lion," replied Roberson.

The Cowardly Lion was a new interpreter who had quit days after arriving at ASP Hill as a replacement for the wounded Reyes. He had earned his nickname by refusing to leave the Humvee during his first patrol. Harsh words from Huss blew the terrified terp out onto the street, where he wept openly.

"We are all going to die!" Joseph screamed.

"Hey, Lion, stop talking, buddy," Huss warned him. "Or I'm gonna make your prediction come true."

"We will die here!"

That night, the Iraqi officers who had seen *The Wizard of Oz* snapped their tongues when they heard the translation. They wanted their piece and acted out the scene where the lion weeps, to the great delight of the advisors. The little tribe had its own form of punishment that bolstered its underlying code.

In tears, Joseph had run into his room and scrawled a note to Troster that read, "I cannot do any more patrols because I am scary . . . I am a coward man." He left soon thereafter.

★

TF Panther finished its tour in early June. Iraqi Battalion 3/3–1 wasn't sad to see Panther leave and neither were the advisors, who had recently noticed a cardboard placard posted at a TF Panther observation post:

> Hit civ. veh w/fruit while driving—15 pts
> Get little kid to chase MRE on a string—20 pts
> Get cursed out in Arabic—25 pts
> Get "Damn, he's a pimp" picture w/two Iraqi women—15 pts
> Win hearts + minds then shoot them to shit—20 pts

The black humor could have been a product of the tough tour of duty the guardsmen had served. Ordered to police a sprawling, lethal sector with 25 percent less combat power than the previous active duty army battalion, TF Panther had been tested from the outset.

Summing up their accomplishments in their yearbook, TF Panther officers invoked numbers. Of the 1,500 detainees brought to Camp Habbaniyah, 750 were "processed," and 400 served "serious jail time." Guardsmen discovered more than 500 IEDs and disarmed 262 of them. The infantry platoons together performed over 400 missions, with tiny Pyro conducting 150 missions with the jundis alone.

More than "500 meters of concertina wire" and "60 tons of barrier material" were emplaced (some dividing Camp Habbaniyah from the Iraqi soldiers). Twenty-three tanks, five Bradleys, and countless Humvees patrolled "the most heavily IED'ed part of highway in Iraq."

Even in humor the commanders looked for tangible events. The base defense unit "successfully destroyed more insurgent sheep than any other unit." When it came to defeating the Anbar insurgency, however, progress was difficult to measure. Most U.S. unit staffs had difficulty articulating "success" in murky counterinsurgency to their troops, and the TF Panther staff was no exception.

"What have we accomplished? Accomplishments mean different things to different people," wrote the intelligence officer. "We must leave here knowing that we did make a difference. We may not see the fruits of our labor for months or possibly years to come, but we did make a difference."

The Panther executive officer invoked football, but in untraditional terms.

> If you read counterinsurgency doctrine, it states that it takes roughly eight years to defeat an insurgency. Using a doctrinal model and a football analogy, a realistic expectation of our time here was to advance the ball 12.5 yards on a 100-yard field. That is the measure of success. Did we advance the ball 12.5 yards, a little more than one first down? The answer to that question is yes.

The commanding officer was equally circumspect. His citizen-soldiers had volunteered when others in the guard hung back, let alone the U.S. citizenry.

> Fighting a war against terrorism is a long-term commitment and is fought on many fronts. We have fought bravely and sacrificed greatly on our front when it was our time to do so. Many years from now you can proudly tell friends and relatives that you were on the front lines of the war on terror.

As TF Panther packed up, Colonel Falah thought it would be good politics to award an American soldier an Iraqi medal for valor in combat. That would signal teamwork to the incoming unit, U.S. Marine Battalion 3/5—"Darkhorse"—his new partner unit. Falah did not know the TF Panther officers well, so he asked his company and platoon commanders to vote on bravery. They didn't choose an officer at all.

They chose lowly Specialist Carl Prine.

Falah presented the medal to Prine in the Panther command post. A picture was taken for Falah's collection of American military linkages. In the background, one of Prine's senior soldiers looks stunned.

★

Team Outcast was also getting short. It was early June, and with just over a month to go before turning 3/3–1 over to a new advisor team, Troster might have tugged on the operational reins. Pullbacks at the sunset of twelve-month tours were common in Iraq, a combination of sheer exhaustion and risk aversion—commanders who didn't want to get a man killed within days of going home.

But Iraqi Battalion 3/3–1 was on a never-ending deployment. They were going to remain on ASP Hill until the war was won, and the advisors vowed to fight alongside their charges until boarding the freedom bird for the United States. Team Outcast finally did receive a few replacements to help it through its final months. Sergeant First Class Stephen Alban, Staff Sergeant Larry Dehart, and Lieutenant Bill Rusher fit into the exhausted team immediately for two reasons: They had understated personalities and they wanted to patrol, demonstrating that personality and grit trumped training when selecting advisors. After watching Dehart correct some appreciative jundis on their weapons handling during his second patrol, Troster joked that a soldier dressed in a pink tutu would be fiercely embraced by everyone on ASP Hill if he had calm creativity inside the wire and bloodlust outside.

"Well, embraced by everyone except Roberson," Troster corrected himself.

Team Outcast's replacements weren't the only new American faces in Khalidiya. Darkhorse Battalion, 3/3–1's new partner unit, began to appear on the streets, sparking rumors among the locals that a Marine invasion of Khalidiya was imminent. U.S. headquarters told the Iraqi battalions to obscure the turnovers of big U.S. units rotating back home, as was occurring between TF Panther and Darkhorse, so the insurgents could not exploit any gaps in the physical or emotional landscape.

The Iraqi battalions increased their patrols ostensibly to support this grand cover-up, but the Iraqi officers privately scoffed at the tactic.

"This thinking is wrong," Captain Dhafer complained to Troster when he was sent into Budimnah yet again to cover for Panther's absence. "Either tell the people the National Guard is leaving as a reward for local cooperation, with just a few Marines coming in to spend money and support us, or say that the National Guard was fired because there are still too many bombs, and now comes a Marine battalion to punish!"

What the Marines were really practiced at was unclear. For ten months, TF Panther had vigorously patrolled Route Michigan with armored vehicles; it was their primary mission. Though some locals called them "the glass talkers"—to lodge a complaint you had to shout through bulletproof glass—the guardsmen made the route relatively safe for the jundis and citizens alike.

Now the Marines were in charge and they didn't seem to care about Michigan. On June 2, Dhafer's Humvee hit a pressure plate mine that had been dropped right on the highway blacktop, blowing the tire clear through the wheel well and searing the turret jundi's legs. When Dhafer stepped out of the vehicle to check the damage, he lurched like a drunk and used his rifle like a walking stick. He realized he was concussed.

"Show yourself!" he screamed in frustration.

Dhafer knew the Marines could not watch every meter of Route Michigan, yet they were responsible for the highway, and he did not see them rumbling up and down the road scaring away the mine planters. That night he asked the advisors if 3/3–1 was being encouraged to watch the highway themselves.

"If the Marines want us to take Michigan," said Troster, "they'll tell us."

On June 4, another Iraqi Humvee struck a cluster of freshly buried bombs in the middle of Route Michigan. The explosion tore the front end off the vehicle. Three wounded jundis staggered out coughing and collapsed in an alley. It took a Marine wrecker crew two hours to rock the half-buried Humvee free from its hole. The Marines stuffed wet T-shirts into their mouths to filter the smoke from the burning tires, which was pouring out in fat, twisted horizontal ropes.

That evening, Alex and some jundis on patrol watched an American unit wearing desert digital camouflage fanning out on foot across the cemetery toward the back door of Sadiqiya, an odd route for a presence patrol and very dangerous.

"Who are they?" a jundi asked.

"Those are Marines," Alex replied.

"They are not watching the highway. We will keep being blown up on Michigan, and they will die by the hand of the Sadiqiya Sniper. They don't know what they are doing," the jundi warned.

The advisors were reluctant to tell the jundis that Darkhorse was a "hot fill" on temporary assignment to Habbaniyah for just two months. Marine Battalion 3/2, the "Magnificent Bastards," was slated to replace Darkhorse in late July. The advisors had assumed that Darkhorse would cling to Camp Habbaniyah. Do their time in zone quietly and ineffectually, to minimize casualties.

Quite the opposite was transpiring. A few days after arriving in Habbaniyah, there were Marines all over the place. They looked like college backpackers determined to hike through the small villages for exotic pictures. They couldn't patrol Michigan like TF Panther did because they didn't have as many armored vehicles, so they had decided to walk into the surrounding towns instead.

★

Colonel Falah was promoted to a staff job in Baghdad during this transition, much to the delight of his advisors. Troster recommended that Lieutenant Colonel Fareed, the steady, quiet battalion XO, move up to take Falah's place as commander of 3/3–1.

Fareed had to be careful not to be seen as challenging the patronage system. An informer to Baghdad's generals could easily sabotage his chances. Fareed called all his officers to a meeting after dinner. Over chai and candy, he asked the staff for candidate recommendations. Alex stood to leave, but Lieutenant Colonel Fareed insisted he remain—the shrewd Iraqi colonel wanted to confirm his mandate, and he wanted the Americans to hear about it.

"Sir, I speak for everyone. You should be our next commander," Major Aamr declared. "You have been a consistent leader. You have earned it."

"I am concerned for the soldiers, not myself," said Fareed.

"And the soldiers will be lucky to have you, sir," Aamr concurred. All seconded the recommendation except for Major Mohammed, who detested social maneuvering.

Lieutenant Colonel Fareed hadn't come in over the top as had Falah—he had put in his time. Still, he had contacts in the Ministry of Defense who told him few officers would want command of an exhausted battalion fighting for its life on a dusty outpost in Anbar. If Fareed wanted it, he could have it.

Fareed put his hand on his heart. "If it is your wish that I command 3rd Battalion, it is only up to God now."

He asked Alex to tell the advisors the next patrol was canceled so they could celebrate. The officers tapped out a few cigarettes and shared a long smoke. Part of the elite group that formed the first units in the New Iraqi Army, the senior officers had been together two long years, and they deserved a few quiet minutes together.

One of their own had made it.

13

Death

★   ★   ★

June 2006

The summer heat came in all at once, as if the door of a giant oven had opened somewhere inside Khalidiya. Average high temperatures reached 110° in the afternoon, with occasional spikes to 120°. The advisors marveled that an egg white could be thoroughly cooked during an hour foot patrol by placing it in a bag against the chest, pressed flat by the searing armor plate and the pounds of hot magazines and smoldering radios. Morning was the only tolerable time to go outside, when the average temperature plummeted to 85°, and you could walk for more than fifteen minutes without downing a thirty-two-ounce bottle of tepid water.

In the early morning hours of June 5, Captain Dhafer received a tip and hastily organized a raid to capture the Harden brothers, lieutenants in AQI who used the threat of assassination to shake down the reemerging merchants and tax other citizens. When the Hardens were in town, shops remained closed and agnostic families left to visit relatives.

Dhafer was first into the house. The Hardens crumbled when facing the raiders. Begging for mercy, they dangled a succulent name in exchange for mercy. Ahmed Mukhlif Humadi, aka "Abu Roma," who was known to be leading a sniper-training cell—and accused by some locals of being the Sadiqiya Sniper—was in town to visit his wife.

U.S. and Iraqi units had been chasing Humadi for more than two years. He was a cunning fugitive, slipping in and out of town to deliver a bomb, take a sniper shot, sleep with his wife, or perform the occasional interrogation before a beheading. Six separate witness statements tied Abu Roma Humadi to multiple bombings and shootings since 2004.

Dhafer said he didn't care about years-old sins. The Hardens told him that Humadi was the bomber who had rung his bell in an IED attack two days earlier.

"If you take us to American jail, instead of your jail, I will also give information on Abu Roma's shooting school here in Khalidiya," one of the Hardens pleaded.

"Tell me where he is sleeping and we may not drown you," Dhafer replied.

Fifteen minutes later, Dhafer had surrounded Abu Roma's supposed location with Humvees. He led ten panting jundis on a full sprint toward the suspect's house. Doc Blakley and Alex ran in trace. Dhafer put his boot into the cupped hands of a jundi and was first over the courtyard wall. The others formed human ladders, clambering up thighs and shoulders until it was just Doc Blakley, who was tall enough to pull himself over the wall.

Inside the house, the occupants were too sleepy to put up a fight. Abu Roma had just shifted to another safe house, but his two younger brothers—Kamal and Hussin Humadi—were home with their mother. Dhafer separated the brothers for interrogation. Some jundis lit cigarettes and shared their smokes with the detainees, softly asking for cooperation. Others smacked the brothers on the backs of their heads. This wasn't planned; the interrogation tactics mimicked the personalities.

Dhafer wasn't a yeller. But whenever he whispered in suspects' ears— threats that were rarely revealed to the advisors—they listened. Hussin, about 20, cracked, giving the location of a 1920 Revolutionary Brigade safe house. Young Kamal, just 16, was tougher. As Hussin was dragged out of the house by jundis on suspicion of aiding his brother's sniper cell, Kamal held his mother tightly and said to the jundis, "God sees you are apostates."

"Careful, or this night I will judge you too, boy," said Dhafer. "Your mother will be left with just one lying son."

His mother cried in protest, "Hussin is not like the oldest!"

"Abu Roma?" Dhafer asked.

"He has cut away his father's name and angered God."

The jundis told her not to cry. They would leave fiery Kamal behind and even Hussin would be home soon to care for her. They roughly tossed Hussin into a Humvee.

"I do not believe you," the mother screamed, weeping inconsolably.

Using captive Hussin as a scout, the patrol drove to the 1920 Revolutionary Brigade safe house. Dhafer and two jundis broke down the door at 0300, stumbling upon four unrelated men sleeping on straw mats. Dhafer put the men in the back of the vehicle with Hussin Humadi, the Harden brothers, and four jundi guards including Hater.

It was a long morning at the detention facility. The Marine guards from Darkhorse who were taking responsibility for the Camp Habbaniyah jail insisted on perfect paperwork, not that legible English writing would clear up the tangled prisoner system. Every Camp Habbaniyah detainee was assigned a number, but this designator changed if he was routed up to a bigger jail. Maddeningly, battalions like 3/3–1 and Darkhorse lost track of prisoners this way. Further obfuscating the trail, Arabic names were spelled phonetically and often morphed several times as prisoners moved through the system. The battalion's "Qasim Khudayir" could be the brigade's "Kasem Kudayeer," eventually admitted to Abu Ghraib's maximum security prison as "Kasim Qu'deer."

Because they couldn't find the name "Hussin Mukhlif Humadi" in the records, and the evidence was thin, the Marine guards set him adrift in under twenty-four hours.

Blakley returned from the long patrol at dawn and checked the board where the patrol schedule and cleanup duties, cheap shots, and tributes were posted. He was on the roster for the following day, June 6. Huss caught him staring at the board.

"What's wrong?" Huss asked.

"Sixth of June, 2006," said Blakley. "I don't like it: 666."

Blakley didn't say anything else, disappearing to get some shuteye.

★

The next morning at 0600, Blakley, Gentile, and Joe the elderly terp accompanied Captain Haadi on a trip into Khalidiya to investigate a suspected bomb at the 20th/Market Street intersection. The tip seemed good, but 3/3–1 had lost enough vehicles for one week so Haadi parked near Route Michigan. The patrollers, including Doc Blakley and Joe, moved up Market Street on foot.

Doc enjoyed the morning patrols in Khalidiya. The smell of baking samoons filled the air, children were up before their parents, and mine triggermen usually were asleep. It was better in the winter when there was more darkness, though. That morning was plenty bright already to be walking down "Thunder Road," as Market Street was sometimes called.

A smiling street vender holding some warm breads waved them over. Doc was so popular in town that he didn't have to pay for food, but he always carried a few dollars along with his boxes of Pop Rocks. He cringed when he reached into his blouse pocket for the plastic bag that kept the dinars dry. Doc still hadn't regained the endurance in his trapezius from January's gunshot. The dime-size bubble of scar tissue was no match for the forty-five-pound bulletproof vest. He looked like he was dancing as he walked, shrugging his shoulders uncomfortably.

"Still hurt," said Joe, who didn't wear armor at all because it made him sore.

Doc Blakley's eyes searched the streets for familiar kids. Then a bullet snapped into the wall a few feet from his face. He ducked, but the angle favored the shooter. The second bullet ripped through Blakley's neck and plunged into his chest.

"Joe . . ."

He lay on the street with Joe shouting, "Blakley! Blakley! Oh my merciful God, it's Blakley!" to the wild-eyed jundis who asked, "Who is it, who is it?"

The jundis did not fire their weapons wildly, or run for cover screaming about snipers. They moved fluidly to covered positions and stared at Blakley. Gentile swerved the Humvee around the Iraqi vehicles and put the brake pedal into the foot well when he reached his fallen partner, shielding him. Gentile needed all his strength to get Blakley inside the truck. He pulled his friend close and felt for a pulse somewhere in the wet.

"Come on, brother."

Blakley exhaled and was gone.

Captain Haadi, the extremely religious officer who had recently joined 3/3–1, ran in a large circle and then fell to his knees on the sidewalk, reaching skyward in prayer. Blakley was his favorite advisor.

In the ASP Iraqi radio room just a few hundred meters upslope, Haadi's high-pitched words ran together like a scream. The old Iraqi radioman, the hypochondriac Mr. Jeebs, burst into tears and rolled on the floor like a wounded animal. Aamr went to help him up, but he crawled out into the sun and curled up on the fresh bed of rocks that he had recently positioned in front of the door to knock the mud from the boots of soldiers entering the radio room.

"No! No! No!" Jeebs wailed.

Troster was inside his hooch.

Outcast Six, this is Outcast Golf, Gentile radioed. *We got a man down. Sniper fire. Over.*

Troster was off and running, his armor flying behind him like a kite. He thought from Gentile's transmission that a jundi had been shot. He and Bennett arrived at Market Street a few minutes later. Joe held his face in his hands and Gentile was shaking. Troster instinctively knew Blakley was dead.

"Blakley's gone, sir," said Gentile.

Troster's face tightened. He opened the door to the Humvee and looked at his medic. *No, no, no.*

"Call the other guys on the hill and tell 'em to get down here," he said softly.

Team Outcast, August 2005. *Standing, from left:* Huss (WIA), Troster, Bennett (WIA), Bozovich. *Kneeling, from left:* Boiko (WIA), Watson (WIA), Rivera (WIA), Gentile, Neary (WIA). *Not pictured:* XO (reassigned), Roberson, Blakley (KIA).

Majors Roberson and Mohammed find an ammunition cache at the water treatment facility. Insurgents buried weapons all over town to avoid house searches.

SSG Blakley with an artillery shell mine. He loved action outside the wire.

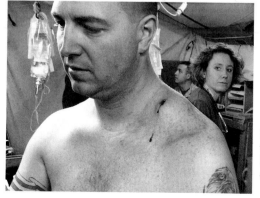

Blakley's sniper wound, January 2006. He returned to action only days later.

SVBIED attack on Michigan that resulted in 3 jundi KIA, 16 jundi WIA, and 1 advisor WIA, October 2005. Body parts from the bomber were discovered 100 meters away. As with so many Iraq engagements, the rest of the ambushers were never found.

Rivera and Watson's Humvee after striking a mine in Abu Fleis, February 2006. Watson, who was severely wounded, was dragged to safety by his Iraqi charges.

LT Khalid, a professional who paid for his own gear and proudly flagged his outpost, was stubborn and confident.

LT "GQ" Ali, a happy officer with a keen tactical sense and impeccable grooming standards.

Team Outcast posing with some of their charges, July 2006.

During a typical night raid, Mohammed interrogates a suspect while Alex translates for the American advisors.

LTC Aamr, CPT Haadi, and MAJ Mohammed disagree with one of Alex's many suggestions, November 2006.

CPT "Bomb" Dhafer, who de-armed more than a hundred mines by hand. KIA in 2009.

Haadi chatting with locals in Abu Fleis while on patrol. He eschewed helmets for ball caps so he could approach as a peer.

Typical mine digger caught with cordless phone detonator and $100 payment. "Car Bomb" Cardenas saw "something in his eyes" that led to the arrest.

The view from the turret on a Khalidiya street in the Kurdish neighborhood notorious for pot shots.

LtCol Todd Desgrosseilliers, commander of the 3/2 Betio Bastards, who roamed Habbaniyah constantly like a politician on steroids.

Team Outcast, November 2006. *Top row, from left:* Newton, Foisy, Stoesser, Smith. *Second row, from left:* Lester, Himes, Povarelli, Caldwell, Akin, Schwarzman, Sylvester, West. *Seated, from left:* Alex, JD, Dupuy. *Missing:* Perez.

Chief Shalal lectured by LtCol "Ogre" McCarthy, the police advisor who was determined to root out corruption in the force.

The author with "Irhabi Hater" Haider whose goal was to kill an insurgent with his knife. He used to mock the author's blade, saying it was "made for mice."

Aamr, Fareed, Mayor Hussein, Shalal, and Ogre. The negotiations to get police into Khalidiya never stopped, even when they shared a joke about their pushy advisors.

The author, Fareed, Sylvester, and Aamr on Team Outcast's last night on ASP Hill.

Using the Snake Eater identification system donated by Spirit of America and Goldman, Sachs to conduct a census. Nighttime loiterers were fingerprinted and the records stored in a proprietary database used to sketch the social network.

TAA militiamen dressed in black join a joint Iraqi Army/Police patrol and claim they will retake the city from insurgents, November 2006.

Operation Sad City, a mass lineup of every male in Sadiqiya that helped break the insurgency. TAA militia dressed as jundis identified the insurgents hiding in plain sight for three years.

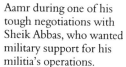

Fareed gives Desgrosseilliers a going-away present. The Snake Eater–3/2 partnership set the standard.

Aamr during one of his tough negotiations with Sheik Abbas, who wanted military support for his militia's operations.

Alex and Sly "soft" interrogate a local while loiterers look on. By 2007, most patrols were walking conversations with locals, and 9 out of 10 mines were discovered before they exploded.

The author with a local boy outside the elementary school in Khalidiya. The I♥NY T-shirts were big hits.

One of four enemy KIA shot by jundis, November 2006. They had money, machineguns, and electric cattle prods in the car. The other bodies were strewn along the road, then gathered up and proudly dropped off at the abandoned hospital in front of a stunned crowd of locals.

The author, his son, and Alex in Connecticut, 2011. Alex, who arrived in the States on a special immigrant visa, is on his way to National Guard training, having been barred from the Marines for excessive tattoos.

Captain Haadi was slumped in the street with his helmet off, crying.

"Get yourself together!" shouted Troster.

"Doc Blakley is dead!" Haadi cried in response.

"More people are going to die if you keep sitting there like that."

The rest of the advisors arrived, except for Neary, who was left on radio watch. One by one they leaned into the Humvee to say good-bye to Blakley. The Iraqis wondered aloud why the Sadiqiya Sniper had shot the American doctor. Hitting a medic who treated the people in town hurt their cause.

The advisors stayed quiet. They knew why the sniper had shot Blakley and they knew the Iraqis knew, but as seasoned hands they also knew that sweeping moral judgments about the enemy were best digested alone, like bitter pills.

The advisors took Blakley to TQ. The last they saw him was on a gurney with piles of clumpy sand in the undercarriage, used to absorb the blood. The duty surgeon examined Blakley and said, "The bullet entered at his collar and . . . Men, it wasn't survivable. Unluckiest shot I've ever seen, and I've seen a lot. He was hit before in the same region. Are the shootings related?"

"I doubt it," said Troster. "But in this war we'll never know."

Zientek met the advisors at the hospital. He pulled Troster and Roberson aside. "Anything I can do?"

"If anyone has information on the son of a bitch who did this, we want in," said Roberson. "I don't care if it's Superfriends or the CIA. We go on the raid, and somebody dies."

Back at ASP Hill, Neary wanted to go see Blakley. Troster drove him to TQ, but the mortuary affairs officer refused them entrance. After a short argument, Troster gave up. He was very worried about Neary. He was inconsolable, and it scared him.

The jundis came to the Horseshoe throughout the afternoon to pay their respects. In many cases it was the jundis who needed consoling. They stood in sobbing clusters as the advisors packed Blakley's gear and stacked it in the courtyard. Eventually Boz and Dehart emerged from their room dressed for the next patrol, and the jundis, realizing there was going to be no memorial service that afternoon, shuffled down to their bunkers arm in arm.

Troster knew his men were grieving. Losing a soldier as popular as Blakley was crushing, but it was important to demonstrate to the Iraqis—and themselves—that the mission continued. Revenge was a remedy, but Troster was careful to dampen expectations. As a DEA agent, he'd seen unsolved murders in shootings with a dozen witnesses.

Troster found Gentile huddled with Huss over a list of Blakley's personal property. Doc was married with three children. Most of the advisors were fathers, and they were heartbroken. Troster pulled Gentile—a father of four—aside and told him to take a few patrols off.

"I want to go back out tonight, sir," Gentile insisted.

"That was pretty tough out there this morning," said Troster.

"I got a job to do. Losing Doc doesn't change that. "

Troster was impressed with the mechanic. Gentile was depressed, but he instinctively knew Khalidiya had lost something, too, and the people would be watching for a reaction.

Up the sandy wash that marked the well-worn path to the Horseshoe courtyard marched Marine Staff Sergeant Saul Cardenas. An infantry volunteer with a month left in Iraq, Cardenas was on loan from Darkhorse, a replacement for Lieutenant Rusher, and was determined to find a firefight.

"How'd you end up with us?" Troster asked him.

"I was told there's work as an advisor, sir," Cardenas replied.

"There's work all right. You'll be living with Mark Huss. Blakley was his roommate," Troster explained. He and Rivera didn't want Huss to be alone even for one night.

"I've been around loss before, sir," said Cardenas.

"You'll be patrolling tonight. That okay?" Rivera asked.

"Oorah!" Cardenas cheered.

Punctuating the conversation, there was an explosion in town. Troster held his breath for the long interval until Boz's voice came through the radio.

Outcast Base, this is Outcast Bravo, radioed Boz. *Had an IED go off about twenty meters away. No casualties, no damage. Continuing the mission. Outcast Bravo out.*

Hearing the exchange, several Iraqi officers told Alex that the regular patrol schedule didn't honor the dead American. "Lieutenant Troster shows no respect to Blakley," said one. "He does not care that he has been killed."

"Troster shows ultimate respect to Blakley by patrolling. What would you have him do? Cry all night?" Alex asked.

"He is a cold man. He never liked Blakley. They fought, you know."

"Blakley wanted to go outside the wire more and Troster wanted him to help treat you," said Alex. "Now you are saying that by patrolling Troster shows no respect? It is the opposite."

That night Gentile got paired with Cardenas on a patrol in Khalidiya. Under the stars, they watched a squad of jundis reattach a power line to a sparking transformer that had been hit by celebratory gunfire from a nearby party. The owner of the power line came outside to yell at the partygoers, the jundis intervened, and before long the soldiers were the target of both parties' rage, to Cardenas's bafflement.

Gentile didn't talk much. Cardenas wanted to say something to comfort him, but the jundis had given up on handyman duties and were trotting back to their vehicles, so the advisors sealed themselves in their own Humvee. It was quiet inside except for the low rumble of the engine and Gentile's measured breathing.

★

The morning after Blakley's death, GQ took four vehicles into Abu Fleis looking for revenge. Near the big bend halfway up the peninsula, an explosion flipped GQ's Humvee on its head, the turret gunner miraculously escaping with everything intact but three fingers. GQ saw the severed digits scattered on the road. He picked one up but his balance hadn't returned. He stumbled sideways and crashed into a wall.

"Get those fingers," GQ panted at his jundis, "and bring them to me."

GQ wrapped the fingers in a kerchief he kept to wipe his brow and tucked them in his pants pocket. The injured jundi sat next to GQ so his lieutenant could dress his bloody hand. One of the jundis remarked that Blakley would have sewn on the fingers right there in the field. Another proclaimed that Blakley had once cured him of the Khalidiya krud in ten minutes.

"Blakley is dead," said GQ. "Call for the QRF."

Insurgents had stitched the route with bombs. A mine blasted Captain Dhafer's lead QRF vehicle on the way into Abu Fleis and his friend GQ. Luckily, it had been buried upside down. Dhafer celebrated his good fortune and kept going.

But a second bomb detonated as they reached GQ's overturned truck. It ripped open the undercarriage of Dhafer's vehicle like a sardine tin, knocking unconscious all the men inside except one, who sobbed uncontrollably about Blakley and bombs.

"I am getting tired of this," Dhafer told Roberson, who had driven in with GQ's patrol. "I feel like someone has slammed my ears with cymbals."

"I'm getting tired of this too, Dhafer," Roberson concurred.

Roberson called for wrecker assistance from Camp Habbaniyah, but the battle space handover between Darkhorse and TF Panther was jumbled and no one arrived. The jundis guarding the smoking accident scene waited for hours in the baking heat. Roberson handed over all the water bottles in the advisor Humvee. Young men came out of the fields they were tilling to watch the rattled patrol melt into the pavement. The jundis tried to buy fruit juice but they had no dinars and no local would extend credit after the kidnapping of 16-year-old Mohamad, whose whereabouts where still unknown. Dhafer contemplated imposing martial law before thinking better of it and calling for the makeshift Iraqi road crew.

In minutes, three Iraqi vehicles arrived better suited for a junkyard parade than the battlefield, including a heavy pickup truck with a welded bumper that looked like a hammerhead shark and a converted Rio flatbed dragging sparking chains like tentacles.

With a terrible groan, the two trucks strained and puttered back to the outpost, dragging the shattered vehicles past the smirking mob. Some men were outright giggling.

Most locals like us soldiers, thought Dhafer, *but they like winners more.*

"Is it always like this, sir?" asked Cardenas, who was with Roberson that day.

"Not always," said Roberson. "Sometimes the bastards shoot at you."

The following day the insurgents proved the XO right. As 3rd Company drove onto 20th Street, intense crossfire erupted from several buildings and a car. A rocket slammed into the running board of Captain Haadi's Humvee, flattening two tires and cracking a wheel disc.

Enemy machine gun and rifle fire spiraled in, quickly concentrating on Haadi's wounded vehicle. Watching from his position two trucks back, Rivera knew that if he didn't drive the ambushers off, Haadi and his men in the kill zone were dead. He wheeled his Humvee to cut around but an Iraqi Humvee beat him to the punch, its PKC blazing as it raced toward the enemy car.

"That's right!" yelled Rivera, thrilled that the jundis were attacking. "Get some, jundi!"

Surprised by the assault, the enemy car retreated into an alley where its occupants ditched. One insurgent trailed blood. The jundis followed, but the droplets gave out. RPGs, a PKC machine gun, two AK-47s, and pounds of ammo filled the trunk of the car.

Battalion 3/3–1 never reported the weapons find. Captured weapons that were turned over to the Ministry of Defense tended to disappear somewhere in Sadr City, the Shiite epicenter of Baghdad. The jundis stashed the weapons in the corner of their bunker, hidden by a bed and some old uniforms in case one of their own weapons went bad.

Jundis knew how to scrounge—that wasn't anything new. But the killer instinct they showed on 20th Street that day was.

★

On the morning of June 10, Captain Haadi had a choice. He could follow his prescribed patrol route, or he could follow yet another suspect local tip about Blakley's killer, all of which had proved bogus in the week after the shooting.

This tip led him to the home of a sheikh who funded the 20th Street Mosque, a sanctuary for overnight foreign fighters sponsored by AQI. Haadi didn't knock. Relations with all the sheikhs were so bad it didn't make a difference. Jundis tossed the home while Haadi drank tea. A jundi came waving a love letter recently written to one of the sheikh's daughters. The 16-year-old author insinuated he had killed an American.

"I have a sniper's eye," the young man had scrawled in the letter.

There was no Arabic metaphor for the term. The letter writer's name was Kamal Muhklif Humadi, the brother of Hussin and the notorious sniper Abu Roma.

Haadi had no idea that Hussin had been arrested by Dhafer on June 5, the day before Blakley's killing, during a search for his oldest brother, Abu Roma. Or that Blakley had been in the room supervising the arrest. Dhafer had left Kamal behind to comfort his sobbing mother, and the boy had screamed in anger. No one linked the timing or established motive; Dhafer had detained thirty suspects over the month, with no written record. The Iraqi officers didn't share intelligence. Once, over yogurt, GQ had scratched a name from his most-wanted list after overhearing that Walid, his own company commander, had captured the suspect weeks before.

"Does your daughter consort with murderers?" Haadi asked the sheikh.

"No. But you do, as God sees it," the sheikh said.

"God the most merciful has taught me not to kill you for having such a loose tongue," Haadi whispered. "We will be back to talk to your daughter."

Haadi immediately departed the sheikh's house to check Kamal's background with his local sources. Love letter in hand, Haadi presented his best source, Omar, with a written list of notorious names. Of these, he asked, who is the shooter?

"Kamal or Ahmed Humadi are the names you want. Kamal is young. He shoots for his brother, who is the sniper leader. They call him Abu Roma," Omar replied.

"I know about Abu Roma. It is rare for blood to run both good and bad," said Haadi. "At best the boy Kamal lies to get credit for killing Blakley. At worst he is the terrorist who assassinated my advisor, a doctor."

"A doctor. Yes, I have heard this terrible thing," Omar commented.

"I will need you to locate him," said Haadi.

"But that is . . ."

"It wasn't a request!"

★

The SEALs and the Iraqi scout platoon, an elite unit from 3/3–1 trained by the SEALs, were the experts in nighttime raids. One day later, at midnight, Roberson joined Lieutenant Rorke, the SEAL platoon leader, and his prisoner snatch team in their blacked-out gun trucks, rolling quietly under an

F-18 fighter plane that was scanning the route with thermal scopes and a powerful magnifier. Riding with the scouts, Omar the source pointed at two houses.

"Which one?" asked Lieutenant Fredo, an Iraqi scout platoon leader who'd picked up his nickname because he wore a thin mustache like the *Godfather* character.

"Both," replied Omar.

Roberson stared at the outline of the housing block in the moonlight. Tonight they would put an irhabi into the ground. He, the scouts, and the SEALs were into the houses before the echoes of the door-breaching explosions faded. Every screaming face got blinded by barrel-mounted flashlights and pushed into the cement floor. Every room, every cupboard was searched. Kamal was gone.

The F-18 pilot radioed Lieutenant Buffalo. *Got a single squirter moving across the rooftop, heading west fast.*

You've got to be kidding me, thought Buffalo. He had led dozens of kill-or-capture missions, and only one other suspect had tried to run away, or "squirt." Even hiding in closets was rare.

Whoever he is, he's guilty, thought Buffalo.

Buffalo and Roberson raced up to the rooftops to join the search. The squirter control unit, which prevented fleeing suspects from escaping the perimeter, had locked down the apartment block. Now it was a matter of finding the snake hole.

Any sign of him? Buffalo panted into the radio.

Negative, radioed the F-18 pilot.

The senior chief petty officer in the SEAL platoon was first up on the rooftops. He knelt next to a water tank and listened. Nothing. He stood up and scanned the rooftops with his night-vision goggles. Nothing. He removed his goggles and stared into the black slick of the open water tank, concentrating on his hearing. A stream of bubbles rippled the surface. Kamal came up out of the water sucking air but instead met the chief's iron grip. The wanted boy was yanked free and slammed on the concrete deck.

"*Ismak!*" shouted the chief, asking for his name.

"*Ismi Kamal.*"

"Kamal what?"

"Kamal Humadi."

Humadi slapped helplessly at the chief's thick forearm. The SEAL straddled him and went to work, binding his prey like a spider immobilizing a fly. In the Marines, medics came from the navy, and the chief assumed Blakley was navy, like him. It was a long journey down the stairs to the Humvees for young Humadi.

The jundis asked the Americans to leave the target site so they could end the matter with a club. Kamal began to babble. He knew the Americans had a capacity for mercy that the jundis rarely harbored. With his wrists flex-cuffed behind his back, he threw himself on his knees and banged his head against American boots for mercy.

"America good," he said. "George Bush!"

Roberson was disgusted. Kamal had the body of a 14-year-old girl, but it had taken only seven pounds of trigger pressure to kill Blakley. Roberson told the Iraqis to blindfold him. There would be no revenge killing.

The jundis protested.

"They say this kid will be out of Bucca in under ten years," an interpreter with the SEALs said.

The Iraqis were wrong. Kamal was set free a few months later.

In mid-June, the Iraqi battalion organized a memorial service for the fallen advisor. It was the first service in the entire brigade to be held at an Iraqi outpost. Blakley's rifle was jammed between his combat boots into some gravel the Iraqis had scrounged from an insurgent construction business—in Khalidiya, that meant any shop open for business.

Blakley's dog tags dangled from the pistol grip of the rifle. The American flag snapped in the silence between each sad speech.

A year later, the tiny group of American advisors couldn't remember their own words, but they remembered those of the new Iraqi battalion commander, Lieutenant Colonel Fareed, who spoke in Arabic and then English:

"The 3rd Battalion thanks you for coming to pay respects to one of our fallen brothers. We share the same blood and the same fight. When Staff Sergeant Blakley gave his blood, it was my blood too. When he died, I died too. We will never forget him. You advisors are our brothers forever."

14

Changing of the Guard

★　　★　　★

June–July 2006

The final weeks for Team Outcast went by in a blink. In mid-June, 3/3–1 was ordered to take responsibility for securing Route Michigan. Troster knew better than to argue with Lieutenant Colonel Zientek this time. Regimental Combat Team 5, or RCT 5, had taken over the battle space from Fallujah to Ramadi and now counted the 3rd Iraqi Brigade as one of its subordinate units. Colonel Larry Nicholson, the RCT commander, was moving from battalion to battalion, hammering home one message: integration. Nicholson, who had a jagged shrapnel scar across his neck from an enemy rocket blast, made it clear that Marine battalion commanders who did not advance Iraqi units in their sectors would not be promoted. The Marines of Darkhorse Battalion, 3/3–1's new partner unit in Habbaniyah, had determined that giving the Iraqi soldiers more battle space would push them up the learning curve, like it or not.

On Route Michigan, Darkhorse Marines slapped together seven-meter-high outposts consisting of sandbags, plywood, and bulletproof glass, spaced three hundred meters apart right on the highway like tollbooths. The giant sand castles were like ovens in the searing summer heat, but they were like fortresses, too. The jundis were expected to live there and keep the insurgents off the road.

"This is different from what Panther did," Lieutenant Colonel Fareed told Troster during an inspection of the posts. "They didn't live on the road, and they had tanks. It's too dangerous."

"This is called outposting," Troster explained. "They can cover each other by fire and observe the road at the same time."

"I'm not sure any of our companies can live here," said Fareed.

"I can think of one," Troster suggested.

"I'll order Mohammed's 4th Company to live on Michigan, if it must be done."

Major Mohammed didn't care about the creature comforts. For ten months, he had lived in an ammunition bunker on ASP Hill with his jundis, sneering at the other Iraqi officers who watched nightly DVDs with the advisors. Happy to be on his own, Mohammed put a squad in each watchtower on Michigan and sent vehicles up and down the highway. The mine attacks that had marked early June stopped.

As Colonel Nicholson left to visit another unit, Zientek told him that the outposts were only a Band-Aid. "It's good the jundis control the main road, sir," Zientek said, "but they're outsiders. The insurgents live right along the road and we have no idea who they are. We need to recruit police."

★

Neary had taken Blakley's loss the hardest. He was talking less and keeping to himself. At dinner, he no longer tried to converse with the jundis in pidgin Arabic.

"What are we doing here, guys?" he asked the other advisors. "Has anyone really thought about how little things have changed? All of us could die. And for what?"

On June 14, he talked about walking off post. It was too noisy for him at ASP Hill. Maybe he'd go down to the spot where Blakley was shot, he said, or walk to Baghdad. Get away for a while. His teammates stood watch over him that night, and the next morning, Troster took Neary to see the doctor at TQ.

The doctor decided that Neary needed more sleep and rest.

"Doctor, we're patrolling two or three times a day," Troster said. "When you go out, it's just you, an interpreter, and one other American. One drives and the other mans the gun. The best I can do is let Neary sleep for a few hours. I can't give him a long shower, a hot breakfast, or Fox News."

Two days later, Neary's bum knee gave out. The doctor told Troster that suiting Neary up in armor was out of the question. "Neary, you're going home," said Troster.

"I'd like to stay, sir."

"You've done your time."

★

Twelve months is too long for advisors in a hot combat zone. Burnout started at about the nine-month mark, and by the last two months most men had exhausted their patience and stamina. Shorter tours boosted productivity in high-tempo missions—the SEAL task unit and the Special Forces advisor teams served six months, while CIA and special operations units that went on frequent raids served only four to six months

The counterinsurgency academics at advisor training argued that it took nine months just to build rapport with Arab officers and to understand the local population. But in Habbaniyah, Iraqi officers rotated into new assignments every six months.

Staff Sergeant Cardenas showed that advisors could earn credibility in a week, as Dehart and Rusher had before him. He loved working with explosives. Days after Cardenas arrived, the storage room was filled with grenades and rockets borrowed from contacts in Darkhorse. To the delight of the jundis, he held classes on how to handle C-4 explosives and demonstrated on patrol by blasting open a suspect's locked gate, gaining the nickname "Car Bomb." On June 20, he noticed a man on the roadside with a cell phone flinch as the Humvee passed. Car Bomb slammed on the brakes, sprinted over to the man, and screamed at him.

"Where is it? *Wain* boom?"

The man pointed to a drainage culvert. Buried there were two pipes packed with explosives.

"That's one of the biggest yet," said Rivera. "How'd you know?"

"I just knew," said Cardenas. "It was in his eyes, man."

Months later, memories of some advisors grew hazy, but the jundis never forgot Car Bomb.

★

On Camp Habbaniyah in mid-June, the Darkhorse commander, Lieutenant Colonel Patrick Looney, tore down the giant wall that had separated the Iraqis from the Americans. Looney sent his men out in squad patrols across the zone, fanning out across the canals and down the trash-filled streets. Watching from their new towers on Michigan, the jundis shook their heads, waiting for a naïve Marine to fall victim to the Sadiqiya Sniper. They didn't know that a "guardian angel" Marine sharpshooter team accompanied every patrol, trotting from one high spot to another.

On June 16, a Darkhorse sniper team saw two local men in a parked car near Sadiqiya videotaping a Marine patrol, a rifle stock visible in the passenger's lap. At long distance, the Marines shot both insurgents dead. In the lap of the dead passenger, the Marines discovered a well-maintained Marine Corps sniper rifle. In 2004, a Marine sniper team had been killed in Ramadi and their weapons taken. The rifle had been awarded to the top AQI sniper, according to Major Mohammed, though there was no way to determine if it fired the shot that had killed Blakley. Now a Marine sniper had taken it back.[1]

An impressed Mohammed quickly partnered with a Marine company commander from Darkhorse who had been stopping by the Michigan towers asking how his men could help.

"You have tanks. We like tanks," Mohammed said.

"Okay," the Marine commander replied. "But I was thinking we'd walk around together. Get to know one another, your jundis and my Marines."

Mohammed ordered his jundis to get out of their towers, and together the joint small unit patrols saturated his zone day and night, looking for mine emplacers. He didn't tell Major Aamr or Lieutenant Colonel Fareed about the missions. If they failed, he would blame it on the pushy, clueless Marines.

In the last two weeks of June, combined patrols wandered the streets thirty-two times without a single contact. Marines from other Darkhorse companies regularly drove into Khalidiya and Abu Fleis and asked to join Iraqi patrols they saw, including a tank platoon that rumbled up during a patrol Troster and Fareed were on that turned into a photo op, with jundis clambering up for a photo with the grinning Marines to send their relatives.

"This is what it was like in Mosul," said a laughing Fareed, who always insisted on removing his helmet for photographs. "Darkhorse treats us as allies."

Inspired by the burst of goodwill between 3/3–1 and Darkhorse—and its effect in calming Khalidiya and Abu Fleis—Troster wrote a memorandum for the record that the Marines stood "in stark contrast to TF Panther."

During the first week of July, Lieutenant Colonel Looney visited Lieutenant Colonel Fareed on ASP Hill. Fareed was on edge, uncertain what the Marine's verdict would be on the fledgling partnership.

"Colonel, we've been thoroughly impressed with 3rd Battalion," Looney declared.

"You have treated us as brothers in this fight," Fareed said.

"We are," Looney concurred. "I'd like to single out Major Mohammed for particular recognition. Thanks for assigning him to those joint patrols. Marines call him the mayor of Sadiqiya, you know."

Fareed had no idea Mohammed was leaving his posts on Michigan, let alone running around town on foot. He glanced at Aamr, who offered a weak shrug. Mohammed could not be tamed. He was both invaluable in the field and a running liability.

"Mohammed is a very good officer," Fareed said.

That was the beginning of the end of company command for stubborn Major Mohammed. Fareed and Aamr were terrific officers who understood the value of individual initiative, but even in the U.S. Army, company commanders were not given untethered reign over plots of ground, let alone an Iraqi Army steeped in hierarchy. Mohammed was eventually assigned a staff operations job in the stifling headquarters building that doubled as ASP Hill's radio room. Mohammed was miserable except during chaotic calls for reinforcements from the hill, when without body armor he was able to hop into the closest available vehicle faster than anyone else. Fareed and Aamr let it slide because he was gone to help the distressed patrol before they could stop him.

★

Troster's team was due to rotate home in mid-July. In his judgment, the Iraqis were ready to patrol on their own once per day, a boost for their confidence and a nice send-off for Team Outcast. They were ready.

On July 4, Troster visited Fareed in the commander's quarters. Fareed did not keep bodyguards around, but Chai Boy was still employed, and he announced Troster. Some Iraqi traditions even the most influential advisors could not bend. Fareed spoke good English and needed no interpreter.

"Colonel, it's the American Independence Day back home. Here on the hill, it's time for the battalion to send out independent patrols. The jundis are ready."

"I am proud to say I agree," said Fareed.

"Also, when the replacement advisors arrive in a week to begin the handover, we won't have enough room for them in the Horseshoe unless the Iraqi officers move down to the bunkers and live with their jundis," said Troster.

Fareed insisted that Troster personally break the news to the company officers about the living quarters. Never eager to deliver bad news, Fareed wanted Troster to take the heat. He was leaving soon anyway.

Troster told the other officers at dinner that night. Some of the Iraqis made sucking noises by pulling air through their teeth, signaling trepidation about both moves.

"I will lead the first alone patrol," GQ said, breaking the silence, "if I can keep showering at the advisor house!"

"GQ, if you patrol on your own," Troster said, "you can shower wherever you want."

★

Two days later, Roberson, Troster, and Huss wandered out to the front gate to watch the Iraqis leave the wire. They handed out flares and smoke grenades, and with mixed feelings watched the Iraqi Humvees roar out into battle on their own.

"Like little birds leaving the nest, huh, boss?" Roberson observed.

"They look good, don't they?" Troster concurred.

As their days in the country dwindled, Team Outcast admitted to tinges of melancholy. Their grand adventure was ending. Some dreaded their homecoming and the niggling reality of life outside ASP Hill. Lieutenant Bennett, who had received a Dear John letter months earlier, wasn't sure if his wife would be there to greet him. Her letters had stopped entirely some time ago. He diverted his attention to his teammates. Before each patrol he prayed for their safety, and it had worked—on his patrols, no advisor had been wounded.

On the evening of July 9, he climbed into a Humvee turret for one of his last patrols. A klick up Route Michigan a mine blast tore up into the seams of the doors and into the turret, splashing Bennett with burning shrapnel.

Troster evacuated Bennett to TQ while Roberson remained guarding the shattered Humvee with a group of jundis. At the hospital, Bennett was anesthetized and operated on. Troster told the surgeon, "I'd like to keep Bennett here for a week so he can fly home with the team."

"I'm afraid he has to get to Germany, Mike," the doctor replied. "One of the shards came awfully close to severing his femoral artery and both legs are pretty nicked up."

"Can you wake him up here, then? I don't want him to wake in Baghdad with a bunch of strangers."

Troster waited for the anesthesia to dissipate, and the first thing Bennett asked was, "How am I down there, sir? I can't feel anything!"

"You're fine, Bennett. Listen, the doctor—"

"Hey! I mean down *there,* how am I? Can you check for me?"

Troster lifted Bennett's sheet and inspected his groin. "Bennett, it's a sight only your wife can love, but everything is in working order."

Troster said good-bye on behalf of the team and left the hospital to seek vehicular support for Roberson, who was still a sitting duck on Route Michigan, awaiting a tow truck to cart away the wrecked Humvee. Troster drove around looking for big trucks. At the west gate of TQ there was a parked recovery convoy that bristled with heavy weapons. Troster beeped his horn.

"Follow me. I'll take you to the dead Humvee," Troster told the convoy commander. "We need to tow it out of there before dark."

"Sorry, sir, I can't," the Marine lieutenant said. "We're awaiting route clearance by the engineers and a brief by my S-2."

"I can give you better intel than some S-2. I live there. Let's go."

"Sir, I'm embarrassed, but it's the base commander's rules and the guards won't let me out."

Troster sped to the explosion site alone in his Humvee. When Roberson heard the story, he spat in disgust. "You understand my frame of reference on Fobbits now?"

"Yeah, maybe you're not a sociopath after all, Walt," Troster said.

Jundis dragged the wreck up to ASP Hill using three Humvees linked like sled dogs. The following night, a huge U.S. flatbed wrecker announced its presence at ASP Hill with a hiss of air brakes. A baby-faced Marine sergeant wandered up to the Horseshoe and said with a Southern accent, "Anyone here got a Humvee needs a tow?"

"Where's your four-vehicle escort?" Troster asked. "And your S-2 officer?"

"Oh, hell, sir. I heard what happened, and it sucks. Then a few of us figured out they don't watch the back gate, so we snuck out with no gun truck escort. We're prepared to go into town ourselves to get it, if that's what it takes. But don't tell nobody because I already got bad paper."

Troster and Roberson didn't know whether to laugh or cry. It wasn't the men but the machine that broke your heart.

Back in the States, the Pentagon personnel machine was still churning out undermanned, ad hoc advisor teams that were ill prepared for their mission. Replacing Troster's team was a nine-man mix of active soldiers, reservists, and National Guardsmen whose civilian jobs ranged from refrigerator repairman to firefighter. In an email, the incoming team leader, Major Mac, a high school vice principal, had asked Troster about living conditions. Was there a nearby dining facility, Internet access, and a gym?

"Look at this, Walt," Troster told Roberson. "Tell me this is a joke."

Just as the 98th Division had tried to warn Troster's 80th Division via email about the nature of the mission, Troster tried to dampen expectations. "The living conditions aren't the important thing," Troster wrote. "You need to prepare your team for combat patrolling. It's a Spartan existence."

Major Mac replied that his chain of command expected him to train the Iraqi staff on the base, not patrol with junior soldiers. The key to independence, according to their advisor training, was teaching Iraqis sound organizational planning.

Troster knew what Lieutenant Colonel Zientek expected. "The 3/3–1 staff doesn't need help planning," he wrote back. "Your team will be combat advising, not training. Prepare for battle."

For the record, Troster composed an after-action report for his seniors. The email exchange had brought back bitter memories, and he wanted to contribute to the historical record of the abysmal advisor staffing and training model. Regarding his own team's training, he wrote, "Soldiers are trained according to a plan dictated by higher, yet 85% of it was not needed." As for the advisor training in Iraq at the Phoenix Academy, Troster recommended it "be eliminated."

Troster concluded his report: "Advisors must live and work with their Iraqi counterparts. Training them to perform missions but refusing to join them on those missions is counterproductive."[2]

★

The new Outcast team arrived at ASP Hill on July 19, 2006. Unit turnover is often frustrating—the old-timers are self-assured, skeptical, and disconnected; the new joins are overeager and chirpy. Between advisor teams, turnovers were particularly thorny. Tactics can be passed on from one unit to the next; personal relationships cannot.

Troster felt that Major Mac had been poorly prepared for the combat mission. Mac was insistent on staff development, having been told by General Casey himself that this was the focus of advising in Iraq. Further, in the public school system the principals set the policy and the teachers taught, without blurring the roles. Troster believed that hierarchy in advisor teams was divisive.

Mac's deputy, Major Steve Sylvester, was a firefighter from Fargo, North Dakota, who served in the Minnesota National Guard. A former football player with a shaved head and a thick light brown mustache, "Sly" Sylvester, a military policeman by training, quickly decided that the team of rookie advisors was set up for failure.

"This is totally different from what we were told," Sly told Roberson. "We didn't train for this mission. We thought advising was training."

"Advising is fighting," said Roberson. "Get used to it."

"Problem is, I'm not in charge of the team."

On July 20, their last patrol as lead advisors to Iraqi Battalion 3/3–1, Troster and Roberson brought Major Mac along on a QRF. An insurgent had fired a rocket at one of the sand castle checkpoints on Route Michigan. The advisors raced down from ASP Hill, arriving in time to find Hater standing sadly over a dead insurgent.

"I chased him and shot him," said Hater. "He ran bleeding inside a house and hid in a clothing hamper. The mother revealed him, so he ran out here. But now he is dead. It is too late to kill him with my knife."

Irhabi Hater unsheathed his long knife and turned it forlornly.

"Have you tried mouth-to-mouth?" asked Roberson. "If you bring him back to life, then you can stab him."

Hater bent over the corpse, uncertain. Then he burst out laughing with the others. It was Iraqi Battalion 3/3–1's first confirmed kill. The jundis had developed hunters' instincts, which to Roberson was absolutely essential in battle. Roberson knelt and searched the corpse for identification and contraband.

"Does this happen a lot?" Mac asked.

"Often enough," said Troster, exchanging a look with Roberson. "The advisor tour is filled with goodies like searching bodies. But like I told you, the way you gain influence and credibility with these guys is in combat."

"We'll make our own assessment of what the battalion needs."

In two hours, it was all over the battalion: 3/3–1 finally had an enemy body and the new senior advisor looked horrified. In Troster's opinion, Mac had refused to listen during the ten-day transition, jeopardizing all that Team Outcast had built.

★

On July 21, Zientek held a final party for Troster's men. Over nonalcoholic Beck's beer and barbequed chicken, the advisors celebrated their tour's end. Troster pulled Zientek aside to air his concerns about the new advisors on ASP Hill. Zientek was not in a good mood. A mine had killed one advisor to the 2nd Battalion and amputated the legs of two others.

"I have reservations about the new Outcast team, Jim," Troster said. "They don't want to patrol."

"They just got here. But I hear you," Zientek replied.

On the other side of the barbeque pit, Roberson gave McNulty a similar assessment. "Those soldiers are going to have to be shoved outside the wire kicking and screaming, Drew. I'm telling you, polish up your boot."

McNulty respected Roberson for his tactical prowess but had struggled for six months to connect with his fellow major. They sipped their non-beers and tried to make small talk. Roberson gestured at the fighting knife McNulty wore on his hip. In a fluid move, Roberson pulled his own knife out of his belt. "See how fast that was?"

During the tough Battle of Fallujah, McNulty had charged into a room and stabbed a jihadist to death.

"That's a great idea," McNulty said, "I mean, being fast with a knife."

"Hell yes, it is," said Roberson, not knowing about Fallujah.

McNulty thought that between Hater and Roberson, the soldiers on ASP Hill had revived the caveman style of warfare.

★

Troster, Roberson, and the other advisors left the going-away party without giving any speeches. In the ten-man team, one had been fired, seven had been wounded, and one had died. They had been hit by fifty mines and had found fifty-one others. They had arrested over 250 men but had no idea how many were actually behind bars. The advisors had left the wire on 1,500 patrols, and Rivera, Huss, and Bozovich had stunningly topped 450 patrols each.

But what counted was that Iraqi Battalion 3/3–1 had improved to the point where a patrol or two were unescorted each day, and they were now the predators, not the prey. Whether Sadiqiya, Khalidiya, and Abu Fleis could be tamed was an open question. Troster believed that saturating Khalidiya with patrols had stimulated local cooperation not because the living standard had improved but because now a growing number of people thought the Iraqi Army would remain in Khalidiya until it prevailed. As proof, Imam Mahish and Sheik Abbas had come forward in April even if that goodwill disintegrated in an instant.

He compared the long tour with 3/3–1 to his work at the DEA. Sometimes neighborhoods improved, sometimes they got worse. If you measured yourself by how many crack dens you raided, you were delusional. The key was the endurance and morale of the force. You had to keep going out, time and again, knowing that in the end what mattered was the spirit of the community. You were, and always would be, an outsider. An outcast.

The thing that counted most was the performance of "their" jundis and the recognition of their peers. They wanted their effort to be judged by other advisors. No one else in the military understood the job. Outsiders didn't count. What Troster's men craved was praise from fellow warrior-kings and pride as they watched Iraqi Battalion 3/3–1 continue to develop from afar.

PART TWO

GOOD-BYE, DARKNESS

15

Change of Pace

★ ★ ★

August 2006

The leader of each advisor team must provide clear tasking priorities for the team and motivate his men. As Major Mac understood his instructions, the priority task was to advise the Iraqi battalion staff about planning procedures to build independence. This meant cutting back on patrolling, while Mac personally focused upon gradually building a personal relationship with his counterpart, Lieutenant Colonel Fareed. Although this one-on-one relationship building left the rest of his team adrift—was each advisor to single out one Iraqi for special attention?—Mac's focus was not unusual. T. E. Lawrence's *Twenty-Seven Articles,* distributed to most U.S. advisors, argued for the slow start that Mac was endorsing.

"Go easy for the first few weeks," wrote Lawrence. "A bad start is difficult to atone for, and the Arabs form their judgments on externals that we ignore."[1]

Mac called Lieutenant Colonel Fareed "saydi," showing respect for the Iraqi's seniority of rank; Troster had avoided the use of "sir" because it implied the advisor was subservient. Mac, on the other hand, wanted to be Fareed's confidant and not suggest that he was Fareed's equal. He was also determined to improve living conditions for his team and the Iraqis. Although he had graduated years earlier from Ranger school, he didn't see field duty outside the wire as the priority.

Mac's boss, Lieutenant Colonel Zientek, had sharply different priorities. As far as Zientek was concerned, if advisors weren't outside the wire sharing the dangers of the streets, they weren't doing their job. But Iraqi senior officers like Fareed rarely patrolled, leaving that to the junior officers and jundis.

Mac felt that his job was to stay by Fareed's side, and that meant staying inside the wire. Every instructor in the stateside training had stressed building a competent Iraqi staff and letting them fight the war.

Zientek and Mac were on a collision path. Something had to give.

★

Back at Marine headquarters fifteen kilometers to the east, Brigadier General Bob Neller, Major General Zilmer's hands-on deputy, had taken a personal interest in the advisory effort. Neller was blunt, with the happy-to-be-fighting demeanor of a bulldog. As far as he was concerned, if advisors were not out in the field, they were useless.

But Neller knew that ten-man advisor teams were too small for everyday duty. So by August he was reinforcing each team with grunts from nearby Marine battalions. If a battalion commander made the mistake of saying this took manpower away from his tasks, Neller would sharply remind him that the main, primary, critical, essential, and crucial task was getting the Iraqi Army to fight its own war. Across Anbar, Marine battalions got the message and sent about ten grunts to every advisor team, including the 1st and 2nd battalions in the 3rd Iraqi Brigade.

Mac's team on ASP Hill, though, was treated as an exception, if not ignored. Mac didn't want a cadre of Marines clamoring to patrol, and Marine augments lobbied to go to other teams staffed by Marines. ASP Hill with its Army occupants was not a popular destination. So in August, the nine soldiers under Mac were augmented by only two Marine infantrymen, Staff Sergeants Dave Cox and Gordon Solomon.

Both Marines developed an immediate dislike for Khalidiya. It was like a town in a Clint Eastwood western, featuring sullen people exhausted by violence. When Cox tossed candy to some kids, they responded by throwing back rocks. Solomon went out on his first patrol and was startled to see the jundis slap around a man who had ducked away when he saw the approaching Humvees. By the rule book, Solomon was supposed to stop the slapping and report the incident. But as he watched, the sobbing man pointed to an old tire on the edge of a trash pile. Captain Dhafer walked over to the tire and knelt down and probed with his knife, soon cutting the wires that led from the explosive to a battery. Dhafer then jerked on the other end of the wire, pulling out a chunk of explosives wrapped in adhesive tape.

In early August, they discovered another hidden mine. Solomon pulled out his K-BAR fighting knife and probed for the wires running to the detonator. Several giggling jundis peered over his shoulder, offering advice. Then came the sharp *tink* of the blade striking metal. Solomon leaped to his feet and screamed, "Run!"

The jundis fled, while Solomon sprinted behind Cox's Humvee, scream-ing, "It's gonna blow! It's gonna blow!"

When no explosion followed, Solomon said, "It's alive, Cox. Honest to God, it hissed at me."

It took an EOD team an hour to disarm a complex bomb that was rigged to two others. They lectured the Marines about breaking protocol. "Don't blame us," Cox said. He pointed at the Iraqis. "They started it."

Cox believed that Iraqi 3/3–1 had the right stuff. The jundis were dis-ciplined, and their endurance was exceptional. The company commanders wanted to fight. The glaring deficiency was a group of four new Iraqi lieuten-ants. They cut patrols short or parked in friendly neighborhoods and drank chai.

"Why don't their company commanders put a boot up their ass?" Cox asked Alex after one frustrating patrol.

"The company commanders don't want to train the lieutenants," Alex explained. "A good lieutenant might be promoted ahead of them."

"So whose job is it to shape them up?"

"I think that's your job, Staff Sergeant," Alex said.

★

Major Mac had a different opinion. He didn't want Solomon, Cox, or any other advisor inserting himself into small unit tactics that should have been corrected by the Iraqi chain of command. Also, he didn't want advisors patrolling in a single Humvee, as Troster had done. Zientek agreed with him in principle, signing an order requiring a minimum of four advisors in two Humvees on a patrol. That way, there was sufficient force for an emergency medical evacuation. But Zientek had permitted Troster to break that rule, because Troster had a hundred patrols under his belt and was determined to accompany every Iraqi patrol that left the wire until the final days.

Mac didn't have that experience, and he had only eleven advisors, not twenty like the other battalion teams. So he cut back to two patrols a day. He made out a roster that split evenly the routine duties like radio watch, pris-oner processing, and food runs. That left scant time to train the Iraqi staff, so the two new Marine grunts were put on every patrol in order to allow the five officers on the top-heavy advisor team time to advise their senior coun-terparts on the Iraqi battalion staff.

Lieutenant Colonel Fareed pulled Alex aside after dinner one night dur-ing the second week of August. "What do you think of the new advisors?" he asked.

"They have cleaned up the advisor house," said Alex. "And we now have computers hooked up to the Internet. Troster didn't care about email."

"Major Mac is professional. He told me his job is to help me," Fareed said. "I told him my staff can execute operations. He can help me best by making life better in the camp for us all. An American major can get supplies I cannot."

A few nights later, recently promoted Lieutenant Colonel Aamr walked in to the advisor command center and found Major Mac on radio watch. "That is a job for a jundi, not the senior advisor."

"We have many duties," Mac said.

"We have many duties, too. But you do not see me on the radio," Aamr retorted.

A week later, Major Mohammed noticed Mac standing behind the machine gun in the turret of a Humvee. He joked that Mac was a "turret major." After that, concerned that he was losing face among the Iraqis, Mac rarely listed himself on the graveyard radio shift and did not man the turret gun.

Mac also told Fareed that the advisors might have to cut back to accompanying the jundis on only one patrol a day, because the team had to advise Iraqi staff on logistics, medical, and intelligence matters.

In response, Fareed cut the battalion daily tempo from six to four patrols. The Iraqis wanted a more comfortable pace. If the advisors wanted to allocate more time to training the staff and improving living conditions inside the camp, that was fine with the Iraqis. Alex thought the Iraqis were testing the new Outcasts, their fourth advisor team in two years; Fareed was probing to determine how many patrols the rookie advisors would require.

★

At Camp Habbaniyah, newly promoted Major Drew McNulty was troubled by the trend on ASP Hill. Iraqi patrols had suddenly dropped after the departure of Troster's team, as Roberson had predicted. By nature, McNulty was a hard-ass, opinionated mud grunt. Zientek wanted McNulty to ride herd on the Outcasts—a headache for Major Mac, who was trying to plot his own course as the new leader of the team. When Troster led the team, he ignored proper radio procedures and routine reporting, and his monthly written assessments were atrocious. But Troster made his home in the field, so McNulty cut him slack.

Major Mac was given no such slack. In mid-August, McNulty sent a team to ASP Hill to teach the soldiers how to run an operations center. "They're not monitoring the radios half the time," McNulty told Zientek. "This isn't how we do business."

McNulty insisted that Team Outcast submit monthly staff assessments on the Iraqis, monitor and report on every Iraqi patrol via the U.S. chain of command, design all company and battalion operations and submit them for U.S. approval, and accomplish an extensive checklist of improvements. Mac was given two weeks to implement the list.

Mac was feeling the heat because the impetus across Anbar was for "active advising," which meant prodding the Iraqi units into combat. That was the philosophy of Marine Colonel Bob Coates, a burly special operations commander who had served several advisory tours in El Salvador and had been brought over in midsummer by Zilmer to give the advisory effort a boost. Coates liked to visit his fifty-odd teams, and his vehicle was struck by mine blasts several times. Advisors who did not embrace the motto "Alone and Unafraid" were replaced or goaded into action.

Team Outcast believed the new reporting requirements were harassment, and they were right. Fed up with being micromanaged from above, Mac met with McNulty to have it out over the advisor's role.

"We need you guys outside the wire, setting the example," said McNulty.

"I'm following the direction provided by my command and the Phoenix Academy," said Mac. "We're building relationships to prepare the Iraqis for independent operations, not do it for them or hold their hands out in the field. That's General Casey's intent. I know it because he told me."

"Whatever guidance you heard in a classroom has zero relevance here," McNulty retorted.

"Are you saying a four-star is irrelevant?"

"I'm saying that we know this local fight better than he does," McNulty replied.

Mac didn't back down. "I'll go out when it helps the mission," he said, "but we have just eleven guys and I'm advising a battalion commander, not a jundi in a turret. It's about trust. I've gone outside the wire with my commander without my rifle to demonstrate that trust."

Finally, in mid-August, Zientek issued a direct order: Team Outcast would accompany at least two patrols per day for a minimum of six hours. Zientek was open to debate and compromise on most advisory issues; patrolling wasn't one of them.

★

The big generator went out again one night during an August heat wave, when temperatures dipped to 110° at night. The 11 Americans and 450 Iraqis cursed collectively. At the generator, Sergeant First Class Robert Akin tried to untangle the nest of cables the jundis had installed to divert power to a dozen small and unauthorized air conditioners.

"I told you to stop sucking the power," Akin lectured the jundis. "You're like stray pups overloading a tit. Now we all suffer."

The advisors wandered the moonlit courtyard in their boxer shorts in search of nonexistent pockets of cool air. Solomon doused the hood of a Humvee with water and slept in the puddle.

Fareed used the blackout to press his new relationship with Mac. He summoned Alex to a meeting with his staff. Even in the heat they drank hot chai.

"The advisors are going to fix the power," said Fareed. "They promised my jundis air-conditioning and lights. Correct, Alex?"

"Correct."

"The advisors must continue to improve our conditions," Fareed declared, "so we can focus on patrols. Alex, you are to explain that to Major Mac."

Fareed and Aamr wanted to increase unaccompanied patrols but didn't want to issue a written order. In the Iraqi Army, when things went wrong, a written order could lead to dismissal.

"We have no support when we go out. No artillery or QRF," Captain Walid complained. "We need the advisors and their radios."

"We have never called for an artillery strike. And the QRF is always ready, including the advisors," countered Fareed. "I will go out myself to demonstrate to the jundis that we can patrol alone many times a day."

Fareed thought he'd struck a fair bargain: He'd increase patrolling and relieve the bureaucratic pressure on Mac, who would reciprocate by providing electric power and other American life improvements.

★

It didn't take long for Fareed to produce. On August 18, an alert jundi driving Fareed's Humvee spotted a suspicious mound on Route Michigan near Market Street. Footprints were clear in the freshly dug dirt, and in the hole lay five artillery shells and a propane tank. Fareed flagged down a Marine tank that was rumbling along the highway, while his jundis raced off to investigate.

"Can you aim your cannon up there?" Fareed asked the tanker, pointing to a group of four men two hundred meters away at the base of ASP Hill that the jundis had detained after tracking sandal imprints.

The four Iraqi civilians went to their knees as Fareed approached.

"Line them up for the American tank," said Fareed. "Good target practice."

One man burst into tears and pointed to a house at the edge of Khalidiya. The jundis ran inside and dragged two men out. The tank rumbled forward like a curious bear. In the background of the tank's roaring engine, Fareed slapped the suspects' faces with their shoes until one urinated and sobbed out his story. The 1920 Revolutionary Brigade paid them $200, enough to feed their families for two months, to dig the hole. Fareed brought them to the American jail on Camp Habbaniyah, where a Marine told him there was not enough evidence for a conviction, the diggers having changed their story. Fareed didn't care one way or the other. He doubted they'd have the nerve to help the insurgents a second time.

★

Lieutenant Colonel Fareed's adventures on patrol continued two days later. An RPG rocketed out of a Khalidiya storefront and punched through the trunk of his Humvee without detonating. The convoy immediately wheeled into an attack formation and encircled the row of stores, surprising the bystanders and the insurgents among them.

The hardest-looking men were lined up against a wall. Whispering about an execution, a crowd gathered to gawk, standing on tiptoes and leaning over balconies to watch.

"You weep for Saddam, but Saddam would kill all of you if a single person ever fired an RPG at his soldiers," Fareed said. "Then he would shell all of Khalidiya to teach the city a lesson. As God hears me, do I speak the truth?"

The suspects agreed that was true.

"We are the New Iraqi Army. For a year we have fought not for ourselves but for you. Terrorists among you call themselves martyrs, but many of my soldiers have died to keep you safe. They are the martyrs in the eyes of God. If you do not believe this, then you have the courage to defy God. If you have the courage to defy God, you certainly have the courage to fight. My name is Fareed, and I am the commander of the 3rd Battalion. Who among you will fight me?"

It was high theater, but the Iraqis took such displays seriously, and some bystanders shouted encouragement. Fareed's speech reverberated throughout the town. Iraq's is a culture of personality. Inside the battalion, the message was clear: If the commander was looking for a fight, so should the company officers.

★

GQ was getting married in September. Most of the battalion officers would attend, and he wanted to ensure they told stories of intrepidity alongside his follicular feats. Abu Fleis was awash in rumors of arms smuggling disguised as fishing. On August 20, GQ led a patrol into Abu Fleis along the dangerous dirt road on the southern bank of the Euphrates, which was generally avoided because big pressure-activated bombs could be quickly buried in the soft dirt and made undetectable. The patrol surprised five fishermen loading heavy rowboats with suspicious supplies including metal shavings.

"Do you live here in Abu Fleis?" asked GQ.

"It is too dangerous to live in this place!" said a fisherman. "We just keep the boats here. Sometimes we sell ferry rides if the Americans close the bridge."

"You sell death. That's what you sell!" said GQ.

The jundis busted up the boats with their rifle stocks, telling the boatmen to find another job.

GQ led a follow-up patrol the next day to inspect the crossing site, which he expected would be empty of smugglers. The repaired boats were resting on the beach in defiance. GQ and the advisors splintered the hulls with explosives, pushed them out into the current, and chopped up the flotsam with machine gun fire.

★

On August 24, the advisors awoke to grim news. Staff Sergeant Dwayne Williams of North Baltimore, a member of the Camp Habbaniyah EOD team, had been killed while dismantling a bomb. Williams was on his third Iraq tour and had neutralized hundreds of bombs, with three concussions and a Bronze Star to show for it. The bomber knew what he was doing.

GQ, though, was undaunted. That morning he led a vehicle patrol down the dirt road back into Abu Fleis, accompanied by advisors. GQ took a look around the sandy spit for boats, but there was nothing but rustling reeds and squawking herons. He hopped back into the lead Humvee, heading back to ASP Hill. Cox was commanding the second Humvee in the file.

From behind, there came an explosion so powerful that the shock wave pushed Cox forward in his seat. He looked in the rearview mirror. The other U.S. advisor Humvee was hanging three meters up in the air. For a second, it seemed suspended in a geyser of dust. Then it slammed down and tumbled over.

Staff Sergeant Matthew Mattern, the driver, was spit out of the armored door, his pelvis shattered. Captain David Coyle, turret gunner, was thrown clear and landed in a paddy with a broken leg. He watched the Humvee sail in slow motion over his head, crashing in an irrigation canal. A new Iraqi interpreter had several broken bones and was screaming in Arabic.

Where is Solomon? Cox wondered about his friend. He sprinted back to the wreck. The twisted Humvee was resting precariously on the front passenger door, smoking. Solomon was on his back underneath the spinning axle.

"Can you hear me, brother?" Cox shouted at Solomon, waiting for him to cough or moan. There was no reply.

Solomon was gone.

Back in the first Humvee, the turret gunner was frantically trying to raise ASP Hill on the radio, but no one responded. GQ gathered up some jundis and plunged into the foliage, searching for the bomber. Major Mohammed, having heard the distressed radio traffic, came barreling up the road, ignoring the danger of another IED.

"Give me the wounded!" Mohammed shouted in English.

Cox helped load the wounded into Mohammed's Humvee.

"You need an escort to get on TQ," Cox told Mohammed.

"I'm not waiting," said Mohammed.

Filled with moaning men, Mohammed's unescorted Iraqi Humvee roared up to the TQ guard shack at sixty kilometers per hour. Marine guards popped out and leveled their weapons.

"Marines!" Mohammed shouted. "Americans hurt!"

Mattern's leg was dangling from an open window. The guards took one look at the blood-soaked interior and waved Mohammed through. He drove across the air base with his hand on the horn. One American walking beside the road pulled his pistol but was too confused to fire.

Back on the Abu Fleis peninsula, the temperature was 120°. The jundis searched homes, stomped through the high grass along the riverbank, and fired randomly in the air. Inside an hour, all the water bottles had been sucked dry and not one insurgent had been found. With everyone out of water, some jundis climbed date trees to suck the juice out of bitter juvenile dates. Others drank from the filthy Euphrates River. Cox hesitated, knowing he would vomit all night, but in the end, he too drank.

McNulty arrived on scene with a quick reaction force from brigade headquarters. "Where the hell is the Outcast QRF?" he demanded of Cox.

"We have no idea," spat Cox.

McNulty was enraged at the sight of Solomon's body. Why had they gone out on dirt roads? Now another advisor was dead. McNulty assisted with the evacuation of Solomon's body to the morgue at TQ, and a few hours later Cox drove back to ASP Hill smoldering with anger.

Mac tried to embrace Cox, saying, "I'm sorry about Solomon."

"Stay the hell away from me, sir!" Cox yelled.

He stormed into his room and took inventory of his friend's gear for shipment to his family. Solomon left behind a wife and son. Cox wanted to cry out or set something on fire or kill an insurgent. On one level, he knew the mine blast was the rolling of the dice in combat. Everyone outside the wire ran an equal chance. You couldn't leave Abu Fleis as a sanctuary. At the same time, there was the human desire to blame someone.

Iraqi Battalion 3/3–1 had been in Habbaniyah one year, and ten-man Team Outcast had suffered two KIA and nine WIA, including replacements. Mac was in a tough spot. When tragedy struck, it was human nature to second-guess. The sudden loss of one advisor and two others evacuated with wounds had shaken the team's confidence in its mission.

★

That night, Cox wanted to go back out on patrol, hoping to strike back somehow. Mac refused to let him leave the wire. Four kilometers to the north, a pair of Harrier jump jets swooped down along the Euphrates with machine guns thundering. Jundis clambered up onto the roofs of the bunkers to snap pictures of the lines of red tracers. Video from an unmanned aerial vehicle circling above Abu Fleis had shown fifteen men dragging heavy objects toward a bomb crater. The Harrier gun runs had ended the project.

Cox, though, was irritated. Why didn't brigade give Team Outcast the chance to roll down the hill for some face-to-face vengeance? At the end of August, Team Outcast on ASP Hill felt abandoned, skeptical of their own leadership, and resentful of higher headquarters.

★

By September 2006, the mood in Washington was darkly pessimistic. Baghdad hovered on the brink of civil war. Every night, Sunni insurgents aligned with al Qaeda in Iraq battled Shiite death squads intent on driving all Sunnis from the city. In Anbar, Major General Zilmer, the top general, and Brigadier General Neller, his deputy, were concerned that AQI had crushed the spirit of the Sunni tribes by repeated assassinations. Few informers had the courage to point out an AQI member, and Sunni insurgent groups like the 1920 Revolutionary Brigade—while much larger than the extremist AQI affiliates—dared not step out of line.

To his troops, however, Zilmer was always optimistic. The command website banner read WELCOME TO THE FIGHT! He treated junior commanders like entrepreneurs because the war was compartmentalized—what worked in Fallujah might not in Khalidiya. He and Neller were waiting for a glimmer to exploit.

One night in early September, Zilmer and Neller sat staring at an enlarged PowerPoint presentation, poring over the ugly statistical trends. Attacks were steadily increasing. It was clear that the insurgency was not dwindling, but the Iraqi forces were; every month the number of jundis in the Iraqi battalions dropped.

"The Iraqis are going backward, Rick," Neller observed.

"It looks bleak," Zilmer agreed, "but we're not going to be the Marines that lost Anbar."

"I want to reemphasize the local recruiting effort . . ."

Zilmer rolled his eyes. It had taken five months to recover from May's disastrous recruit riot in Habbaniyah. Another Iraqi Army recruiting drive in the Habbaniyah area in July had netted a total of zero interested Iraqis.

"We need to keep attacking, Bob. I suppose that includes continued shots at recruiting Anbaris for the army. What about cops?" asked Zilmer.

"I'd like to plug the gap in Habbaniyah," Neller said. "The insurgents use Route Michigan to zip back and forth between Ramadi and Fallujah. Habbaniyah is their rest stop. They're hiding in plain sight, but the cops are holed up in Coolie Camp."

"So who'll organize the cops?"

"Ogre. He and Habbaniyah are meant for each other."

Lieutenant Colonel Bob "Ogre" McCarthy, 42, was a former player-coach of the Marine Corps rugby team. He had an outsize personality, a thick build, and a bald head not from hair loss, his colleagues joked, but because he'd run through too many walls. Neller pulled him out of his staff job in early September.

"Get your ass to Habbaniyah to run the police advisors," Neller told McCarthy. "You're assigned a squad of National Guard MPs and a few retired contractor cops. Need anything else?"

"What I need, I'll get, sir," said Ogre.

"Right now you don't have much to advise. One corrupt chief named Shalal and a few dozen cops. Your job is to build police, and don't get killed. Clear enough for you?"

"Uncomplicated orders for an uncomplicated man, sir."

Chief Mohammed Shalal, who ran the shadowy Habbaniyah police department—which had retreated into Coolie Camp abutting Camp Habbaniyah—and did not venture into Khalidiya, was widely suspected of cutting deals and shaking down contractors. But he had political connections in Ramadi, the capital of Anbar Province. So he hung on to his job, while his police force was ignored by both sides as irrelevant to the fight.

When Ogre arrived in September 2006, fifteen Kansas National Guardsmen were acting as advisors to Shalal and his cops. The police advisors did not accompany the cops, called *shurtas,* on patrol. The shurtas rarely left the Coolie Camp station, and the advisors lived on the main base at TQ.

"The shurtas pretty much do nothing, sir," a guardsman told Ogre. "Shalal runs a one-man show. His subordinates avoid us."

Ogre moved the team from TQ into Camp Habbaniyah and immediately invited Chief Shalal to a meeting. Shalal wore the blue pants and white shirt of a shurta, but he was twice the size of most of his cops and looked like he would have fit in on one of Ogre's rugby teams.

"Colonel Shalal, I hear things are bad—*muh zien,*" said Ogre. "How can we fix this problem?"

"But I do not know what the problem is!" Shalal protested.

"The problem is you," said Ogre. "You will stop taking money from your men, remove the ghosts from your roster, send your police to Jordan for training, and move back into Khalidiya. In return, I'll let you keep your job."

Shalal was astonished. "Mr. McCarthy, I am not Ali Baba. I do not take money from my men."

"You take forty dollars from each man each month."

"This is offensive. And Khalidiya is impossible. No shurta can survive in Khalidiya. The insurgents will kill us."

Ogre put an arm around Shalal. "You and I will prove that statement wrong."

"*Insha'Allah.*"

As Shalal left, Ogre added, "Colonel Shalal, they are my shurta, too. All four hundred of them. Or is it three hundred? Or thirty?"

"I will get you the exact number," said Shalal.

Ogre's facial features had been disfigured by years on the rugby pitch, and his ears had swollen from repeated collisions. "See how big my ears are? They make lies sound that much worse."

The next morning, Ogre arrived at the police station in Coolie Camp, a two-room apartment surrounded by a crumbling wall scarred from shrapnel of a recent attack by a suicide bomber.

"*Ana ismi* McCarthy," Ogre told the startled junior police. "I am your new advisor. You are brave men. I will bring engineers to build defenses to match your strength. Life is about to get better for you."

The shurtas told Ogre that life had been easy before the 2003 invasion. Under Saddam, the sheikhs picked their own cops. Serious crime was rare. The shurtas resolved petty arguments, pocketed a few dinars from store owners in return for chasing away the thieves, and referred serious matters to tribal councils. As a shurta, you took home $50 a month. You got by.

Then the United States invaded. The Americans who occupied Habbaniyah fired tank rounds, drove in armored vehicles, lived in a walled fort—and expected shurtas with a few pistols to arrest the powerful Baathists who were plotting insurrection. By 2004, the Khalidiya police station had been destroyed and three police chiefs assassinated. The insurgents in Habbaniyah knew every cop by name and family. Many cops became informers for al Qaeda and Sunni insurgent groups like the 1920s, which had gradually infested the force.

In late September 2006, an elderly Coolie Camp policeman died. When the shurtas lined up in a funeral procession, a bomb destroyed the lead police truck, lifting it up over a three-meter wall and sending the engine block onto a farmhouse. Three shurtas were killed.

Over the past year, several cops on Shalal's payroll had been caught consorting with enemy agents, and one dead insurgent was carrying a police ID card. Shalal was the subject of a dozen intelligence reports. If you wanted to stay alive as a cop in Habbaniyah, you did what Shalal told you to do.

★

Up on ASP Hill, thanks to Mac's efforts, life was better for Team Outcast and Iraqi Battalion 3/3–1. The September sun was cooler, with highs below 112°, and once a week it rained. The jundis rushed outside with their dirty fatigues and soap to wash their laundry with their feet, while they danced and grinned at the clouds.

Soon they would have trailers with showers and air-conditioning in their bunkers courtesy of their new advisors. Mac tapped into equipment sources and money Troster hadn't known existed. He arranged for Internet connectivity, enabling the team members to keep in touch with their families, check sports scores, and download music. The power grid was strengthened and all fourteen Iraqi vehicles were provided with regular tune-ups. To the delight of Fareed, his command post received computers and air conditioners—courtesy of Mac.

When three Marine infantrymen were sent to Mac's team as casualty replacements, he assigned them to the two daily patrols. In return, they were exempt from the dull, routine jobs inside the wire, like monitoring the radio at four in the morning. Gradually, ill feelings developed between the three Marines and the soldiers who did the brunt of the patrolling—as Zientek had ordered—and those advisors who instructed the Iraqi battalion staff and carried out the tedious daily chores of improving the living conditions on ASP Hill.

★

The streets of Khalidiya remained lethal. On August 25, Captain Hamid, the 1st Company commander, was shot in the buttocks while standing on Route Michigan. On August 26, a sniper put an armor-piercing bullet through jundi Khalef Goaon's armor chest plate, killing him instantly. On September 16, an insurgent fired a rocket at one of the sand towers on Michigan and was killed by his own back blast. A few months earlier, the dead insurgent had scorched the back of his head while firing an RPG. He had just returned from convalescing in an AQI safe house in Syria. He was a slow learner.

On September 27, Captain Dhafer heard shots fired on 20th Street and vectored his patrol to the scene. An agitated shop owner was holding a hot-barreled AK-47. The vendor had shot an insurgent digging in a mine. The dead man had used the spot once before to blow up an Iraqi Humvee, and angry jundis had responded by shooting up the neighborhood.

"I told him never to dig in front of my store again," said the vendor.

Both sides were chipping away at each other. Bombs and snipers took a toll, but the continued patrolling was affecting the attitudes of the people. From January through June, Battalion 3/3–1 had one mine explode for every one they found. From July through September, due to a marked increase in local warnings, 3/3–1 discovered fifty-one mines and had only four detonate.

The increasing local cooperation was also manifest in recruiting. The jundis were telling their friends that life on ASP Hill—and on the streets of Khalidiya—was better. Soldiers present for duty in 3/3–1 swelled from 400 to 550, enabling Lieutenant Colonel Fareed to increase the battalion's presence in the towns.

In early October, a sweet-smelling, well-dressed man strutted right through Dhafer's foot patrol formation on 20th Street. Irritated, Dhafer followed the man into a house and dragged him out, along with a frightened teenager who blurted out that the fancy dresser was a recruiter for the 1920 Revolutionary Brigade. After a few slaps, the recruiter led Dhafer to a stash with five RPG launchers and several warheads.

"Next time a city slicker prances in the middle of your men, shove a rifle barrel up his ass," Staff Sergeant Cox said later. "You can't tell who's a suicide bomber."

"The people will tell us," said Dhafer.

"Bullshit. We need local police," said Cox.

"Shurtas?" Dhafer said. "During the day, they hide in Coolie Camp. At night they sleep in their own beds. They're worthless!"

★

By October 2006, Ogre had removed forty ghost shurtas from the payroll roster, plus a lieutenant who had shown up for exactly one day's work. Yet at the October 7 pay call, the lieutenant was again in line, this time with the rank of captain. During the same pay call, a 14-year-old boy in an oversize police uniform slapped his fake ID card down on the police advisors' desk. The ID said he was 20 years old, a military veteran, plus he had two years' service in the Iraqi police. Shalal vouched for the ID, while his henchman, Major Saleh, waved a handful of old pay stubs.

"This is ridiculous," Ogre said.

Ogre and his interpreter pulled the trembling boy aside.

"My brothers gave Colonel Shalal four hundred American dollars to join the police," the boy said. "Now my brothers will beat me, and my family will lose the money."

Advisors like Ogre had no authority to fire—or promote—police chiefs or Iraqi Army officers. If the Americans gathered hard evidence against an Iraqi official, which required two eyewitnesses willing to testify in open court, they could prepare a charge sheet for the Iraqi judicial system to consider. This had resulted in less than a half dozen successful prosecutions in Anbar in 2006. Lacking witnesses, Ogre could clamp down only on Shalal's most obvious chicaneries and bide his time.

In mid-October, a cop from Coolie Camp rushed up to the Camp Habbaniyah gate with his unconscious daughter in his arms. Riyam Abbad, nine, had been struck in the head by a heavy iron gate. Blood was spilling from her ears and nose. Skirting regulations, Ogre rushed her to TQ hospital, where the chief navy surgeon determined that she could die unless treated at a special care unit in Baghdad. But it was against regulations to treat Iraqi civilians in U.S. field hospitals.

"Her grandfather is a minor sheikh," said Ogre. "Can we bring her in, sir?"

"I can't take a local directly, but there's a workaround if she's as important as you say," said the surgeon.

The surgeon persuaded two C-130 pilots to fly in rainy conditions to test new gear and procedures. Upon landing, the girl received care in a U.S. hospital and gradually recovered. Ogre's stature among the shurtas skyrocketed.

His next task was to convince the cops to attend police academy training in Jordan, where they learned proper policing and the instructors vetted them, finding a tenth of the cops dirty. A local Coolie Camp sheikh had seven sons on the police payroll, lieutenants all.

"If you want to keep collecting thirty-five hundred dollars a month for your seven sons," Ogre told him, "you need to send them to Jordan."

"Who will protect my family when they are gone?"

"Give me the insurgent names," said Ogre.

"I will send them," said the sheikh, "but I will not give names."

Combat progresses one or two steps forward and then one step back. A week later, Ogre called in some Marine Corps favors to reassure his shurtas, who were terrified of venturing into Khalidiya because of Abu Roma's sniper team. Ogre asked a Marine sniper team to provide overwatch inside Khalidiya for a shurta patrol. But Roma's sniper team got off the first shot, killing Marine Corporal Jonathan Simpson. Two years earlier in the Battle of Fallujah, Simpson's cousin Abe had been killed. Back in the States, two brothers had lost two sons.

Simpson's death sent Ogre into a foul mood. Shalal mistakenly concluded that Ogre's nerves had been shaken. So he strode into Ogre's office and accused the police advisors of skimming money from the Iraqi police payroll.

"You hold all our money," Shalal said. "What happens to the missing dinars?"

Ogre exploded. "You accuse my men of stealing? They risk their lives for you. Fuck you! I'll put my fist right through the back of your lying skull, you dirty little fuck."

So much for tact, diplomacy, and never showing emotion, as recommended in advisor training. Ogre thrust his face forward. For a moment, it looked like Shalal would draw his pistol. The Iraqi police officers were stunned by the blaze of anger. Shalal was a large, powerful man, but he didn't know how to handle Ogre's outrage.

"You have insulted me," said Shalal. "I shall never forget this day."

"If you ever come here and spill out more lies," Ogre said, "I'll rip out your tongue, and your lying minions in Coolie Camp can feed on it!"

Shalal stormed out. But he had backed down in public. The shurtas later said Ogre had won over the force—and made a mortal enemy.

The police still refused to patrol inside Khalidiya. Ogre had four hundred obedient, submissive policemen who sat around substations abutting Camp Habbaniyah and wandered into friendly markets.

Ogre needed a way to get his shurtas out into contested cities like Khalidiya and Abu Fleis. He wanted to integrate shurtas into 3/3–1 patrols. The jundis could advise the shurtas. "To get cops in Khalidiya, I need 3rd Battalion to hold their hand," Ogre told Mac.

"Um, I'll talk to Colonel Fareed," said Mac without enthusiasm. Like the Iraqi officers, Mac held the police in low esteem. At best, they were worthless; at worst, they were spies for the insurgents.

In late October, Ogre was invited to a meeting where several senior Iraqi Army officers were sipping tea with a sharp-featured man dressed in a blazer and business shoes. The civilian introduced himself as Azziz and claimed to be a spokesman for the Khalidiya Tribal Council. Ogre hadn't been told that Azziz was actually Sheikh Abbas, who had made an overture to work with the Iraqi Army six months earlier, when he had approached GQ. But then commandos from special ops had a 16-year old member of Abbas's tribe, and he pulled back in protest. Now Abbas—calling himself Azziz—was back. Ogre didn't know the history because Troster was gone and the advisor team turnover had been so chilly that Mac himself had little understanding of past tribal overtures.

"If my people give information on a person," said Abbas, "the jundis and shurtas must kill or send him away forever. If he comes back, we will never give you more information. So we risk, and you jail."

Ogre studied the polished sheikh. Americans overused the word *wasta*—power and influence—but in this case Ogre thought it fit. Whoever this mysterious sheikh was, he had guts. The al Qaeda cell had gradually gained control over the twenty-five thousand residents of Khalidiya by taking over the local economy, from fuel sales to day jobs. Abbas wanted his town back.

"I'll rebuild the police station inside Khalidiya," said Ogre, stunning the crowd of senior Iraqi Army officers. "But 3rd Battalion must patrol with the shurta."

Having failed to win support from the 3rd Battalion advisors to sponsor police patrols, Ogre approached the Iraqi officers directly. He arranged a summit among Habbaniyah sheikhs, the Iraqi Army, and his police force. In return for the invitation, the sheikhs had promised to offer some tribesmen as police recruits. Before the meeting, the uneasy participants mingled in a small supply room piled with ramen noodle packets. Standing in line to use the microwave oven was Mr. Azziz, aka Sheikh Abbas, but instead of country club attire, he wore a traditional dishdasha and kaffiyeh. He ignored Ogre.

"*Salam Aleykum,* Mr. Azziz. We met the other day," Ogre greeted him.

"I do not think this is possible," said Sheikh Abbas.

"You don't remember? I am easy to forget. You are a sheikh, correct?"

"I am many things," Abbas replied.

Lieutenant Colonel Fareed was on leave, so Lieutenant Colonel Aamr was there representing 3rd Battalion. He liked Ogre from the start, but after fourteen months in Khalidiya was skeptical of grand plans with flaky locals. Aamr pulled Ogre out of the cramped room.

"I hear you are recruiting shurtas," said Aamr. "Where will they live?"

"I will build a station in Khalidiya," Ogre replied.

"In Khalidiya! They will be truck-bombed."

"We will control the streets. The shurta know the irahbi. They will point."

"Will they point to themselves?" Aamr asked.

As soon as the meeting began, instead of volunteering tribesmen, the local sheikhs recited long-winded gripes about the American occupation. Ogre was surprised they undercut his plan. "We cannot send our sons into Khalidiya," said one sheikh. "They will be killed by the foreign fighters. The soldiers cannot see them under their noses."

"We cannot see them?" bellowed the 3rd Iraqi Brigade intelligence officer. "The police are the terrorists!"

"Liar!" cried Shalal.

Ogre unholstered his pistol and set it on the table. Every family had an AK-47. The pistol was a symbol of power in Iraq, a control agent. "I am going to ask all the Americans to leave the room. If the Iraqi patriots cannot settle their differences, we have a hopeless task."

As the Americans exited, Aamr tugged at Ogre's trouser. "You are a very fine actor."

"I'm not coming back until you agree to work together," said Ogre. "The sheikhs, the shurta, the jundis."

Aamr chuckled. "We'll need food and water to last many nights."

★

In early November, Saddam Hussein was sentenced to death by hanging. While Shiites in Baghdad celebrated, many Sunnis were livid. After hearing the news, Sammy and Fosi al Fadawar, two brothers who had proclaimed themselves the "toughest mujahideen in Khalidiya," met with two Syrian AQI fighters in Khalidiya. The foursome decided to retaliate by kidnapping some jundis. They dressed in black, stuffed hundred-dollar bills into their pockets to bribe the checkpoints, and donned body armor and ski masks. They loaded their car with two PKC machine guns, four AK-47s, hundreds of bullets, a cattle prod, handcuffs, blindfolds, a hacksaw, a pistol, several knives, and a change of clothes.

Although it wasn't clear if they had been drinking or smoking hash, their behavior was bizarre. They drove through Khalidiya, playing a blaring tape from a radical imam, and stopped on 20th Street and fired their guns into the air.

"The puppets are afraid to fight real Iraqis!" one of them screamed. "God is great!"

"The jundis are on the highway. If you are so brave, why do you not attack them?" asked a bystander.

"We will do more than that!"

The four drove down Route Michigan, stopped outside a tower check-point, unleashed a string of bullets into the sandbags, and raced off toward Sadiqiya, with two Humvees full of jundis in pursuit. The lead Humvee came up over a rise and bumped into the insurgent car, which had turned around and was bearing down on them. In the turret, jundi Farat could not believe his eyes after chasing ghosts for a year. Farat jerked back the machine gun trigger, steering the bullets across the hood of the enemy car into the windshield. He did not straighten his finger until the gun was dry and the barrel was glowing pink.

Staff Sergeant Cox and several jundis climbed out of their Humvees and sprinted toward the smoking car. One insurgent popped open a door. Cox and his jundis poured four magazines into him.

When the echoes faded, Cox shouted, "Nice shooting, Farat!"

"I killed those fuckers!" shouted Farat in English. "*Allahu Akbar!*"

The pulpy bodies were dragged from the car and positioned for a picture. The jundis hugged one another and danced. The Marine gunners leaped from their turrets to take pictures and ruffle Farat's hair. He was taught the flying high five and the exploding fist. Lieutenant Hussein, a rookie officer nicknamed "Crazy Eyes" because of a lazy eye, was fiddling with the cattle prod that he thought was a flashlight. When the giddy jundis jostled their new lieutenant, he tripped the On switch. A jundi was blown off his feet, screaming about lightning.

When the cheering died down, jundi Farat crumpled to his knees and vomited uncontrollably. He apologized, but Cox rubbed his back and told him he had nothing to apologize for. "You've done your job today, jundi," Cox said.

Cox wanted to burn the bodies as a message. The jundis wanted to show them off. They loaded the bodies in an open trailer and drove slowly along Market Street. Curious boys darted in and out of the huddle trying to get close to the Iraqi soldiers, screaming that jundis had killed the Fadawar brothers. The streets were alive with shouts of congratulations and praises to God. They left the bodies to be claimed at the local hospital that had recently reopened after a two-year closure. It seemed a fitting symbol. The Iraqi troops had delivered both healing and death.

16

Sabbatical

★　★　★

October–November 2006

11 Oct 2006

From: Commander, Marine Corps Mobilization Command (IRR)
To: Major Owen O. West
Subj: Ordered to Partial Mobilization

1. YOU HAVE BEEN ORDERED TO ACTIVE DUTY IN SUPPORT
OF THE NATIONAL EMERGENCY DECLARED UNDER PRESI-
DENTIAL PROCLAMATION 7463 OF 14 SEPTEMBER 2001 . . .

I t was called an "involuntary activation." Actually, Marines don't have to be
dragged into a fight. But saying "I have been ordered to go" provided a bit of
cover on the home front, even though our wives and bosses remained skeptical. In mid-October, I left my New York desk job as a commodities trader
for Camp Pendleton, California, where I had spent five years in the 1990s as a
Marine infantry officer. I received required training that ranged from combat
first aid to the trafficking of humans and sexually transmitted diseases. The
navy doctors checked my teeth, pricked my shoulders, and tapped my knees,
and in late October, I was off to Anbar Province as a casualty replacement for
Solomon. Since my first tour in Iraq in 2003, many of my fellow Marines had
deployed two more times. As an advisor, I hoped to follow their example.

At Camp Fallujah, Colonel Coates, who was running the advisor effort in
Anbar, introduced me to Lieutenant Colonel Zientek, who happened to be in
Fallujah for a meeting. Zientek was gruff and to the point. All of his battalion
advisor teams had taken casualties, and one—Major Mac's Team Outcast in
Habbaniyah—was especially shorthanded.

"Ready to get back in the fight?" Zientek asked. "It's a highly kinetic environment. Khalidiya is watching your jundis, and the jundis are watching you. Your job is to get outside the wire twice a day. Straight, hard infantry work. No weekends. Just get after it."

I had read the new Army-Marine manual on counterinsurgency. For a field manual, it was theoretical, filled with opaque guidance for advisors at the battalion level. "Tactical success guarantees nothing," the manual stated. "As important as they are in achieving security, military actions by themselves cannot achieve success in COIN. Insurgents that never defeat counterinsurgents in combat may still achieve their strategic objectives."[1]

Yet Zientek, with his nonconflicted personality, believed that the advisor's first job was to show the Iraqis how to defeat the insurgents in combat. His guidance was not opaque. There was his way, and there was his way.

Major McNulty pulled me aside. He told me that enemy activity in Habbaniyah had just set an all-time record, with thirty-six attacks in the last few days of October. When I asked about the local mood in Khalidiya, McNulty winced. Later he told me that he'd seen both good and bad reservists in Iraq, and he wanted to stifle any bookish interpretation of warfighting I'd carried overseas in my seabag.

"The mood?" McNulty repeated. "Look, the boss is open to suggestions about how to get the job done but not discussion about what the job is. We're active advisors here. Meaning, there's a fight on, and the performance of 3rd Battalion is on you. The last team leader, Troster, got that. This one . . ."

What distinguished advisor teams was not being Marine or Army; it was how each team interpreted its primary mission. One interpretation stressed training the Iraqis in staff procedures, decision making, and accountability. The other emphasized patrolling and combat leadership. Having served as an infantry platoon commander and a recon platoon commander, I had no doubt which mission Lieutenant Colonel Zientek had just issued.

This minor clash in advising philosophy on ASP Hill reflected the confusion at the highest levels of the U.S. military about how to defeat the insurgency. The new counterinsurgency field manual deemphasized killing guerrillas, yet the daily progress reports were measured by enemy activity. The manual argued that if U.S. soldiers improved everyday life in places like Khalidiya, then the insurgents would lose the support of the people. While true in theory, in practice that meant soldiers were saddled with tasks befitting the Peace Corps more than the Marine Corps.

The Marine command in Anbar was more than a bit conflicted. The delicate balance counterinsurgency required was reflected in General Zilmer's "Flat Ass Rules" posted on unit walls throughout Anbar:

Habits of Thought

1. Sturdy Professionalism
2. Make yourself hard to kill
3. No Better friend, no worse enemy
4. First, Do no Harm
5. The Iraqi People are not our enemy, but our enemy hides among them

You have to look at these people as if they are trying to kill you, but you can't treat them that way. So (a) Be Polite, (b) Be Professional, (c) Have a plan to kill everyone you meet.

On the one hand, generals and colonels mouthed all the right platitudes about winning the people through good works. On the other hand, when discussing the war, Marines like Zilmer, Neller, Coates, Nicholson, Zientek, and McNulty said things like the people respect winners; bullies listen best with hands around their necks; if someone shoots at you, he dies; strength is a Marine's charm. Major Mac didn't understand that Marine culture had created a powerful undercurrent that pulled against the field manual doctrine.

★

I settled into ASP Hill, another creature looking for a place to bed down. Relaxing in a shower pan ringed with wool blankets was Pyro, the team mascot, and her litter of puppies. I eventually settled into an abandoned room that housed the team freezer and a large cardboard box that was used as a makeshift gladiator pit for scorpion fights.

A few days after I was posted to ASP Hill, Major Mac received another assignment. Zientek ordered me to take command of the team. Any awkwardness about Team Outcast's leadership change was smoothed over by Major Sly Sylvester's less-than-diffident manner. Although he was now my deputy on paper, he wasn't shy or deferential. He just wanted to patrol.

"It's time we got back to real Army business," Sly told me as we drove down to Camp Habbaniyah for a meeting. "West, you take care of these never-ending meetings and I'll organize the patrols outside the wire."

After an hour of jawing and arm wrestling, the National Guard firefighter from North Dakota and the Marine reservist commodities trader from New York City agreed to split the meetings and patrolling fifty-fifty.

"How can we advisors help the jundis root out the insurgents?" I asked Sly.

"Anyone who tells you an American can uncover insurgents has never patrolled in Khalidiya," Sly explained. "Trying to pick off insurgents by constant patrolling is tough. You can nail only a few."

"Like trying to kill rats in a garbage dump with a slingshot," I commented.

"I know that you have rats in New York, but I have a hard time picturing you patrolling dumps," said Sly, who had a wry sense of humor that was similar to Lieutenant Colonel Aamr's. "But yeah, we can keep the rats ducking for cover. The jundis need to patrol vigorously so the insurgents won't regain momentum."

That night I studied Troster's patrol record. It was clear they had been hit again and again by mines but did not pull back. That persistence was now paying dividends. In September and October 2005, 3/3–1 had discovered mines when they exploded. A year later, in September and October 2006, there were more total mine incidents, but insurgents were able to detonate just one bomb for every ten discoveries, a rate that was four times better than the national average. I asked Sergeant First Class Tod Caldwell, the intelligence advisor, for his opinion on the statistics.

"Two things are happening, sir," Caldwell explained. "The jundis don't go anywhere without talking to the locals first, who are finally giving out tips, and the insurgents have to plant more bombs as a result."

"But if the insurgents are able to plant bombs at will, that means they still have freedom of movement," I observed.

"I said the people give up bombs. I didn't say they give up the bomb makers."

I accompanied the next three patrols into Khalidiya and Abu Fleis. In combat, infantry units can be quickly judged by "continuing actions," small decisions that improve the odds—dispersion between men, the use of terrain when under fire, weapons carriage. It was clear that Battalion 3/3–1 was a well-trained professional force. The jundis could fight. The ghosts of advisors past walked with them. That meant the new Team Outcast could focus on breaking the insurgency's hold on Khalidiya instead of tweaking patrol formations.

We advisors were culturally blind, so the Iraqi soldiers measured progress for us. Like hundreds of other advisors in country, with a few patrols under my boots I wondered what effect we realistically had in the end on our mentored units. That question was answered a few nights later, when I was invited to a late-night goat grab—a stringy hunk of goat is placed on a communal tray to be finger-plucked as a symbol of solidarity—with the senior Iraqi officers in the battalion. Their sleep cycle made advising challenging. Lieutenant Colonel Fareed, Lieutenant Colonel Aamr, and Major Mohammed often stayed up until three a.m. talking.

"We do our best thinking when you Americans are sleeping," Aamr joked. "Which is a lot."

"From what I've seen, we do our best patrolling when you powerful officers are sleeping," I countered, grabbing another bit of goat and rice with my finger scoop. "This is what we Marines call talking guns. You think, we shoot."

Aamr and Mohammed howled. Deep into the night the trio told me the story of 3rd Iraqi Battalion and its most successful operations. When I suggested an ambush patrol, Aamr said, "You want to patrol like Roberson, but I do not think you are as brave as him."

"Something to shoot for, I guess."

"This should not be a goal. He is the reason your team is called Outcast! A strange man, this officer." Aamr laughed.

I concluded that the strongest possible influence an advisor could have was to establish a permanent mind-set in a foreign combat unit. Battalion 3/3–1 had been imbued with an uncommon fighting spirit by a steady stream of uncommon but aggressive advisors preceding me. The Iraqis often spoke of Prine, Barnes, Huss, Boz, Troster, Cox, and the true outcast, Roberson. Their ethos had permeated the Iraqi ranks.

Their way became our way.

★

The next step in turning out the enemy network was to win the cooperation of the fickle tribal leadership. On November 10, the Marine Corps birthday, Ogre approached me on Camp Habbaniyah, where I was celebrating with a beer ration Zientek had wangled.

"I need you to convince 3rd Battalion to patrol with my shurtas," Ogre declared.

"I just got here," I said.

"I got to Habbaniyah forty-five days ago, and I've got my own freaking police force," Ogre boasted. "Think big, or die trying. Literally."

"I'll tell you what I know so far," I replied. "Jundis hate shurtas."

"Listen, I need you to get Colonel Fareed to come to my next meeting with the sheikhs and the police. The last one was Kabuki theater. Aamr will tell you it was a goat rodeo, and he's right. This time, I have money. Watch them dance for me."

"You're drunk," I retorted.

"On one beer?" Ogre wondered. "Brother, only thing I'm drunk with is belief!"

On November 13, Lieutenant Colonel Fareed attended Ogre's Camp Habbaniyah meeting, and Sly and I tagged along. The small room was packed with tribal sheikhs, Iraqi cops, a U.S. public affairs officer looking for a *Stars and Stripes* story, and the rarely seen "mayor" of the Habbaniyah area, the paranoid Hussein Ali Hussein, who attended to sniff out civil improvement funds. Hussein was young and paunchy, with glasses that signaled wealth to the locals, whose concept of optometry was based on satellite television. Hussein was never clean shaven. He moved in a constant rush, as if his life depended on fidgeting. He lived in Coolie Camp, where the police presence had improved enough under Ogre to initiate small U.S. spending projects. In one case, the shurtas were supposed to guard a soccer field while locals collected the trash and received a dollar per bag. The funds, provided by the SEALs, were funneled off to the cops' families and the field looked no better, but it did spark recruiting for the police.

"Looks like the *Star Wars* bar scene in here," Sly observed when we entered the meeting.

Ogre called the participants to attention, and after an opening speech outlining his plan to put cops into Khalidiya, several of the sheikhs feigned a walkout. "Do the sheikhs in this room want construction projects?" Ogre asked.

Four sheikhs verbally clawed over one another, each boasting of contracting experience and destitute flocks, until Ogre shouted them down.

"All I hear is give me, give me. Until you persuade the shurtas—your own sons—to patrol Khalidiya, I will not discuss projects."

"They will be murdered!" shouted one sheikh.

"We will protect them," said Lieutenant Colonel Fareed.

"You live in a base on the hill!" a sheikh protested. "In Coolie Camp, we must protect ourselves."

Fareed explained, "We will fight with you as brothers. I tell you before God when I see the blood of my soldiers, I see Iraqi blood, not Shiite blood."

"Colonel Fareed's military uniform says martial law. The blue shirt of the shurta says rule of law. That is our future," said Ogre. "It is settled. Third Battalion will patrol Khalidiya with the shurta. I say to the sheikhs in the room, if the patrols go well, I will find hundred-dollar bills for public works contracts."

"It is true that we are helping God by helping you. We will allow patrols in Khalidiya," a sheikh concluded. "But Sheikh Abbas must bring his tribesmen. They are the key to the revolution."

"Revolution?" Ogre repeated. "In the American Revolution, we fought for our freedom. Are you prepared to fight for your own liberation from al Qaeda?"

"Sheik Abbas must bring his men," the sheikh insisted.

Each sheikh at the meeting promised to send his tribesmen into Khalidiya as police, but when the meeting adjourned, Lieutenant Colonel Fareed grabbed my elbow as we were walking back to the Humvees.

"Sheikhs do not mean what they say, Major," Fareed said. "Don't believe them."

"What about this Sheik Abbas I'm hearing so much about?" I asked.

"Abbas. Major, this man I do not know, and I do not trust," Fareed explained. "But we will show the shurta how things work in Khalidiya."

★

GQ was placed in charge of the first joint patrol with the Habbaniyah police. On November 14, he led a patrol to Coolie Camp to pick up the shurtas and escort them into Khalidiya. The shurtas claimed to know nothing about the scheduled patrol. Shalal, the police chief, was nowhere to be found. The jundis returned to ASP Hill cursing the shurtas.

On November 15, GQ tried again. This time the police said they had no ammunition and no training. So for the next two days, the jundis schooled the shurtas at ASP Hill, focusing on medevac drills. The shurtas were more interested in firing AK-47s, but the jundis saw no reason to dip into their own limited ammo supply. The jundis used captured insurgent stocks as target ammunition, and they were better shots than the insurgents. GQ saw no reason to change that by putting shady cops, who he believed sympathized with the insurgents, on target.

After the training, Sly asked GQ how the police looked. "If we fight each other, we can beat them," GQ replied.

On November 18, the first joint Iraqi Army–police patrol roared into Khalidiya. The shurtas wore uniforms, but their faces were covered by black ski masks for fear of being recognized by insurgents in town, including many former school friends. In the backs of white police pickup trucks, several cops were shouting into handheld loudspeakers. Hearing the cops, locals lined the streets of Khalidiya, waiting for something to happen. We advisors remained hidden in the background in case of an attack. This was a show of Iraqi solidarity, not American engineering.

"God is great!" the cops shouted. "Terrorist cowards, your end is near!"

The patrol honked its way down Michigan. Suddenly, several Opel cars carrying masked civilians darted out of Khalidiya and joined the motley formation. The convoy slowed to walking speed as cops jumped from their trucks and happily greeted the anonymous newcomers. They were local civilian tribesmen from a group called Thawar Al Anbar (TAA), the paramilitary wing of Sheik Abbas's tribal council. The TAA was in the business of revenge killing. Some were hefting wooden clubs and beating on the sides of their pickup trucks, while the police cheered and handed over their microphones. Even the jundis seemed buoyed by the presence of the tribesmen, like youngsters in a bar fight welcoming the help of wild-eyed strangers.

"The sons of Khalidiya are here to protect you," the TAA fighters shouted into the borrowed speakers. "We will destroy the terrorist cowards!"

We were standing outside our Humvees at a roadside parking lot, bemused by the carnival atmosphere, when unfortunately the 1st Iraqi Division commander, Major General Tariq, and his advisor, Colonel Juan Ayala, happened to drive by the chaotic scene on their way into Camp Habbaniyah. Tariq stopped, asked GQ what was happening, and drove away in a confused rage. He hadn't been briefed about the joint operation with police and was shocked that GQ had no idea who the TAA were. We knew we advisors were going to hear about it soon enough.

On 20th Street in downtown Khalidiya, the TAA members handed out leaflets reading, "God has called upon the people of Khalidiya to join the Al Anbar revolutionary fight against al Qaeda. If you have hurt or killed sons of Anbar, it is God's wish that now you shall die."

Giddy boys grabbed stacks of the papers and raced off to post them across the city. As the masked TAA members visited with several encouraging shopkeepers, GQ tried to persuade the police to head back home before things got out of control.

"We need them to stay!" shouted the people. "We need police!"

Some TAA fighters posted flyers listing sixty-three local men on the walls of Khalidiya's central mosque. Above the names, two weeks' notice was given for their confessions to be posted on the mosque wall, or they would be hunted down and killed.

Next, the TAA militiamen stormed an Internet café run by "E-mail Umar," who was listed on the poster. Apparently he was suspected of killing a tribesman. Coincidentally, Umar was also sought by 3rd Battalion for assassinating their best source, Omar the Teacher, who had been a trusted source for Captain Haadi. E-mail Umar wasn't at the café, so the TAA clubbed his 60-year-old father, smashed the store windows, and broke the computer screens.

"Anyone who again emails a terrorist or visits the sinner websites in this shop shall be executed, praise God!" shouted one TAA fighter.

E-mail Umar's father rushed over to GQ, holding up his broken hand and wailing piteously. GQ pulled a TAA leader into an alley that was quickly walled off by jundis.

"Any more bullying by your men," GQ threatened, "and you're on your own. I'm in charge here, not you. Now go home."

"It is my town," said the man.

"If you plan to walk around without a mask, you need my jundis."

The TAA leader offered his hand but GQ refused to take it. He whistled at his men, and they vanished in cars and on foot using back roads. GQ was convinced that many of the TAA had mined his troops in the past. Now he was supposed to shake their hands? He quickly gathered up the police and with his jundis escorted them back to Coolie Camp.

That night on ASP Hill, Lieutenant Colonel Fareed was equally conflicted. Over several glasses of tea, he told me he was affronted by "unemployed farmers and smugglers"—the TAA—in his battle space.

"If they are so tough," Fareed told me, "why have they hidden for a year while my jundis have done the hard fighting?"

"The list of sixty-three names on the mosque shook up the town, though," I said.

"That shows how much inside knowledge the tribes have," Fareed agreed. "We will tolerate these 'Sons of Iraq,' but they do not fight for Iraq at all. They fight for themselves."

Higher up in my own chain of command there was similar disapproval regarding TAA involvement in security matters. An email chain was waiting for me when I checked my account at the Horseshoe.

"The police were walking up and down the streets of ASR Michigan, some in uniform, *some in black track suits, ski masks (faces covered) and sneakers,*" Colonel Ayala had written to Zientek. "It looked like a parade of insurgents . . ."

Ayala's aversion to the sudden emergence of a tribal militia like TAA was understandable. In Baghdad throughout 2006, local militias—Shiite and Sunni alike—had been waging murder campaigns to rid their neighborhoods of minority ethnicities and religions. Now in Habbaniyah the TAA had popped out of nowhere, and the Iraqi soldiers were commingling on patrols.

We advisors at the battalion level saw it differently. In Khalidiya, there could be no security without homegrown forces, and the rosters of the police and TAA were the same. The local people did not distinguish between the Iraqi police and the TAA, and neither did the jundis. Battalion 3/3–1 was willing to let the TAA wage a war to kill or jail enough insurgents to dominate the city.

From Ogre's point of view as a police advisor, he wrote that TAA involvement was a "step in the right direction." I agreed and proposed more joint patrols with the police and their plainclothed brothers.

Zientek saw both sides of the argument. "Although not ideal by our standards, this first step at a joint IP/IA patrol in Khalidiya is being deemed a small success by the battalion MTT (West) and PTT (McCarthy)," Zientek wrote Ayala. "To tell you the truth, sir, I do not have a baseline to judge from. Every time that I have come across IPs . . . their actions were outside of what we expect of the IA."

In the absence of overarching policy, Zientek established rules for 3rd Battalion. We could support the TAA but could not conduct further joint operations with them. If TAA wanted army protection on their operations, they'd have to put on blue uniforms and become police.

★

The joint army-police patrols stumbled the following week. Six Iraqi Army officers, including GQ, were jailed by the Ministry of Defense after a drawn-out investigation of a shooting at GQ's October wedding. The officers had been dancing and firing bullets into the air when one of the soldiers tickled another. An errant shot had killed GQ's brother-in-law.

Lieutenant Colonel Aamr was dragging his feet in finding a replacement for GQ to lead the joint patrols. When I asked him why, after five days, there had been no further patrolling with the cops, Aamr blamed the chief of police.

"Shalal is a liar," Aamr said. "I know he gave machine guns to the irhabi. The hell with the police."

"Colonel Aamr, Ogre is going to put Shalal out of his misery soon," I reassured him. "But we need the police to point out the insurgents. We're trying to train shurta, not Shalal."

It turned out soldiers were not the only Iraqis with celebratory trigger fingers. On November 23, Captain Dhafer drove a patrol down to the Coolie Camp police station to bring them into Khalidiya, but the cops refused to leave their station. "We are low on ammunition," a police captain explained. "We have lost many bullets over the last few days."

Dhafer knew about it. He had heard wild celebratory fire by the police several times at night since the Khalidiya parade. "Tomorrow I may return with ammunition," Dhafer promised. "If your men waste it in the air, I'm coming back for you personally."

"We have many police here. You better bring your whole army, if you make such a threat," said the captain.

"But you have no bullets, remember?" Dhafer retorted.

The following day, though, the joint patrol was again canceled. The police were on strike. A drunken police captain had rampaged through Coolie Camp the night before, battering his way into houses looking for women to rape. A SEAL patrol sneaking through town heard screaming. They captured the inebriated cop and hauled him back to Camp Habbaniyah.

"I will kill the Iraqi puppet soldiers," the Iraqi captain screamed. "My police kill Americans. All of you will die when I am free."

The SEALs added the threats to a charge sheet they prepared and locked the drunken captain in the American jail. Hearing this, the cops in Coolie Camp went on strike, refusing to report for work.

Ogre called an emergency meeting in Camp Habbaniyah to discuss what to do about the police boycott. I accompanied a grumbling Lieutenant Colonel Aamr, who was sick of coddling the police, to the meeting, where Mayor Hussein warned that keeping the police captain in jail risked a backlash.

"The shurta may never come to work again in Coolie Camp, let alone Khalidiya!" shouted Mayor Hussein.

"I know the shurta better than you, Mayor," Ogre replied. "They are not quitting."

Aamr slammed an open palm on the desk. "Then why won't they show up for joint patrols? Why do they not heed you, Colonel McCarthy? Because they are mixed up with the enemy!"

Aamr stormed out of the meeting.

Lieutenant Colonel Todd Desgrosseilliers, the fiery commander of Marine Battalion 3/2—the Betio Bastards, the partner unit for 3/3-1—caught up to Aamr in the parking lot. With his thin mustache, wiry build, and wicked smile, Desgrosseilliers looked like a crazed 1970s cross-country runner. He had been awarded the Silver Star during the Battle of Fallujah in 2004, where despite being twice wounded he'd led a shock troop that killed dozens of insurgents in a series of house-to-house firefights. Desgrosseilliers toured the Habbaniyah battlefield with a bayonet affixed to the barrel of his carbine. In the U.S. war colleges, frustrations with the conduct of the war were mounting, and it had become popular for senior officers to dismiss as antiquated so-called kinetic focus. Since their arrival in August, the Betio Bastards had eleven men KIA and dozens more wounded, including several double amputees. In Desgrosseilliers's mind, Habbaniyah did not deserve coddling.

"We must keep up the tempo," Desgrosseilliers told Aamr. "If police stumble, my Marines will support you. What do you need?"

The Betio Bastards were the best U.S. partner the Iraqis ever had, and Aamr hated asking for more, but no Iraqi could resist a wish list. "Our vehicles are broken. It is hard to increase patrols."

"I will lend you my Humvees."

"These are the words of a brother," said Aamr. "And a rich one!"

"We've been trying to get them fixed at TQ, sir," I told Desgrosseilliers, "but the regs prevent the mechanics there from fixing Iraqi Humvees."

"The bureaucrats have no interest in winning this thing!" Desgrosseilliers barked. "You guys need something, come to me, or else it'll just get shot down."

I knew that I was responsible for managing 3/3–1's relationship with U.S. units. As we drove back up ASP Hill together, I asked Aamr if he was comfortable leaning on the Betio Bastards, considering the troubled partnership with TF Panther I heard so much about during the goat grab.

"He who has the biggest gun is always welcome at my table," Lieutenant Colonel Aamr said. "And anyway, Desgrosseilliers thinks like an Iraqi."

In Habbaniyah, Desgrosseilliers was king. He traveled his battle space often, intent on knowing everything from the size of a sheikh's family to the price of black market benzene. In a war where many officers were cautious about setting goals, Desgrosseilliers was openly determined to win.

Unlike previous U.S. dispositions, Desgrosseilliers's Marines were deployed in twelve outposts spread across five kilometers. India Company, led by Captain Joe Burke, had four outposts just west of Khalidiya. In mid-November, Burke had proposed that squads of jundis move in with his men. The jundis would gain access to stacks of DVDs and overflowing care packages. The Marines would teach them tactics and in return learn about culture and expand their intelligence gathering.

Sly and I thought it was a great idea. Labeled the "Jundi Advisor Group," more than a hundred jundis volunteered to "teach" the Marines how to hunt insurgents. The first squad of jundis returned from their five-day stint with bulging pockets of chewing gum, new ponchos, and exotic tales of aggression. The jundis, enraptured by the cocky toughness of the Marines, had walked through bad neighborhoods including Sadiqiya without vehicles or officers. After a week with the Marines, the jundis were eager to build their own network of informants instead of relying on their officers.

They also returned to ASP Hill with requests for a unit slogan. The Marines loved nicknames and mottoes. They had ribbed the jundis over their battalion shoulder patch—a fuzzy bird of prey beneath a parachute, supposedly signifying special operations. Actually, it looked like a chicken under an umbrella. The advisors and the Marines called it "Super Chicken."

Jundi Irhabi Hater proposed a new symbol—a falcon clutching a snake. The battalion nickname "Snake Eaters" was tabled during dinner. When the Iraqi officers heard it was a U.S. Special Forces slogan from Vietnam, the nickname was boisterously approved.

"Yes, we hunt snakes—terrorist snakes who crawl on their stomachs!" shouted Captain Dhafer. "We are indeed the Snake Eaters!"

17

Everyone Is an Insurgent
Until He Is Not

★ ★ ★

November 2006

The Snake Eaters were in a tactical rut. Except for the jundis who were embedding each week in the Betio Bastard squads, the rest of the battalion employed a predictable pattern of vehicle patrols, which were always spotted by young lookouts in the employ of the insurgents. As a result, bomb emplacers were in no danger of being caught, especially at night, when there was no way for locals to notify the Snake Eaters that men were digging outside their houses since the cell phone towers in town had long ago been destroyed. Local informants could not hop in their cars and drive to a 3/3–1 checkpoint at night on Michigan to warn the jundis without being fired upon. So they had to await sunrise, when the insurgents were hours gone. This explained why the number of mines in Khalidiya continued to climb even as tips prevented their detonation.

Over dinner with the Snake Eaters officers one night in late November, Sly and I suggested adding some creative tactics to give the jundis a better chance of capturing or killing an insurgent in the act. We had to clamp down on the enemy's ability to move freely. Major Mohammed immediately volunteered to lead a foot patrol into Khalidiya. He was a staff officer now and spent his time planning patrols and monitoring radios at HQ, which he hated. His path back outside the wire was on foot.

An hour before midnight on November 26, a jundi point man used his rifle barrel to lift a strand of barbed wire that marked the border of ASP Hill. Major Mohammed took the lead as the patrol passed under the wire. He was not wearing body armor and set a fast pace. The fifteen-man patrol stretched like an accordion as it snaked through the hardened dunes toward Khalidiya. So the dogs that patrolled the wasteland would not hear them, Mohammed hiked toward the loudest generator in Khalidiya to cover their movement. By the time they reached the edge of town, Mohammed was moving so quickly that the jundis were panting. Well behind them in the file, the advisors were laboring under their heavy equipment as well.

"This is all kinds of stupid," said Sly, who was built like a hockey player. "We're strung out so far, the sun will come up before we get to the point man."

Sly, who knew his way around combat patrolling, saw no sense in a foot race through a dangerous city at night.

When the advisors caught up with him, Mohammed was interrogating some local curfew breakers. When he saw the advisors, Mohammed took off again at a blistering pace. Sly caught him by the elbow and hissed, "Hey, slow it down, Mohammed. We're not accomplishing anything like this."

"This is not about you," he shot back.

Mohammed was showing off for his jundis. He knew the American rules meant the relief of any advisor who did not wear every piece of body armor on patrol, which hampered their movements. The Americans were angry and embarrassed to be asking the jundis to slow down.

Eager to tap into the word on the streets, Mohammed stopped another small cluster of locals, and they all talked under the steady hum of the generators while the advisors recaptured their collective wind.

"The people are more friendly," Mohammed came back to tell the advisors. "But if they give us the names, and we arrest the terrorists, they will just go free. It is better to kill them. If we don't, the TAA will, the people tell me."

As the patrol approached Michigan, a black-clad figure darted away from the highway and sprinted past the shouting jundis into town. The advisors were closest to the figure, but they couldn't chase the shadow in all their gear and could not shoot him either, which was illegal without absolute certainty as to the man's intentions.

"Next time, I will put a jundi in back," Mohammed lectured the advisors. "He won't miss a chance like that."

This kind of fleeting encounter was common, where the Americans fought like turtles and the insurgents like rabbits. The jundis fell somewhere in between. The insurgents initiated almost all of the fights. They commonly sprinted to safety when they were surprised. The Americans chose heavy armor over mobility. Patrolling without the turtle shell of heavy armor was a grave offense that led to court-martial.

That night I had to submit a significant event report, which was required for patrols with enemy contact. The report needed a personal protection addendum, where I had to testify that every American in the patrol wore full body armor. Across Iraq, casualty statistics were meticulously scrubbed for evidence of armor protection. Naturally there were hundreds of examples of lives and limbs saved by the heavy armor, reinforcing the policy, but that was circular reasoning. Lost was the fact that more soldiers were hit because they couldn't move quickly, and more insurgents survived because they were rarely detected, let alone caught.

We needed to keep up with our jundis on foot at night, when our chances of being struck by an IED were minimal anyway. So I put in for a waiver for advisors to remove their flak vests and helmets at night according to the team leader's discretion.

Major McNulty looked over my request and laughed. "They'll never let you do it," he told me. "Day, night, doesn't make a difference. Next you'll be asking to be treated like a major in the Marine Corps."

★

In addition to mixing in foot patrols to keep the insurgents off balance, we advisors lobbied for air support to fill the gaps between patrols in Khalidiya. Lieutenant Colonel Zientek dispatched an ANGLICO (Air Naval Gunfire Liaison Company) team—Marines who were experts in controlling aircraft with radios and computers linked to receive real-time video from aircraft and unmanned aerial vehicles (UAVs)—to join Team Outcast on ASP Hill. This provided overhead surveillance of our area and frightened the insurgents.

On the night of November 28, a Marine F-18 was vectored to Khalidiya to support an ambush patrol led by Captain Dhafer. Dhafer hid in a graveyard overlooking the southern edge of town while the aircraft searched for suspicious movement. The pilot spotted five men rushing back and forth between a house and a car parked in a courtyard, which was rare. He illuminated the courtyard with an infrared beam. The shaft of invisible light was revealed in the night-vision goggles of the advisors, who guided the Iraqi patrol to the suspect house. Five male teenagers were sitting in the living room, drinking chai.

"Why are you going back and forth to the car in the courtyard?" Dhafer asked.

The boys looked startled. "We haven't been out to the car tonight."

When the jundis roughly zip-tied the boys, they broke down. They had a bottle of booze in the car and were sneaking drinks behind the backs of their parents.

"We have satellites now that watch this town all day," Dhafer warned them. "I saw the five of you running to take a drink on my television. Tell your friends that when they move, we watch."

As we walked out, I commented, "So much for secrecy, Dhafer."

"Secrecy?" Dhafer retorted. "It is more important they know who has the power. None of those men will ever dig again."

"How do you know they were insurgents?"

"Everyone is an insurgent until he is not," he quipped.

During the last week of November, an ANGLICO Marine was controlling an unmanned drone just after dark when he spotted three men digging a mine into Abu Fleis Road. A vehicle patrol led by Captain Haadi was vectored to the site. Hearing the Humvees, the diggers raced into a nearby house. Haadi and his men burst into the house a few minutes later and found four senior members of the 1920 Revolutionary Brigade relaxing on a couch. In the background, women scrambled to hide shovels and wire. The men refused to talk to Haadi. But he didn't mind—the evidence was strong for once, and he was thrilled. All four were bound by the jundis and patted down for delivery to jail, and then Haadi kept them on their stomachs on their floor for over an hour so they could hear the thunderous controlled detonation of their mine by EOD.

"How did you find us?" one of the men asked, breaking the silence.

"You must ask God about that when you are in prison," Haadi replied. "This is my town now, and I am always watching, like a falcon. I am a Snake Eater."

Later that night, Haadi celebrated the arrest over chai and cigarettes at the 3rd Company bunker. A wooden ammunition crate was broken up and used as fuel for a fire that was quickly surrounded by happy jundis seeking relief from temperatures in the 40s.

"We are the hunters now," Haadi told his men.

"In America, we call this the predator-prey relationship," I told Haadi. "There can be no doubt in town that the Snake Eaters are the predators."

To underscore the proud feeling of battlefield dominance on ASP Hill, we advisors held a small ceremony for Irhabi Hater and Jundi Farat, who had killed the Fadawar brothers. They were praised for their bravery and steady aim, and awarded military equipment: knee pads, rifle-mounted flashlights, and state-of-the-art bandages that had been donated by my fellow traders at Goldman Sachs.

"I will kill many more, to get a GPS next time!" said Hater.

"If you kill five, Hater, you get a CamelBak," I said, to clapping from the jundis.

Hater was swollen with pride. He took stock of me. "Major West, perhaps you will wrestle me for the CamelBak right now?"

The jundis cheered Alex's translation and clustered tightly around me and Hater to see how this would turn out. It was my turn to take stock of Hater. He removed his shirt. He was a big kid, and if I wrestled him, there would be no good end to it, no matter the outcome.

I smiled. "In the Marines, we don't wrestle, Hater, we fight."

Hater pursed his lips and eventually fell for my bluff, wagging his finger at me, laughing. "In Iraq, we do not fight our brothers. You Americans are too violent!"

★

The jundis weren't the only hunters in Khalidiya. Though the joint army-police patrols had stalled, the TAA had not. On the afternoon of December 1, "Captain King"—a Marine intelligence expert brought in by Lieutenant Colonel Zientek to help manage local information and whose real name was never revealed—drove up ASP Hill waving a cluster of dirty papers.

"Remember when the TAA posted those warnings on the mosque saying they'd kill anyone on the list who didn't confess by today at noon?" King said. "Well, a few dozen have confessed. They pledged allegiance to the TAA and promised never to support AQI! Now Sheikh Abbas wants the police to arrest some of the others tonight, like he promised in the flyer. Can your Snake Eaters provide military cover for the shurta?"

Until then, I had shared the Iraqi officers' skepticism about Sheikh Abbas's TAA. Now here was King with a ream of signed confessions of some of Khalidiya's most-wanted insurgents. I met with Lieutenant Colonels Fareed and Aamr, and they agreed to back up the shurtas on a raid that night. The plan was for the Snake Eaters to surround a few of the suspects' houses with Humvees while the police went inside and made the arrests. Aamr started to draw up the operation. I called Zientek to inform him.

"I don't like this," said Zientek. "If the TAA kills someone, you're in deep."

"These are Iraqi police we're working with, sir," I explained.

"Police and TAA are the same, and you know it. Third Battalion will have no control over what goes on in those houses. You'll be left holding the bag on scene if this goes bad. You trust the TAA?" he asked.

"I trust that our short-term interests are the same," I reassured him.

An hour later, as the Snake Eaters were rehearsing the upcoming raid by using a barracks building to simulate a target house, Major McNulty called me. "The boss is pretty unhappy. My advice is to stand down, as painful as that may be."

"In the end it's the Iraqis' call, right?" I asked. "We advise, they decide."

"We both know that's not true," McNulty said.

I trotted outside the Horseshoe to find Fareed inspecting his jundis at the gate, telling them how important this operation with the police was.

"Colonel Fareed, it would be a very good thing to stay home tonight," I announced.

"But you supported this," he told me.

"I now think it is a bad idea."

"Sheikh Abbas and his tribe will lose belief in us. I have promised," Fareed protested.

"Colonel Fareed . . ."

"I can see by your face that you are in pain," he said. "All right. If my advisor says I must cancel this operation, I will cancel."

Right then I knew how effective Troster's team had been.

Two miles away, just inside the sandbagged entrance to Coolie Camp, First Lieutenant Khalid was awaiting final instructions from ASP Hill on escorting the raid force into Khalidiya. But there were no police that he could see. In their place were three carloads of hyperactive masked militiamen with blankets covering their laps. Khalid figured they were hiding weapons. Zientek's instincts had been correct. The operation was a TAA hit, not a police action. After talking to Fareed on the radio, Khalid broke the news to the militiamen, "The operation is canceled."

The TAA hit men cursed the jundis and disappeared into the night with their headlights off. A few hundred meters down Route Michigan, taillights popped on. The TAA cars reversed and raced back into Coolie Camp.

"You have lost your courage in three minutes!" Khalid teased the TAA leader as the militiamen headed back to their homes.

"You are naïve if you think you can succeed here without us," the man warned.

"For one and a half years, my jundis have gone into town again and again," said Khalid. "You say you are the answer, but driving into Khalidiya at night is different when it is real, isn't it."

18

Women and Children Last

★ ★ ★

December 2006

"U nity of effort" is a central tenet of counterinsurgency. In practical terms it means comity between parties that have separate bases of power and goals. Ogre's weekly police meeting provided the classic example in the Habbaniyah area. The participants who came together to try to work toward a common goal on December 3 were representative of the different power bases: two Marine colonels, two Iraqi Army colonels and their advisors, two high-level Iraqi cops, and two sheikhs.

Before the meeting, Lieutenant Colonel Zientek pulled Ogre and me aside for a quick tutorial. "I can't get concrete guidance from headquarters on how to handle the TAA," he said. "The Iraqi generals want us to play ball with TAA, but if they kill an innocent civilian and you're on scene, you face courts-martial. So joint patrols with TAA are out."

The regulations were clear: Advisors were supposed to report any Iraqi soldier who used physical force on a captive suspect, including open-handed slaps. In fact, the advisors were expected to step in physically to prevent it. This was tricky ground. When does an advisor turn against the man he is advising? A half century ago, in Vietnam, it was a matter of individual conscience when an advisor intervened. In Iraq, advisors were ordered to impose the Western rule of law in situations where no one knew what the "rule of law" meant. So senior officers like Zientek tried to shield the junior advisors, like me, by laying down ironclad rules to keep us away from the murk. I never heard of an advisor turning in an Iraqi soldier for using excessive force during an arrest.

After Ogre called the meeting to order, Lieutenant Colonel Fareed said,

"I have heard a rumor that TAA is planning to enter my battle space at night. Nothing happens in Khalidiya without our knowledge."

"We don't understand why you canceled the raid," Abbas told Fareed. "We want to kill the terrorists."

"You're not real soldiers. Militias are causing problems in Baghdad," Fareed explained. "We cannot have the same here."

"As God the most merciful knows, the terrorists are not real soldiers, either. There are foreign fighters in Khalidiya," said Abbas. "Help us to kill them."

The police chief, Shalal, had not regained stature after Ogre had insulted him. His replacement was inevitable unless he found new benefactors. So he spoke up in favor of the TAA.

"Thawar Al Anbar are good people," Shalal declared. "They have lost fathers and sons. I am working with them to stabilize Khalidiya—"

"All I need is sixty days," interrupted Abbas. "Then I will disband the TAA." No one believed him.

"The police are the proper tool, not TAA," said Lieutenant Colonel Aamr. "But they are afraid to patrol with us. It's one excuse, then another. Nothing changes."

Shalal protested loudly, "My police have no equipment and no fuel to patrol."

"Then we will go together, army and police, to the petrol station and we provide you with fuel," Lieutenant Colonel Fareed retorted.

Shalal laughed. "You don't understand how things work in Habbaniyah."

Lieutenant Colonel Desgrosseilliers of the Betio Bastards shot out of his chair. "You watch how to talk to that man! His men and mine are getting killed every day!"

Desgrosseilliers had no patience for two-faced local Iraqi "leaders" like Chief Shalal. A dozen of Desgrosseilliers's Marines had died in Habbaniyah. A week before, a young member of his personal security detail had been killed by a suicide car bomber west of Sadiqiya. He leaned over the table and pointed at Shalal's eyeball. "I'm sick of your shit, you coward!"

"Do not yell at my face," said Shalal.

"I'll scream in your face! Want to settle this like a man?"

Shalal was stunned. For three years, U.S. units had treated him as royalty, even giving him a patchwork National Guard unit to command on ASP Hill until it was "overrun" by insurgents. Now, for the second time in a month, a Marine colonel was challenging him to fight in front of the group. "Police are not Marines!" he pleaded. "The IED in Khalidiya today would have blown my truck apart."

"Your men can ride with mine in Humvees into Khalidiya," Fareed argued. "The TAA is also welcome, but with no weapons. They will point out the guilty."

"Absurd—my men must protect themselves," Abbas protested. "We will go into Khalidiya without you, and you will never know."

"Habbaniyah belongs to my battalion," Fareed said. "Your militia will ruin everything! If you come in, my jundis will shoot you down."

Ogre stood up, and the room settled down.

"Sheikh Abbas, you know as well as I do that there are no secrets in Khalidiya," Ogre said. "This is the resolution. Colonel Fareed's jundis will escort the shurtas to the fuel station. Then we will begin joint patrols again. The TAA can give information."

No one was satisfied, but no one wanted to get into an extended shoving contest with Ogre. We had reached what the counterinsurgency field manual called unity of effort.

★

The joint patrols with the police restarted, although the bickering continued. The police insisted upon being driven into Khalidiya in Iraqi Humvees. The Snake Eaters, who were starting to feel like chauffeurs, were determined to find out why the police never had fuel for their vehicles.

Habbaniyah had two gas stations—one was government run and one was private. On December 5, Lieutenant Colonel Aamr led a vehicle patrol to the government station, which was located at the base of ASP Hill at the foot of a small, sandy cliff. Aamr's patrol slowly drove past the long queue of cars and wheeled up to the tiny manager's hut that was built like an individual bomb shelter.

"Who gets to the head of the line?" Aamr asked the proprietor, tilting his head at the men at the front of the line who looked tougher than the rest.

"I don't know," said the owner. "It is not my business."

"Who takes the most fuel?"

The proprietor nervously eyed the queue. "Sir, I have a family. The longer we talk, the more they want to kill me."

The proprietor refused to discuss anything further, so Aamr instructed him to fill up the police vehicles anytime they needed fuel or his insurgent-infested operation would be shut down.

"But, sir, I always fill up the police cars. And their families' and friends' too!"

A disgusted Aamr drove to the private station two kilometers east on Route Michigan, where the owner was selling fuel at a modest markup. "I set a ration of five liters of fuel a day for everyone in line," the owner told Aamr. "That is the fair way."

"There are wealthy men in Abu Fleis," Aamr said, "who burn through five liters every day in their generators and cars."

"They send their chai boys to stand in line each day."

"Why sell to them? You know they are the ones who kill innocents."

The owner laughed. "Sir, I swear before God, I would have to live on the moon if I did not sell to them! They would kill me the same night."

"Do the police ever buy here?" Aamr asked.

The man laughed. "They get benzene sometimes, but they never pay!"

That night Aamr and I worked out the math. Habbaniyah residents consumed more than 240,000 liters of fuel each month. The Iraqi government supplied Habbaniyah with a 120,000-liter truck delivery, split between the government station and the private one. The black market supplied the rest. Judging from the Khalidiya street price charged by insurgent agents, they netted a monthly profit of about $200,000. The profiteers had a huge incentive to pay $100 to each digger who would plant a mine to prevent the Snake Eaters from gaining control of the streets—and of the fuel business. The fifteen bombs the Snake Eaters encountered each month cost the profiteers less than 1 percent of their revenues.

The Snake Eaters approached Lieutenant Colonel Desgrosseilliers, asking for the Betio Bastards' help in putting an end to the thugs who controlled the fuel queues. The problem was, the Snake Eaters didn't know an insurgent from a friendly local.

"Let's get Abbas involved," Desgrosseilliers suggested. He gave Sheikh Abbas a dozen decals that showed the fighting mask worn by Russell Crowe's renegade general in *Gladiator*. If your car had a sticker, Marines were your big brothers, and anyone you fought was an enemy. A few days later, several trucks displaying the decals drove past rumbling Marine tanks that patrolled Route Michigan on their way to the government gas station.

The TAA tribesmen questioned each man waiting in line. They quickly identified four known insurgents controlling the crowd, threw them onto the street, and beat them with clubs and the butts of their AKs. Other drivers cheered this local resistance. Soon positive rumors about the TAA were all over Khalidiya.

Ogre and Desgrosseilliers butted heads over the TAA. Ogre was worried about his friend becoming entangled with a militia. "I've spent months sorting out the shurta," Ogre told Desgrosseilliers. "Boosting the TAA could undercut the authority of my cops."

"From what I hear, the TAA *are* the cops," Desgrosseilliers said. "Let them police themselves."

"It's dangerous, man," Ogre warned.

"It's a war."

★

Snake Eater officers also encouraged the tribesmen to use vigilante tactics. In mid-December, a TAA squad charged into a Khalidiya house and beat to death four insurgents. None of the advisors was in town at the time, and when Sly and I checked the patrol schedule, we saw that a Snake Eater patrol scheduled for that time slot had been mysteriously canceled.

"Maybe the TAA sneaked into Khalidiya between patrols," Dhafer told me with a straight face. "It is not a bad thing. I hear Muj Mom is next on their list."

"Muj Mom" was a 50-year-old woman who lived in a stately compound on 20th Street. After her husband was killed by a U.S. tank in 2004, Muj Mom had opened her house to al Qaeda transients. Her neighbors claimed she slept with insurgents in return for bombs and money. When the jundis arrested her son in early 2006, she had chased the Humvee down the street like a "crazed dog," according to Dhafer. After that, she stood on her stoop defiantly whenever the jundis walked by.

On December 3, Captain Haadi had been leading a foot patrol near Muj Mom's house when a bomb exploded a meter away, flinging him over a small wall. He suffered a concussion but returned to duty. Four witnesses fingered Muj Mom. For Americans to arrest a female required permission from a general. In twenty-four hours, we had approval and a rough plan of action: A female American doctor from TQ had volunteered to accompany us to her house in daylight to squelch local sensitivities about men arresting a woman.

"It won't work," said Lieutenant Colonel Fareed. "Khalidiya will lose its dignity if we arrest her."

I was surprised. "You've been watching her for a year, and she almost killed Haadi a few days ago!"

"Even with a woman doctor arresting her, the men in town will feel ashamed. They know in their minds what Abu Ghraib is like."

"Colonel Fareed, she'll be treated well. You know that."

"It is the sex! Khalidiya will think this woman is being raped, and the people will hate us for allowing you to take her," Fareed said. "It is better to have the TAA kill her. But you won't permit it. So we are stuck."

★

In Iraqi towns like Khalidiya, females were the third rail. The U.S. servicemen had adjusted to the male-dominated Iraqi culture, typically avoiding Iraqi women altogether. When you raided a house at night, no good could come of quizzing a hysterical female. The women were placed together in a room and left alone. In the daylight it was just as bad. Some women were alarmed by the slightest glance, scattering like startled birds as the sheepish advisors offered lame apologies to old men who loudly sucked their teeth at an imperceptible transgression.

There was a minority belief, expressed mostly by U.S. officers, that to ignore women was to ignore 50 percent or more of the battlefield intelligence. Perhaps an astute female interrogator could convince a wife to give up insurgents who were not relatives. The Iraqi soldiers were dismissive of this theory. Convincing women to betray males was preposterous.

"Even the smartest ladies, what can we offer them in return?" Captain Dhafer said with a laugh when the topic came up at an ASP dinner. "We cannot give money because they will shame their families and be called prostitutes. Women have no power."

Captain Haadi thought Dhafer was wrong on the last point. His top source, Cleopatra, was a widow who had taught at Baghdad University. She lived in a large house in Abu Fleis and counseled members of the 1920 Revolutionary Brigade and, hedging her bets, Haadi.

In mid-December, an extremely upset Haadi appeared in my room. He was shaking when he briefed me on Cleopatra, who had a tumor the size of a baseball growing in her neck. "You must help this woman, Major. Her irhabi friends can do nothing for her. She is ready to switch sides if she can live."

"Captain Haadi, you know we're told never to make a promise to an Iraqi," I said flippantly. "You never forget."

His eyes welled. "You must do this thing! I have never asked for anything!"

"Haadi, this is against the rules."

"I am asking now!" Haadi insisted.

I emailed navy doctors Michael Thompson and Ted Edson at the TQ hospital. They had broken regulations a few months earlier for Ogre to save the little girl with the fractured skull. "We can't help her on TQ," Edson wrote. "We'd have to break down walls to get her on a flight. Is she worth it?"

"She could become 3rd Battalion's most important source. It will have a direct battlefield impact," I wrote.

Edson called me a few hours later. "I called in a few favors and we might be able to pull this off. It's going to take heavy lifting, but we're here to fight the insurgency, same as you."

At midnight the next evening, we drove into Abu Fleis and knocked on the outer door of the widow's compound. Cleopatra's living room smelled of chai and cinnamon candies. She was elegantly dressed but looked gaunt. She smiled faintly and pointed to a silk-covered couch. We heavily armored advisors sat awkwardly on the lip of the sofa, hoping we wouldn't get it dirty.

"Relax, please. Have some tea," she said in English. "I never thought I'd have American soldiers sitting in my living room. This is a fine evening."

"We really need to get you out of here, ma'am," said Sergeant Brian Schwarzman, Team Outcast's medic. "Wherever we go, things tend to happen."

She laughed. "My friend, nothing will happen to you when you are with me."

Her son was a big kid who demanded to escort his mother back to TQ air base, where her helicopter journey would begin. "I will be with her the whole way," he said in English. "I must protect her. There is no choice in this matter."

"That won't work," I said. "Your mother seems like she can take care of herself."

The boy looked at his mother and they both laughed. "This is quite true," he admitted.

When they embraced, I saw her growth. It was the size of a cantaloupe. When she was safely inside the Humvee, I quietly asked Haadi, "What happens if she dies in our hospital? Our own jundis still believe Americans are perpetuating the war." When an insurgent was freed from prison, or a mine turned up in a suspicious spot, jundis occasionally spread rumors that we Americans were purposely extending the war to benefit oil and defense companies.

"Many in Abu Fleis will say we kidnapped and killed her," said Haadi.

At the field hospital, Edson and Thompson were waiting. Once she was inside the facility, her mannerisms became Western, and she happily chatted with Edson.

"If she makes it, this is going to have a huge impact," I told Edson.

"It better!" he joked.

At the U.S. Army hospital in Baghdad after a flight on a U.S. plane, a surgeon cut away the growth and expertly sutured Cleopatra's neck. Tests showed no traces of cancer. A few weeks later, Haadi told me she was eating again and in the best of spirits. "So can you get intel from her?" I asked.

"It is better than that," said Haadi. "She is telling her people that they are wrong about me. She loved how she was treated in Baghdad. Much more, I cannot say, but I have a dozen new sources."

Haadi never told me how many members of the 1920 Revolutionary Brigade came over to his side, but he believed they stopped placing mines in Abu Fleis.

★

By the end of 2006, the security situation in Khalidiya had improved enough to conduct medical outreach. Aamr and Fareed remembered Troster's attempt of a year earlier that had quickly devolved into a gunfight. Now they set their sights higher and asked for a half dozen doctors to treat an entire Khalidiya neighborhood.

On December 7, a makeshift clinic was set up in an elementary school on 20th Street that was surrounded by a high wall. The Snake Eaters, the Betio Bastards, and the SEALs provided medics—including a female doctor—while the Iraqi police made their first large-scale show of force since the parade through town a month earlier.

The Betio Bastards donated a psyops Humvee mounted with an enormous speaker that could broadcast throughout town. Once the school was secured, with soldiers on the wall and Humvees blocking the roads, Fareed grabbed the microphone from a psyops officer and announced, "This aid clinic is sponsored by your countrymen, soldiers, and your police. Help us rid Khalidiya of terrorists and there will be more. We have brought a woman doctor."

The line of women grew so quickly that the Humvees in the security cordon expanded the perimeter two blocks. Some of the people suffered from grotesque maladies. The Hunchback of Khalidiya, a tiny woman whose spine was rigidly bent like a fishhook, rested on her side in the street, awaiting her turn. A young woman was cradling an eight-day-old baby no larger than a canteen.

Two advisors were especially riveted by the scene. Lance Corporal Tim Smith, who had graduated from his Kentucky high school only a year earlier, moved forward to help organize the crowd, which was starting to get unruly. Gunnery Sergeant James Newton, a tough Marine who had volunteered for advisor duty as a filler between regular combat tours and was built like a football guard, grabbed him by the arm.

"Jesus Christ, look at them," said Smith.

"We're not going to be able to treat them all," Newton explained. "Get back on your guard post. We got company coming."

A group of Iraqi police carrying an old man in a wicker chair shoved their way past the women to the head of the line and set him down at the school entrance, where another policeman patted him for a suicide vest and waved him through. Behind him, other men, less old and less infirm, cut the line.

"The shurta have collected a few local sheikhs and tribesmen," Ogre told me. "They get priority treatment."

"What's wrong with them?" I asked.

"They're terminally selfish," Ogre quipped.

The SEALs created a second line for women only. Clothing was handed out to the neediest families. My wife had sent a large package of bubbles. As a demonstration, I blew a few to the delight of the children and reached back for the box to hand out the containers to the kids, but some kid had stolen it.

Having let the first ten men in line see the doctor, the jundis were rewarded with information on the location of two bombs and asked the advisors to let even more men inside.

Lance Corporal Smith had seen enough. He hopped off the wall overlooking the crowd and stormed over to the men waiting their turn. "Get the hell out of here. You ain't sick."

"At ease, Smith," I said.

"Sir, we're just gonna sit here and watch this? It's wrong!"

"Get back to the truck, Smith," said Gunny Newton. "*NOW.*"

As the operation was coming to a close, one of the SEALs stood atop the wall and led a wild throng of children in a dance routine. If they ably mimicked his moves, he tossed candy and blankets. Soon his bag was empty, and the older boys who continued for a few minutes to dance for free felt ridiculed.

Rocks sailed over the wall. Pebbles at first, small symbols of irritation, but soon large stones came flying. The crowd surged up against the schoolyard gate, sensing that the clinic was about to close.

"This is bad. Get the trucks ready to roll," Sly ordered. "We're outta here."

Ours was the last Humvee to leave the compound. Stones were coming in waves. In the Humvees ahead of us, the turret gunners tucked down into their trucks as they ran the gauntlet of flying rocks. Space opened between our vehicle and the next, and it was immediately filled with screaming locals who blocked our exit. The Humvee was immobilized. I was on foot with Newton and Sly, and shouldered my rifle.

Gunny Newton roared. Everyone in the crowd stopped. He was the largest man in Khalidiya. Newton charged out in front of the Humvee. The tough street kids looked at him in horror and fled. Sly and I hopped into the Humvee, and with Gunny as our escort, we drove out of town without being hit by a single rock.

"Thanks, Gunny." I said.

"Not a problem."

At ASP Hill, Lieutenant Colonel Fareed was overjoyed. "The people are embracing us. We received over fifty names. It will take a month to arrest them. We must do this again soon."

"It was a disaster," I said.

"A disaster? Oh, you mean the stones they threw at you. That's nothing. You're just Amerikees, that's all."

19

I Fought the Law and I Won

★ ★ ★

December 2006

On the 8th, Captain Haadi halted his vehicle patrol on Route Michigan in front of a three-story marble-encrusted house three hundred meters east of the entrance to Abu Fleis. The owner, who was nicknamed "Yahoo," was a wealthy Baathist who, prompted by Cleopatra, had contacted Alex via email. Yahoo was willing to trade insurgent names for information on upcoming construction projects sponsored by the Americans that Lieutenant Colonel Desgrosseilliers had recently promised if the roadside bombings stopped.

"Tell the advisors to wait here," Haadi told Alex.

He walked into the house alone, leaving four advisors and a dozen jundis out in the open on Route Michigan, within range of Abu Roma's snipers. Haadi walked out an hour later and offered no apology.

"The next time you drink stupid juice for breakfast, Haadi," I threatened, "we stay home."

"As God hears me declare it, it was the right thing," Haadi replied. "You'll see."

The following night, Haadi revealed his plan—an ambush patrol using Yahoo's dominant roof, which he had negotiated the previous day. The same group slowly rolled down ASP Hill onto Michigan on a routine four-vehicle patrol. Near a bend in the road, at Haadi's signal, twelve of us hopped out of the trucks and hid in a ditch. The Humvees kept moving, gunning their engines to attract the lookouts. On foot the ambush team humped in single file down a crusty wadi, arriving undetected at the back door of Yahoo's large home. We knocked and Yahoo whisked us inside.

"*Ya hala,*" he said, welcoming us. "You are on time."

Haadi and Yahoo plopped down on a plush crimson couch and sipped hot chai.

"Guess you know what you're doing after all, Haadi," I admitted.

"You ask for an ambush, I give you best ambush," said Haadi. "Go upstairs and see."

Haadi and Yahoo gestured at the stairs, and the rest of us—one advisor, one terp, and ten jundis—hiked up to the flat roof. We sat down behind a low concrete wall that ran around the edges of the roof and checked our weapons. The jundis were fairly accurate shooters with their AKs, as was Alex.

Two large condenser units were centered on the roof deck. They weren't running. It was a cool night, and the occasional *clack* of AK-47 barrels striking the cement sounded like thunder claps. With my NVGs, the roof provided a dominant view in all directions. Three hundred meters to the west on Route Michigan sat the Snake Eaters' guard tower at the intersection of Abu Fleis Road, invisible in the dark to the squinting jundis, who had no goggles. Alex powered up the ten-million-candlepower infrared spotlight, while I screwed a magnifying lens onto my NVGs.

Alex switched on the spotlight. Invisible to the naked eye, the thick infrared beam, as seen through my NVGs, illuminated the scene. The jundis took turns looking through my goggles, gasping as Alex shone the bright light down the street and along the walls of nearby houses. After a few minutes, he put down the infrared light to answer our handheld radio.

"Captain Haadi wants to go across the street and hide inside the school," Alex told me. "He may catch a sniper setting up for the morning."

Staff Sergeant Blakley had died right in front of Haadi, and the Iraqi captain carried the tremendous pain of that day on his face like a shrapnel wound whenever snipers were mentioned. Haadi was convinced that Blakley's killer, Kamal Humadi, and his mastermind brother, Abu Roma, had once stored weapons at the high school. Haadi had recently uncovered a weapons cache on the school grounds and believed Roma was back to his old tricks. On any other day I would have been happy to accommodate Haadi's request, but he had worked hard to get us into Yahoo's house undetected.

"This is a great spot," I told Alex. "Now Haadi wants us to leave?"

"No. Just you, me, and him. The jundis stay here as overwatch," Alex explained.

"If he's up for it, I am. But I don't want the jundis firing, or we'll all get clipped."

I positioned the jundis along the rooftop wall, then joined Haadi and Alex on the first floor. They were having a hushed argument on the staircase.

Haadi angrily wagged his finger at me. "Too danger, Major!"

I realized immediately that Alex, who craved adventure, had set the whole thing up. Haadi didn't want to leave on a three-man patrol chasing ghosts that night—Alex did. And now Alex was telling Haadi it was the advisor's idea.

I shook my head at Haadi and roughly pulled Alex aside. "If you ever do that again, I will fire you. You lied. If we can't trust you, you're useless."

Alex's eyes welled up. "I am sorry, sir. I know you like small patrols . . ."

"Your job is to translate, Alex. Is that clear? You burned us."

I stormed back up to the roof and saw the flash of an RPG ignition. Insurgents were attacking the Abu Fleis tower checkpoint on Michigan. The sharp bang of the ignition reached the rooftop, followed by two deep booms as rockets exploded against the tower wall. I folded the night-vision monocular over my eye and took a kneeling firing position at the lip of the roof next to the jundis.

"Fire on my tracers," I said.

Alex translated and grabbed the spotlight. Through my monocular, I could clearly see three insurgents three hundred meters away on Abu Fleis Road firing AK-47s while a third fiddled with an RPG launcher. I switched on the laser pointer fixed to my barrel, centered the glowing blurred dot on the tallest insurgent, and fired three times. A red-hot ember leaped toward the insurgents, followed by two more.

"Kill them!" I shouted. "Kill them! Kill them!"

The jundis cut loose on full automatic. The barrels of their AKs jerked in the air, sending up long bursts of tracers that looked like antiaircraft fire. From a distance, Yahoo's house must have resembled an exploding star. Alex calmly kept the infrared light focused toward the insurgents. When the spotlight caught them, they were shooting in all directions, having no idea where the crazy crisscross of tracers was coming from. All three enemies were still standing. I had pulled my first burst. Buck fever.

I wedged my barrel grip into a crack in the wall, centered the laser dot on an insurgent, and fired twice more. Both times the weapon bucked away from the trigger finger instead of moving with it—a reliable indication that I had held steady on the target.

On Route Michigan, the Humvees roared toward Abu Fleis, with the jundis in the turrets wildly firing their machine guns. The bullets sprayed like an untamed hose. In three minutes, the jundis had expended five hundred rounds. I wasn't able to raise my head to get off another shot.

When the firing died down, Haadi's men searched the ambush area, finding dozens of spent cartridges but no blood trails. Haadi and his jundis were happy. Alex and I were glum. When we returned to ASP Hill, I took a glowing chemlight out into a field and shot it three times out of three. My rifle was properly battle zeroed and my laser pointer was accurate. Somehow I must have jerked my shots, even though it didn't feel that way.

The next afternoon, however, the Snake Eater scout platoon interrupted a funeral in Abu Fleis for a 17-year-old boy named Ayad. The mourners acted strangely, avoiding the salutations of Lieutenant Fredo, the scout leader. One man oddly insisted the dead boy had had no influence over his own sons. The boy's father, Hadithi, explained that his son had been executed by al Qaeda and dumped on Abu Fleis Road.

"When did this happen?" asked Fredo.

"Last night. Ayad's two friends brought him home. He was already dead. They survived."

"I should like to congratulate those brave boys," said Fredo.

"They are not here. In hospital in Ramadi, I think."

Lieutenant Fredo had a dark complexion, and when he was angry he turned black. He took the man aside and said coldly, "Tell me the truth and show me the body."

The father broke down and admitted that his son was part of a local insurgent gang. He had been shot during the attack on Abu Fleis tower. Fredo inspected the body. There were small bullet holes in his neck and armpit.

The next day, Captain Haadi asked me to accompany him on patrol to collect my gift.

"What gift?" I asked.

"The father wants to give you something as an apology."

"Apology? I shot his son." I was mystified.

"His son was a terrorist who tried to kill my men!" Haadi shouted.

Americans treated the relatives of known insurgents, including wives and fathers, as faultless for their wayward sons. The Iraqis believed the stronger the bloodline, the more complicity in the insurgency. Families were harassed, not consoled.

★

Haadi met Hadithi, the trembling father, in the courtyard of his home and offered him a cigarette. He was fat and tired. Haadi waved me inside, but I demurred. At night, I had shot a tall man holding a deadly rocket grenade launcher who was trying to kill jundis. Now here was a father who had just lost his 17-year-old. I had two boys back in New York City. I didn't want to see this man. I pulled security with Haadi's jundis on the street while Alex went inside to give me a report. A few of the jundis, who were chuckling, gestured to get my attention, then chanted in English, "Kill them! Kill them!" poking fun at my rooftop order.

Inside the courtyard, Hadithi sobbed. "I hate my son! He has brought great shame."

Hadithi had been a police officer in the '90s and now was without a job.

"You get me names of insurgents, and I will get you work," Haadi told him.

Hadithi brightened. "You have this connection?"

Haadi pointed to me. "He does."

Hadithi offered to testify against a man named Basim Khalifh. "He has been very busy lately," Hadithi revealed. "He was friends with my son."

"Bah. He's well known. You give me nothing. No one knows where he lives."

Hadithi pointed at a sprawling compound across the street and went back inside. Haadi searched several nearby houses as a diversion, then entered Basim's home. The insurgent had fled, but two hundred pounds of soap and fertilizer were found in a well, along with several barrels of kerosene.

"That is for our heat," an old woman protested.

"If this is true, where is your siphon? Tell Basim that God is watching, and God favors us," Haadi warned her.

The search operation over, Haadi drove to a large home in Abu Fleis where a widow had long accused SEALs of shooting her 10-year-old son in the back. That accusation was unfounded, but during their investigation, the advisors discovered that bullets from the Camp Habbaniyah shooting range often pelted the neighborhood accidentally.

The old widow stuck to her story about rampaging U.S. Navy commandos. She held out her nervous son for inspection. He was shaking badly and struggled to lift his shirt to show his scars. Behind the house, three boys were playing soccer. They said their friend had been hit on the field by a bullet that had come from the sky. They excitedly pointed out two bullet holes in a tree they were using as a goal post.

Haadi took a $20 bill from me and handed it to the old woman. "God has made his choice. Now you must do the same. Who follows the example of the Prophet, the terrorists or my soldiers?"

"You do, sir," she said.

On the way out of Abu Fleis, Haadi told me the small peninsula was about to come over to our side. It struck me as an unfounded boast. He pointed at the spot by the garages along Route Michigan where Rivera and Watson had been hit. "This would not happen today. The people would not allow it."

"These 'people' just attacked our tower," I observed.

"The people who count, I mean."

It had been a draining patrol, but Haadi had one more errand. He stopped by Yahoo's home on the way to the ASP and took a few jundis inside. The rest of us waited outside for thirty minutes and took an inaccurate potshot for good measure. When Haadi returned, I said, "This is getting to be a bad habit, Captain Haadi."

"He learned that we killed the terrorist Ayad and he wanted a photograph with us. He asked to become a regular source for 3rd Battalion and I told him maybe," Haadi explained.

"Maybe? After one kill, now we're getting picky, Haadi?"

"You don't understand, Major. We have the power here. If a man wants to be part of the future, now he comes to the Snake Eaters. I told him Saddam's men have come over. There are hundreds of men helping us. Important men."

"There are?" I asked.

"He now thinks there are," Haadi quipped. "That's what matters."

In mid-December, Sly and I took a Sunday morning off to evaluate Haadi's assertion that local allegiances were shifting. We knew that about fifty insurgents had switched sides to join Sheikh Abbas's TAA, some had left town, and others were dead. The Snake Eaters had recruited some reliable informants. But we had no way of knowing how many insurgents remained.

The enemy was facing the same challenge with locals who had become informants. To differentiate their sympathizers from their turncoats, insurgents in Khalidiya had diagrammed the names and locations of local citizens and recorded in detail their loyalties. We learned this when a partial census of Khalidiya was discovered on an enemy thumb drive earlier that month.

We wanted to do our own census, but we didn't know how. The army's counterinsurgency manual was heavily influenced by the writings of David Galula, a French military officer who had written *Pacification in Algeria,* which describes his victory over local insurgents. Galula insisted, "A thorough census was the first step in controlling the population."[1] In 1956, Galula had instructed his lieutenants to paint a number on each house and record the occupants in notebooks, a rudimentary but effective census. In Vietnam, the mobility of the Vietcong guerrilla forces was eventually crippled by a laborious hamlet-level census completed by hand in 1968. In Iraq circa 2006, cheap technology was available to radically improve this critical counterinsurgency ingredient.

The U.S. military had the best mapping technology in the world. Combined with a GPS, a communications link, and a basic database, a census could have been completed in months. Yet a census was absent from America's war plan. After forty-four months in Iraq, the U.S. military had scant institutional memory when it came to Iraq's people, its stated focus of effort.

For two weeks in December, Sergeant First Class Caldwell completed the painstaking task of numbering on a digital map every house in Habbaniyah. I had the suspicion that we were repeating past efforts. I was subsequently depressed to discover that every U.S. unit in Habbaniyah preceding the 3rd Iraqi Brigade, beginning with TF 1–34 Armor in September 2003, had labeled buildings and attempted to chart interpersonal relationships. These ranged in form from simple Excel spreadsheets to poster boards with mug shots, but between the huge variance in phonetic spellings and the prolific use of false identities among the locals, these well-intentioned attempts were of little use to the next incoming unit.

Year after year, there was no systematic handoff. Every unit stationed in Habbaniyah—from the 1–34 Centurions to the 1–506 Curahees to TF Panther to the 3/5 Darkhorse to the 3/2 Betio Bastards—complained about the intelligence handed off from the prior unit. Each unit started from scratch, devising its own tracking system because the U.S. high command saw little utility in a centralized system. Hundreds of houses we visited had been previously searched, and hundreds of men we questioned had been previously detained. After every exhausting patrol, most information the jundis gleaned evaporated. Sly and I became convinced that if we captured all of this individual intelligence, building the battalion's institutional memory—from recurrent bomb sites to those locals who always seemed to pop up after a short firefight—we could gradually strip the local insurgents of their ability to hide in plain sight.

With a map-based handheld scanner—text, fingerprints, and digital photographs—the Snake Eaters could complete a biometric census of the twenty-five thousand military-age males in zone in about three months. In late November, I had emailed Spirit of America, an American nonprofit known for responding rapidly to material requests from deployed U.S. troops. By late December, Lieutenant Colonel Fareed and his officers were curiously inspecting two laptops and three prototypes of the Snake Eater photo/fingerprint scanner.

We took the scanner out on a few patrols and recorded about thirty loiterers each time, including their actions, their mosque affiliations, and their best friends. We finally had a counter to the fake IDs each man carried on his person, but our database was strictly local; we had only a few units given to us by Spirit of America. We needed a national platform. We gradually entered a couple hundred facial pictures, fingerprints, and addresses into our private database, but we never succeeded in persuading the high command to turn our small tactical bluff into a strategic reality. Iraq never had a census.

★

On December 16, I discussed my frustrations about the local population census with Captain Dhafer while on patrol in Khalidiya. If we mapped out the social network, I asserted, we could corner the names that popped up again and again.

"Then what will you do? Arrest those who are always near a bomb site and who are mentioned whenever we ask insurgents who they take as friends?" Dhafer asked.

"Well, something like that, yes," I said lamely.

Dhafer, who was always in a good mood, threw his head back and laughed. "I know now why I like you. You want to treat insurgents as prisoners of war!"

"The ones we narrow down, yes."

"Ah, but here is the problem!" exclaimed Dhafer. "The thing that makes the people angriest is not arresting the innocent man. It's releasing terrorists from jail."

"I doubt it," I said, believing that false arrests through the years had created local animosity.

Dhafer led me to a group of men clustered in front of a Market Street clothing shop. Unlike during Troster's tour, most of Khalidiya's shops were open for business when I arrived. And the locals freely engaged the Iraqi soldiers. At Dhafer's bidding, they swarmed me. So many locals were speaking simultaneously that Alex had trouble translating. There emerged a theme: We Americans needed to keep detainees in jail longer.

"You broke our country," one man said, "so why do you let bad men out of prison? Because you don't want to fix it!"

We traveled west down 20th Street. I told Dhafer to keep his mouth shut, letting the locals initiate the conversation this time. The results were similar outside a school. A crowd quickly gathered, and the spokesman, who climbed atop a propane tank to make his point, first complained about the past American mistakes, and when I asked about unfair imprisonment, he ranted about our prisoner policy.

"Al Jazeera has shown that you free terrorists to extend the war," he said.

"What do you mean?" asked Alex.

"Why are the guilty not kept in jail?" the local demanded. "The good people are coming forward to identify them, and in a few days they are back! Do you think this information comes without danger? You make us very angry with your stupidity!"

★

As we walked away, Dhafer asked if we could pay a visit to Imad Hamid in Sadiqiya as a means of driving the point home to me. Imad was a sore spot for Dhafer; he had arrested the 20-year-old insurgent two times already. The first time was in January 2006 for sprinting away from an explosion; Dhafer caught Imad with several $100 bills in his pocket, which he claimed were the day's wages in the chicken-selling business. He was released for lack of evidence. Then again in June, when Imad planted a bomb that destroyed an Iraqi Humvee and injured several jundis. The insurgent had videotaped his work, and it was enough evidence for the Americans, who placed him in the Camp Bucca Theater Internment Facility (TIF), a national jail like the infamous Abu Ghraib. An Iraqi judge soon released Imad, arguing that the videotape was nonsense. Dhafer did not find out about the release until five months later, when he saw Imad during a patrol in Sadiqiya I was accompanying.

"I arrested you twice last year," said Dhafer.

"I served six months. I damned the insurgency," Imad replied.

"He is a good son of Iraq," his mother added.

"If he does this again, I will end his life!" Dhafer threatened. "I will burn his house down!"

It was an empty threat. Every day in Iraq, troops encountered suspected insurgents who had been previously arrested. When I first joined the team, I had read Troster's after-action report excoriating the "ridiculous evidentiary justice system" that had "no place in a wartime environment."[2] Most detainees were let go because their crimes could not be proved to the satisfaction of corrupt Iraqi judges, or to U.S. military lawyers. We didn't have prisoners of war in Iraq, only criminal suspects entitled to many of the same rights as in the States. Most detainees were set free within a few months. The advisors called it "catch and release."

Catch and release was especially hurtful because Iraq was a police war, and imprisonment was the dominant military weapon. In 1968, U.S. troops in Vietnam killed ten guerrillas for every one they captured. In Iraq, it was the opposite. Coalition units killed few insurgents—the enemy had learned from the Shia and Sunni uprisings in 2004 not to engage in a shooting war with the Americans—but they had become good at using citizen tips to track down the perpetrators. In sixteen months, the Snake Eaters had killed fewer than ten insurgents. Yet they had arrested over three hundred. The same was true of U.S. units like the Betio Bastards, which in six months had killed few insurgents but had imprisoned over 350.

Accusations against detainees were vetted by lawyers at three separate commands. In the end, just 5 percent of the cases—those considered ironclad—were referred by the top U.S. lawyers to the Central Criminal Court of Iraq (CCCI), where an Iraqi panel decided on the sentences. The CCCI in turn had ruled on just sixteen hundred out of over thirty thousand detainees in 2006. Half were set free.

The imbalance was staggering. In 2006, the Iraq Ministry of the Interior reported twenty-five murders per day but had fewer than eight hundred convictions for the entire year. By contrast, New York State averaged two murders per day but imprisoned twenty-four-hundred criminals per week. The American and Iraqi jails together held at most about thirty-five thousand prisoners—by some estimates just half the number Saddam Hussein released from prison in the mass exodus of 2002.

The U.S. military was suffering from cognitive dissonance at the top. The senior generals understood that arrests were the primary military weapon—and believed that the citizens, soldiers, and battalion-level JAGs were probably correct in their conclusions of guilt—but publicly they advocated the opposite course, including mass releases, and abdicated responsibility to an Iraqi justice system that did not yet exist. It was true that Abu Ghraib and Guantánamo had boosted the insurgency, but by institutionalizing catch and release, the high command had mistakenly fused high-level public relations onto grassroots counterinsurgency tactics, where it was self-defeating.

★

Returning to ASP Hill that evening, Captain Dhafer cornered me in the Horseshoe's food stockroom, piled high with plastic-wrapped salty treats. It sometimes doubled as a souk for the Iraqi officers. They liked to visit because the smells were exotic, whether it was microwaved Pop-Tarts, giant bowls of chocolaty Cocoa Puffs, or a steaming pot of Colombian coffee. I offered Dhafer some pretzel sticks but he took only one, savoring it like a cigar.

"The people of Khalidiya are ready to give many names," Dhafer claimed. "Are we ready to put them in prison?"

"If their evidence packages are solid . . ."

"Major, this is what worries me. We want to develop a plan with TAA to arrest twenty men. But if they do not go to jail, the people will go back to hiding. There is very much risk for them. Some are foreign, but most are brothers and fathers!"

I didn't have the heart to tell Dhafer that another mass prisoner release was planned to coincide with the hajj, the annual pilgrimage to Mecca that would commence in late December. I'd done some research into the judicial system, and the findings were grim. The American-run prisons in Iraq were nearing capacity—we had released twenty-five thousand in two years from the TIFs alone—and the Betio Bastards warned the Snake Eaters about an effort being run out of U.S. headquarters in Baghdad called "expedited release." In reality, it was simply an effort to better scrub evidence packages at the crowded TIFs. But the message to the infantry battalions was clear: If you arrested someone, you needed hard evidence commensurate with prosecuting a street crime in the States because our leaders in Baghdad doubted there were that many bad guys.

I said good night to Dhafer and logged in to my secure email account to see what we were up against. After a known insurgent had returned to Khalidiya because of an early release from jail, in mid-December I had emailed Coalition Forces (CF) lawyers demanding to know how strong these evidence packages had to be to get a conviction. A CF lawyer sent me some unclassified trial summaries as examples of flimsy cases, and I immediately understood Troster's fury.

> CF located a weapons cache consisting of 155mm artillery shells, rockets, assorted antiaircraft ammunition, and 7.62mm ammunition on the defendant's property. CF presented two witnesses, a sketch, and photographs . . . The prosecutor recommended that the court dismiss the charge as the weapons were found outside the defendant's house and the house was not surrounded by a fence . . . DISMISSED the case.

> CF searched the defendant and found two Senao cordless phones. The serial number of one of the Senao cordless phones matched the Senao base station that was attached to the IED. CF presented two witnesses, a sketch, and photographs. The prosecutor recommended dismissing the charge because there was no telephone expert to verify that the serial number on the mobile phone matched the serial number on the phone's base station despite photos of the two items displaying matching serial numbers . . . and DISMISSED the case.

> CF searched the defendant's vehicle and found three Motorola radios wrapped in PE-4 explosives that were ready to be detonated and a fuel canister with PE-4 attached to two blasting caps. At the hearing, the Coalition presented two witnesses and photographs. The prosecutor recommended that the court dismiss the charge as the Coalition did not present the vehicle's ownership papers . . . the trial panel . . . DISMISSED the case.

★

Iraq was a civil war fought out along sectarian lines. In the summer of 2006, Bez Boz, the Baby Falcon, had been spotted at a checkpoint by a friend from

Baghdad. "Mustafa, you are a soldier!" the man said. "This is very big news. And trouble for you." Bez Boz lacked the will to kill the man right there, instead choosing to flee. He was not seen again on ASP Hill.

In mid-December, our loyal terp, Reyes, returned from leave to tell us he had moved his family. Reyes was a Shiite from Najaf, and when he had returned home to visit his young wife and child, a longtime friend threatened him.

"You are helping the invaders," he said.

"I am hunting men who would destroy the shrine of Ali if they could," Reyes replied.

"You will be hunting for your own head if you continue."

Reyes abandoned his house, moving his family north to Samarra with relatives.

Later in the month, GQ and the rest of the officers in his wedding party returned to ASP Hill from jail, the careless shooting having been put to rest. In Mosul, they had run into a stern military judge who refused to allow a tribal settlement. GQ was distressed by the incredible bad luck marriage had brought—every month the Snake Eaters snatched bad guys and fed them into a justice system that was broken precisely because there *were* no judges in Iraq. "Then one day the sun came right into our cell," said GQ, "and we knew God had forgiven this terrible accident." While the judge was on vacation, his greedy clerk accepted one million dinars as an unrecoverable bail payment.

"It will take me years to pay my family and friends back," GQ told me.

"We'll get your money back and keep you out of it," I offered.

"Do not do this, Major, or there will be consequences. Let it be. It is the Iraqi way."

On December 19, Major Mohammed's brother, a Sunni colonel who worked in Baghdad, was killed by al Qaeda assassins. The killing had occurred at home, in front of his family. Mohammed stuffed a canvas bag with clothing and equipment and hitched a ride to Baghdad.

A week later, Mohammed sat in a car in Ghazaliya, a shabby Sunni neighborhood in Baghdad where he had tracked his brother's murderers. The weapons in the borrowed car glistened with fresh rifle oil, slicking up the vinyl seats. The three passengers watched the mosque across the street. Echoes from the minaret drowned the idling engine.

"It's a long sermon," the driver observed.

"Takfiri sheep need someone to think for them," said Mohammed, seated next to him. He was often repulsed by his own people—during Iraq's improbable, electrifying silver medal performance in the 2006 Asian Games, he had cheered against the national team—and railed against Iraq's swift sectarian deterioration. In truth, he understood its emotional underpinnings. The entire country was driven mad with revenge. And so was he.

"I must thank you again for coming. You are my only brothers now," Mohammed told the men in the car. He had known them since childhood.

His brother's assassin emerged from the mosque courtyard and squinted to block the sun. He was a big Syrian nicknamed "Abdullah Syria." Wearing long Western-slicked hair that fell over the collar of his white Adidas sweat suit, the Syrian stood out in the flock.

He walked down the sidewalk, trailed by three bodyguards carrying AKs. Mohammed's car lurched forward, crossed the littered median, and slowed. "Leave Syria to me," said Mohammed.

The Syrian's three bodyguards were carrying machine guns. Bullet belts were gaudily strewn across their shoulders. Machine guns and ribbons of heavy ammunition might impress the congregation, but to a professional soldier they signaled amateurism.

Mohammed's crew gunned down two bodyguards, while the third ran away. The Syrian also tried to run, but Mohammed shot him in the back. He crumpled to the sidewalk.

When Mohammed reached the man, he knew he'd popped a lung and probably his heart. He wished he had a camera. The man was moaning softly.

"God is great, donkey," Mohammed said. He stuffed the rifle barrel into the Syrian's ear, pulled the trigger, and ran back to the car. Noticing a rifle barrel over the wall of the mosque aimed at him, he fired a single shot to keep the man down, then fired the rest of his magazine into the air.

Before hopping back into the car, he yelled, *"Jaish al Mahdi! Jaish al Mahdi!"* as loudly as he could to confuse the situation. The Mahdi was the Shiite militia that terrified Baghdad Sunnis. As his car sped away, he heard people screaming, "It was the Mahdi Army!"

Now he could go back to fighting.

20

Good-bye, Darkness

★　★　★

December 2006

On Christmas Day, Lieutenant Colonel Fareed, Sly, and I met with Sheikh Abbas, the SEALs, and Lieutenant Colonel Desgrosseilliers to discuss Operation Sad City Roundup, an ambitious operation to arrest several insurgents in Sadiqiya. Desgrosseilliers's Betio Bastards would isolate Sadiqiya with tanks at night, while teams of Marines on foot would flush any snipers. Fareed's Snake Eaters and the SEALs would swoop in and raid several houses. Abbas's TAA fighters, dressed as jundis, would identify the insurgents.

Abbas had finally agreed to the terms for TAA participation as originally outlined by Zientek. His militiamen would act as unarmed sources, not hit men. Weeks of joint patrolling had convinced the tribesmen that the jundis were competent warriors.

"I recommend one change. We should capture them in the day," Abbas said. "If you go at night, you'll only get three or four. Many do not sleep in the same house each night."

Fareed and Desgrosseilliers exchanged a bemused look. Fareed tapped his most-wanted list. "Are you telling us you know where most of these men are during daylight?"

"Of course I do," Sheikh Abbas retorted.

"Searching all these houses will take days," said Fareed.

"They are not in houses," Abbas explained. "For one year they have been right in front of you, but you have never seen them. They have grown so confident that they hang together like dogs. That will change with my men. We should gather up every man in Sadiqiya, and we will point to the terrorists."

"Are you saying we're to put the entire city in a lineup?" Desgrosseilliers asked.

"I am," Abbas replied.

"Do you think this will work?" Desgrosseilliers asked me.

The current rumor was that Marine headquarters in Anbar was about to ban all contact with the TAA. I supposed Desgrosseilliers wanted to see where I stood.

"I don't know if it will work, sir, but I know we have to try," I said.

"Of course we do. Lieutenant Colonel Fareed, what is your opinion?" Desgrosseilliers asked.

"How can I say no to the Papa Nicks?" Fareed joked.

Desgrosseilliers had just returned from visiting his outposts, and he was dressed in Santa pants. I was similarly dressed, having delivered more head-lamps and blood-clotting bandages to the Snake Eaters courtesy of my fellow traders at Goldman.

"There is one thing," Fareed continued. "If we arrest many irhabi, I am worried the prisoners will be released. Major West has told me of this release program."

"I have my own answer for expedited release. It's called 'rapid depar-ture,'" said Desgrosseilliers. "If your officers take the time to help the TAA write good statements, we'll add our own intelligence, and the detainees won't be coming back anytime soon."

Rapid departure was not an official program, but by emphasizing the need to beef up detainee packages—and preparing his higher headquarters to receive some very bad actors—Desgrosseilliers was himself counterbalancing the bias toward release we felt at the top.

Desgrosseilliers wasn't the only one who was fighting catch and release. On December 14, Lieutenant General Ray Odierno had assumed command of the troops in Iraq and asked the Marine leadership in Anbar what they needed. Generals Zilmer and Neller wanted to halt the relentless stream of released prisoners flowing back into Anbar. Odierno approved the request. The mass release was canceled; for the time being, no prisoners hailing from Anbar would be freed, a huge morale boost to the Snake Eaters and the citi-zens of Khalidiya.

On December 26, the night before Operation Sad City, I emailed Zien-tek the details. His reaction was muted. First Battalion had been attacked by several SVBIEDs, and an advisor, Corporal Josh Schmitz of Spencer, Wis-consin, was dead.

"I'm looking at the Sad City plan now, and I don't see any principles of Marine Corps operations," Zientek told me over the phone. "There's no mass or concentration—you're outnumbered and spread out. There's no maneuver. The security plan calls for tanks, but Sadiqiya is known for its snipers."

"Well, there's surprise, sir," I said weakly.

"In a daylight raid?"

"The targets hang out at the truck stop just beyond the 611 Bridge," I explained.

"Are you telling me that the most-wanted men in Khalidiya just sit out there in the open every day like the Sopranos, shooting the shit?" Zientek asked.

"That's what TAA tells us."

Suddenly it sounded preposterous to me, too. Day after day our patrols passed the truck stop. The men just sat in their open garages leaning back in their cheap plastic chairs, like hundreds of other men along Michigan who watched life pass by.

"Take care of your people, Major," said Zientek.

★

On the morning of December 27, Lieutenant Colonel Fareed gathered his company commanders outside Ogre's headquarters on Camp Habbaniyah. They spread out ten extra uniforms in the sun and waited. TAA fighters were supposed to dress as jundis, but they were nowhere to be seen.

"I do not think they will be coming," Fareed told Ogre.

"*Habbibi,* do you doubt me?" said Ogre, using a term of affection.

"I do not doubt *Hadji* McCarthy," Fareed joked.

Finally Sheikh Abbas rolled up in police cars with his gang and was greeted like a long-lost brother by Fareed and Aamr. The TAA militiamen left their guns in their cars and dressed in the ragged chocolate chip uniforms provided by the Snake Eaters. Fareed had brought extra-large sizes because he assumed the militiamen were fat. Instead they looked like emaciated jundis. They had gone hungry over the years of al Qaeda rule.

Marines from Betio Bastards left their patrol bases along Route Michigan and moved into overwatch positions encircling the city, carefully checking the traditional sniper hideouts. As a squad of Marines spread out down a narrow alley, there was a sharp explosion, and Lance Corporal William Koprince was dead.

Lieutenant Colonel Aamr gathered the Iraqi raid force on the Camp Habbaniyah airstrip. "A brother in the Marines has been killed by a mine in Sadiqiya. It is up to us to ensure his death brings fruit."

Seventeen vehicles filled with jundis and TAA roared out of the camp and quickly surrounded the truck stop in Sadiqiya. Jundis swept the city, hauling every military-age male back for inspection. In thirty minutes, hundreds of men were marched in rows down to Route Michigan. Anyone who sauntered up to gawk was grabbed. Soon the town was deserted. A queue of a thousand men staring at their feet stretched for four hundred meters.

One of the Iraqi armored vehicles rolled slowly along the line. TAA "jundis" peered out the dirty portholes, occasionally rapping excitedly on the glass. When an insurgent was identified, he was yanked from the line and handcuffed.

Once the first hundred men were inspected, Fareed gathered a few sprightly citizens and announced, "Run and tell the rest of the men in Sadiqiya to report here if they want to retrieve their relatives."

"Sir, the whole town's here!" one of the men protested.

That day, thirty-one men were detained in Sadiqiya and driven to the Bastards' detention facility, where jundis sat side by side with TAA fighters, critiquing their penmanship as they filled out witness statements and drank sodas. Lieutenant Colonel Desgrosseilliers was mourning the loss of Koprince, but his mood brightened when he saw the names. He lit a cigar. "See, we got three high-value targets, including your most wanted. What a day!"

The Snake Eaters' number one target was Abu Roma, the sniper. I saw a bunch of jundis crowding around one of the insurgents for a group picture, like hunters standing over a trophy kill. They wanted me to take the picture, but Americans were not allowed to photograph detainees.

Lieutenant Fredo, the scout commander, pleaded, "Please, Major, it's Abu Roma!"

"Who?"

"Ahmed Mukhlif Humadi. His brother, Kamal, killed Doc Blakley. For years soldiers have been looking for this terrorist. We captured Abu Roma! He is the Sadiqiya Sniper! Praise God!"

Fredo wiped tears from his eyes. The jundis broke into a frenzied dance. Hand in hand they encircled Roma and sang. Then one jundi tried to attack the sniper but was held back by his mates. "Help me, God, to kill this man!" the jundi shouted.

"Get those jundis out of here," I told Alex, "or we'll all be locked up here tonight."

I spent some time looking at Roma's case. He had an astounding eight intelligence reports in his file, dating back to 2005. He was a mousy little man with big ears. Looking at him, I doubted he was the mythical Sadiqiya Sniper.

One of the SEAL interpreters wanted to investigate Abu Roma even further. He had been on the raid when Roma's brother Kamal was captured and believed the brothers were indeed snipers. He volunteered to impersonate an insurgent and fish for information.

The SEAL terp was roughly tossed into Abu Roma's cell, as if he too were an insurgent. During the night, Roma bragged about bombs he had planted, but by morning, running out of time, the terp was forced to press for information about his brother.

"I was picked up with my sniper cell," he told Roma. "Know any snipers?"

"There is a very strong group here," said Roma.

"Do you or your family shoot?"

Roma stopped talking. He sat in the corner of the cell and picked at the bars with his long fingernails. Eventually the terp called for the guard. "God will show you no mercy," he told Roma when he rejoined the SEALs.

★

By day's end, eighteen suspects were quickly shipped to the Regimental Detention Facility under Desgrosseilliers's rapid departure program, including Abu Roma and one of the Bastards' most wanted, "Nasty" Afrid, a kidnapper whose expertise was beheading. As Desgrosseilliers had predicted, their evidence packages were so strong that all eighteen suspects were forwarded to the TIF.

The other thirteen men were returned to the streets, mostly because they were local drones who had been given a good scare. TAA watchmen vowed to become parole officers and that night visited the imam in Sadiqiya to drive home the point that his boys better never again support insurgents.

The following day, December 28, the Snake Eater scouts and the SEALs repeated the mass arrest operation on a smaller scale in Abu Fleis. Eight men were arrested, bringing the Snake Eater total to fifty-six arrests for December, the highest monthly number of captures in its history. Of those fifty-six suspects, fifty-three were ultimately incarcerated in the TIF, a rate of 95 percent—about three times better than the average for U.S. units in Anbar. Citizens' testimony had become detailed and accurate; they, too, had learned to gather overwhelming evidence.

The TAA declared that Khalidiya was next. On December 29, the Snake Eaters sent out patrols as usual, with instructions to take some spot surveys in advance of the mass arrest operation. As Sly and I walked the streets of Khalidiya with Captain Dhafer, it was clear that something was different.

Some of it you could articulate—boys beating on pots and pans to celebrate our arrival instead of warning about it; grown men sharing a laugh with the advisors—but mostly it was an undercurrent, a human vibration the jundis immediately tuned in to but we Americans couldn't pinpoint.

"Can you believe it, Major?" Dhafer asked, smiling.

"I'll believe whatever you tell me to believe, Dhafer."

"We cannot do an operation because there is no one to arrest," exclaimed Dhafer. "The war is over here. Over!"

That seemed a bit much. An old man approached with a list of names, his sons or nephews fanning out behind him like a flock of geese. "We give you these names because they are the worst," the patriarch said, handing the note to Dhafer. "But you will not find them. They have left."

Sly and I looked at each other. The people had found their courage, and the insurgents had no place to hide. Al Qaeda supporters stood exposed. After three and a half years of the heaviest bloodshed in Iraq, the local Sunni tribes had come over. The insurgency in Khalidiya was finished.

21

Twitchings

★　★　★

January–February 2007

t would be tidy to end the Battle for Habbaniyah with a single event, but in guerrilla warfare, capitulation is not clean. Pinpointing the end of an insurgency is like pinpointing the end of a marriage. Captain Dhafer was convinced the battle was won on December 27, 2006, but it had started to wither before that, and it would continue to twitch for some time.

As the new year arrived, TAA raids similar to Operation Sad City were taking place throughout the Habbaniyah area. In retaliation, insurgent suicide bombers drove a series of car bombs into 2nd Battalion's Route Michigan checkpoints in an area known as the Shark's Fin, near Fallujah, killing four jundis and wounding five. The Snake Eaters struck back two days later during Friday noon prayer, encircling the Farooq Mosque in the middle of Abu Fleis, which harbored the most notoriously unfriendly congregation in the Habbaniyah area, including Mukhabarat secret police retirees who owned the large farms and employed the most people. With the help of the local branch of the TAA, a dozen known insurgents were peeled from the mosque compound. Surprising the Snake Eaters, the crowd that gathered on the street to watch did not protest but cheered.

★

In mid-January, Ogre engineered the firing of Police Chief Shalal, a real feat considering that as an advisor he did not have official authority. In handing sovereignty to the Iraqis in 2004, the United States had failed to retain the ability to hand-pick military and police leaders, even though we paid their salaries. It was a costly mistake. At the top, frustrated general officers watched helplessly as senior Iraqi officers and ministry officials embezzled and stumbled. At the bottom, majors and lieutenant colonels like Ogre ignored the press releases and threw their weight where it was most needed. After months of maneuvering with the provincial governors, Ogre had finally replaced Shalal.

It was an especially painful firing for Shalal, who had skimmed subordinate salaries for years. The TAA was encouraging its young men to join the police force. Two hundred and nineteen local recruits were screened for training in January 2007, exceeding the hundred-man quota Ogre had been given by Brigadier General Neller.

When he saw the January numbers out of Habbaniyah, Neller, who four months earlier had told Ogre to "build the police and don't get killed," wrote in an amused email: "Enough. I asked for a hundred more, not 200+. Ogre's Army has enough shurta."

Ogre wanted to keep tabs on Shalal, so he visited occasionally. He was treated as a guest in Shalal's home, and acted like one. "We are better this way," said Shalal.

"We have a saying: Distance makes the heart grow fonder," Ogre concurred.

Ogre suspected that his new chief, named Khalid, was secretly the TAA operations officer. But he was decisive and blunt, and he didn't back down from a fight. After Khalid was named chief, Iraqi cops loyal to Shalal blocked his car on the way to the district station. "You are not the rightful chief," the cops declared. "Turn around."

Khalid exited the vehicle and punched one of the police officers in the jaw, knocking him down. The others backed off.

TAA's influence within the leadership ranks of the Habbaniyah police was not limited to Khalid. Sheikh Abbas was named chief of the new Khalidiya police force. Ogre was building him a new station house downtown. In the secure working environment, the building went up so quickly the locals called the rising strands of rebar a "mirage."

Abbas converted dozens of reliable TAA fighters to serve under him as cops in Khalidiya station. They were issued snappy blue uniforms and plotted for the day when they could patrol without black masks shielding their identities. TAA was swiftly legitimizing operations because the Marines were about to put it out of business. On January 16, 2007, Marine headquarters asserted that TAA engaged in illegal acts and issued an order banning further contact with the tribesmen.

Before the memo worked its way down to battalion advisor teams, TAA grabbed three suspected insurgents at the government gas station in Khalidiya, roughly interrogated them, and dumped them at Lieutenant Khalid's checkpoint on Route Michigan. "These are insurgents," said a TAA fighter.

The young Iraqi lieutenant questioned the battered captives and set them free. One man refused to leave. He had been kicked in the ribs, and his hand had been slammed in a car door. "You must help me get medical treatment," the injured suspect said.

Khalid drove the man to ASP Hill, where over tea and ice packs he revealed the names of fuel thieves. "I will become an informant if you let me stay the night," he told the Snake Eaters. "I cannot sneak back home tonight or they will know I have been talking to you."

"People sneak around all the time," Lieutenant Colonel Aamr said.

"Not anymore," the man countered, stunning his audience. "We know you are watching from the sky now. And the people are telling on us."

Against the wishes of the advisors, the Iraqi officers let the man spend the night.

At sunrise, Lieutenant Colonel Aamr rapped sharply on my door. He looked ill. "This man who slept here? He died last night."

"How'd he die?" I asked.

"We gave him blankets, chai, and let him sleep with the doctors. He just died," said Aamr. "What do you think about putting the body in the lake?"

"*Mejnan.*" That's crazy.

"Then we shall bury him on the ASP? Will the dogs not dig him up?"

Brigade policy set a four-hour detainee hold limit. After that, the suspect had to be freed or turned over to the Americans. We'd broken that rule to help the man, but in the Marine Corps, at least, the second mistake—covering it up—was much worse than the first. "Colonel Aamr, the best thing to do is let the command know immediately. Did you notify brigade?"

Aamr raised his eyebrows. "Of course I didn't. They will ruin us."

Compared to U.S. battalions, whose commanders were in daily contact with brigade commanders miles away, Iraqi battalions were isolated. Third Brigade headquarters was right across Route Michigan, yet messenger boys were the favored communication link. The battalions preferred it that way—they were basically independent units—and so did the brigades, where senior colonels could still claim credit while distancing themselves from failure.

"The brigade has been encouraging cooperation with the TAA. You and Fareed have been resistant. But you followed orders to build a relationship. The two of you should drive down and angrily tell the brigade commander that this is the result, and you want to know what he plans on doing about it," I suggested.

"This could work," said Aamr.

Sly, who came over to help, joined in. "Even better, bring the body."

The Snake Eaters visited brigade headquarters and were immediately absolved of any wrongdoing, but the next time Aamr saw Sheikh Abbas—now Chief Abbas—in Ogre's weekly meeting, he complained about the dead man.

"Never again must the TAA put us in this position," lectured Aamr.

"We did what the Amerikee told us," said Abbas, pointing at Ogre and me. "We got information before this man died. Much information!"

"Brother Abbas, we didn't order any hit," said Ogre.

"No, but you told us to get information," countered Abbas.

"So we Snake Eaters say the dead man is the brigade's responsibility, the brigade says it's the division's responsibility, the division says it was TAA's fault, and TAA says they were doing what you advisors told them." Aamr laughed. "Who do you fault?"

"I take my orders from George Bush," Ogre deadpanned.

"It is the Iraqi way!" said Aamr.

★

In February 2007, Team Outcast received transfer orders to an Iraqi national police unit in Baghdad. The Marine command had determined that the military advisor ranks in Anbar were to be filled exclusively by Marines. The Outcast soldiers, one of the few army teams in the province, were bitterly disappointed. They wanted to finish out their tour with the Snake Eaters.

Their last operation together in early February was memorable. Instead of rotating in and out of ASP Hill on three-hour shifts, Iraqi foot patrols remained in Khalidiya for three straight days, moving from house to house, where they were welcomed by homeowners to rest and eat. Jundis rotated every six hours at rally points within the city. Their control of the city was total. Observing the seventy-two-hour infiltration patrol, which was executed by Fareed, Aamr, and the Iraqi company commanders as professionally as a U.S. infantry operation, I was compelled to snap a few pictures to show all those who had mentored the Snake Eaters over the last three years how good they looked.

Abbas's police from the new Khalidiya station joined them on the beat. Several of the cops were unmasked now. Backed by machine gun–toting jundis, cops questioned and released most men with stiff warnings. The jundis were stunned that the cops knew many of their peers by name. Two foreigners were detained on the basis of excessive beard length.

"In America, we call it 'style police,'" I told Aamr after the operation, when we were discussing the bearded detainees. "Who were they?"

"Just two fools who did not get the memo, as you say," Aamr said with a chuckle.

"Do you really think the insurgency is dying?" I asked.

"With unmasked shurta patrolling their own streets, the insurgency is finished."

"The TAA is no longer needed in Khalidiya, after all."

"But they are, Major. We need them as police!"

The Snake Eaters were now independent operators, but after three years, most Iraqi soldiers could not imagine life without American advisors. They deeply distrusted their own ministries and had come to rely on U.S. intervention in everything from pay problems to air-conditioning to tracking bodies at the Baghdad morgue. "The Green Zone has the most insurgents in the country. You know them by the suits they wear," Captain Haadi liked to say. "We Iraqis cannot flourish without advisors. You rebuilt Japan after destroying it, and you will rebuild us."

It was a symbiotic relationship. The advisors linked their own effectiveness with the ability to fight both the guerrillas outside the wire and the bureaucrats within. The latter perception resembled Munchausen syndrome, and it occasionally resulted in stagnation. Just before Team Outcast departed, U.S. high command ordered American units to stop providing fuel to the dependent Iraqis. There was plenty of domestic fuel in Iraq. If the United States was ever going to transition the fight, fuel was a logical place to start.

The Iraqi officers were despondent. Given the high-level corruption, they declared, fuel would trickle down to ASP Hill in droplets. "We will have to stop sending vehicle patrols into Khalidiya," Lieutenant Colonel Fareed told me. "The insurgents will return."

Thoroughly alarmed, we advisors circumvented the order, stealing fuel from TQ to ensure continuous patrol coverage in Khalidiya. In the most daring operation, an advisor tried to learn how to drive a giant Iraqi fuel truck that the jundis had painted in U.S. yellow drab, but he couldn't master the clutch. A jundi mechanic drove the hulk to TQ and, when the fuel farm was in sight, the advisor switched places and managed to stop the truck within range of the last long gas hose.

The next day, U.S. logisticians flagged the phony requisition. We were told to knock it off. I was certain the Iraqis would stumble without us and wrote a self-important memorandum for the record claiming that without advisors providing fuel, operations would cease.

We were caught red-handed during the next heist and left with empty tanks. The Snake Eaters sat immobilized for a day, waiting to see what the Americans would do next. The following morning a funny thing happened—

several Iraqi fuel trucks appeared on ASP Hill—the Ministry of Defense had realized the Americans were not bluffing about self-sufficiency. The new fuel program sputtered along for two weeks, but by the time Team Outcast was turning over with the incoming team of Marines, the Iraqis had their own fuel system in place.

"You're gonna put us out of a job," I told Lieutenant Colonel Aamr.

"Major, you have not had this job for months now." Aamr laughed. "We just like your company."

★

On Team Outcast's last day on ASP Hill in early February 2007, Major Mohammed sat next to me on a squeaky bunk bed in the Terp Honeymoon Suite in the Horseshoe, where the advisors had gathered for a small going-away party. By then, the interpreter room looked like a rich college kid's dorm room—it had an Xbox tournament arena and a stash of Victoria's Secret catalogs.

Mohammed generally avoided the place, but he wanted to pay his respects to the advisors. The fact that one of the terps had managed to smuggle a liter of Black Label whiskey poured into a resealed Scope bottle back on the Iraqi leave convoy didn't hurt.

The terps acquired their taste for alcohol before it hit their tongues, Mohammed contended. Just hanging around the Americans was enough. For them, drinking alcohol wasn't an act of rebellion. It was a natural ingredient of the good life—the American life—like the iPod. Mohammed was bitten the old-fashioned way. Evening drinking in the souk was a badge of Arab sophistication, he said, that had to be earned.

Each man was rationed a single splash of whiskey. We drank from canteen cups and signal flare hammer caps. The advisors hadn't had alcohol in six months. Some of the men shivered. The Iraqis clapped them on their backs like old salts and gleefully inquired about their watery eyes.

"You take care of business?" I asked Mohammed. He had taken an extended bereavement leave to mourn his brother. I doubted his time off had been recorded in the personnel files at the Ministry of Defense, if they kept records at all, but if anyone deserved extra pay, it was Mohammed.

Alex translated. Mohammed shook his head, dumbfounded. Like most Iraqis, Mohammed feigned confusion if a question was too pointed. But he liked American colloquialisms—his favorite phrase was "stick it where the sun don't shine"—and recognized this one.

Eventually he broke into a smile and stroked his thick mustache, signaling a forthcoming promise. "I have one man to kill," he said in English.

Mohammed proudly told the story of the hunt for his brother's killers, with the crowd in the tiny room huddled around him.

"For every good man that is killed," Alex amplified at the story's conclusion, "four assholes are killed in retaliation. In fact, with a birthrate over six, Iraq needs war to keep the population from soaking up the two rivers!"

One of the advisors added, "Maybe if you guys took less leave there'd be less killing and this country wouldn't be so screwed."

Alex translated before I could stop him.

Mohammed looked at all of us and said in Arabic, "You have been here seven months. We have been fighting for three years straight, and we'll be fighting for another five. You stop your lives to come here, and I thank you for that, but this *is* my life. I'll be fighting when you are playing with your grandchildren, telling them to bring batteries, benzene, and magazines when it's their turn to come here and fight."

When the last droplets of alcohol were lapped up, the crowd broke apart to take pictures at the outpost's sandbagged entrance. I followed Mohammed to the fighting positions overlooking the lights of Khalidiya, just a few hundred meters downslope. We could hear the hum of the generators and the wild dogs barking.

"I wish I could stay here longer, to see this through," I told him. "Maybe I'll be back. As you said, you'll still be fighting ten years from now."

"To see what?" asked Mohammed.

"To see Iraq when it's better."

"If better, why we still fight?"

We stood in silence. It was well past curfew in Khalidiya, but shadows crisscrossed in the spills of the larger lights.

"Do not come back," Mohammed eventually said. "This is not your country. When America goes, we will talk bad about you."

"I'm not asking for a thank-you. We fight because we believe in Iraq, same as you," I insisted.

"If Ali were to return, we would kill him again. We are terrible people."

I had no response, and it seemed to please Mohammed, who was a natural antagonist. He fished a pack of cigarettes from his pocket and tapped out a stick, though he knew I would not accept.

I shook my head. It wasn't the cigarette. It was the whole thing.

"Good-bye, Major."

"Good-bye, Major."

I shook his hand and left him there, smoking a cigarette on the perimeter.

"Major West," he called out after me, hand over his heart, "I will never forget the advisors."

I joined the team posing at the outpost guard gate, arm in arm with the Iraqi officers, smiling broadly for the cameras. In the flash-lit safe zone at the spiked end of the antitruck serpentine, we exchanged gear, compliments, and promises to stay in touch. We were the outcast offspring of New Iraq, and my thoughts were with Major Mohammed and the sleeping city below him.

EPILOGUE

B y the winter of 2007–2008, Iraqi Brigade 3–1 was rated as one of the two
best units in Iraq. The Iraqi command gave the Snake Eaters and the
rest of the brigade a special rating as a quick reaction unit. They were
relieved of their responsibility in Habbaniyah and used as an elite shock troop
in Diyala, Basra, Baghdad, and Mosul, where they patrol to this day without
advisors—as they have for close to four years.

It took the Snake Eaters three years to develop the tactical expertise necessary for high-level independent combat operations. After six months of basic
training (don't kill yourselves) and three months of special urban "counterinsurgency training" (don't kill the people), the Snake Eaters deployed for
seven months of on-the-job combat training in Mosul with an eager U.S.
partner (here's how you kill the enemy). In Habbaniyah, the tactical mentoring slowed during the contentious nine-month partnership with TF Panther,
though the baptism by fire did cultivate a taste for self-reliance. Nine months
of joint operations with Marine Battalions 3/5 and 3/2 followed—a critical
development phase during which the Snake Eaters were treated as equals and
performed as such.

When Team Outcast handed off the baton in February 2007, the battalion was three years old. It would take another six months of stability operations before its soldiers were comfortable operating outside the umbrella of
U.S. medical and logistics support.

It was doubtful that the new Iraqi units being built in Baghdad could
move as quickly from the assembly line to operational independence. The
soldiers who formed the core of the 3rd Iraqi Brigade were former Special
Forces lifers who eschewed politics and religion. In 3rd Battalion, there was

very little turnover because, on balance, morale was excellent. The officers believed in the advisor system, the jundis were among the first to volunteer for the New Iraqi Army—a superior talent pool—and their advisors had instilled in them an appetite for risk, an intolerance for mediocrity, an aversion to corruption, and a belief that they were tougher than the guerrillas—and every other Iraqi unit in country.

★

This culture proved to be the undoing of many officers. As the rapid reaction force starting in 2008, the Snake Eaters became enmeshed in religious politics and the incurable graft that pervaded the Iraqi senior officer corps and ministries.

Caught in the crossfire of Shiite political factions while deployed to Baghdad, Lieutenant Colonel Fareed was moved into a high-level staff position. Major Mohammed, who had steadfastly refused promotion, was promoted and transferred. In Mosul, Lieutenant Fredo gave a bottle of water to a parched protester while overwatching an anti-Maliki march and was jailed for one hundred days. Lieutenant Colonel Aamr and Major Haadi complained to their superiors about illegal payoffs. Aamr was set up by an angry general. Aamr, a top-tier career officer who would make a superb colonel in the U.S. military, was placed on probation for months on suspicion of theft. His career appeared to be finished.

The saddest story belonged to "Captain Bomb" Dhafer. Haadi and Dhafer's companies were supporting a U.S. Special Forces attempt to capture Mosul's number two most-wanted terrorist, an al Qaeda captain. Haadi had been hit by a mine in Diyala a year earlier and was still not fully recovered from his gruesome wounds. He could no longer dart around the battlefield. Haadi tried to stop his best friend from going into the suspect house first—Dhafer had walked point for three years. Enough was enough. No man can survive on the edge that long. Dhafer would not listen and entered first. The terrorist on the second-floor landing shot Dhafer in the chest, right above his plate, and he died in Haadi's arms.

The American soldiers blew the terrorist up.

That night, Haadi, who was a wreck, sobbed into a cell phone to Alex, "It was just like Blakley!"

I sent a few thousand dollars to a Western Union drop in Baghdad so Haadi could put a down payment on a small property for Dhafer's young son. Alex and I didn't hear anything for weeks. "I think Haadi was killed in Baghdad, sir," said Alex, who was by then in the United States training to become a U.S. Marine.

Alex was struggling with his own tragedy. After going close to two years

without leave as a terp in Anbar, he had gone home to Baghdad and decorated his room with Marine Corps paraphernalia. During the wave of sectarian cleansing that turned neighbor against neighbor, a moving crew forced
his family out of their home. Seeing Alex's flags, a hit squad invited his
older brother back to retrieve some belongings. They removed his eyes and
dumped the body. A year later, Alex's ten-year-old brother was still getting
taunting phone calls asking him if he had the guts to come get his brother's
eyes back.

I had sponsored Alex with a special immigrant visa, and he was living
with my family in New York City. In our other lives, we had a plan to show
the murderers what guts really look like. For now we were worried about
Haadi, who had gone missing.

Turns out that Haadi had been restricted for insubordination. When he
was freed, he delivered the money to Dhafer's wife in a nice ceremony. I was
confident the money wouldn't go missing.

A year later, Haadi, too, was placed on probation as a thief and, when that
didn't stick, the powers that be flipped the charges, labeling him a whistle-
blower.

I had also filed an immigration package for Reyes, the young Iraqi medic-
turned-terp, but in 2010 lost contact with him and his young family. They
had fled sectarian murderers in 2007, 2008, and again in 2009. Alex and I
were very worried. Reyes, if you're out there, pop smoke and we will get
you, *habbibi*.

In the fall of 2011, Alex and I finally got some good news via a phone
call with Haadi. Aamr had been cleared of all charges and had been given his
own battalion to lead. Mohammed had so impressed his new unit with his
relentless warrior spirit that his legend had spread. Fareed remained the quiet
professional, and was well regarded by the brass. Fredo had been promoted
to captain, and was still leading special operations troops.

"As for me, I have been promoted to personnel officer of the Snake Eaters," said Haadi, "but you will not guess who is the battalion commander."

"Tell us," said Alex. "Mohammed?"

"Walid."

"The advisors will be shocked," Alex told him.

"The advisors. Those were the best days. Now all Americans are leaving
my country."

I had Alex ask Haadi if he thought the rapid American drawdown was
a good thing. Most of us who served in Iraq—and the Iraqi soldiers themselves—always expected a small force of Americans would remain in Iraq for
a decade more.

"We will see, Major," was all Haadi said.

★

The 3rd Battalion advisors also sacrificed outside of Khalidiya.

The army kept Chris Watson on active duty for two more years as he struggled to heal in the hospital system, but he never made it back to the police force; his legs were too mangled. Traumatic brain injury screenings eventually became mandatory in the army. After an intense two-day battery, the doctors wrote a definitive report: The massive explosion caused long-term TBI damage that needed care.

But when Watson left the military in 2008, he learned that the Department of Veterans Affairs had its own screening. There, a doctor asked Watson to drop his trousers.

"Now what in the world does my ass have to do with my brain?" asked Watson.

"This is a full examination," said the doctor.

Years in the Army and police department had dulled a sharp revulsion to bureaucratic waste. The examination over, the doctor pronounced Watson's brain completely healthy. Across the country, soldiers and Marines who hadn't once felt their ears pop were being treated for TBI. Watson had a two-hundred-pound double-stacked mine detonate right beneath him. It was against his code to beg for pity, so he thanked the doctor and left.

His doctor in Virginia was a good guy. It pleased him when Watson attended group counseling sessions. Most attendees were from the nearby reserve quartermaster unit. Boiko might have stood up and cut loose with some real trauma, but Watson stayed silent. No two units fought the same war in Iraq. He didn't judge them, and he hoped others would never judge his team. But from then on they could talk out their childhood trauma without him.

A few years after he returned to the States, Huss also attended a group therapy session sponsored by the VA. He was trying to scrub from his mind the daily flashbacks triggered by the October 2005 SVBIED.

Like Watson, Huss couldn't relate to a single man there, so he never went back. They were all fakers. None had seen real combat. Some had never even deployed!

Back home in Iowa, Huss told the story of that Khalidiya car bomb only once. He was traveling in a car with three childhood buddies. After he finished, they stared at him. Stared at him like the Fobbits at TQ and the PTSD patients at the VA.

He vowed never to tell it again.

★

Two years later, Huss did tell the story again, to me. So did two dozen other men whose feats are not included here. The mentorship of the Snake Eaters was a multiyear effort by five separate advisor teams of soldiers, National Guardsmen, and Marines. I'm sorry I could not include all of them in this book. They sacrificed much more than I did.

Those Outcasts who returned to combat include Lieutenant Colonel Andy Milburn and Major Rocco Barnes, who advised the Snake Eaters in 2005, before Mike Troster's team arrived. Together they served five tours in Iraq and three tours in Afghanistan. Rocco was killed in Afghanistan in 2009 while acting as senior advisor to yet another team of Marines. As a civilian, he was a bodyguard for movie actors, and he had told me he was 45 when I called him to talk about going back with the Marines. He was actually 51. Ageism was the only thing about him that was Hollywood. The rest of him was pure warrior.

Marine Corporal Tim Smith, a member of my team, won a machine gun battle with a Taliban unit in Afghanistan but was shot in the arm and seriously wounded. Gunner Kenison, who kept a watchful eye on Troster's team when they first arrived in Iraq, was shot in the jaw in Afghanistan.

Shawn Boiko, Saul Cardenas, Dave Cox, Jeffrey Foisy, Andrew Himes, Jay Kajs, James Newton, Wayne O'Donnell, Walt Roberson, Brian Schwarzman, William Stoesser—and many men from the other 3rd Brigade advisor teams—volunteered to go back overseas into the fight. The war may not be shouldered wide, but it's deep.

★

While writing this book over the past four years, I've tried to figure out how much influence an advisor team really has on its unit, and whether institutional expectations match those limitations. I have again read the field manuals taught in our Army and Marine schools where we train advisors. The manuals have an upbeat, culturally correct tone, suggesting that our soldiers and Marines will succeed as advisors based on their tact and sensitivity. The manuals need drastic revision; they are misleading a generation of advisors.

Advisors are needed because battalions like the 3/3–1 Snake Eaters have failed in both Iraq and Afghanistan. An advisor must of course treat everyone with due respect, but not with deference. If the leaders of the host nation units were doing their jobs correctly, there would be no need for advisors.

The major difference between Troster's and Mac's teams was not tactical patrolling versus staff training. The real difference was attitude. Troster was intolerant of 3/3–1's lack of self-confidence; his goal was instilling a spirit of dominance. Mac was forbearing in matters about the spirit and morale of 3/3–1; his goal was to teach good officership and staff independence.

The goal of any advisory team must be to imbue the host nation unit with a sense of aggression. An aggressive unit by definition believes it can dominate its enemy. Once a unit has that core belief, then an internal code of conduct takes hold, shaping the actions of everyone in the unit. Once a unit is focused upon the enemy, it develops a sense of pride in its accomplishments and a sense of shame at poor performance. Advisors don't have the legal authority to fire poor leaders, but they can shape the unit ethos and make it difficult for poor leaders to remain in power.

No matter how we entered Iraq and Afghanistan—and will undoubtedly enter future small wars—all roads out lead through the advisor. On patrol with the Snake Eaters, I always felt the presence of dozens of advisors past, and when I connected with them, our experiences in Khalidiya were different, but one belief was constant: Advisor teams work. I only wish our predecessors had seen the Snake Eaters in 2007 and the eventual turnaround.

Success has a thousand fathers. Iraq was an American-led war and we want American heroes. But the sudden reversal in Khalidiya was not an American story. For years before the arrival of Iraqi soldiers, U.S. generals and diplomats had been meeting with displaced Anbari sheikhs in Jordan. U.S. colonels in Habbaniyah had shared chai with an endless stream of local tribesmen. U.S. soldiers had distributed millions of dollars to locals. Looking back, it seems foolish to believe that American forces alone could have protected the indigenous people in Anbar Province from the hard men among them.

When the 3rd Iraqi Battalion joined the fight, together with their U.S. partners and advisors they were able to put a lid on the local insurgency in Khalidiya. But its defeat depended on the people who had enabled the enemy for years. Why and when the people of Khalidiya summoned the courage to point out their oppressors and decided to switch sides is a mystery. That's the truth—despite well-intentioned doctrine at the top and acts of incredible courage at the bottom.

Special credit is certainly due to Generals Zilmer and Neller, regimental commander Nicholson, battalion commanders Fareed and Desgrosseilliers, and advisor teams led by Troster, Zientek, and McCarthy. But as a commodities trader, I prefer conditions to cause. The real credit for the turnaround goes to all the grunts—U.S. soldiers, sailors, guardsmen, Marines, Iraqi shurtas, and especially those wonderful, ever-enduring jundis—who stuck it out for forty-two months before the tide turned.

★

In July 2009, Alex called Haadi in Mosul to check up on him and get the latest scoop on Khalidiya. The Snake Eaters had been closely following events in Khalidiya since departing eighteen months earlier, and some of us advisors closely followed the Snake Eaters. Alex and I were stunned to learn that just one bomb had exploded in Khalidiya in two years, a personal vendetta by a cop, not a return to the bad old days. Habbaniyah had supposedly returned to its prewar role as a sleepy agricultural waypoint on the route to Baghdad, and Lake Habbaniyah was again a popular domestic vacation spot.

"I am bringing my own family to the lake," Haadi told Alex. "It is that safe."

I had my doubts. Security was one thing; cavorting with children in a lake less than a kilometer away from the site of hundreds of bombings and dozens of sniper shots was another. Then in August I read a *New York Times* article about hundreds of Iraqis, Sunni and Shia, who now gathered on the shores of Lake Habbaniyah near ASP Hill to dance by the waves to pounding tunes spun by a Western-style DJ.[1] I was floored by the report, and emailed it to the advisors.

"My jaw is on the floor right now," Troster replied.

"This means so much," wrote Huss. "Every day I struggle to tell my family what I did over there. I have a lump in my throat."

"Cool," Roberson joined in, and that was it.

But it was Cox who spoke for us all: "I'm sitting here with tears in my eyes, because only we understand what we and the Iraqis worked for, and how hard it was every day, and who was lost along the way. But together we did it! I just hope the politicians don't screw the pooch . . ."

ACKNOWLEDGMENTS

I wrote this book to show what ordinary soldiers can accomplish when used in an extraordinary way. I'm an ordinary writer. This book has taken nearly four years to research and write partly because of extraordinary circumstances, and I owe thanks to many.

Like many advisors, I was a reservist, immediately returning to work as a commodities trader a week after my homecoming from Iraq in 2007. I believed the advisor model was working in Iraq and could work in Afghanistan if the Pentagon properly prioritized.

My father, Bing, had seen the same thing during his multiyear service in Vietnam. In *The Village,* he chronicled a squad of Marines sent into a Vietnamese village to partner with local fighters. These Combined Action Platoons were successful but the program was scrapped at the end of the war, along with the entire advisory program. Thirty-five years later, that dismissal cost us in Iraq. Dad and I remained captivated by advising, and in May 2007 we proposed an advisor model for Iraq and Afghanistan, an abbreviated version of which appeared in *Slate.*

"You should write a book," my dad told me.

I didn't see how I could do it. I had taken four leaves of absence from my job in a decade. My wife, Susanne, had endured the birth of one boy while I was away, and the antics of three when I was home. I wrote a few op-eds describing what I had seen in Iraq, but the realities of my job and my family responsibilities soon separated me from the defense policy debate. Besides, I was a part-time troop who fought in one city. I didn't fight the Washington wars, where real persistence is required.

Inspiration is tricky for writers to pinpoint. Writing is part of my genetic code, and I'd always been very proud of my dad's service in Vietnam, and his memorialization of a small band of Marine advisors. A year later, Alex was living in my New York apartment, and he insisted that I write a history of the Snake Eaters. I wasn't going to let the opportunity slip by a second time, and thank both Alex and Dad for issuing the challenge.

Hearing all proceeds were going to fund the education of children of U.S. and Iraqi servicemen, Susanne, a former teacher, agreed to the project. There were nights we wished we had not. I had written two novels before we had kids, typing when she was off running or visiting friends. Now I was writing during my train commute and late at night, snatching any available weekend block for phone interviews between coaching duties. The untold reality of military deployments is that the families have it much harder than their infantrymen, who are generally happy to join the fight, and the same was true of my bursts of writing. Suz, without you this climb would have been a ten-year expedition.

While most of the events were related to me after the fact, I checked and rechecked with each fighter in an attempt to best capture the tiny battles as they unfolded. No two men remembered the same details. Armed with patrol logs and hundreds of reports, I sometimes checked my dates to confirm the men were in the same firefight. Many vignettes were thrown out as a result, and that was tough the news to break to various principals.

Still, the first draft exceeded six hundred pages when I emailed it to Alessandra Bastagli at Free Press. She was a superb editor, providing the clarity and blunt direction this Marine needed. Over the course of nine more months of research and editing, during which Suz was again forced into many nights of double duty, the core narrative was revealed. More than anyone else, Alessandra whipped this book into shape. I'll never forget that.

Tightening the book obviously required major cuts. My biggest regret is that many soldiers, Marines, Guardsmen, SEALs, and Iraqi soldiers and police were omitted from this text. All of you contributed to this victory. I'd like to cite all the advisors attached to the 3rd Iraqi Brigade, 1st Iraqi Division, including Bill McCollough's, Ford Phillips's, and Tom Chalkey's teams from our brother battalions; Craig Wiggers's team that succeeded ours; Captain Joe Burke and India Company 3/2; Rocco Barnes, Andy Milburn, and Jay Kajs, who preceded Mike Troster as Snake Eater advisors; and Matt Alford, Robert Akin, Tod Caldwell, Pierre Dupuy, Jeffrey Foisy, Andrew Himes, Shaun Lester, James Newton, Wayne O'Donnell, Milton Perez, Anthony Povarelli, Brian Schwarzman, Timothy Smith, William Stoesser, Steve Sylvester, and Andy Wilson from my own team. Schwarzman and Caldwell deserve special recognition as our MVPs: Smith rode in the turret every day, and Newton and Sylvester were the brave, steady hands.

Finally, thanks to all the people who contributed their time, especially Aamr, Chris Ahn, Alex, Rocco Barnes (R.I.P.), John Bennett, Shawn Boiko, Daniel Bolger, Greg Bozovich, Shawn Bronson, Mike Buckley, Tod Caldwell, Sal Cardenas, Phil Carter, Juan Castillo, Kevin Charter, Matthew Cooper, Dave Cox, Larry Dehart, Rorke Denver, Todd Desgrosseilliers, Dhafer (R.I.P.), Paul Eaton, Theodore Edson, Clay Fisher, Ed Fonseca, Mark Gentile, Antonia Greene, John Gronski, Haadi, Thomas Hallowell, Mark Hampton, Alan Higgins, Thomas Hobbs, Mark Huss, Brian Hutcherson, Russell Jamison, Jay Kajs, Pat Keane, Jon Klug, Loris Lepri, Robert "Ogre" McCarthy, Bill McCollough, Chuck McGregor, Patrick McHenry, Drew McNulty, Andy Milburn, John Nagl, Joseph Neary, Bob Neller, Neo, Michael Noonan, David Petraeus, Chris Phelps, Joshua Potter, Stan Price, Carl Prine, Reyes, Eliezer Rivera, Walt Roberson, Bill Rusher, Bryan Schwarzman, Frank Shelton, Neil Smith, Tim Smith, Michael Stolzenburg, Colin Supko, Kyle Teamey, Mike Troster, Erich Wagner, Chris Watson, Bing West, Andy Wilson, Jim Zientek, and Rick Zilmer.

NOTES

Introduction

1. Barack Obama, "Address to the Nation," August 31, 2010, www.whitehouse
   .gov/the-press-office/2010/08/31/excerpts-president-barack-obamas-address-
   nation-end-combat-operations-iraq; Associated Press, "Obama's Speech at
   Camp Lejeune, N.C.," *New York Times,* February 27, 2009.
2. U.S. Department of State, "Translation of Letter Written by the Terrorist abu
   Musab Zarqawi," February 2004, www.au.af.mil/au/awc/awcgate/state/31694.htm.

1: Into the Haze

1. George Bush, "President Addresses Nation, Discusses Iraq, War on Terror,"
   White House News Release, June 28, 2005.
2. Clay, *Iroquois Warriors in Iraq,* p. 84.
3. Ibid., p. 32.
4. Cloud and Jaffe, *The Fourth Star,* p. 249.
5. Lawrence, "Twenty-Seven Articles."
6. www.alertnet.org/thenews/newsdesk/MOU625502.htm.
7. www.commongroundcommonsense.org/forums/index.php?showtopic=37654;
   www.democraticunderground.com/discuss/duboard.php?az=view_all&address
   =104x4800822; http://icasualties.org/iraq/iraqideaths.aspx?hndPeriod=Sep-05.
8. Associated Press, "Baghdad Blasts Kill 31 as Zarqawi Declares War on Shiites,"
   September 16, 2005.

4: Ambush

1. Gen. David Petraeus, "Commander's Letter," Multi-National Force Iraq,
   March 15, 2007.
2. Callwell, *Small Wars,* p. 41.

5: Survivor on Steroids

1. Affourtit, *Communion in Conflict,* p. 41.

7: Ranger Danger

1. Hubert Lyautey, *Du rôle colonial de l'armée* (Paris: Armand Colin, 1900).
2. Mark Mazzetti, "U.S. Generals Now See Virtues of a Smaller Troop Presence in Iraq," *Los Angeles Times,* October 1, 2005.

8: Bombs Away

1. White House, "National Strategy for Victory in Iraq."
2. Ibid.
3. Petraeus, "Learning Counterinsurgency."

9: Outcast

1. Kilcullen, "Twenty-Eight Articles," p. 4.

12: Running on Empty

1. Oppel and Hassan, "Iraqi Recruits Said to Balk at Postings."

14: Changing of the Guard

1. Oliva, "Darkhorse Snipers Kill Insurgent Sniper."
2. Michael Troster, "After Action Report," July 2006.

15: Change of Pace

1. Lawrence, "Twenty-Seven Articles," article 1.

16: Sabbatical

1. Department of the Army, *Counterinsurgency.*

19: I Fought the Law and I Won

1. Galula, *Pacification in Algeria,* p. 99.
2. Troster, "After Action Report," p. 3.

Epilogue

1. Duraid Adnan and Timothy Williams, "Lake Habbaniya Journal," *New York Times,* August 24, 2009.

BIBLIOGRAPHY

Affourtit, Thomas D. *Analysis of a Culture in Conflict: Comparative Personality Determinants Between U.S. Marine Advisors and Vietnamese Soldiers*. Technical Report 79–2. Fairfax, VA: Interaction Research Institute, February 1979.

———. *Communion in Conflict: The Marine Advisor in the Middle East*. Technical Report 0306. Fairfax, VA: Interaction Research Institute, 2006.

Anderson, Steve. "Ten Myths of the War in Iraq." Briefing slides, Multi-National Force—Iraq, April 27, 2007.

Ayala, Juan. "Reflections." *Marine Corps Gazette*, March 2008.

Bolger, Daniel P. "So You Want to be an Adviser." *Military Review*, March–April 2006.

Boot, Max. "Can Petraeus Pull It Off?" *Weekly Standard*, April 30, 2007.

Bremer, L. Paul, III. "How I Didn't Dismantle Iraq's Army," *New York Times*, September 6, 2007.

Callwell, C. E. *Small Wars: Their Principles and Practice*. 3rd ed. Lincoln: University of Nebraska Press, 1996 [1896].

Center for Army Lessons Learned. *Transition Team (TT) Training Collection and Analysis Team Initial Impressions Report*. Fort Leavenworth, KS, May 2006.

Charlie. "You've Been Selected for an ETT." Abu Muqawama blog. www.cnas.org/blogs/abumuqawama/2008 /02/you've-been-selected-ett.html.

Clay, Steven E. *Iroquois Warriors in Iraq*. Leavenworth, KS: Combat Studies Institute Press, 2007.

Cline, Lawrence. *Pseudo Operations and Counterinsurgency: Lessons from Other Countries*. Carlisle, PA: Strategic Studies Institute, Army War College, 2005.

Cloud, David, and Greg Jaffe. *The Fourth Star: Four Generals and the Epic Struggle for the Future of the United States Military*. New York: Crown, 2009.

Coalition Provisional Authority. "An Historic Review of CPA Accomplishments 2003–2004." www.iraqcoalition.org/.

The Continuing Challenge of Building Iraqi Security Forces. Hearing before the House Armed Services Committee, 110th Cong., 2007.

Cook, John L. *The Advisor: The Phoenix Program in Vietnam*. New York: Schiffer, 1997.

Cordesman, Anthony H. *The Iraq War and Lessons for Counterinsurgency*. Washington, D.C.: Center for Strategic and International Studies, 2006.

———. *Iraqi Force Development: Coalition Reporting as of the Fall of 2005*. Washington, D.C.: Center for Strategic and International Studies, 2005.

———. *Iraqi Force Development: Conditions for Success, Consequences of Failure*. Washington, D.C.: Center for Strategic and International Studies, 2007.

———. *Iraqi Force Development: Summer 2006 Update*. Washington, D.C.: Center for Strategic and International Studies, 2006.

———. *Strengthening Iraqi Military and Security Forces*. Washington, D.C.: Center for Strategic and International Studies, 2005.

Davidson, Janine. *Principles of Modern American Counterinsurgency: Evolution and Debate*. Washington, D.C.: Brookings Institution, 2009.

Demas, Nicholas. "Memorandum for the Record." September 25, 2005.

Development of the Iraqi Police Service. Hearing before the House Armed Services Committee, 110th Cong., May 24, 2007.

Dixon, Paul. "'Hearts and Minds'? British Counter-Insurgency from Malaya to Iraq." *Journal of Strategic Studies* 32, issue 3 (2009).

Donovan, David. *Once a Warrior King: Memories of an Officer in Vietnam*. New York: McGraw-Hill, 1985.

Dunne, Jonathan P. "Cultures Are Different: Modifying Maslow's Hierarchy for Contemporary COIN." *Marine Corps Gazette* 93, no. 2 (February 2009).

Fall, Bernard. "The Theory and Practice of Insurgency and Counterinsurgency." *Naval War College Review,* April 1965.

Felter, Joseph, and Brian Fishman. "Al-Qa'ida's Foreign Fighters in Iraq: A First Look at the Sinjar Records." West Point, NY: U.S. Military Academy, Combating Terrorism Center, 2009.

Fox, Joe, and Dana Stowell. "Professional Army Advisors—A Way Ahead." *Infantry Bugler,* Winter 2007.

Galula, David. *Counterinsurgency Warfare: Theory and Practice*. Westport, CT: Praeger, 1964.

———. *Pacification in Algeria, 1956–1958*. Santa Monica: RAND, 2006.

Gant, Jim. "*One Tribe at a Time: A Strategy for Success in Afghanistan*." 2009. http://blog .stevenpressfield.com.

Gentile, Gian P. "A Strategy of Tactics: Population-centric COIN and the Army." *Parameters,* Autumn 2009.

Goodwillie, James G. "Memorandum to BG John P. McLaren," 5th IA Division MiTT After Action Files, September 27, 2005.

Gordon, Michael R. "The Conflict in Iraq: Road to War." *New York Times,* October 19, 2004.

———. "Grim Outlook Seen in West Iraq Without More Troops and Aid." *New York Times,* September 12, 2006.

Gray, Wesley R. *Embedded: A Marine Corps Adviser Inside the Iraqi Army*. Annapolis: Naval Institute Press, 2009.

Helmer, Daniel. "Twelve Urgent Steps for the Advisor Mission in Afghanistan." *Military Review,* July–August 2008.

Hickey, G. C. *The American Military Advisor and His Foreign Counterpart: The Case of Vietnam*. Santa Monica: RAND Corporation, 1965.

Highley, Sam. *COIN/PA: Leveraging Military Public Affairs to Fight Insurgencies*. Air University, April 2006.

Jaffe, Greg. "A Camp Divided." *Wall Street Journal,* June 18, 2006.

Jones, Joseph W. "Advancing the Military Transition Team Model." Master of Military Studies thesis, Marine Corps University, 2008.

Kilcullen, David. "Counterinsurgency Redux." *Survival* 48, no. 4 (December 2006).

———. "Twenty-Eight Articles: Fundamentals of Company-level Counterinsurgency." *Small Wars Journal* 1, March 2006.

Kitson, Frank. *Gangs and Counter-Gangs*. London: Barrie & Rockliff, 1960.

Krepinevich, Andrew F. "The Future of U.S. Ground Forces: Challenges and Requirements." Testimony before the Senate Armed Services Committee, April 17, 2007.

Lawrence, T. E. "The Science of Guerrilla Warfare." Introduction to "Guerrilla Warfare" *Encyclopedia Britannica,* 14th ed., 1926. www.pegasus.cc.ucf.edu/~eshaw/Lawrence.htm.

———. "Twenty-Seven Articles." *Arab Bulletin,* August 20, 1917.

Lessard, Laurence. "Operational Leadership Experiences." Fort Leavenworth, KS: Combat Studies Institute, 2007–2008.

Luttwak, Edward. "Dead End: Counterinsurgency Warfare as Military Malpractice." *Harper's,* February 2007.

Manchester, William. *Goodbye Darkness: A Memoir of the Pacific War*. Boston: Little, Brown, 1980.

Mansoor, Peter. "From Baghdad to Kabul: The Historical Roots of U.S. Counterinsurgency Doctrine." *Origins: Current Events in Historical Perspective* 3, issue 1 (October 2009).

McCallister, William S. "A Means to Structure Analysis." *Small Wars Journal,* August 9, 2007.

———. "Anatomy of a Tribal Rebellion." *Small Wars Journal,* August 30, 2007.

———. MNF-W Engagement Model Slideshow, June 20, 2007.

Montagne, Renee, and Steve Inskeep. "Future Iraqi Advisers Face Hard Lessons." National Public Radio, *Morning Edition,* March 27, 2007.

Montgomery, Gary, and Timothy McWilliams. *Al-Anbar Awakening, Iraqi Perspectives: From Insurgency to Counterinsurgency in Iraq 2004–2009.* 2 vols. Quantico: Marine Corps University Press, 2009.

Nagl, John A. *Institutionalizing Adaptation: It's Time for a Permanent Army Advisor Corps*. Washington, D.C.: Center for a New American Security, 2007.

Navarro, Eric. *God Willing: My Wild Ride with the New Iraqi Army*. Washington, D.C.: Potomac Books, 2008.

O'Hanlon, Michael, and Jason Campbell. "Iraq Index." Washington, D.C.: Brookings Institution, October 1, 2007.

Oliva, Mark. "Darkhorse Snipers Kill Insurgent Sniper." *Marine Corps News,* June 22, 2006.

Oppel, Richard A., Jr., and Khalid W. Hassan. "Iraqi Recruits Said to Balk at Postings." *New York Times,* May 2, 2006.

Petraeus, David H. "CENTCOM Update." Washington, D.C.: Center for a New American Security, June 11, 2009.

———. "Learning Counterinsurgency: Observations from Soldiering in Iraq." *Military Review,* January–February 2006.

Phelps, Christopher E., Michelle Ramsden Zbylut, and Jason Brunner. "Selecting and Training US Advisors." *Marine Corps Gazette,* March 2009.

Progress of the Iraqi Security Forces. Hearing before the House Armed Services Committee, 109th Cong., June 23, 2005.

Ramsey, Robert D. III, ed. *Advice for Advisors: Suggestions and Observations from Lawrence to the Present*. Fort Leavenworth, KS: Combat Studies Institute Press, 2006.

———. *Advising Indigenous Forces: American Advisors in Korea, Vietnam, and El Salvador*. Fort Leavenworth, KS: Combat Studies Institute Press, 2006.

Ray, James F. "The District Advisor." *Military Review,* May 1965.

Ricks, Thomas E. *Fiasco: The American Military Adventure in Iraq*. New York: Penguin Press, 2006.

———. "General Affirms Anbar Analysis." *Washington Post,* September 13, 2006.

———. "Situation Called Dire in West Iraq." *Washington Post,* September 11, 2006.

Ryan, Sean. "Security Forces Assistance in Counterinsurgency and Stability Operations." Fort Leavenworth, KS: Joint Center for International Security Force Assistance, 2007.

Sepp, Kalev I. "Best Practices in Counterinsurgency." *Military Review,* May–June 2005.

Shay, Jonathan. *Achilles in Vietnam: Combat Trauma and the Undoing of Character.* New York: Atheneum, 1994.

Sheehan, Neil. *A Bright Shining Lie: John Paul Vann and America in Vietnam.* New York: Random House, 1968.

Sloan, Stephen, and Sebastian L. V. Gorka. "Contextualizing Counterinsurgency." *Journal of International Security Affairs* 16 (Spring 2009).

Smith, Neil, and Sean MacFarland. "Anbar Awakens: The Tipping Point." *Military Review,* March–April 2008.

Stafford, Darlene, and Henry Griffis. *A Review of Millennial Generation Characteristics and Military Workforce Implications.* Alexandria, VA: Center for Naval Analysis, 2008.

Tran, Mark. "Iraqi Police Cannot Control Crime." *Guardian,* May 30, 2007.

Status of Iraqi Security Forces. Hearing before the House Armed Services Committee, 110th Cong., March 6, 2007.

U.S. Department of the Army. *Counterinsurgency* (FM 3–24, MCWP 3–33.5), December 2006.

U.S. Department of Defense. News Briefing with Brig. Gen. Dana Pittard from Iraq. August 28, 2006. www.defense.gov/transcripts/transcript.aspx?transcriptid=3703.

U.S. Marine Corps. *Iraq Culture Smart Card.* www.fas.org/irp/doddir/usmc/iraqsmart-1104.pdf.

U.S. Military Transition Teams in Iraq. Hearing before the House Armed Services Committee, 109th Cong., December 7, 2006.

Voorhies, David. "MiTT Happens: Insight into Advising the Iraqi Army." Fort Benning, GA: Combined Arms Tactic Directorate, April 20, 2007.

Wagner, Erich. "Guardsmen and Jundis: A Historical Comparison of the USMC's Experience of 'Native Troops' in Nicaragua, 1927–32 and Iraq, 2004–2008." *JCOA Journal,* Fall 2008.

West, Bing. *The Strongest Tribe: War, Politics, and the Endgame in Iraq.* New York: Random House, 2008.

———. *The Village.* New York: Harper, 1972.

Wheeler, Kurt, ed. *Al Anbar Awakening: An Oral History.* 2 vols. Quantico: Marine Corps University Press, 2008.

White House. "National Strategy for Victory in Iraq," November 30, 2005. georgewbush-whitehouse.archives.gov/infocus/iraq/iraq_strategy_nov2005.html.

Wright, Donald P., and Timothy R. Reese. *On Point II.* Fort Leavenworth, KS: Combat Studies Institute Press, 2008.

INDEX

ABOUT THE AUTHOR

OWEN WEST is a former Marine major who has served two combat tours in Iraq. A graduate of Harvard College and Stanford Business School, West is managing director at Goldman, Sachs where he trades energy. His first novel, *Sharkman Six* (Simon & Schuster, 2001), won the Boyd literary award for best military novel. His second novel, *Four Days to Veracruz* (Simon & Schuster, 2003), debuted when he was in Iraq. He is the coauthor of the screenplay adaptation of *No True Glory: The Battle For Fallujah* (Bantam, 2005), and has written dozens of articles on military affairs and adventure sports. In 2005, he won the Marine Corps Leadership Essay Contest. He serves on the board of the Marine Corps Scholarship Foundation and is a member of the Council on Foreign Relations.

OWEN WEST is donating all of his proceeds from *The Snake Eaters,* net of agency fees, to the Marine Corps Scholarship Foundation and to the families of fallen advisors and the families of the fallen Iraqi "Snake Eaters." For more information on the Marine Corps Scholarship Foundation, please visit www.mcsf.org.